THE

CHINA LOBBY MAN

The Story of Alfred Kohlberg

◦⧏⧐◦

by
Joseph Keeley

ARLINGTON HOUSE   NEW ROCHELLE, N.Y.

Contents

Acknowledgments

To the many people who assisted in the preparation of this book I am deeply grateful. Space does not permit a discussion of specific contributions nor even a listing of all those who helped in some way, but I am particularly indebted to:

Mrs. Alfred Kohlberg, Mrs. Harry Geballe, Miss Anna E. Murray, Mrs. Irene Corbally Kuhn, Mrs. J. B. Matthews, Robert Morris, Miss Freda Utley, Eugene Lyons, Dr. Walter H. Judd, General Albert C. Wedemeyer, Major General Charles A. Willoughby, Miss Edna Lonigan, Isaac Don Levine, William F. Buckley, Jr., Lyle H. Munson, Rabbi Benjamin Schultz, Louis F. Budenz, Dr. B. A. Garside, N. C. Nyi, Edward Hunter, Dr. Maurice William, Herbert Romerstein, Charles W. Wiley, James F. O'Neil, Lawrence Fertig, Richard M. Nixon, Charles Edison, E. A. Blackmore, William Loeb, Karl Baarslag, Rodney Gilbert.

Author's Foreword

I was privileged to know Alfred Kohlberg and many others mentioned in this book who tried to prevent the disastrous events that have succeeded one another since World War II. These men and women were voices crying in the wilderness but their voices were drowned out by strident shouts and cries from the left.

For more than a decade I had the opportunity to observe Alfred Kohlberg at work, and since he was a neighbor in Bronxville, I frequently saw him at play, as host at gatherings at his home. His big stone house was the scene of many interesting meetings of people with one thing in common, a staunch opposition to the Communist conspiracy.

It was because of my friendship for Alfred and my understanding of what he tried to do that, after his death in 1960, his widow asked me if I would be interested in writing this book. If so, she said she would give me access to all his records. This she did, opening up a fascinating store-house dealing with the great and the near-great of our time. Not to mention some of the greatest scoundrels of all time.

Most fascinating of all was a series of volumes that Alfred had prepared for his grandchildren, one volume for each grandchild. Each was a labor of love, the pages individually typed and illustrated with personal photographs and other mementoes, all assembled by hand and beautifully bound. However, this was not the traditional family album but literally a fact book.

Alfred Kohlberg was of course annoyed at the vicious smears that were aimed at him during his lifetime though he publicly shrugged them off. However, he *was* concerned about what his grandchildren might come to think of him in the future, when they read what had been said and written about "the China Lobby man."

As an indication of what might be expected, Ida Kohlberg told me of a grandchild coming home from school in tears. He wanted to know if it was true that his grandfather had stolen millions of dollars. The youngster's teacher, moved by a strange compulsion, had quoted Senator Wayne Morse to these little children. In one of his more ridiculous outbursts the Senator had charged that the China Lobby had received $654,000,000 from Chiang Kai-shek, and while he did not mention Kohlberg by name, everyone knew that Kohlberg personified the China Lobby.

What did the teacher mean? Had grandpa stolen all that money? Ida explained to the child that his grandfather had stuffed the money in a shirt pocket and forgotten about it. The shirt had been sent to the laundry and apparently the money had gone down the drain. The little boy got the picture and laughed.

In discussing her late husband with me, Ida Jolles Kohlberg spiced her accounts with the same delightful humor.

Unfortunately, she did not live to see this book in print. A few weeks after she had read the manuscript, Ida Jolles Kohlberg died of emphysema on February 10, 1968.

To the memory of that wonderful woman
this book is respectfully dedicated.

Introduction*

by William F. Buckley Jr.

How pleasant it would be to have an altogether frictionless evening, a surcease from work, a contented hour given over to celebrating the personal and public accomplishments of a brave man. But evenings which bring together spirited people moved by a common impulse—in this case, the impulse to save the people of China from total despair—cannot take that course, and probably should not. We seldom give ourselves over completely to serenity. I think of a great Christian prayer, serene, beatific, but before it is quite over, we find ourselves asking our Maker to be so thoughtful as to "cast into hell those evil spirits who roam through the world seeking the destruction of souls." Amen. And anyway, to take no notice of the basic frictions which animate this kindly, dogged, energetic, modest, and intelligent man, would be to render an imperfect tribute to Alfred Kohlberg. He is one of the few men who would be bored to death by any evening given over exclusively to the recounting of his virtues and attainments. I know him well enough to venture to say that the first thing that went through his mind on being asked whether he would consent to being honored by us was, "Hm. A good opportunity to state again the case against the recognition of Red China."

It is not as though others, of different political persuasion, behave less opportunistically. I think of another testimonial dinner, held within the past year, in this very room, to honor the retiring president of Sarah Lawrence College, Dr. Harold Taylor. The theme of the evening was "The Liberal Spirit

* Remarks at the Alfred Kohlberg testimonial dinner, July 26, 1960.

in American Life." Dr. Taylor, a distinguished philosopher, will be remembered as a man who spoke out most ardently in the recent past in resistance to the reign of terror which Alfred Kohlberg and his friends were instrumental in inflicting upon us, a reign of terror which threatened the country with the direst evils, perhaps the greatest of which, Dr. Taylor often seemed to be suggesting, would be the silencing of Dr. Taylor. At that meeting, many cups ran over with thanksgiving, for the part Dr. Taylor took in the liberation of our nation from the threat of Senator McCarthy and Roy Cohn. There were present other veterans of that great war, filing into this room on their crutches, faces held together by plastic surgery, to commemorate their years together in the trenches. For instance, Mrs. Eleanor Roosevelt, who spoke at the dinner, rounding out her extraordinarily long day. Another speaker was Mr. Archibald MacLeish, a blithe spirit from the world of poetry, who finds recreation in lime-rick-type assaults upon American conservatives; and the formidable Dr. Robert Oppenheimer, whose Promethean mind has roamed the cosmos in discontent, ever since the pygmies told him that fire was not for him alone to play with. And who presided? The tiger himself, the man who declared that CBS would *never* surrender, Mr. Edward R. Murrow. At that gala, much attention was given to the frictions that disturb the Liberal Spirit in American Life, an uncommonly large number of which appear to be generated by people in this room.

Let us, then, think back to some of the causes that bring us together. We are always being reminded that these are changing times, and that it is the duty of modern man, lest he sin against reality and consign himself to irrelevance, to accommodate those changes. What does it mean, "the times are changing?" I am less and less certain. The views of many men certainly appear to have changed. In November of 1945, Mr. Dean Acheson stated, "Never in the past has there been any place on the globe where the vital interests of the American and Russian people have clashed or even been antagonistic. And there is no objective reason to suppose that there should now or in the future, ever be such a place. We understand and agree with them that to have friendly governments along her borders is essential both to the security of the Soviet Union and for the peace of the world."

Fifteen years have gone by, and Dean Acheson now seems destined to emerge as among the principal anti-Communist irreconcilables in public life. Unfortunately, we had, in the interim, lost China. Among other things, we thus supplied the Soviet Union with another friendly government along her borders—consistent with our objective of providing for the security of the Soviet Union; on the assumption that to do so was to make way for peace in our time.

When Mr. Acheson was chased out of public life by an unusually emphatic act of public resolution, the landslide of 1952, he departed as the symbol of a futile, epicene anti-Communism, to make way, we were assured, for a vigorous, purposive, clearheaded anti-Communism. So the people believed—but not all of them. On election eve a Yale professor who was watching the returns with me over the television said wearily, after listening to Mr. Eisenhower's victory speech: *"Mark my words, before Eisenhower is through, he'll make Dean Acheson look like Custer's last stand."* I think in foreign policy that is substantially what has happened, most especially since the death of John Foster Dulles. Mr. Eisenhower has been pretty good where China is concerned (indeed, he tends to be pretty good on everything to which he does not turn his attention). Would that he had not undertaken to solve the farm problem. The solution is costing us

2-3 billion more than under Mr. Truman. I say "pretty good" because those few symbols of hope for the Far East that are left to us—non-recognition of the Red Chinese Government by the Government of the United States, non-recognition of the Red Chinese Government by the United Nations, the continued independence of little Quemoy and Matsu—are with us still, even though pressure mounts to abandon hope. Seven years later, the symbols remain, but is the restoration of freedom to China any nearer than it was in 1952? If times were better one could ask for something more, something more substantial than merely the survival of our symbols, because, after all, it is deliverance, not the mere hope of it, that gives meaning to those symbols; we might, then, under different circumstances, judge the President more critically for having found no way to press for deliverance and, more, for not having shown the spirit to make the search. Meanwhile Tibet is gone, Laos teeters on the edge, the North Koreans, scrupulously violating every term of the peace treaty, brag of having fought the West to a standstill; in Cuba the Communist revolution goes forward; the Hungarians, having written with their blood the code to the dissolution of the Communist conquest, have despaired of our blindness—but the list is too long, and too depressing, and too obvious to those here to warrant retelling; but by whatever road one travels in assessing the foreign policy of the Administration, one ends up at Camp David, where Khrushchev came after wending his way about the land, after subduing prominent members of the American press and the business community, after suppressing the insurrection led by the mayor of Los Angeles and bringing California to heel through Governor Pat Brown, who greeted Khrushchev with the words, "We who respect you, we who admire you, welcome you to California." Indeed, we mourn for Dean Acheson who, at least, enforced the Monroe Doctrine.

The trick of it is that individual people change, "things" don't. The premises of Soviet Communism were the same in 1945, when Dean Acheson was making preposterous assumptions about Communism, as they are today, when Dwight Eisenhower is making preposterous assumptions about Communism. And in between the premises were the same; the same when we lost China in 1949; the same when Dwight Eisenhower was hinting at the liberation of the Soviet satellites in 1952. The metaphysics of Soviet Communism did not change during that period. What did happen during that period is that the Soviet Union acquired control over, roughly, half the world, developed the hydrogen bomb, girded the moon with a rocket, and was cheered by San Franciscans. But these circumstantial developments do not alter—or do they?—the essential moral and intellectual relationships of men and ideas. We still pray, do we not, that the Lord will thrust into hell Satan and the other evil spirits who roam through the world seeking the destruction of souls? Or does Camp David render that prayer obsolete?

People change; their ideas change; their resolution; their power; their character; their qualities; their blood-counts: but truths, the great dogmas of the West are totally unchanged, and these Alfred Kohlberg had perceived by 1945, and has never let go of them, and never will; and if our nation had been guided by him, there would be with us tonight men and women from the interior of continental China, come to pay him tribute for the part he played in making possible the overthrow of the oppressor.

What has he done? And how? He does not have a vast publishing empire—unless you count a mimeograph machine and the estimable Miss Murray as a rough equivalent. He does not have a vast fortune. He is not a Senator, or a Congressman, or a general. He has been a businessman, a philanthropist, a publisher. But his instrument is the letter.

How many letters has he written? I do not know. I do know that a month or so ago he wrote one to the *New York Times,* and that directly under the date, he wrote "My 467th unpublished letter to the *N. Y. Times*"—which evidently so moved the editor of the letters section of the *Times* as to cause him to publish it. The next editor will face the same problem.

It was, by the way, a typical letter from Alfred Kohlberg, who has the sharpest eyes in America for the legerdemain of the mythmakers. He wrote:

> "Dear Sir:
> "Your editorial in today's issue entitled 'Red China's Trees' is apparently based in part on a dispatch in yesterday's paper by a Canadian correspondent telling about the planting of trees in Communist China. That dispatch reported 540 million fruit trees planted in the bed of the Yellow River in Honan and Shantung Provinces.
> "I have only crossed the Yellow River in its lowest course, in Shantung Province, on the Tientsin-Pukow railway, where it is approximately one mile wide. Presuming that width and a length of something up toward 500 miles in Honan and Shantung Provinces, there might be 500 square miles in the bed of the Yellow River. This equals 320,000 acres which, divided into 540 million trees, makes 1,687 trees per acre. In my native California, 40 fruit trees per acre is more or less standard procedure, so that your correspondent reports trees planted 42 times as close as in California.
> "Maybe he should have taken pencil and paper and figured this out before he swallowed the figure which

the Communist Chinese propaganda bureau sent him.

Very truly yours,
"ALFRED KOHLBERG"

How many letters has he written? Again, I cannot say: but I can say that I myself count it a day lost when I do not see a letter Mr. Kohlberg has written to the President, or to Khrushchev, or to Allan Dulles, or J. Edgar Hoover, or Mrs. Roosevelt, or de Gaulle, or Churchill, or you, or me, copy to the *New York Times,* the *New York Herald Tribune,* the CIA, etc. I do not blame the poor editors of *The Reporter* magazine for their frenzy about the China Lobby. Alfred Kohlberg has enormous firepower. He is like the lone living survivor in the beleaguered fort who goes about from dead man to dead man pulling rifle triggers to persuade the enemy that the fort is bristling with armed men. *The Reporter* cannot wholly be blamed if, on seeing a thousand bullets whiz by, they assume they are shot by a thousand men.

In the spring of 1954, which you will all recall was during the period when, as Richard Rovere likes to put it, the lights went out, Mr. Kohlberg wrote a letter—and sent it to every college president in the United States. Dear Mr. President, said Mr. Kohlberg, I hereby volunteer to appear as your Commencement speaker this spring, and enclose herein text of my address; but let me warn you, I am available only on a first-come-first-served basis. The speech was an unforgettable sequence of hysterical pronouncements on the theme of our reign of terror, woven together to make a single *cri de coeur;* and it belongs in the national archives. College presidents do not seem to smile much any more, or at least not when anybody spoofs them; and no one is witness to any smile on the face of any college president on reading Alfred

Kohlberg's proposed Commencement Address. The speech, even in those days, when so many academicians were cooperating so zestfully in the prodigious effort to transmute a heightened awareness of the problems of internal security into a reign of terror—the speech was wonderfully, giddily exaggerated, fatally overdrawn. Anyone caught reading a book by Thomas Jefferson was nowadays whisked off to jail; it took an act of raw physical courage to give money to Harvard University now that the chairman of a congressional investigating committee had served his displeasure upon it; no professor would dare to buy a foreign car for fear of reprisals by the American Legion: but then the Kohlberg touch. After each apocalyptical phrase, a tiny number, and a corresponding footnote below. Every one of those preposterous statements, it developed, had been uttered by an egregious figure in the academic world, by men like Robert Hutchins, Bertrand Russell, Henry Steele Commager. Alfred Kohlberg had simply brought together into a single address the jeremiads on our time of the principal witness of the academic world, to the Diminishing Freedoms of the American Citizen, the theme of the commencement addresses of the past four years and, inevitably, the theme of the next Commencement Service. No one, as I say, availed himself of the services of Mr. Kohlberg; but wasn't there, that first week in June of 1954, a note of self-consciousness, a little touch of restraint, in the rhetoric of the academic orators as they addressed the graduating classes and exhorted them to go out in the world and fight Joe McCarthy?

But merely because Alfred Kohlberg *does* know how to smile, it is a mistake, as near to a deadly mistake in the relationships of controversy as one can make, to assume that he is a frivolous man. The editor of *The Reporter* recently wrote that one cannot be a conservative unless one is solemn.

(If there is a correlation between solemnity and con-
servatism, heaven knows *The Reporter* would be a conservative journal.) But Alfred Kohlberg is skittish only in the
sense that Gilbert K. Chesterton could be said to have been:
he is a man totally engaged. He is concerned with the fate
of men who have fallen prey to tyranny, and with the careers
of those who cooperated in that catastrophe, and he seeks to
bring hope and relief to the former, and for the latter,
justice; and these ends he labors after with the instruments
at his command—his wit, his perseverance, his mimeograph
machine.

Should he lose hope? Should *we* lose hope? As recently
as two weeks ago, a kind and courteous gentleman, the retired chaplain of Yale University, returned from the Far
East which he visited in his new capacity as executive director of Yale-in-China, an evangelical educational project
of great distinction, and recommended that we recognize
Red China, since recognition is after all "inevitable." Is it
indeed inevitable? I do not see why; and I do not say that
because I am philosophically disinclined to concede that
anything is "inevitable." I believe it is inevitable, for instance, that, in support of recognition of Red China, the
argument will be used that recognition is inevitable. But
recognition of Red China—the betrayal of Free China—is
no more inevitable than, say, the victory of Communism all
over the world. That is not inevitable. Is it?

It is only inevitable that men will continue to misunderstand, and that the issue of recognition of Red China
will increasingly become a fetish, one of those devices—
like summit conferences—through which, substituting procedure for policy, we propose to dissipate evil spirits. The
pressures for recognition have become thunderous, and
some of the arguments were surely constructed by Rube

Goldberg. Last spring when word reached the West of the invasion of Tibet and the horrors it brought, the *New York Post* was constrained to deplore the brutalities of the Chinese Communists. The editorial went as follows: We must deplore the brutalities. The exact nature of the brutalities cannot be known because there were not present any American journalists. The journalists could not be there on account of our failure to recognize Red China, which, by the way, why the hell haven't we? If the rape of Tibet has in a single series of logically connected sequences been made to argue for the recognition of Red China, it becomes possible to explain the course of American foreign policy; and it becomes easier, much much easier, to understand what is meant by the "inevitability" of recognition.

But with the progressive disintegration of thought, it becomes correspondingly important that we persevere. Important for brave and learned and courageous men like Professors Karl Wittfogel, Richard Walker, and David Rowe to go on teaching; for principled and resourceful statesmen like Walter Robertson and Walter Judd and Francis Walter to go on leading; for penetrating and incorruptible craftsmen like George Sokolsky and James Burnham to go on analyzing; for devoted citizens like Alfred Kohlberg to go on writing those letters.

Mr. Kohlberg's efforts will be unceasing. That *is* inevitable. We shall not hear the end of him. I count that among the certitudes that govern my existence. If any of us ever strays, to find himself in the shadow of hell, we will find a letter pinned on the gates, addressed to us by name, copy to the *New Tork Times*. "Before you go any further," Alfred Kohlberg will have written, "are you aware that Satan has belonged to 23 Communist fronts?"

Chronology

1899   Open Door Policy announced by Secretary of State Hay.

1905   Russian-Japanese War.

1911   Overthrow of Manchu Dynasty. Sun Yat-sen emerges as China's leader.

1915   Japanese 21 Demands.

1921   July 1: Chinese Communist Party established.

1922   Comintern proposes admission of Communists into Kuomintang.

February 6: Nine-Power Treaty, Washington Conference.

1924   January 21: Death of Lenin.

1925   March 12: Death of Sun Yat-sen.

1927   Japan's Tanaka Memorial.

Communists break with Kuomintang.

Trotsky calls for revolutionary intervention in China.

April 12: Chiang Kai-shek arrests Communist leaders after occupying Shanghai.

December 3: Stalin emphasizes importance of Chinese revolutionary movement.

1928   July 12—September 1: Comintern Sixth Congress sets line for China's Communist Party.

1931   September 18: Japanese invade Manchuria.

November 7: Provisional Government of Chinese Soviet Republic established with Mao Tse-tung as President.

1934   The Long March by Communists from Kiangsi to Shensi (Yenan).

1935   March 16: Germany denounces Treaty of Versailles, starts to arm.

1936   December 12: Chiang Kai-shek captured.

1937   Negotiations conducted between Communists and Kuomintang for a united front against Japanese. Japan invades China.

July 7: Marco Polo Bridge incident.

July 11: Start of Soviet-Japanese clashes along borders of Siberia, Manchukuo, Korea.

August 21: Non-Aggression Treaty signed between China and the Soviet Union

August—November: Battle for Shanghai.

December 12: Japanese sink USS *Panay*.

1938   September: Czech-German crisis.

September 29: Munich Pact (Peace in our time).

1939   January 29: U.S. Communists demand end of U.S. isolation.

August 23: Hitler-Stalin Pact.

September 1: Germany invades Poland.

September 1: U.S. Communists demand United States remain neutral.

September 1: Mao denounces "imperialist" war.

September 3: England and France declare war on Germany.

September 17: Red Army invades East Poland.

1940   Mao Tse-tung writes "New Democracy."

September 2: U.S. Communists create American Peace Mobilization.

September 27: Germany, Japan, Italy negotiate tripartite pact.

1941   January 6: President Roosevelt proclaims Four Freedoms.

April 13: Russo-Japanese Neutrality Pact.

August 14: Atlantic Charter.

June 22: Hitler attacks Soviet Union.

November 26: Secretary of State Hull hands Nomura ultimatum that Japan withdraw from China and Indo-China.

December 7: Attack on Pearl Harbor.

December 8: United States declares war on Japan.

December 8: China declares war on Germany, Italy.

December 11: Germany, Italy declare war on United States.

1942 March: Eugene Dennis of CPUSA calls for playing down war in Asia to support USSR.

October: Communists call for second front.

October 10: Britain and United States voluntarily renounce extraterritoriality in China, ending 100-year evil.

1943 February 2: Germans surrender to Russians at Stalingrad.

July 14: Bisson article in IPR's *Far Eastern Survey* marks change in Communist line, signals attack on Nationalist government.

November 22—26: Cairo Meeting between Roosevelt, Stalin, Churchill, Chiang Kai-shek.

November 28—December 1: Teheran Meeting between Roosevelt, Stalin, Churchill.

1944 June: Wallace, Lattimore, Vincent, Hazard make trip to China.

June 6: D-Day.

August 18: General Pat Hurley sent to China as President Roosevelt's envoy.

October 13: General Stilwell recalled.

October 28: General Wedemeyer named to replace Stilwell.

1945   January 8: Hurley accredited as Ambassador to China.

February 4–11: Yalta Meeting: Roosevelt, Stalin, Churchill.

April 5: USSR denounces pact with Japan signed April 13, 1941.

April 12: Roosevelt dies.

April 25: Founding conference of UNO starts at San Francisco.

May 9: VE-Day.

July 3: James F. Byrnes named Secretary of State.

July 17-August 2: Potsdam Conference: Truman, Churchill, Stalin; Attlee later replaced Churchill.

August 6: A-bomb at Hiroshima.

August 9: A-bomb at Nagasaki.

August 9: Russia declares war on Japan: invades Manchuria.

August 14: VJ-Day.

August 14: Sino-Soviet Pact, based on Yalta Agreements, signed.

August 26-October 11: Negotiations between Chinese Communists and Nationalists. Talks finally collapse and strife begins.

October 20: Outer Mongolia in Soviet-sponsored plebiscite votes independence from China.

December 15: President Truman calls on Chiang to accept Communists into his government.

December 20: General Marshall arrives in China as Truman's special envoy.

1946   July 11: J. Leighton Stuart named Ambassador to China.

July 17: American China Policy Association started.

October: *Plain Talk* launched.

December 25: New Chinese Constitution adopted.

December 18: Truman proclaims "hands off" policy.

1947 January 7: Byrnes resigns as Secretary of State, is succeeded by Marshall.

January 29: Marshall abandons China mission.

August 24: Wedemeyer submits report condemning Communist actions in China. Truman, Marshall suppress it.

1948 Chiang's position seriously declines.

October: Manchuria falls to Reds; they occupy Mukden.

1949 January: Fall of Tientsin, Peiping to Reds.

January 21: Dean Acheson becomes Secretary of State.

May 25: Shanghai falls to Communists.

August 5: State Department issues White Paper disclaiming responsibility for China debacle.

July-December: Nationalist forces withdraw to Formosa.

October 1: Communists announce formation of Chinese People's Republic.

October 2: USSR withdraws recognition of Chinese Nationalist Government and recognizes Red China.

December 8: Nationalists move capital to Formosa.

1950 January 5: President Truman says we will not defend Formosa.

January 6: Britain recognizes Red China after breaking relations with Nationalist Government.

January 11: Senator Taft accuses State Department of being guided by leftists in its China policy.

January 12: Secretary Acheson in speech says Korea

outside our defense perimeter and reaffirms we will not help Formosa.

January 14: Chinese Communists seize U.S. consular property in China. We recall our officials.

January 24: Alger Hiss found guilty.

February 9: Senator McCarthy makes Wheeling "numbers" speech.

March 8: Tydings Committee begins hearings to investigate State Department employee loyalty.

June 25: South Korea invaded by North Korean troops with Russian tanks and arms.

June 26: President Truman orders U.S. forces to repel North Korean attack. Orders Navy to defend Formosa.

November 26: Chinese Communist troops intervene massively in Korea.

1951   April 10: General MacArthur removed from command.

April 19: MacArthur addresses Congress.

May 3: Russell Committee (MacArthur Hearings) begins work.

June 14: Senator McCarthy attacks Marshall in Senate speech.

June 25: Russell Committee ends hearings.

July 25: McCarran Committee starts hearings investigating IPR.

1952   June 20: McCarran Committee hearings end.

CHAPTER ONE

The Man Behind the Headlines

THE TAXI JERKED TO A STOP AT THE SENATE OFFICE
building, and a short, round-faced man clambered out.
Paying the driver, he straightened up and gazed for a
moment at the dome of the Capitol across Constitution
Avenue. Then he turned and started briskly toward a
door.

As he did a car horn sounded, insistently. He looked in
the direction of the noise and saw a woman beckoning to
him. Looking more closely he recognized her—Mrs. Helen
Lombard, an attractive widow he had met on a previous
trip to Washington. He had been introduced to her in the
office of Benjamin Mandel, Research Director of the
House Committee on Un-American Activities.

"Alfred Kohlberg!" she cried as he approached. "I bet
I know why you're here."

"You know?" he asked taking her hand. "I don't know myself. I just thought I'd take my chances on finding someone."

The woman laughed. "Don't be so coy. I know you're calling on Joe McCarthy."

Kohlberg shook his head. "I had a letter from him a week or so ago, but I had no intention of calling on him."

"Well," said Mrs. Lombard, "he's looking for you everywhere. As a matter of fact he had the wrong address or misspelled your name and couldn't find you. I just sent a young Naval Intelligence officer, whom I'm chauffeuring around here, to tell him where he could reach you. If you'll wait here a minute he will be back and can take you in."

Moments later the lieutenant returned and escorted Kohlberg to a basement room. It was a dingy, disorderly place and several people were studying papers, typing, or talking together in casual fashion. Kohlberg, looking about, found it hard to believe that this unlikely spot was a command post for a battle that was being reported all over the world in big black headlines. Here Senator Joseph R. McCarthy, with the help of his staff, was trying to counter the highly publicized attacks being made before the Tydings Committee.

Senator McCarthy was absent when Kohlberg came on this scene but the little New York businessman was soon the center of attention. Usually Kohlberg was one of the most inconspicuous of men, but here he was a celebrity. These people, with some knowledge of Communist subversion, were well aware that this was a Very Important Person indeed in the anti-Communist movement. This was the man who had dared to challenge the mighty Institute of Pacific Relations, and among people who take an interest in such things he was known as one of the most outspoken critics of our foreign policy and the people responsible for it.

In short, this was a man who knew the answers and

McCarthy's staff took advantage of his visit to pepper him with questions. Most of these, Kohlberg noted, dealt with two luminaries of the IPR—long-time adversaries of his—Owen Lattimore and Philip C. Jessup. After answering a long series of questions, he finally begged off. He told his inquisitors he had a lot of information in his files in New York, and if they would give him a little time, he would get it together and send it to them or deliver it in person.

When it became evident that Senator McCarthy would be delayed, Kohlberg left, but later that day he phoned the Senator and asked if he would join him for dinner at his suite in the Mayflower Hotel where they could talk privately. McCarthy accepted the invitation and asked if he could bring along his secretary, Jean Kerr, and a friend who was helping him, Charles Kersten, a former congressman. Kohlberg cordially invited him to do so.

"At dinner that evening," he later indicated in his personal notes, "Joe asked me to give him the story of the China sellout step by step and in chronological order. This I did during a two-hour, leisurely eaten dinner. Jean Kerr took brief notes, not in shorthand, yet the following week in a speech on the Senate floor the Senator told the story of the sellout of China just as I had told it to him there, almost without error."

The date of that first meeting of Kohlberg and McCarthy was "about March 23rd or 24th, 1950." This date should be noted carefully in view of subsequent attacks that were made against the two men. Six weeks before, Senator McCarthy had made his controversial speech in Wheeling, West Virginia, in which he had accused the State Department of harboring Communists. Because of this an investigation of the State Department had been started by the Tydings Committee on March 8, 1950. However, it soon became evident that the real aim of these hearings was to discredit both McCarthy and his charges. So obvious was the bias of Senator Millard Ty-

dings and his Democratic colleagues that they became
known as a "whitewash committee," intent on clearing
the State Department.

Shortly before Kohlberg met McCarthy there had been
another indication of this bias. Testifying in executive
session on March 21, Senator McCarthy had character-
ized the influential "China expert" Owen Lattimore as "a
top Russian espionage agent." This appraisal, supposed to
have been confidential, was promptly leaked and it appeared in Drew Pearson's column the next day. Word of
McCarthy's charge quickly reached Lattimore, then in
Afghanistan, and he immediately started home to testify
in his own defense.

McCarthy, of course, was cast as the "heavy" in this
melodrama. Much of the press portrayed him as a bluster-
ing barbarian who was seeking to destroy the reputations
of innocent people. At the height of the hearings, and
thanks largely to Owen Lattimore, Alfred Kohlberg got
similar treatment. He was described as "the man behind
McCarthy" and "the China Lobby man." As such he
achieved the ephemeral fame of newspaper headlines,
feature articles, and editorials, and the references were
usually far from flattering.

Ironically, the leftists and the liberals who attacked Alfred Kohlberg used guilt by association as their major
weapon. To them it was enough to say that he was "the
man behind McCarthy." To these evangelists of the liber-
al-left this was proof positive that Kohlberg was a scoun-
drel, but even this tenuous charge was a smear.

For reasons that will be discussed in later chapters, Alfred Kohlberg had compiled a mass of information about
people who had operated within the framework of the
Institute of Pacific Relations. There was no secret about
this, and he had been circulating such information for
several years. Indeed, hundreds of people—newspaper
editors, politicians, and others—were on his mailing list.

What McCarthy wanted and what Kohlberg gave him was the same material he had been circulating since 1944. While the left wing complained bitterly that McCarthy was using the facts supplied by Kohlberg, they also sneered that Kohlberg's information was worthless, "warmed-over charges" that had been "discredited."

Kohlberg, for one, did not think they had been discredited. At the height of the controversy, Lattimore threatened to sue McCarthy if he would repeat his charges against him without senatorial immunity. Kohlberg publicly ridiculed this as a bluff. In a letter sent to newspapers on August 18, 1950 he said:

"On March 18, 1947, I published the statement that Mr. Lattimore 'maintains liaison with heads of the Communist Party; reportedly operative for Soviet Military Intelligence.' On May 23 I repeated the above. I am financially responsible, yet Mr. Lattimore doesn't sue me."

One of Lattimore's staunchest supporters was the columnist Drew Pearson, who was probably the first to imply that Kohlberg was actively backing McCarthy. This story had its origin at the time Kohlberg and McCarthy first met. As the Senator was leaving Kohlberg's suite, he invited him to a party at Pearson's home. Kohlberg declined and may have missed a chance to get a free hat. At least the Senator showed up later with a hat Pearson had given him. The columnist was at that time being sponsored on radio by a hat manufacturer and his products were presumably being handed out to build good will. However, if Pearson didn't give Kohlberg a hat, he gave him some publicity.

The following Sunday, listeners to Pearson's broadcast heard him ask a series of questions, such as "Who paid for Senator McCarthy's secret headquarters. . . ?" and "Who paid for the 200 phone calls made from the room?" Kohlberg, "who made millions in China", was then named as a contributor to "certain very vocal senators."

Kohlberg was asked about Pearson's charges by a reporter for the *New York Compass,* an ultra-leftist paper of the time. Was it true that he was financing Senator McCarthy? Annoyed at the line of questioning, Kohlberg cut off the interview with this question:

"Do they say who supplied funds to defend Alger Hiss? When they tell me that, then I will make public my contributions."

He then wrote to Pearson telling him he was wrong. He explained that he had contributed nothing whatever to Joe McCarthy. "I was so naive," he said, "that I thought the Senate would provide the staff he had there. I further told Pearson that as long as he had called my attention to it I was going to send a contribution to the Senator. This I did a few days later, sending him a check for $500.00."

Kohlberg reports that Pearson made no correction but there was an interesting sequel. On April 11, McCarthy wrote Kohlberg as follows:

> I want to thank you very much for the check in the amount of $500.00 which you forwarded to help cover the cost of investigators, etc., in my current fight against Communism in the State Department.
>
> As you know, the left-wing columnists, commentators, etc., have been waging an all-out war to smear me personally and discredit the investigation in every way possible. One of the completely untrue and rather fantastic claims is that the investigation is being financed by what is called the China Lobby. I gather that by the "China Lobby" they refer to the recognized Chinese Nationalist Government. What makes this claim doubly ludicrous is the fact that those who have been working toward the communization of China have spent vast sums in this country but as far as I know the Nationalist Government has spent practically nothing.
>
> For some reason I gather this segment of the press is attempting to identify you with an imaginary

China Lobby. I know that if it were to appear that you contributed to hiring investigators, etc., in the amount of $500.00, they would be able to twist and distort this in the minds of the American people. Therefore, even though I am frankly in need of funds to hire additional investigators, I feel I should return this to you rather than give those who have been perverting the freedom of the press and the airways even a remote opportunity to make it appear that there is any semblance of truth to the fantastic claim that this investigation is prompted by any China Lobby. I am sure you will understand my position in the matter. With kind regards, I am sincerely yours, Joe McCarthy.

While Pearson seems to have pioneered in reporting that Kohlberg was McCarthy's financial backer, the idea soon caught on. The *New York Compass* immediately spread the word and the *Daily Worker* for April 11, 1950, told its readers some horrifying "facts" about Kohlberg in a major feature under a five-column banner headline, "The Man Behind McCarthy."

"Brain-truster of Sen. Joseph R. McCarthy's 'Communist-scare' shenanigans," the comrades were told, "in the Owen Lattimore case is a New York millionaire who amassed at least part of his fortune through semi-slave exploitation of Chinese women. He is Alfred Kohlberg, 1 West 37th Street, importer of Chinese textiles and self-proclaimed leader of Chiang Kai-shek's lobby in Washington. . . ."

Red readers were given a good Marxist explanation for Kohlberg's actions. They were told he was anxious to start a shooting war to get Chiang Kai-shek back on the mainland so Kohlberg could once again exploit Chinese women. "Kohlberg," the *Daily Worker* piously proclaimed, "could make no business deals with the new China government on the basis of this slave system."

The next attack on Kohlberg came two days later in the *Washington Post.* This was an editorial titled "Kohlberg's Klan," an exercise in what the *Post* sometimes calls "McCarthyism."

"Kohlberg," it said, "is, indeed, the so-called China or Chiang Kai-shek lobby, and as such is perhaps the moving spirit in a cabal of no mean proportions. . . . The rabid ex- and anti-Communists who have sold so many of our policy-makers that they are God's elect in the conduct of the Cold War, have rallied to his standard, and doubtless have given him a point or two in his scurrilous operations. He is a Pied Piper who has gathered to his cause a lot of disgruntled ex-officeholders and Republican diehards. . . . They are, together, a rabbit warren of conspirators and 'knife-him' artists in and out of government against the good name and standing of reputable men. . . ."

Shortly after this editorial appeared Kohlberg got a phone call from Alfred Friendly, who identified himself as a reporter for the *Washington Post.* Because of the vicious editorial and expecting that there would be more of the same, Kohlberg refused Friendly's request for an interview. This, of course, did not keep Friendly from writing about him. Said Kohlberg: "Not being able to get an interview, Mr. Friendly drew on his imagination for material. And his imagination proved extremely unfriendly to me and to Senator McCarthy but most friendly to Lattimore." The title of Friendly's article was "The Man Behind the Man Who Is Against Lattimore."

Had Kohlberg been willing to see Friendly, it is possible that certain errors in the piece could have been avoided. However, from the general tone of the piece, Kohlberg was probably correct in assuming that it didn't greatly matter whether one saw a *Washington Post* reporter or not—the story would come out pretty much the same way in either case.

One part of Friendly's lengthy story does merit attention because it posed several questions that puzzled many people. Why, he asked, did "one man's view on foreign policy—utterly at variance with those of four successive Secretaries of State" became "the canon of orthodoxy for a large segment of a major political party"? How did this man, "a private citizen, relatively obscure, and by his own admission without pretensions to being a scholar or (until recently) a statesman" get Senators to do his bidding?

"How does it happen," the article asked, "that Alfred Kohlberg, a successful New York merchant, but by no means an industrial giant or tycoon, could build up his charges to make them form almost the entirety of Senator McCarthy's key case against Owen Lattimore?"

They were good questions, all, and in this book an attempt will be made to answer them.

One of the questions that Friendly asked himself, and then answered, dealt with motives.

"Why Kohlberg's burning passion and unremitting fight?"

The answer: "To suggest that he is motivated by a desire to save his big business in China seems, to this reporter, to underestimate Kohlberg's character. His crusade must have cost him immense time that he might otherwise have devoted to his business and it has clearly cost him large amounts of money."

This at least gave Kohlberg more credit than many other writers did.

For example, the *New Republic* for April 24, 1950, carried a piece entitled "The Men Behind McCarthy" which not only came close to plagiarizing the *Daily Worker's* title, "The Man Behind McCarthy," but expressed some of the same ideas. The writer, Edward A. Harris, of the *St. Louis Post-Dispatch* imputed to Kohlberg, "This owlish, sharp-tongued busy New Yorker," the same mercenary motivation as had the *Daily Worker:*

"... Chinese women in the cottage system of piecework

finished handkerchiefs and other linens for his importing firm. Presumably this source of cheap labor has been closed to Kohlberg by the fall of the discredited Chiang government."

The *St. Louis Post-Dispatch* made it a practice to treat Kohlberg with this kind of interpretive journalism. Ordinarily he took this sort of thing in stride, but now and then he would lose his temper and express his feelings. The editor of the *St. Louis Post-Dispatch* on one occasion received, and published, one of Kohlberg's missives:

"This letter is to thank you for the recent articles and an editorial about me in your paper. . . . My effort to induce our Government to oppose the extension of Communist conquest in Asia and extend aid to the anti-Communist forces in China has heretofore brought me criticism from the Far Eastern Division of the State Department, especially Messrs. Alger Hiss, Donald Lee, John S. Service, Andrew Roth, and Lauchlin Currie, all named by witnesses as connected with espionage and the stealing of documents. It has also brought me criticism from the *Daily Worker* (listed as subversive by the Attorney General) and *Political Affairs* (also listed). I have always feared that my efforts were unavailing, but the criticism from these sources I have considered a small feather in my cap.

"Now to add the *Post-Dispatch* as another feather, even though of a slightly lighter hue, is most encouraging."

Who was Alfred Kohlberg?

The headlines that carried his name have long since been forgotten by most people, but even when he was most active, relatively few people knew who he was. As a long-established importer of Chinese textiles he was well known in the mercantile community in this country and abroad. However, he did not have many of the qualifications that are usually essential to make a person "newsworthy." He had none of the academic merit badges, earned or honorary degrees, which indicate that a person has wisdom, publicity value, or a strong sense of philanthropy. Indeed, Kohlberg never finished college. He had no political standing, even the kind exemplified by an appointment to an honorary committee by a governor or mayor. He never appeared in *Who's Who In America,* and until the time of the Tydings hearings few newspaper morgues contained many clippings under the heading, Kohlberg, Alfred.

On the face of it, he was just a little businessman who obviously did not know his place. Why, not only did he criticize such eminent scholars as Owen Lattimore and Philip C. Jessup, and the distinguished businessmen who served as trustees of the Institute of Pacific Relations; he even had the nerve to tell President Truman, General Marshall and Secretary Acheson how to conduct our foreign policy. Publicly!

From this one might picture Alfred Kohlberg as a big, burly extrovert, accustomed to elbowing his way and to shouting down opposition. Actually, he was a mild-mannered, unassuming little man who rarely raised his voice. He was short, less than five-and-a-half feet, somewhat overweight in his later years, and he was prematurely bald with a fringe of brown hair. He was soft-spoken, and usually had a smile that involved his sharp brown eyes as well as his mouth. One writer, favorably inclined to Kohlberg, called this smile "enigmatic." Another, in an article for a publication that he had no use for Kohlberg, described it as "an agile smile," which had "no warmth in it." How Kohlberg was portrayed always seemed to depend on whether he was being viewed from the right or the left.

Kohlberg dressed neatly and conservatively, but in his later years, after he had suffered his coronary attacks, he took to wearing a long, heavy overcoat to keep warm, even in fairly mild weather. People sometimes glanced curiously at the short rotund man with the long coat but until that time few people ever gave him a second look. However, his personality made itself strongly felt on short acquaintance. When he talked there was no mistaking the force of the man. He would listen quietly, attentively, and then react with solid good sense, never with bombast. A few words, quietly spoken, were usually enough to set forth a sound premise or demolish the argument of an opponent.

Most of his work was done with the written word, and for years he laboriously set down by pen or pencil every word of his vast output. This copy was later typed by his secretary. Even when he acquired a dictating machine he would occasionally revert to writing by hand, especially if the message was an important one. The written word was Kohlberg's major weapon because he was given little opportunity to get his message across to radio or television audiences. On several occasions he made radio and television appearances, but these were usually local. The networks for the most part showed little interest in what he had to say even though he volunteered. The usual response to letters he wrote offering to speak or debate were to the effect that schedules were filled and "don't call us; we'll call you."

Even so, over the years he succeeded in making his point. There is an indication of this in two yellowing newspaper clippings found in his files. One was from the *New York Daily News,* which has the largest circulation in the country. Under date of August 7, 1957, the *News* made this comment:

"During the past decade our State Department has run up an alltime record for diplomatic errors and bonehead plays in China and South Asia. One man whose predictions have proved correct and whose warnings have gone officially unheeded is New York's Alfred Kohlberg, first and most effective kicker apart of the Commie-ridden Institute of Pacific Relations."

The other clipping was from *The Lagrange Daily News,* which probably has the largest circulation in Lagrange, Georgia. Dated March 3, 1951, this editorial said: "Some guy named Alfred Kohlberg sent a letter to the *News* the other day. . . . Now when somebody writes a letter like this on pretty stationery, with all kinds of impressive branch offices, I usually read it just for curiosity. But seldom does the *News* print such a letter. . . . This one is different in some respects. It is entitled 'An Open Letter' and it is addressed to the Honorable Dean Acheson, Secretary of State, Washington, D.C.

"Kohlberg, no matter what he is or why he is motivated, poses some interesting questions. . . ."

The editorial then listed some of the questions, most of which concerned the fighting then going on in Korea. "Why," asked Kohlberg, "do you prevent General MacArthur's strategic air force from bombing the industrial areas of Manchuria, and the Communist staging areas for supplies and troops in Manchuria?"

The editor concluded with this thought:

"These all look like pretty good questions to me, Alf. Tell us if you get an answer and what some of the answers are."

But even though Kohlberg asked countless questions about our foreign policy, and about policy-makers who seemed bent on turning Asia over to the Communists, he rarely received any answers.

In time, however, answers were forthcoming. They were supplied by the Senate Internal Security Subcommittee in the course of its investigations of the Institute of Pacific Relations, and they completely vindicated the inquisitive little businessman. Unfortunately, by the time the conspiracy was revealed it had succeeded. The "diplomatic errors and bonehead plays" had turned hundreds of millions of once friendly Chinese into a force dedicated to our destruction.

CHAPTER TWO

A Family Album

IT MAY HAVE BEEN HEREDITY THAT CAUSED ALFRED Kohlberg to "go west," so far west that in time he became involved in China and China's recent history. The same westward-ho compulsion seemed to drive all four of his grandparents. When they started west from Germany, prior to the Civil War, they did not end up on the east coast of the United States as did so many of the immigrants of the time. Their travels took them all the way to California.

The Germany they left seemed to offer little opportunity or hope, particularly for Jews. The Revolution of 1848, which had shaken all the German states, had been put down, but unrest caused many to flee. Among the refugees were four young people who were destined to become Alfred Kohlberg's grandparents. Two of them,

Selig Kohlberg and Rose Meinberg, met in this country and were married in the early 1850's. They moved to Annapolis, Maryland, where Alfred Kohlberg's father Manfred was born in 1856. Selig Kohlberg had a small dry-goods store, but prior to the Civil War he gave it up and moved his family to Washington. There they remained until the war was over, when, packing their belongings, they embarked on a sailing ship to California. Selig Kohlberg opened a dry-goods store in San Francisco, but he became ill and Manfred had to leave school at the age of thirteen and run the shop.

Shortly after Selig Kohlberg and Rose Meinberg arrived in America, Alfred's maternal grandfather-to-be, Selig Wurtenberg, started out from Herstella, in Westphalia. The year was 1849 and news of the California gold rush intrigued the nineteen-year-old youth. To get to the rich gold country with the least delay he booked passage on a sailing vessel that was making the voyage by way of Cape Horn.

At about the time that he was boarding ship, a young girl of sixteen or seventeen, Natalie Wichelhausen, was also setting out for California from Germany, with her parents. Selig and Natalie met in San Francisco in 1854 and were married. Meanwhile Selig had prospered and the young couple returned to Germany. Their first child was born there but after the excitement of gold rush days in California, Germany bored them. After four years they returned to America.

As their ship approached San Francisco they found it greatly changed, and Selig Wurtenberg liked it less. After a year or so he headed for the wide open spaces of Mendocino County, a hundred miles north of San Francisco. Learning that the farmers there, in the vicinity of Ukiah, were growing wheat, he started a flour mill. However, the mill burned down, and he then built a brewery since many of his neighbors were raising hops. Eventually he shifted from brewing beer to selling it, and Alfred Kohlberg once wrote that his most vivid recollection of his grandfather Wurtenberg was as a barkeeper, proudly running his saloon in the neat little town of Ukiah.

Here Alfred Kohlberg's mother Marianne was born. Ambitious and anxious to get more of an education than that provided by the local grammar school, Mary, as she was usually called, was graduated from normal school in 1877 and became a teacher.

It was on a trip to San Francisco, made by stagecoach in those days, that Mary Wurtenberg met Manfred Kohlberg and they became engaged. However, marriage had to be postponed because Manfred was supporting his invalid parents and his two sisters. After the parents died, Manfred and Mary were married on February 21, 1886. Alfred was born the following year, on January 27, 1887, at 222 Van Ness Avenue. Another child, Alice, was born on April 11, 1889. Alice, now Mrs. Harry Geballe, still lives in San Francisco.

When Alfred reached school age, being smaller than most of the boys in his class, he soon learned about the tendency of some to pick on those who can't or won't defend themselves. He realized that he either had to submit or fight back. After having been beaten a few times he started to defend himself. As he put it, with obvious pride, "I became good enough so the bullies looked for some easier mark to pick on."

The boy attended the Turk Street School, then Hamilton Grammar School and, later on, Lowell High School. At Lowell he became interested in track and made the team. While in high school he cultivated two related interests that were to have a significant bearing on his later life. He became a printer and an author. The Kohlbergs then lived in an apartment on Pine Street and here Alfred set up a printing press that had cost him five dollars. It had a bed large enough to print a magazine, and he produced a publication called *The Westerner*, with a circle of readers restricted to family and friends.

Kohlberg graduated from Lowell in 1904, and matriculated at the University of California in August of that year. As part of his extra-curricular work he got a job as a reporter for the *Oakland Enquirer* and then for the *Oakland Tribune*, covering campus news. His most noteworthy journalistic feat, however, was for the *Daily Californian*, the campus newspaper, and for this he was almost expelled. One of his professors made some caustic comments on football and officials who encouraged it. Kohlberg sent a *Daily Cal* reporter to interview him, and the professor expanded on his original theme, even denouncing the Governor of California. The story was a sensation but Kohlberg was threatened with expulsion and was barred from the professor's class.

Kohlberg's academic career was brought to an unexpected close in his sophomore year through an act of God. On the morning of April 18, 1906, he and a roommate in a little boarding house in Berkeley were awakened at about 5 A.M. by a horrible shaking which made them think the house was coming down. Alfred was experiencing an earthquake—the *great earthquake*. Telling of that memorable occasion, he wrote:

"We got dressed and began to think about what to do next. Somebody suggested that we go to San Francisco and see what had happened to the big buildings there which were mostly made of brick. We went down and took the first train to San Francisco at about 6 A.M., arriving there before 7 A.M. From the ferry buildings we walked up Market Street and with one or two other boys I walked to where my father's business was located.

"The buildings were damaged to some extent, some were demolished, others had some of the cornices knocked off, fronts fallen out. The amount of damage was not really too large. However, we began to hear that fire was spreading in different parts of the city but we did not wait to see because we had to get back to Berkeley in time for final cadet drill that very day. So by 8 o'clock we took the ferry boat and train back to Berkeley not realizing that the city was going to burn down that day."

And burn it did. Rumors that the city was ablaze from one end to the other intruded on the morning's drill. The boys learned that gas and water mains supplying the city had been broken by the quake and the spreading fires could not be quenched. What the boys did not know at the time was that the fire would rage for three days, that it would destroy 30,000 buildings in an area of 497 blocks, and would have a toll of 500 dead and missing.

The students became increasingly restive, particularly those whose homes were across the bay, and as soon as the drills were over there was a rush to the trains. Since they were in uniform they were passed through guard lines onto the ferry. By this time the city was a vast sea of flames and young Kohlberg was faced with the job of getting to his home. Moving where the heat was bearable he followed an indirect course for miles. When he finally reached his home he found his father. The rest of the family had been sent to safety, to Golden Gate Park, and at nightfall he and his father joined them there.

Alfred then learned that the cadets from the university had been ordered to duty; so he reported. The colonel ordered him to stand by, to serve as his orderly. For five days, from Wednesday through Sunday night, he was kept on guard duty. Unable to find out anything about his folks, he asked for permission to return to San Francisco. Permission was refused so, without saying anything further, he went to the armory, turned in his rifle, and took the train and ferry to San Francisco. And so ended not only his career as a cadet but his academic career. He never returned to the campus as a student.

Fortunately, his home had been spared and his family was safe. However, his father's shop was destroyed and he was working in nearby Fillmore Street where the city had set up an emergency printing plant. Important in this were Alfred's printing press and type, now requisitioned by the authorities. Alfred found his father in charge of the plant, which was turning out passes, food orders, and other official papers. Alfred pitched in and his father gracefully bowed out, leaving the boy in charge.

Several days later, when the city was able to get bigger presses into operation, Alfred decided to continue with the business. He formed a partnership with one of the workmen his father had hired. Business boomed and the little plant ran day and night, as people stood in line to place orders. Alfred worked the night shift and slept during the day. His partner did the opposite. After ten days of this, Alfred made a disturbing discovery. The only money deposited in the bank was that which he took in. He went to his father for advice.

"If your partner has stolen from you," the older man said, "that's too bad, but you're young and there's lots of time for you to overcome that. But if he has stolen from you he will steal from your customers and you will be a partner in that stealing. His reputation will be your reputation. So there is only one thing to do. That is, get rid of him immediately. Either you must buy him out or he must buy you out, but it must be done this afternoon without fail."

The two Kohlbergs went to see the partner, who insisted that he wanted neither to buy nor to sell. The father then said, "In that case I'm going upstairs now to the judge to get an order to dissolve the partnership." The three went to the judge's chambers in the same building and the judge agreed with the solution recommended by Alfred's father. Kohlberg Senior then made a specific offer: "We'll give you all the assets except the original printing press." The partner accepted, taking all the money that was in the bank.

Proving the father's wisdom, six weeks later a sheriff came into the shop. He was looking for Alfred Kohlberg because his former partner had run away leaving some debts, and he wanted Kohlberg to settle these accounts. Papers were produced proving that the partnership had been dissolved and the sheriff went off looking for the true culprit.

Kohlberg never forgot what his father taught him about guilt by association—that if you become a partner of a crook "his reputation becomes your reputation."

Years later, in 1955, he discussed the incident of his printing partner and applied it to President Roosevelt's partnership with Stalin:

"This new partnership," he wrote, "was reduced to writing and signed with 24 other partner nations on January 2, 1942. It was called the Declaration of Washington. This was modified at Teheran and Yalta and Potsdam and Moscow until it was finally shot full of holes. In the process one-third of the world went down the flume, including several of the original signers, such as the Republics of Poland and China and the Kingdom of Yugoslavia. . . . I still think my Dad was right."

Kohlberg's printing business continued through 1906 and 1907, and it prospered. He had three full-time employees and started to think of himself as an established businessman. A sudden change came in 1908 when a bubonic plague scare hit San Francisco. To head off what could have been a disastrous epidemic, the Chamber of Commerce began a drive to kill rats and to rat-proof houses. Hundreds of thousands of circulars were needed and Kohlberg got the contract. However, Kohlberg ran an open shop and the unions announced that they would have nothing to do with the rat drive. Kohlberg went to the printers' union and agreed to sign up but he held out for one non-union employee. The union agreed to accept him and on that basis Kohlberg signed up. But as soon as this was done the union reneged and demanded that Kohlberg fire the employee. Kohlberg in disgust decided to have nothing more to do with union-controlled industry. He sold his shop and went to work for his father.

Within a year he was selling to stores in the San Francisco area. The line consisted of fancy dry goods, such as ladies' neckwear, belts, and so on. He started moving in ever widening circles and in time was traveling all over the state, even "as far as Los Angeles, which we then considered one of the smaller towns."

Alfred's territory was extended to Dallas, Texas, in 1910, for a special reason. In 1909 a pretty, dark-haired young lady from that city, Selma Bachrach, came to San Francisco to visit her aunt. Alfred met her and the following year he traveled to Texas to see her. They became engaged and were married on July 26, 1911. They set up housekeeping in San Francisco, and a son, Robert, was born the following year.

Unfortunately the business was proving unprofitable. The father started investing in real estate and the son persuaded him to concentrate on that and retire from jobbing. Then Alfred opened an office and became a western states representative for a number of New York firms.

It was at the Panama Pacific Exposition of 1915, at San Francisco, that Alfred Kohlberg discovered China—in the form of an exhibit from that country featuring laces and silks. Impressed, he called on the local firm that had installed the display but they could tell him little about it except that it had been prepared by a firm in Chefoo, China. Kohlberg offered to sell the goods and they gave him some samples. When he found that San Francisco buyers liked the stuff he decided to offer it in a wider area. That fall he started on a trip east and ended up in New York. Returning, he headed north, to Spokane.

There he found bad news awaiting him. A letter informed him that the man in Shanghai, with whom Kohlberg's orders had been placed, refused to deliver the goods. All the time and money he had spent on his eastern trip were thus wasted. Finally he made up his mind to return to San Francisco to try to raise enough money to go to China himself. He borrowed $650 on his life insurance and turned other assets into cash. This gave him just enough money for the long trip to the Orient.

Disembarking at Yokohama, he spent six weeks in Japan which he described as "a strange and exotic land, then humming with industry, some of it produced by the European war and coming from markets which had formerly looked to the European countries for their supplies."

After making some tie-ups with Japanese manufacturers, he took a small boat to Tientsin in North China. From the start China appealed to him. He fell in love with the country and its people, and wrote of "its swift-running rickshaw coolies as opposed to the plod, plod of the Japanese coolies; China with its swarming population; China with its good-natured laughing street coolies as opposed to the more serious crowds in Japan; China immediately took itself to my heart." He found a firm willing to do business with him, and gathering samples of the line he planned to sell in the United States, he started for home.

As soon as he got through customs he went to a hotel where he deposited all his luggage except one wooden case. While in the Orient he had learned there was a great shortage of snap fasteners in the United States, and they were being made in Japan to fill the vacuum created when German fasteners became unavailable because of the war. Sensing that there would be a market for them, he had filled his big case with them, and this he loaded into a cab in Seattle and took to the Western Dry Goods Company, one of his customers.

When he arrived at the store he told the buyer he had a lot of fasteners and did Western want to buy them? The buyer excitedly asked where they were.

"Downstairs," said Kohlberg, "in a taxi."

"Bring them up," cried the buyer. "I'll take them. Never mind the price."

With the money from that one transaction Kohlberg was able to pay all the expenses of his trip to the Orient.

Two days later he was back in San Francisco, ready to embark on the career that was to make him wealthy. However, war fever was gripping the country and Alfred was eager to enlist. He asked his father if he would take care of his wife and child if he went into the army, but the old man discouraged him. "Just do your duty," he advised. "When your time comes in the draft you will be called."

His draft notice finally did arrive, early in November 1918, and he started frantic preparations. Then the matter was resolved on the 11th, by the Armistice.

With travel restrictions lifted, he started on another trip to the Orient in March 1919. This time he took a different route, and it took him through Korea at the time of the uprising against Japan. Although it was a non-violent protest, it was being put down ruthlessly by the Japanese military. One aspect that Kohlberg noted was the many Korean prisoners, their arms tied behind them, being herded around by Japanese troops.

On the return trip the ship was so crowded that he had to share a cabin with two men, one of them sick with dengue fever. On reaching San Francisco Kohlberg became sick, with symptoms suspiciously like the fever of his cabin mate, but his illness was diagnosed as tuberculosis. Since he was returning to New York his doctor suggested that he go to Saranac Lake for treatment. He left his wife and Robert behind and when he reached St.

Louis a telegram was handed to him informing him that his wife had died suddenly of nephritis. He returned and after the funeral he postponed the trip to Saranac. This proved fortunate. Another doctor diagnosed Alfred's case and said it was not tuberculosis, but dengue fever. This proved correct.

He went back to New York where his brother-in-law Harry Geballe had been running the business. There he was soon joined by his sister, the Geballe's infant daughter, and his son Robert. After a few months the Geballes were about to leave for California when word came that the father, Manfred Kohlberg, had died suddenly. As though this was not enough, the day after the funeral Robert became sick and it was learned that the boy, like his mother, was a nephritis sufferer.

In time, a change came about in Kohlberg's business. At first he had dealt mostly in silks and laces, but after 1930 these gradually declined in importance. Instead, handkerchiefs dominated the business. These were made of Irish linen, bought in Belfast and shipped to China to be made up in designs prepared by experts working for Kohlberg in the United States. The delicate embroidery was done by an army of Chinese women, working through contractors, in a cottage industry that spread over a large part of southeastern China. Kohlberg made it a point to go among these people and to pay them decently for their work.

So extensive was his business that he was referred to in the United States and China as "the handkerchief king." Since the name Kohlberg was synonymous with quality handkerchiefs his business was mainly a matter of handling orders that came to the company virtually unsolicited. There came the Depression of course, but apart from this the business ran smoothly until Pearl Harbor. During World War II Alfred Kohlberg, Inc. just managed to stay in business, after a succession of years, starting about

1922, when sales ran from a million to two million dollars a year.

After World War II he re-established lines with his Chinese suppliers and business continued almost normally until the Chinese Communists seized the country in 1949. In 1957 Kohlberg decided to close up shop. The business, which for years had occupied the building at 1 West 37th Street in New York City, was liquidated and Kohlberg moved to a suite of offices upstairs where, with a small staff, he devoted himself to public affairs.

In the sweep of time between 1919 and 1951, he suffered several personal tragedies, probably the greatest of which was the death of Robert. When the boy died of nephritis on May 22, 1924, the father was heartbroken. Repeatedly in letters to members of his family he referred to the son he had lost, and each year, unless he was in a distant part of the world, he visited the boy's grave on the anniversary of his death and on his birthday.

Meanwhile he had remarried. His second wife, Charlotte Albrecht, had worked for him for several years but had left his employ because of illness. They were married in 1921 and had four children, Marjorie, Roberta, Alfred, and Laurence. Soon after Laurence's birth in 1927, disagreements arose. There was a separation in 1931, followed by a divorce the following year. The parents shared custody of the children until 1941, when a judge ruled that the children were old enough to decide where they wanted to live. Marjorie and Alfred, Jr. elected to stay with their mother, while Roberta and Laurence went with their father.

In 1933 Kohlberg was married again, this time to Jane Myers Rossen of California. On their return from a wedding trip to Europe they moved into the big house at 84 Dellwood Road, Bronxville, New York, that he had bought after his second marriage.

Ten years later Alfred's mother died in San Francisco at a time when he himself was seriously ill. He suffered another tragedy eight years later, when Jane Kohlberg died in her sleep.

In June 1952 he married Mrs. Ida Jolles, who had been widowed eleven years previously, and whom he had met in China in 1941. Owner of a world-famous needlepoint establishment, the Jolles Studios, with headquarters in Vienna, Mrs. Jolles had been forced to leave Austria to escape the Nazis. She was in China to start a needlepoint factory and met Alfred at the office of her business representative in Shanghai. After that she saw him on such occasions as when they were being shown some of the refugee camps and feeding stations of the Joint Distribution Committee. There were, of course, other meetings.

The marriage was a happy one, since the two had much in common. For one thing, Ida Jolles Kohlberg was an excellent business woman in her own right. But there was more. Mrs. Kohlberg had seen Nazism at first hand in Europe, she recognized that Communism was akin to that evil, and she proved to be a stalwart ally in Alfred Kohlberg's fight against it.

CHAPTER THREE

International Incident

MOST AMERICANS WENT TO WAR WITH THE JAPANESE when the Nipponese struck at Pearl Harbor. Alfred Kohlberg declared his personal war on Japan much earlier, and was one of the first American casualties of the war, having been shot by a Japanese soldier in 1939.

He became directly involved soon after the outbreak of the Sino-Japanese War, which started at the Marco Polo Bridge outside Peiping on July 7, 1937. Fighting had begun in Shanghai in August of that year, and he arrived there from Swatow in October. The heaviest part of the fighting was then over but there were still skirmishes on the outskirts of the International Settlement and bombs were still being dropped directly along the Whangpoo River across from the downtown section. From the rooftops Kohlberg could see the fighting that was taking place and he was able to watch the troops scurrying around in the distant trenches.

Saddened by the plight of his Chinese friends, he had, in August 1937, cabled $2,500 to Clarence Gauss, American Consul General in Shanghai, to be used to help them. When he arrived in Shanghai, Mr. Gauss told him that this money had been used as the nucleus of a fund, raised locally, which had already helped tens of thousands of Chinese, uprooted from the fighting zone, to return to their homes in the surrounding countryside.

The plight of the refugees in and near Shanghai was pitiful. Kohlberg estimated that "possibly an extra million" squeezed themselves into the International and French Settlements during this crisis.

Like most Americans, at the time of the Mukden Incident of 1931, and afterwards when the Japanese seized Manchuria, Alfred Kohlberg had believed their propaganda, which was that they were going to restore peace so that business and life could go on in spite of the so-called Civil War in China. He thought that once the Japanese had pacified Manchuria all would be well. But by 1937, seeing what was taking place, he had a clear picture of what the Japanese were up to—the conquest of all China.

"Once I was thoroughly convinced of that," he said, "everything became clear and doubt vanished from my mind as to the rights and wrongs of the Sino-Japanese War. What I saw in Shanghai only served to confirm the opinion I had slowly come to by that time."

The following year, 1938, he was again in China, once more going to Hong Kong, Swatow, and Shanghai. On this occasion he ran across something that he thought had special significance. As he described the incident:

> On arriving in China, immediately after the signing of the Pact of Munich in September 1938, I got the impression that something funny was going on,

which was confirmed when I met a man by the name of Vlassos on the boat going from Shanghai to Swatow. Vlassos was a Greek aeronautical engineer, married to a Chinese wife, and working for the United Aircraft Company at the airfields in Free China, servicing planes which United had sold to the Chinese Government.

He confirmed my suspicions about the absence of the Russians at Munich by telling me that the Russian aid to China, which had started in 1937, had ended very suddenly in the summer of 1938. It was apparent to me that there could be only one explanation for this, and that was that the Russians had made a deal with the Japanese.

It was also apparent to me that the Russians would not make a deal with the Japanese, who were their real enemies on the east, if they could not at the same time make a deal with the Germans, who were their real and more important enemies on the west. By the time I had returned to the United States I had worked out a complete theory to explain a Russian-Japanese-German agreement.

This he gave to the press in San Francisco, and later, to the press in New York. The *New York Times* of November 25, 1938, published the story under the head, "Soviet Aid to China Reported Ended."

In an attempt to underscore his findings he addressed a memorandum to Dr. Stanley Hornbeck, political adviser of the Far Eastern Division of the Department of State. Dated February 2, 1939, and headed "The Real Explanation of Munich," his memorandum presented the thesis that Hitler and Stalin were planning a deal and that the old Bolsheviks who opposed this alliance with the Nazis were having a hard time, indeed imperiling themselves.

Kohlberg offered an interesting bit of evidence to support his theory:

"By the early summer of 1938 this process of liquidation in Russia was almost complete and word of the
coming German-Japanese-Russian alliance had
leaked from the inner circles and come to the attention of Marshal Bluecher, Supreme Commander of
the Russian-Siberian Army. Being strongly opposed
to such an alliance (as had been the high command
of the army in Russia proper) Bluecher took it on
himself to stop the conclusion of such an alliance by
starting an attack on Japan in late June and early July
at Changkufeng Hill on the Korean-Manchurian-
Siberian border. This attack, within a few days, developed into a first-class war and ended with the
Russians in command of the hill after the almost complete annihilation of an entire Japanese division. Instead of resulting in breaking off negotiations with
Germany and Japan, it brought about their swift conclusion and the removal of Marshal Bluecher from his
command. . . ."

Continuing, he noted that both the Germans and the
Russians had been changing their propaganda line, gradually diminishing the violence of their attacks on each
other and aiming instead at England, France, the United
States, and certain individuals and elements within those
countries. "The next moves on the international chess
board," he said, "may be expected to develop in the form
of attacks by Germany, Japan, and Italy against the British
and French Empires."

Long afterwards he wryly pointed out that no one had
taken him seriously at the time. More than six months after
he wrote to Dr. Hornbeck, the Ribbentrop-Molotov agreement was made public on August 23, 1939. Then the
whole world understood that Russia and Germany had
come to an agreement, thus setting the stage for World
War II.

When Kohlberg arrived in Hong Kong in 1939 he
learned that the U.S. Navy would be sending a destroyer

up to Swatow within a few days. He was told he would be allowed to travel on this ship, the first vessel to make the trip since the Japanese occupation. At Swatow he found that the Japanese had closed the harbor to all shipping. A curfew had been imposed and Japanese troops patrolled the streets. As an American, Kohlberg was able to secure permits allowing him and some of his associates to travel upcountry to bring back goods that had been made for him, and held, because the port was closed.

These trips were made in small boats. On the morning of August 31, 1939, Kohlberg's party started up a branch of the Han River in whose delta Swatow is located, leaving the city at dawn. Their destination was 35 miles from Swatow and they had traveled half this distance when a Japanese sentry on the bank of the river fired at the party. Kohlberg was hit in the leg, receiving a very bad gash; the bullet just missed the bone. The boat immediately put in to shore and landed at the sentry post, where Kohlberg showed a pass and got a first-aid dressing from the sentry.

They then started up-river again but his wound became so painful that Kohlberg ordered the boatman to turn around and head for Swatow. Soon after this a Japanese speedboat came along and arrested them. They were held from 2 P.M. until 9 P.M., at which time they were allowed to go after they signed a release. The trip back to Swatow in the dark was dangerous but they eventually arrived there safely. Kohlberg reported to the American destroyer where a pharmacist's mate re-dressed the wound and gave him an anti-tetanus shot. The diplomatic moves that followed were thus described by Kohlberg:

> The very next morning the American Consul General came to me and after my protest was filed we began to get results rather quickly. The shooting occurred on August 31, 1939. The Ribbentrop-Molotov or Hitler-Stalin Pact had been made public on August 23, 1939, and the war in Europe began on September

1, 1939. The Japanese, not knowing the insides of the Ribbentrop-Molotov Agreement, feared that Germany and Russia had come to terms and left them out in the cold. All of a sudden they thought it advisable to cultivate the good will of Great Britain and the United States, whose friendship they had spurned from 1937 on, and then came the Kohlberg incident. So the Japanese ordered their authorities to make every possible reparation to me.

It began with the Japanese Consul General coming to call to apologize on behalf of His Imperial Japanese Majesty and on behalf of His Imperial Majesty's Commander for the area. The Consul General spoke pretty good English, having been stationed in the United States at one time, so I sat him down after he had finished his apologies and told him it was fortunate that my leg was not worse than it was, but that much more serious things impended. I told him I had had 25 years of business and travel in Japan and China and had many friends in both countries; that it hurt me greatly to see my Japanese friends fighting my Chinese friends; but bad as that was I told him I saw something even worse in the future and that was a war between his country and mine. And all of it, I told him, will be the fault of the Japanese Army, because they are running hog-wild, causing all this trouble and seeking more. "All that your diplomatic services are allowed to do," I told him, "is to make the apologies after the army makes the mistakes." I called his attention to the mistakes made in my case by the army, particularly in arresting me after shooting me.

To my surprise he agreed with me completely, and said: "I wish you would come and tell this to the political chief of the army, Colonel somebody-or-other." I agreed to do so. The next morning he called for me in his car and took me to see this colonel, and he acted as interpreter. Before going to see the colonel I had arranged that the chairman of the American group in Swatow, Mr. Fred Maloof, was to accompany me, so that he would know everything that went on.

To cut this story short, the net result of my talk with this colonel was that Japanese transports were made available to American shippers, both import and export, and the harbor remained open until Pearl Harbor itself put an end to everything. This gave me the great satisfaction a week or so later, when I was suffering with an infected leg in the hospital in Hong Kong, of thinking how useful I had been to my competitors in getting the port opened for them.

Shortly after Pearl Harbor, Kohlberg tried to settle his score with the Japanese by offering his services to the Navy as a kamikaze pilot. This, it might be noted, was before the Japanese started using that suicide technique.

Kohlberg had become an expert pilot by 1930. His global travels in early commercial airlines made him an air enthusiast, and he decided to buy his own plane and learn how to fly. His first craft was a Stinson that could accommodate three passengers and a pilot. It was a closed-cabin job, a monoplane with a high wing. He found a pilot in Captain Bill Sievert, a World War I flier, and he lost no time in putting the ship to use. His first trip was to California to see his parents, and he started taking flying lessons on the return flight. His family was spending the summer on Cape Cod and he used to fly there every weekend. He also took some of his customers aloft, though only a few of those who were invited took him up on his standing offer to take them flying.

This hobby preoccupied him for years. He had a succession of planes and he became a skillful pilot. He boasted of his weather judgment and maintained that he never got lost. During his eleven years of private flying, from 1930 to 1941, he logged tens of thousands of miles.

World War II curtailed his flying to some extent but it

did not end his aerial activities. After all "there was a war on" in Europe and elsewhere and aviation was an important part of it. Kohlberg, aware of the implications of the war in Europe through having seen the other face of it in Asia, was becoming increasingly involved. As a Jew, he felt that Jews in Americà had a duty to help their co-religionists in Europe and he was active in raising funds for the Joint Distribution Committee, a predecessor of the United Jewish Appeal. In 1939 when the latter was formed he was made chairman, first of the handkerchief group, and then of the entire handkerchief, glove, and linen division.

"By dint of personal calls day after day on all the members of the trade," he said, "I organized them into a rather closely knit group and raised several times the amount of money they had been providing for relief of Jews in Europe."

Then he added, "I was rather rough in my approach and was accused of browbeating them into giving contributions. I did it with the best of intentions, however, always making the largest contribution myself."

But fund-raising was not Kohlberg's true forte, especially when Hitler made his move into Norway and Denmark and then sent his *Wehrmacht* pouring through Holland and Belgium into France. The disastrous news from the fighting fronts day after day so aroused him that finally, on Memorial Day 1940, he flew to Toronto to try to enlist in the Royal Canadian Air Force. Although he lied a few years off his true age of 53, he was rejected. He asked the Canadians to reconsider and was referred to Ottawa. He flew there that very day.

Although it was late when he reached Ottawa he took a chance on finding someone at RCAF Headquarters and met a Wing Commander, Homer Smith. Kohlberg explained the reason for his trip but was informed that the RCAF had more volunteers than it could handle and there was no chance at all for a man over 50. Unbeknownst to Kohlberg, however, Wing Commander Smith appealed to top authority on behalf of the American. Early the next morning he phoned Kohlberg saying that Billy Bishop, Air Marshal of Canada, wanted to see him. But unfortunately, Kohlberg's age was against him and he did not get his hoped-for chance to serve.

Kohlberg's offer to serve as a kamikaze pilot for the U.S. Navy was made when the Japanese struck at Pearl Harbor. Two days after that attack, Artemus L. Gates, Assistant Secretary of the Navy, received a letter which said, "I am 47 years old, have 846 hours of certified solo time all on single engine jobs of 450 horsepower or less, mostly cross-country, including some blind flying. I feel competent, after a little checking, to fly anything and am willing to dive into any objective my commander would consider worth-while. Can you use me?"

The letter, incidentally, was addressed to the Assistant Secretary as "My dear Dye," and "Dye" knew the sender was quite serious in making this offer. His surprised reaction is indicated in this reply:

"I have your offer very much in mind. In fact I have not been able to forget it since you wrote me early in December, but to date I just don't know where such 100 percent unselfish services can be used. Perhaps the opportunity will develop, but I think our battle in the Pacific is going to be a long war."

The "long war" dragged on and in 1943 Kohlberg again offered his services to Assistant Secretary Gates, this time with a specific suggestion:

"The enclosed article in last night's *Sun* suggests to my mind the possibility of flying a fair-sized plane with a full load of explosives directly into the submarine hangars at L'Orient. It would be extremely interesting to see what an explosion in that confined space would do to their bomb-proof hangars."

Friend "Dye" again rejected the offer.

Meanwhile Kohlberg had been serving in the Civil Air Patrol. He was assigned to a base at Pascagoula, Mississippi, but his stay was brief. He flew two patrols a day, out over the Gulf of Mexico, looking for submarines. However, he never spotted a sub. Not much interested in going through needless motions, he was not reluctant to leave the CAP.

CHAPTER FOUR

The China That Was

WHEN THE COMMUNISTS STARTED THEIR PROPAGANDA campaign in this country against the Chinese Nationalist Government, they had an enormous advantage. To most Americans China was indeed "the mysterious East," and pro-Communist propagandists exploited this ignorance to the utmost as they hacked out books, magazine articles and newspaper stories that were loaded with distortions. The basic theme of their propaganda was that the Nationalists were corrupt, incompetent, and cowardly, and only in areas held by the Chinese Communists was any effort being made to fight the Japanese.

This line had become generally accepted in the United States when the Honorable Walter H. Judd, of Minnesota, made a speech in the House of Representatives in which he reminded Americans of certain facts, and told them how much they owed Chiang Kai-shek. In this speech, delivered March 15, 1945, Dr. Judd said:

"Mr. Churchill and Mr. Roosevelt made the basic decision right after Pearl Harbor to hold defensively in the Pacific while disposing of Germany and Italy in Europe. So we poured 98 percent of our supplies into Europe and less than 2 percent into east Asia, and less than 10 percent of that went to the Chinese. Up until a few months ago, when we finally began to consider the Chinese armies of sufficient importance to make an all-out effort to be of assistance to them, they had only two-tenths of 1 percent of all the supplies that we sent abroad to our armies."

Then, taking cognizance of the Communist line that Chiang was unworthy of help, the congressman continued:

"Now suppose that Mr. Roosevelt and Mr. Churchill had reversed their decision, had decided to beat Japan first and then sent 98 percent of our aid to Asia. Where would England have been? She would have gone long ago. Nobody would have cursed the British as cowards and worthless because they could not fight without arms. And Russia could not possibly have held as she did at Stalingrad, and she could not be doing what she is doing now if she had not had help—lots of it. China did not get much help."

While most Americans believed in giving top priority to the war in Europe, and concentrated on winning that war, as Dr. Judd pointed out, the Russians placed things in a different perspective. In Communist planning, the postwar world was constantly kept in mind, and in the Kremlin's brave new world China occupied a dominant position. Indeed, the "final victory" that Communists never cease boasting about is based on the premise of a Communist China. Here is how Lenin explained it in 1923:

"In the last analysis, the outcome of the struggle will be

determined by the fact that Russia, India, and China, etc., constitute the overwhelming majority of the population of the globe. And it is precisely this majority of the population that during the past few years has been drawn into the struggle for emancipation with extraordinary rapidity, so that in this respect there cannot be the slightest shadow of doubt what the final outcome of the struggle will be. In this sense, the final victory of socialism is fully and absolutely assured."

This threatening prediction was ignored by many American policy-makers and "molders of public opinion" during and after World War II. Indeed, some of these people operated actively in behalf of the Communists who were trying to seize control of China, and much of the work was done in our own State Department.

In his efforts to alert the American people to this situation, Alfred Kohlberg frequently quoted a diplomat of an earlier day, the American Secretary of State, John Hay, who at the turn of the century made this observation: "The storm center of the world has gradually shifted to China. Whoever understands that mighty empire socially, politically, economically, and religiously, has a key to politics for the next five hundred years."

The Open Door Policy of John Hay, which attempted to preserve the territorial and administrative integrity of China, was also a favorite theme of Kohlberg's. Why, he used to ask, did we go to war over this basic issue, and win this war at a fabulous cost in American lives and treasure, only to permit the Soviet Union through its Communist stooges to acquire the control the Japanese had been seeking and slam the door on the rest of the world?

Actually, China had long been a target of Russian expansionism. The czars had penetrated and colonized Chinese territory long before World War I, and ambitious plans for further Russian expansion awaited only a victorious conclusion to that conflict. The Boshevik Revolution of 1917 changed matters to some extent, as the new Communist regime piously proclaimed that it was renouncing privileges that Imperial Russia had obtained in China, and intended to help China in her struggle for independence. Which of course meant that the Communists intended to undermine Western influence and eventually establish a Soviet China.

There was a revolutionary base on which to build. The Manchu dynasty had been overthrown in 1911 and the revolutionaries under Dr. Sun Yat-sen agreed on Yuan Shih-kai as President of their new Republic. However, Yuan soon made it plain that he intended to start a new dynasty, and Dr. Sun and his Kuomintang rebelled and had to flee the country. For several years China was in a chaotic condition, aggravated by World War I and the depredations of various warlords, and it was not until 1923 that a start was made toward a stable government. Important in this was a young member of the Kuomintang, Chiang Kai-shek. Chiang had taken part in the 1911 revolution, in 1923 he was Chief of Staff in the Headquarters of the Commander in Chief of the Kuomintang forces, and in 1924 he had the opportunity of learning about Communism at first hand on a mission to Moscow which lasted four months.

The kind of chaos and anarchy that existed in China at the end of World War I was made to order for the Communists, particularly since Sun Yat-sen had established two instruments which they felt could be exploited. One of these was Dr. Sun's *San Min Chu I,* the Three Principles of the People, which constituted the heart of his doctrine for the guidance of the new Chinese nation. The other was his Kuomintang Party. Even though Dr. Sun had specifically rejected Communism, the Communists were sure they could make it appear that the Three Principles were essentially Communist doctrine. As for the Kuomintang, the Communists were confident they could infiltrate and control it, especially since Dr. Sun had given them an opening.

Making a mistake that has been made many times by otherwise astute leaders, Sun Yat-sen decided that it was possible to collaborate or coexist with Soviet Russia. Indeed, he had little choice since the West refused to help the new China that was coming into being. But acceptance of aid and advice that Russia offered led to the inevitable—before long a Trojan Horse of formidable proportions was installed within the Great Wall of China.

China's Communist Party was officially formed in July 1921 when the First Congress of Chinese Marxists was held in Shanghai. To get the Party going, Moscow sent one of its Comintern agents, Gregory Voitinsky. Among the early officials of the party was the assistant librarian of Peking National University, one Mao Tse-tung. Another helper in those days was a Soviet agent of Dutch background, Sneevliet, who operated under the name of G. Maring. The persuasive Maring met with Dr. Sun in Kweilin in 1921 and convinced him that Russia's New Economic Policy was essentially the same as China's Program of Industrialization.

In December 1921 Lenin dispatched his personal representative, Adolf Joffe, to Shanghai where he met Dr. Sun to discuss cooperation between the Russian Communist Party and the Kuomintang. Out of this meeting came the famous statement:

"Dr. Sun holds that the Communistic order or even the Soviet System cannot actually be introduced into China because there do not exist here the conditions for the successful establishment of either Communism or Socialism. This view is entirely shared by Mr. Joffe, who is further of the opinion that China's paramount and most pressing problem is to achieve national unification and to attain full national independence, and regarding this task, he has assured Dr. Sun that China has the warmest sympathy of the Russian people and can count on the support of Russia."

Next on the Chinese scene was a fabulous character, Michael Borodin. Born in Russia, he had been taken to America by his parents when he was a child. Under the name Berg he operated a business school in Chicago, but having become a dedicated Marxist he went to Russia after the Revolution and became an agitator under the name Borodin. After serving as a Soviet agent in Mexico, Scotland, and Turkey, he turned up in Canton where he was warmly welcomed.

Charmed by the crafty Borodin, Sun Yat-sen made him adviser to the Kuomintang, and the Russian used this position to get Chinese Communists formally admitted into that important body. During this time, needless to say, relations between Russia and China were amicable because Moscow was getting exactly what it wanted— gradual control over the country through Russian influence on China's leaders.

A change came soon after Sun Yat-sen's death on March 12, 1925. In December of that year a group of Chinese leaders met and demanded the expulsion of Communists from the Kuomintang and the dismissal of Borodin and his Russian associates. This move was opposed, curiously enough, by Chiang Kai-shek. This was not because he had any of Dr. Sun's illusions about the possibility of coexisting with the Communists. His stay in Russia had thoroughly convinced him that the Reds were never to be trusted. But since he was about to start a massive military campaign against the northern warlords, he did not wish to encourage an open break with the Communists. He did, however, remove much Communist influence from the army by sending the Russian military advisers home.

Concentrating on the troublesome warlords, he wiped out those who refused to cooperate with the Nationalist

Government. This task was pretty well completed in 1928 but the Communists provided some serious diversions that complicated the task. In Hankow they had set up a separate government in 1927, and Chiang had to drive them out. In Shanghai there was a serious uprising, and here Chiang struck back ruthlessly, killing hundreds of Communist students and workers. Other trouble spots were Nanking, Canton, Nanchang, and Swatow, where Communist uprisings had to be put down by force. In the course of these troubles, thousands of Chinese Reds were executed.

Meanwhile a number of incriminating Communist documents had fallen into Chiang's hands. These told how the Reds intended to eliminate the Kuomintang Party, replace it with the Communist Party, and set up a Soviet state. These he subsequently published to justify the actions he took against the traitors involved. The Kuomintang was purged of Communists, and Borodin and his Russian associates had to get out of the country. The widow of Sun Yat-sen, who had favored the Communists, went to Moscow, where she became useful as a symbol. Indeed, Mme. Sun is still proving helpful to the Communists, currently speaking up for Ho Chi Minh against American actions in Vietnam.

Chiang's successful action against the Communists took Moscow by surprise. Since he had kept his opinions about Communism and Communists to himself, the Kremlin considered him as tractable and subservient as other Chinese who had been indoctrinated in Moscow. Indeed, Chiang was looked upon in Moscow as a means to their end of establishing a Soviet China, and there is reason to believe that 1927 was supposed to mark the advent of a Red China. Many Communist functionaries, including America's gifts to the conspiracy, Earl Browder and Eugene Dennis, started turning up in China at that time, possibly with the idea that the Red uprisings were going to bear fruit.

In thwarting the plans of the Kremlinites, Chiang Kai-shek of course earned their hatred. Moscow, which had looked upon him with tolerance, now called for its Chinese stooges to wage all-out civil war against him. Chiang then gave the Red hierarchy further reason to hate him. Seeking to survive, the Communists had taken control of a small area of Kiangsi Province and gradually built up an army.

In 1930 Chiang started an offensive against them, but the Reds fought back doggedly, for four years. Meanwhile, in 1931 they held a congress and adopted a constitution for a Soviet China, with Mao Tse-tung as President. After six tries, Chiang dislodged the stubborn Communists from Kiangsi in 1934, but as he moved in for the kill they eluded him in one sector and started their famous "Long March." This took a host of Reds, including women and children, to Shensi Province, 2,000 miles distant, where 20,000 of them made Yenan their capital. Through this maneuver they made themselves virtually inaccessible to Chiang and managed to survive.

Chiang has been criticized for having allowed the Communists to escape him, but at the time of the "Long March" Communism was only one of his problems. His battles with the warlords had been costly in men and money and in 1931 he also had the Japanese to contend with. In September of that year Japanese troops had invaded Manchuria, following the explosion of a bomb on the tracks of the South Manchurian Railway near Mukden —the famous "Mukden Incident." By the end of 1931, Chinese forces had been forced to withdraw to south of the Great Wall, and on March 20, 1932, the Japanese attacked Shanghai. After two weeks of bloody fighting they took the city, only to relinquish it when world opinion resounded against them. However, a year later they were again on the offensive, this time in the provinces just below Manchuria.

Aware that his government was in no condition to wage a major conflict with the Japanese at this time, Chiang did his best to avoid war. This gave the Chinese Communists the opportunity they had been seeking to stir up trouble. Through mass demonstrations, violent speeches, and the printed word, they denounced Chiang Kai-shek as pro-Japanese and harped on the theme that since Chiang could not be trusted the Chinese people should look to the Communists for help and guidance. What was not made known to the Chinese people was the fact that Moscow was appeasing the Japanese even more abjectly than the Kuomintang. Despite repeated provocations on the part of the Japanese, the Russians kept avoiding any moves that could have involved the USSR in war with Japan.

Out of this situation a new Communist line was developed, as usual with the idea of giving aid and comfort to Soviet Russia. Increasingly worried by the possibility of a two-front war, with Germany on one flank and Japan on the other, the Russians took steps to counteract the threat. In 1935 the Comintern advised Communist Parties in all countries to establish and work in harmony with united-front groups of all kinds opposed to fascism. Under this dispensation, even the detested Chiang Kai-shek and his Kuomintang were needed as allies.

To make certain that he would in fact become a partner, the Communists staged the famous Sian incident of December 1936. The author of a novel dealing with foreign intrigue might well dismiss such a plot as too fanciful, and indeed, the story has never been fully clarified. However, the Generalissimo was kidnaped in Sian by some of his officers, headed by Chang Hsueh-liang and Yang Hucheng. Communist leaders were present and, by a strange coincidence, an American woman, Agnes Smedley, was in Sian on that historic occasion. Miss Smedley was an active propagandist for the Communists and was later identified as an important cog in the Sorge spy machinery.

Chiang was held prisoner for two weeks during which time his captors demanded that he stop harassing the Communists and start fighting the Japanese. When he refused the Communists decided to kill him. At this point, it is said, orders came from the Comintern to release him and this was done. One story in explanation of this is that the Comintern has learned that an arch-rival of Chiang's, Wang Ching-wei, was on his way to China from Germay, where he had reached an understanding with Hitler. Fearful that a Nationalist Government headed by Wang would get the help of Germany and Japan in crushing the Chinese Communists, and would permit the Japanese to apply pressure against the entire Russian border, the Comintern decided to play along with Chiang Kai-shek.

No agreement between the Communists and the Nationalists was announced at the time Chiang was released, unharmed, but it was assumed that this action signaled the start of a united front. Formal action came later when on February 10, 1937, the Chinese Communist Party's Central Committee came forth with detailed proposals. On September 22, 1937, agreement between Nationalists and Communists was reached, and a statement was issued pledging these four points:

"1. The Communist Party shall strive for the realization of Sun Yat-sen's three principles of the people, which answer the present-day need of China.

"2. It shall abandon the policy of armed insurrection against the Kuomintang regime, and the policy of Red propaganda, and the policy of land confiscation.

"3. It shall abolish the Soviet Government and institute a system of democracy, so that the nation may be politically united.

"4. The Chinese Communist Party will stop calling its

armed forces the Red Army, abolish their existing military designations, integrate them into the National Revolutionary Forces, subject them to the jurisdiction of the National Government and await orders to march to the front to fight the Japanese."

These pledges the Communists proceeded to dishonor from the start, and while the Soviet Union gained from the agreement, it had tragic consequences for China and the Chinese people.*

China's all-out declared war with Japan began on the night of July 7, 1937, when Japanese troops fired on a Chinese detachment near the ancient Marco Polo Bridge outside Peiping. Chiang's fears about starting a full-scale war with Japan at this juncture were soon justified. The Japanese quickly took Peiping, following which Shanghai was overwhelmed after three months of bloody fighting in which the Japanese had every advantage in the way of modern weapons against the poorly equipped Chinese. Nanking then fell to the Japanese and its inhabitants were slaughtered. After four months of bitter fighting the Japanese seized the temporary capital of Hankow. In this battle, 230,000 Japanese with artillery and air support overcame more than a million poorly armed Chinese troops, and after this disaster the capital was moved 500 miles up the Yangtse River to Chungking.

However, as though to make up for these calamities, and to keep him fighting the Japanese, the Kremlin spoke well of Chiang for a couple of years. This good opinion was shared and disseminated by people everywhere who normally allow the Kremlin to do their thinking for them. Indeed, as proof of the high esteem in which Stalin held

---

*Mao Tse-tung's plans for "a new China" were utterly incompatible with these pledges. What he had in mind was spelled out in a pamphlet called China's New Democracy. Called the most important document for the understanding of world Communism produced outside of Moscow since 1917, it is presented as Appendix A.

Chiang at this time, he signed another of his widely used non-aggression pacts with him.

The situation changed when Hitler and Stalin negotiated *their* non-aggression pact on August 23, 1939. There was no longer any necessity for the united front so the Chinese Communists had no reason to pretend that they liked the Nationalists. Fighting broke out between the two forces, and Communists all over the world again denounced Chiang. In Kohlberg's words, the switch in the party line again made him "a heel." And in Communist eyes he remained a heel until Hitler turned against his erstwhile ally Stalin on June 22, 1941. Then, once again, Soviet Russia needed all the help it could get, so once more the Communists became solicitous of the Generalissimo, and again they spoke well of him.

The entire business was of course an act. The Chinese Communists throughout all these zigs and zags of the party line behaved exactly like Communists. Even while going through the motions of patriotic Chinese fighting the Japanese invaders, they were thinking and acting in terms of Communist goals. This is proved by a secret directive that Mao Tse-tung sent to Communist officers in 1937, when the Communists were supposed to be cooperating with the Nationalists:

> The Sino Japanese War gives the Chinese Communists an excellent opportunity to grow. Our policy is to devote 70 percent of our effort to our own expansion, 20 percent to coping with the Government, and 10 percent to fighting the Japanese. There are three stages in carrying out this fixed policy:
>
> The first is a compromising stage, in which self-sacrifice should be made to show our outward obedience to the Central Government and adherence to the Three People's Principles; but, in reality, this will serve as camouflage for the existence and development of our party.

The second is a contending stage, in which two or three years should be spent in laying the foundations of our party's political and military powers, and developing these until we can match and break the Kuomintang, and eliminate the influence of the latter north of the Yellow River.

The third is an offensive stage, in which our forces should penetrate deeply into Central China, sever the communications of the Central Government troops in various sectors, isolate and disperse them until we are ready for the counter-offensive, and wrest the leadership from the hands of the Kuomintang.

In employing this treacherous strategy, by the time World War II ended Mao's Communists had acquired control over an area of roughly 300,000 square miles with a population of approximately 116,000,000. This they did without suffering military losses at all comparable with those sustained by the Nationalist armies. Despite incessant Communist propaganda that inflated the achievements of Mao's Red Army army into heroic proportions, the fact is that they caused the Japanese relatively little trouble. In one respect they were actually helpful to the Japanese who used to deploy their trainees against Communist forces to give them actual combat experience without subjecting them to serious risks.

In this connection, an interesting point was made by Congressman Judd in the 1945 speech quoted earlier in this chapter:

"I was working in our hospital in Fenchow, Shansi Province," he declared, "when the Japanese finally captured the city on February 17, 1938. In the next two weeks they pushed on west seventy-five miles to the Yellow River, which separates us from the Communist province of Shensi. There the Japanese have been within a hundred miles of the Communist capital, Yenan, for just over seven years, and have not made a single major effort to get that Communist capital. I wish somebody would explain that. . . ."

At the end of 1938 the Japanese controlled virtually every part of China that had any economic value. By October the major ports were in Japanese hands, isolating China from the rest of the world. By seizing the Yangtse and Yellow River valleys they secured the nation's most important source of food. They confiscated most of the country's industries and they controlled the major railroads.

Supplies needed by Chiang to carry on the war dwindled to a trickle. After the fall of France in 1940 Western nations no longer tried to deliver goods through Burma and Indochina. Russia sent equipment for awhile, but these shipments dropped off as the Soviet Union became increasingly embroiled in Europe and started making deals with its former enemies. When the Kremlin signed a non-aggression pact with Japan in April 1941, making the Soviet position fairly secure in the East, there was even less reason for giving China any aid.

Meanwhile the United States, traditionally China's good friend, took an ambiguous position with regard to Japan, one which encouraged the militarists of that nation in their moves in Asia. In what seemed to be a probing action, the Japanese in 1937 made an aerial attack on a U.S. gunboat, the *Panay,* anchored at Nanking in a spot designated by the Japanese themselves. The United States did nothing about it, and meekly waited three months before it even sent Japan a bill for damages. Our State Department, in an action hardly befitting a great power, instructed its diplomats to avoid going any place or getting into any situation that might lead to trouble. Above all, they were told, they had to run away from hostilities. The Japanese were delighted at this display of neutralism which to them looked very much like cowardice.

But the fact is, the United States was not neutral. We were feeding the Japanese war machine with American steel and American oil, and this trade continued until the summer of 1941 when an embargo was declared.

On the other side of the ledger, there was much popular support for China in the United States. Chiang was promised aid short of war, and a little aid was indeed forthcoming—a loan of $20,000,000 in March 1940, and another loan of $25,000,000 in September of that year. We were more generous in sending experts of various kinds to China, including some whose expertise and loyalty were seriously questioned years later by official investigating agencies—Owen Lattimore, Lauchlin Currie, and John Carter Vincent.

Of far more value to Chiang Kai-shek and the Chinese people were the Flying Tigers. They showed up in China in 1941, at about the time that Britain opened the Burma Road at the insistent urging of the United States. Claire Chennault, a veritable "rock of a man," who headed this fabulous volunteer group, had been in China since 1937 but had spent most of his time until 1941 building airfields, trying to get planes and pilots, and cutting the red tape that seemed to tangle every move he tried to make. Now, with the backing of Washington, the Flying Tigers were in business with their shark-nosed P-40's, and the Japanese no longer controlled the skies over China.

Things were changing in the United States too. There was a widespread feeling that this country ought to stay out of war, a feeling recognized by President Roosevelt when he said, "I hate war," as he spoke of helping the allies with aid "short of war," and when he promised "again and again and again" that American boys would not be sent to fight on foreign soil. Even so, the drift toward war was obvious. This was accelerated when the Japanese advanced into Southeast Asia and took over Indochina after the fall of France. When Japan continued this advance in spite of warnings, the United States, in the summer of 1941, placed an embargo on oil, scrap iron, and other supplies that Japan needed for the war, and froze her credits in the United States.

This brought on a flurry of diplomatic action, as Ambassador Nomura and special envoy Kurusu met with Secretary of State Hull offering concessions—even offering to pull out of Northern Indochina if the credit freeze and the embargo were lifted. In an attempt to counter this, China's T.V. Soong and Hu Shih met with the President. A letter from Chiang Kai-shek, saying in effect that China was at the end of her rope, was handed to the President.

In their efforts to persuade the President to take a hard line against the Japanese, Chinese diplomats received support from strange and curious quarters. Harry Dexter White, who was later shown to have collaborated with Soviet intelligence, sent a telegram to Edward C. Carter, Secretary General of the Institute of Pacific Relations, urging him to "come to Washington." White also drafted an appeal to the President arguing against what he called "a Far East Munich." White, as Under Secretary of the Treasury, worked closely with Henry Morgenthau, Jr., and a letter over Morgenthau's signature called on the President for "iron firmness" in dealing with Japan. A cable came from Owen Lattimore, then in Chungking, stating that the Generalissimo was "really agitated" at the prospect of any appeasement of Japan. Also "agitated" over the prospect of a peaceful settlement with Japan was Lauchlin Currie, who met with Edward C. Carter when the IPR head came to Washington in response to White's urgent summons.

In the light of what was later disclosed about these people through the hearings of the Senate Internal Security Subcommittee that investigated the IPR, one may well wonder about the real reason for their fears that the United States might not go to war with Japan. For while Chiang Kai-shek stood to benefit from such a war, the one who stood to benefit more was Josef Stalin.

In any case, on November 26, 1941, Secretary Hull handed Ambassador Nomura an ultimatum which is supposed to have been drafted, at least in part, by Harry Dexter White. This called on Japan to withdraw all military, naval, air, and police forces from China and Indochina. This meant a humiliating surrender and could have caused a revolution in Japan. It also would have meant the end of Japan as a bulwark against Soviet expansion in Asia.

There could be only one answer to this note and it came on December 7, 1941, at Pearl Harbor.

Chapter Five

The ABMAC Affair

IN THE SPRING OF 1943 ALFRED KOHLBERG WAS SUR-prised to get a summons to Washington from no less a personage than Lauchlin Currie, administrative assistant to President Franklin D. Roosevelt. Sitting across from this nervous little man, who continually fussed and fidgeted, Kohlberg heard a strange tale, which he set down in his memoirs.

"He told me of reports of the hopelessness of the Chinese National Government and its armies, the lack of will to fight, corruption, etc. I listened with my mouth open, I am sure. I had never been so honored with a briefing by so high an official."

It may be assumed that Kohlberg was not the only one to hear this kind of story from a man who was later shown to have played an important role in the fall of China and who now chooses to live in South America. Testifying before a Senate Committee in 1954, John C. Caldwell, who headed the United States Information Service in the Far East, declared:

"In 1943 and 1944 when OWI employees for the Far East, particularly for China, were employed we were brought here to Washington from the New York overseas office for orientation, and the orientation consisted of your seeing two people. The two people were Mr. Laughlin [sic] Currie and Mr. Owen Lattimore, only the two. From these people we were to get our basic philosophy, you might say."

At the time that Kohlberg and Currie were having their meeting a profound change was taking place in Sino-Russian relations. The background of this was unknown to the businessman at the time but in view of what was divulged later concerning President Roosevelt's assistant, it may be taken for granted that Currie was aware of it. As we saw in the preceding chapter, the Chinese Communists had formed a united front with Chiang Kai-shek in 1937, with the Kremlin's blessing, but by 1943 the situation was different. Stalingrad had been successfully defended, and with U.S. aid making it obvious that Nazi Germany would be defeated in the west, the Communist line changed.

Now Stalin was able to put things in the proper Communist perspective. Lenin's dictum about the importance of controlling China once again became paramount. The united front in China was no longer vital, so Mao Tse-tung and his followers stepped up their divide-and-conquer tactics against Chiang. And Communists and Communist dupes all over the world took their cue from their Kremlin masters. Attacks were begun on people and policies that since 1937 had been tolerated or even praised.

The start of the attack on the Nationalist Government of China was signaled by an article in a little magazine called *Far Eastern Survey*, published by the Institute of

Pacific Relations. The issue of July 14, 1943, carried an article by T. A. Bisson, an IPR staff member, entitled "China's part in a Coalition War," the basic theme of which was that there were "two Chinas." One of these, according to Bisson, was feudalistic, chained to the past, and oppressive, while the other was a democratic China which truly expressed the will of the Chinese people. The "feudal China" was of course the China of Chiang Kai-shek. The brave-new-world China, naturally, was the one that had Mao Tse-tung as its head. And setting forth a line that was to be echoed and re-echoed for years, until it was utterly discredited, Bisson set down these words concerning Communism in China:

"By no stretch of the imagination can this be termed Communism; it is in fact the essence of *bourgeois* democracy, applied mainly to agrarian conditions." (Italics in the original.)

There were immediate repercussions. In a letter of July 20, 1943, to Owen Lattimore, then with the Office of War Information, W. L. Holland, Research Director of the IPR, made this comment:

"What do you think of Bisson's article on China in the current *Far Eastern Survey?* As you can imagine it has caused a considerable storm among some of the official Chinese here. While I disagree with some of Bisson's terminology I think the article is fundamentally sound and says a lot of things that many people feel ought to have been said before this. . . ."

Soon afterwards, on August 8, Moscow's key policy publication, *War and the Working Class,* carried a long article by Vladimir Rogov, Tass correspondent in China, which also attacked the Nationalist Government. The Chinese Government, according to Rogov, contained "appeasers, defeatists, and surrenderists," and they were trying to destroy the Communist armies and foment civil war. The Rogov article later was reprinted in the *Daily Worker.*

However, as Kohlberg sat facing the President's assistant he had no way of knowing that he was getting the same line that would, in a matter of weeks, appear in print as official Communist doctrine. He was, however, deeply disturbed to hear about all the corruption among China's leaders, particularly among the military, and their lack of will to fight. And he was especially concerned to learn that there was corruption in the medical services because he had a special interest in that field.

This had developed over several years. Always touched by the sad plight of so many Chinese, Kohlberg had looked about for some practical way of helping them. With the appraising eye of a businessman he had investigated some of the philanthropic agencies operating there, making on-the-spot checks of what they were doing and giving due attention to how much they spent to get results. Many he ruled out because, while they did a good job, they spent too much on overhead. He finally settled on ABMAC, the American Bureau for Medical Aid to China, as an organization that seemed to operate most efficiently in an area where its services could do the greatest good for the Chinese people. He not only contributed money to ABMAC but took an active part in fund-raising drives, applying "in modified fashion" the aggressive methods he had earlier employed in raising money for the United Jewish Appeal.

At the time the Japanese attacked Pearl Harbor, the ABMAC setup had undergone a change in that its funds were coming largely from United China Relief, which had been taken into the government-organized National War Fund, a bureau which raised money for the aid of all the allied nations. Under this arrangement, ABMAC received an average of $2,000,000 annually for its work in China from 1942 to 1945 inclusive. However, in accepting this money it also had to submit to certain controls.

Sharing in the responsibility for these disbursements

was Edward C. Carter, who was not only the Chairman of
United China Relief's Program Committee, but also the
head of the Institute of Pacific Relations. The significance
of this interlocking arrangement was to come out later, but
until that time Kohlberg's relations with the ubiquitous
Mr. Carter were fairly cordial.

Actually, Alfred Kohlberg was far better acquainted
with conditions in China than was Carter, particularly as
they concerned ABMAC. In 1941, as a director of the
organization, he had made an extensive survey trip of
ABMAC's operations in Free China, following the com-
pletion of a business trip which had taken him from
Shanghai to Swatow and then to Hong Kong.

After a couple of days spent in preparation in Hong
Kong, meeting such people as Dr. Robert K. S. Lim, head
of the Chinese Red Cross Field Service, and getting the
necessary credentials, Kohlberg started his 1941 inspection trip for ABMAC in an old Curtiss-Wright biplane
which carried freight over the Japanese lines to a point
near Kukong. These flights were purposely made when
the weather was so bad that there would be little if any
Japanese ground fire, and first-class pilot that Kohlberg
was, he said he could not understand how the pilot ever
found his way to the first stop, a small, dimly lighted air-
strip 60 miles from Kukong.

Since an understanding of what occurred on that trip
has a bearing on what happened after his meeting with
Lauchlin Currie two years later, the following, in the form
of an introduction to the detailed report to Kohlberg's
fellow directors of ABMAC, is presented:

> "The following morning a 3½-hour bus ride
> brought us to the provisional capital of Kwantung
> Province at Shao Kwan. This bus deserves descrip-
> tion as it is typical of wartime passenger travel in
> Free China. This particular greyhound of the road
> had a locally built body of heavy boards and iron

bolts on an ancient Dodge chassis. Into this contrap-
tion 32 persons fitted themselves with all the bag-
gage that 32 people would think of bringing along. In
fact so perfectly were we fitted into each inch of
space with the overflow comfortably packed on top
of the bus that even a Times Square subway guard
would have viewed the result with admiration. Yet
such is the good nature of the Chinese and such the
spirit in which they accept the hardships of wartime
that there was not an unpleasant argument to mar the
general good nature of the bus as we jounced our way
gaily over the war-torn road to Shao Kwan and the
looked-forward-to comforts of a railway. Two days by
rail landed me in Liuchow, Kwangsi Province. From
Liuchow, two days by car (ambulance) brought me to
Kweiyang, capital of Kweichow Province, and the
new medical center of Free china."

He described bomb-damaged Kweiyang and the work
of the Medical Relief Corps of the Chinese Red Cross. An
important function of the medical schools was to train
men for army service. Some idea of the magnitude of
China's medical problem may be ascertained from Kohlberg's figures. To serve both the army and the civilian
population in areas where the army was operating, the
medical service had a total of 108,000 men, of whom only
400 were qualified as doctors. At Kweiyang a three-month
course was given which taught soldiers how to set frac-
tures, sterilize and dress wounds, treat common illnesses,
and provide needed preventive measures.

In his report Kohlberg described an aspect of China's
scorched earth policy that few Americans knew about:

The so-called roadless area . . . is a strip of land
nearly 2,000 miles long running along the whole
front of Japanese occupation in China. Its width varies from 20 to 120 miles depending on the terrain. In
this area all roads and railroads have been destroyed

—not only is the road surface destroyed, but all embankments as well, and the land put back in cultivation. Thus the Japanese planes can identify nothing and the Japanese mechanized machines have no roads to use. These roadless areas are the Chinese lines of resistance. In these areas the fighting occurs. In this area the Red Cross Army units operate. After receiving attention at the first-aid stations close to the very front the wounded and sick, if unable to walk, must be carried by stretcherbearers back across this roadless area to the road head where ambulances wait to take them to the nearest hospital. This trip sometimes takes a week or even two, and the number of head, chest, and abdomen casualties who die en route or arrive at the hospital too far gone to be saved is appalling.

Yet this roadless area has made it possible for China's poorly equipped army to hold at least one million well equipped Japanese soldiers bogged in China. Here they cannot advance and dare not withdraw to undertake the tempting adventures Japan's military gangsters see dangling before their eyes in the Indies or in Siberia. . . .

China hopes for military supplies under the Lend-Lease Act, for a continuance of medical supplies and transport from the American Red Cross, and, not least, the continuance of the aid of the American Bureau for Medical Aid to China which served so well the urgent needs of China's war wounded the past three years. [ABMAC] realizes how vital to America is China's struggle. If Japan should succeed in conquering this one-quarter of the earth's population, we and our children and our children's children would have a hostile Japanese military empire of 700,000,000 human beings facing us across a constantly shrinking Pacific Ocean. If China is victorious we may again return to days of peace.

No effort to aid China short of our maximum is worthy of America today.

This was followed by a detailed report in which Kohlberg told of his travels over much of China in behalf of ABMAC—the people he met and the work being done in schools, laboratories, and hospitals aided by his organization. Then there was the war itself. Bombings were frequent and he noted that "much of the time had to be spent in air-raid shelters."

There were also such items as, "General Dick Loo [Surgeon-General Loo Chi-teh] told me 1,250,000 treated in army hospitals, of these 250,000 died, 750,000 returned to army, 100,000 still in hospitals. Apparently 150,000 discharged cured but unfit." A further notation was to the effect that 80 percent of the wounds were in upper and lower limbs. Most of those who suffered head and chest wounds never made it to the hospitals.

Having learned at first hand something about the sacrifices being made by Chiang's troops, it is little wonder that Alfred Kohlberg listened in amazement as Lauchlin Currie talked about corruption, incompetence, and lack of will to fight. Things certainly must have changed drastically in the two years since Kohlberg had made that trip to Kweiyang. But the little man in the big job seemed to know what he was talking about, and further, he told Kohlberg he could check what he told him with Americans in Chungking.

There was no denying that critical reports were coming out of China, Indeed, that was why Kohlberg was going there. A cable had been received by ABMAC in New York on February 13, 1943, sent from Chungking by Dwight Edwards, the Field Director for United China Relief in Chungking. This made serious charges against the Emergency Medical Service Training Schools supported in large part by ABMAC, and against Dr. Robert K. S. Lim who was responsible for the EMSTS. Edwards accused Dr. Lim's schools of "a very great waste in the use of AB-

MAC's funds" and made the grave charge that Dr. Lim
was "under heavy suspicion on the part of the highest
authorities in the Chinese Government." In view of this,
and because Dr. Lim's actions laid United China Relief
open to "charges of looseness," the cable recommended
that no more money go to him. Another disturbing element in this was an action taken by UCR in arbitrarily
cutting the ABMAC appropriation for the Army Medical
Corps by $640,000 for the year starting April 1, 1943.

Officials of ABMAC studied the charges and on April
13, noting that some of Edwards' charges were contrary
to known facts, they called on United China Relief to take
no action on Edwards' recommendations until the situation was properly investigated. A week after this the executive committee of ABMAC adopted a resolution
empowering Alfred Kohlberg, who was going to China on
business, "to examine all correspondence, reports, accounts and other data in the possession of the Chungking
office of ABMAC or its representative Dr. George Bachman. . . ." He was also authorized "to investigate the services being performed by the agencies in China aided by
ABMAC. . . ."

On the basis of his personal knowledge of China and
because he knew Dr. Lim and the work he was doing,
Alfred Kohlberg was critical of the Edwards charges and
prepared a memorandum which questioned certain aspects of them. One criticism was that Dwight Edwards
was trying to assume too much responsibility in the running of ABMAC's affairs. This seemed to strike a sensitive
nerve because it brought a prompt retort from Edward C.
Carter, who was not only the Chairman of the Program
Committee of United China Relief but also the Secretary
General of the Institute of Pacific Relations.

The fact is that the IPR and its satellites made it a
practice to move in on any organization where it could
wield influence, a fact that was to be abundantly proved

by the McCarran hearings of 1951-1952. But Carter apparently did not like to have attention called to this strategy.

After his conference with Lauchlin Currie, Kohlberg had to wait in Florida for almost a month for the airplane to which he had been assigned. This happened to be a new DC-3, military designation C-47, which was being lend-leased with a full cargo to the Chinese Government. The pilot was a Baltimore-born Chinese, Moon Chin, with Al Mah, a Canadian-born Chinese, as co-pilot. Moon Chin was a first-rate airman who had been Chiang Kai-shek's personal pilot, and the one who had brought Jimmy Doolittle out of China after the bombing of Tokyo in 1942.

The plane took off from Miami on June 27, 1943, and flew via Puerto Rico and Trinidad to Brazil. It made the Atlantic crossing to Ascension Island and then went on to the African coast. Moon Chin occasionally allowed his passenger to fly the plane for a few hours while they were crossing Africa and India, and the trip ended at Calcutta where Kohlberg became sick with an intestinal upset. He finished his flight to Chungking in a Chinese National Aviation Corporation passenger plane. He reported:

> In Chungking I gathered up what information I could mostly from American sources. I found it all most discouraging, with stories of corruption, of lack of will to fight, etc. Instead of believing these and going home satisfied, I believed them but determined to check them first hand for myself before going home to report.
>
> My determination to do this met with violent opposition from the United China Relief Director in Chungking and from ABMAC's own representative there. The more they objected, however, the more firm I became in my determination to see for myself.
>
> I asked the Chinese Surgeon-General to get me a permit to visit one of the fronts, which I picked out.

> He told me it was quite impossible, as any permission
> to visit the front had to be by request of the American
> Embassy and the Embassy couldn't do anything in
> under six weeks at the least. So without permission I
> started out by mail truck to Kweiyang. I had been
> told in great detail of corruption at the medical head-
> quarters there, hence it was my first spot to check.
> After a week there I found the stories all either un-
> true or exaggerated.

In a detailed "travelogue" submitted as a report to AB-
MAC, Kohlberg told of his trip to the 6th War Area. It was
a rugged ordeal for a man then 56 years old. A war-weary
train, reached by rickshaw, got him as far as the "roadless
area," but from that point the going was hard. It meant
travel by sampan, river steamer, horseback, and on foot.
Occasionally in his report Kohlberg referred to his horse-
manship, or lack of it. One such reference was, "From
here about 51 *li* of riding, that very nearly killed your
representative, brought us to a receiving station."

All this travel was, of course, only a means to an end,
and that was to find out as much as possible about the
situation in China and the contributions being made by
ABMAC to the Chinese war effort. This meant inspections
of military hospitals and dressing stations, studies of battle
statistics, interviews with officers responsible for medical
matters, and numerous other details. A 22-page single-
spaced report, subsequently submitted by Alfred Kohlberg to ABMAC, indicates that this was no VIP junket.
However, there was a certain amount of pomp and cir-
cumstance.

When he reached Changsa he reported that as an
American arriving at the Chinese fighting lines, "I was
received with all honors." Sometimes, he noted, even a
brass band was on hand to greet him or send him on his
way. After his front-line tour he returned to Changsa
where he decided to give a dinner to his medical and

missionary friends. The high spot of this was instant coffee since he happened to have a bottle of this rare delicacy with him. Also handed out to his guests were "the last of my cigarettes."

After this treat, the commanding officer, Lieutenant General Chang Teh-nun, presented him with a picture which he himself had painted, "The Scholar's Retreat." This was inscribed with a long dedication to Kohlberg in the upper right hand corner. For years this painting hung in the sun porch of the Kohlberg home in Bronxville but it evoked a sad memory. "I regret to say," said Kohlberg, "General Chang Teh-nun was court-martialed and executed the following year for disobeying orders in the great battle for Central China which was fought in 1944."

Before leaving Changsha, Kohlberg made a speech in which he referred to the untruths he had heard in Washington and Chungking and the far different situation he had found on the spot. This speech was reported and published in newspapers throughout China. Leaving Changsha he went to Henyank, then to Kweilin, and from there to Kunming.

In the course of these travels he encountered one of China's greatest problems, inflation. He paid as much as $8.00, American, for a package of Camel cigarettes. A cake of Palmolive soap cost more than $2.50, and a two-pound can of coffee sold for upwards of $50.00.

"If spent for imported commodities," he said, "the U.S. dollar bought an average of two cents' worth." He pointed out that inflation was not uniform everywhere. "In Kunming it is more than 150 times, in Changsha much less. But everywhere it is still getting worse."

When he reached Kunming he finally met Dr. Lim, who had been removed as Director of the Emergency Medical Service Training Schools three weeks before. He showed Dr. Lim the reports concerning the ESMTS hoping to get "the dirt" from him, but the doctor refused to talk. "All I

had been able to get out of him," said Kohlberg in his
report, "was that the charges were a fait accompli and he
had no hard feelings toward anyone."

Kohlberg did get a lot of significant information from
two other men, both Americans. One was General Claire
Chennault, head of the famed Flying Tigers, who was
extremely conscious of the untruths that were circulating
and knew who was responsible for them. Another source
of facts was Brigadier General T. S. Arms, who was in
charge of the infantry training school under Lieutenant
General Joseph W. Stilwell. Even then Stilwell displayed
a hatred of Chiang Kai-shek which was later to lead him
into alliances with the pro-Communist State Department
officials responsible for our suicidal China policy, but
General Arms obviously did not share Stilwell's extreme
views. Arms gave Kohlberg the facts about one vicious
rumor that was being circulated to the effect that Chiang
Kai-shek was stockpiling vast quantities of tanks and guns
obtained from the United States, saving them for use
against the Chinese "liberals" instead of using them
against the Japanese:

> "I asked why we permitted such hoarding. He
> laughed and said he had heard some good ones but
> this took the cake. He said that up to that date all the
> arms and ammunition that had come in had gone to
> him and to the artillery training school; that they
> were not fully equipped as yet, and until they were,
> nothing would be flown in (the air route over the
> hump to Kunming being the only route in) for any
> force except the Air Force whose minimum require-
> ments were the first priority. He explained that noth-
> ing but Air Force supplies had come in since May,
> due to the monsoons. After the monsoons ended, he
> expected the resumption of his equipping; and after
> that was completed, he explained, General Stilwell
> was to get full equipment for two of his divisions, and
> then, after that, 50% was to go to Stilwell, and 50%

to the Chinese Army—sometime in 1944. At that moment, he said, not one tank or gun or rifle or bazooka or cartridge had been turned over to the Chinese Army under lend-lease, hence none could be hoarded."

On returning to Chungking, Kohlberg immediately sought out Edward C. Carter, to try to get some action on his complaint against Dwight Edwards. Carter proved to be an artful dodger. Kohlberg finally found him with Edwards, Dr. Bachman, and William L. Holland, of the IPR; but Carter took him aside and told him he couldn't do anything about his complaint. It seems he was not in China on behalf of United China Relief, but was doing some work for his other organization, the Institute of Pacific Relations. However, Kohlberg insisted that, as long as Edwards and Bachman were present, he wanted to register his complaint in their presence. This was done but "Carter maintained a noncommital and impartial attitude," according to Kohlberg.

A few days after this Kohlberg attended a meeting of the United China Relief Chungking Committee and was surprised to find Carter addressing the meeting as Chairman of the Program Committee of UCR.

Unable to get any action from Carter, and indignant at the pattern of lies and evasion he had encountered, Kohlberg flew back to New York, retracing the route he had taken to get to China. The long trip did little to cool his anger. Speaking about it later he said:

"To me it smelled like treason because I couldn't see anyone benefitting from these lies but the Japanese. The possibility of Communist motivation had not occurred to me."

When he reached home he was sick. Thinking he was merely over-exhausted from his ordeal he stayed home for a few days to rest up but he got worse. Finally a doctor was called who diagnosed his illness as intestinal flu. But when his temperature climbed to 106° he was taken to Presbyterian Hospital in New York where it was found that he had malignant malaria. During his lengthy stay in the hospital, word came that his mother had died in California.

While recovering he dictated his lengthy report to ABMAC. Recalling this, Miss Anna E. Murray, who was his secretary for many years, said that he had a little black notebook and constantly referred to it as he dictated. "And all the while the perspiration was pouring from him."

After setting down his report which dealt with ABMAC operations in China as he had found them, Kohlberg turned his attention to the individuals whose actions had disturbed him. One of these was Dr. Bachman of ABMAC. He wrote to him, asking him to clarify certain statements he had made and received a prompt reply. However, Kohlberg obviously was not satisfied with the answers and Dr. Bachman was recalled.

Kohlberg's prime target, however, was Dwight Edwards, the United China Relief official. Edwards, he charged, had not only meddled in ABMAC matters which were none of his business, but he had also engaged in political meddling which jeopardized relations with the Chinese. This meddling had resulted, among other things, in the resignation of the very able Dr. Lim. This had caused a chain reaction, arousing the resentment of the Chinese medical profession and causing a serious curtailment of activities in a vital area.

It is interesting to note that in undermining Dr. Lim, Edwards had aligned himself, possibly unwittingly, with a cabal which had circulated vicious rumors against him. These were listed by Dr. Lim in a letter he sent to ABMAC's New York headquarters late in 1942: "Rumors that the Generalissimo had dismissed me; that General Ho Ying-chin did not support our program; that ABMAC was dissatisfied with the EMSTS and had sent Dr. Bachman out to investigate; that I mishandled supplies and funds; that I contemplated joining the British Army in India, thus implying my desertion of the group here, were whispered about in Chungking and were, I believe, reported in Washington. . . . They also made a charge that I was a Communist acting under orders from the Communist Party and that the purpose of the training schools was to insinuate Communistic propaganda in the army through their medical officers who came for training."

These rumors culminated in an official government hearing at Chungking which completed vindicated Dr. Lim, and Kohlberg felt that it was necessary for ABMAC to divorce itself completely from anyone or any organization that would engage in such smear tactics. "I proposed," he said, "that if these men were not recalled to give an accounting of themselves, ABMAC withdraw from United China Relief. I was voted down on this drastic step, so decided if I wanted to carry on the fight I had best resign from ABMAC, which I did on December 31, 1943."

Shortly after this Kohlberg filed formal charges against Edwards with the directors of United China Relief in New York. The organization appointed a committee to hear his charges, composed of such men as Henry Luce, James G. Blaine, Paul Hoffman, and Edward C. Carter. Kohlberg quickly concluded that the committee was going to do nothing about his charges.

"When I came to the hearing they told me they had very limited time to listen to me; and it was apparent that they had very little interest in the charges that I made. I cannot exactly recall the charges at this time, except that he was responsible for untruths about the Government of the Republic of China which were having a very deleterious effect on Chinese-American cooperation in the war effort. I made no charge of Communism against him, as it had not occurred to me that the Communist question was involved. After the limited presentation I was permitted to make, the committee took the matter under advisement, dismissed me and went on to other business."

A few days after this he received a summons from Charles Edison, former Governor of New Jersey and Secretary of the Navy under President Franklin D. Roosevelt. Mr. Edison had just been elected the new chairman of United China Relief and he was interested in Kohlberg's charges. In fact, the two men spent the day discussing them. But Kohlberg declared that on that very day, without notifying Mr. Edison, the committee made its report and stated that he, Kohlberg, had not sustained his charges. Which was probably true since he had been given virtually no opportunity to do so.

Although he resigned from ABMAC, Alfred Kohlberg assisted and supported the organization unofficially. Personally aware of the excellent work it was doing (and which it continues to do on Formosa and in Korea), Kohlberg kept on contributing to it and even engaged in a certain amount of fund-raising. In 1951 he rejoined the ABMAC Board of Directors and not only made substantial financial contributions to the organization but solicited help from others. For example, in November 1955 he circularized his friends, asking for contributions for organizations in which he had a deep personal interest.

"The first of these," he wrote, "is the Jane Myers Kohlberg Memorial Fund, which supports a health program in 19 schools in Formosa. It is administered by the American Bureau for Medical Aid to China (ABMAC) of which I have been a director off and on for more than fifteen years. . . ."

When he died one of his largest bequests was to this organization, which had been instrumental in making him aware of a world he had never imagined. This made possible the Alfred Kohlberg Memorial Research Laboratory, a magnificent three-story building which has become the leading center for medical research on Formosa. Dedicated in 1963 by Alfred Kohlberg's old friend Dr. Loo Chi-teh, it is currently carrying on more than 30 research projects, in neurophysiology, pharmacology, immunology, biochemistry, pharmaceutical chemistry, hematology, metabolism, cardiology, pulmonary physiology, nephrology, and medical education.

Recalling some of the incidents of the 1940's, Dr. B. A. Garside, Executive Director of ABMAC, made an interesting observation concerning Alfred Kohlberg:

"He saw things as black or white. There were no middle shades. We used to argue, but never with any bitterness, and it so happened that in time we found he had been right, especially about people.

"He used to attend all sorts of meetings, including those held by Communists. He knew them and seemed to like them as individuals, and they seemed to like him. He'd pick up their literature and discuss it with them in a friendly way. What he didn't like were people who pretended to be what they were not."

Unfortunately, Alfred Kohlberg was fated to meet more and more pretenders as time went on, and they turned up in unexpected places.

CHAPTER SIX

The Amazing Dr. William

Of all the strange chapters in the history of East and West there can be none stranger than this, that the founder of the Chinese Republic and the spiritual leader of the new China found in the writings of an unknown American author so clear a statement of the solution of the hardest problem in his political philosophy that he made the American formulation his own.

The foregoing, written by the eminent historian James T. Shotwell and published in the *Political Science Quarterly* for March 1932, refers to an odd facet of recent history that is relatively unknown. The American author referred to by Dr. Shotwell was a Brooklyn dentist, Dr. Maurice William, and but for a book he wrote, China probably would have become a Communist nation long before it did.

By a strange quirk of fate, it was the same Dr. William who provided a turning point in Alfred Kohlberg's life by opening Kohlberg's eyes to the significance of what he had encountered in China and Washington in 1943.

Dr. William had been a socialist prior to World War I. In fact he was a charter member of the Socialist Party in 1900. However, he became disenchanted with certain aspects of socialism and wrote a book which he titled: *The Social Interpretation of History: A Refutation of the Marxian Economic Interpretation of History*. Unable to find a publisher for it he had a few hundred copies privately printed in 1921.

In the normal course of events nothing more would have been heard of the book, but in some curious manner a copy of it fell into the hands of Dr. Sun Yat-sen. One story has it that this copy of the book was forwarded by a Chinese student in this country and the wrapper identifying the sender was lost when the package was opened. Be that as it may, the book reached the great Chinese leader at a crucial moment, when he was trying to make a decision as to China's political future.

This was in 1924. Dr. Sun had cancer and knew he did not have long to live. He therefore started to give a series of lectures setting forth a philosophy by which the Chinese people could live. These would later be known as the San Min Chu I, or Three Principles of the People.* Dr. Sun had been strongly influenced by Karl Marx's ideas on economics and this influence was apparent in his early lectures. Then the rest of the series was cancelled without explanation. The reason was that Dr. William's book had reached him, the ideas intrigued him and he wanted more time to study them. As Dr. Shotwell expressed it:

"Dr. Sun saw at once in the arguments of Dr. William a confirmation of his own innate tendencies with reference to socialism, for which he had hitherto found no

*The final and most authoritative version of the San Min Chu I is presented as Appendix B.

statement in terms of logical or systematic reasoning. Dr.
William supplied him with a conception of socialism
which renounced the class war as historically and
economically false, and in the text of the San Min Chu I
whole passages of Dr. William's book were embodied en
bloc.... However it came about, the reading of *The Social
Interpretation of History* by Dr. Sun Yat-sen may yet turn
out to be one of the most important single events in the
history of modern Asia. ..."

When Sun Yat-Sen resumed his lectures he presented
the third and last of his Three Principles. This dealt with
the people's livelihood, but instead of presenting a pro-
Marxist viewpoint in that important sector, as had been
expected, he was pro-democratic. He rejected Marx's
materialistic concept of history and the theory of the class
struggle.

It certainly was not what the Communists wanted, and
expected, after all the help they had given Sun Yat-sen.
The USSR had loaned the Chinese Government several
million dollars when Western nations had refused assistance, and it had sent advisers. They were sure that Sun
Yat-sen would proclaim a doctrine which, sooner or later,
would mean a Communist China. As Dr. Shotwell pointed
out, "It required more than an ordinary act of courage for
the leader of the revolution at a time that was still critical
to come out frankly and fearlessly in contradiction to the
militant philosophy [of the Soviet Union]."

The Communists, of course, looked upon Sun Yat-sen's
reversal as an act of betrayal.

Dr. William had no knowledge of this. Then one day,
some four years later, a friend told him he had read an
article in *Asia Magazine* telling how his book had caused
Dr. Sun's historic switch. Amazed, the dentist went to the
Chinese Embassy and the Chinese there were astounded
that he had no knowledge of what had happened and had
received no official recognition for his contribution. He

was told that the book had been translated into Chinese and was in wide use as a reference on American democracy. Indeed, it was promoted as "the book that changed Sun Yat-sen."

Honors that were long overdue were paid Dr. William and he was made a life member of the Kuomintang, the only non-Chinese ever to be so honored.

This, then, was the man who was to set another powerful force in motion by enlightening Alfred Kohlberg. As a fellow-official of the American Bureau for Medical Aid to China, Dr. William knew about Kohlberg's 1943 trip, the reason for it, and the antagonisms that had developed because of it. He also knew about some of the personalities involved. It was obvious to him that Kohlberg had no understanding of the basic reason for the anti-Chiang propaganda he had encountered. Indeed Kohlberg went on the assumption that since it helped the Japanese it was somehow Japanese-inspired. Dr. William proceeded to set him straight.

"Dr. William," said Kohlberg, "asked me why, when I complained about the untruths that were being circulated about China, I did not put my finger on the central source for most of the untruths. That is, on the Institute of Pacific Relations, of which I was a member, to which I was a contributor, and also a member of its Finance Committee. I told him I saw no Communists. I had heard these stories from Americans, and I knew nothing about any such stories coming from the Institute of Pacific Relations. He said to me, 'Don't you read the publications of the Institute of Pacific Relations?' I said that I did not because I didn't have time and found them to be academic mishmash with very little practical value, and for years I had not bothered to read anything they sent me.

"He showed me some of their recent publications, for 1943 and 1944, carrying the very same lies that I had been complaining about. He particularly called my atten-

tion to an article by T. A. Bisson, published in July 1943,
[This was the famous 'China's Part in a Coalition War' in
the *Far Eastern Survey*.] which had nearly all the lies
about which I had been complaining."

Kohlberg then went to the offices of the Institute of
Pacific Relations to secure back numbers of the publications they had sent him but which he had discarded. The
reaction he got proved to be another surprise. Even
though he was an official of the organization he was
blandly told that they could not sell him the back issues
he wanted. All they had available were a few recent items
of an innocuous nature.

"At this point," he said, "I gave up." Which doubtless
is what the IPR people expected him to do. But he retired
from the lists only temporarily. With the same stubborn-
ness that motivated his trip to the front lines in China
when he was told he would not be allowed to go, he
decided to get to the bottom of the IPR's strange actions.
His son Larry, then home from Amherst on vacation, suggested that he try the New York Public Library, just up
the street from his office. And there he found complete
files of the publications he wanted.

Since the library was so convenient he spent a lot of
time there. Saturdays and Sundays were given over to his
research, and in addition he devoted two or three after-
noons a week to the job.

"I skipped most of what they published," he later
wrote, "and tried to limit myself to the articles that had
to do with China, either politically or militarily. After I
had read through that mass of material I then turned to
the *New Masses*, a Communist weekly, and to *The Communist*, a Communist monthly, and read the articles they
had on the same subject matter; that is, the political and
military situation in China.

"From this it became clear that the IPR and the Communist publications had switched their attitudes toward

China radically each time there had been a radical change in the world situation affecting China. In 1937 the Communist were praising Chiang Kai-shek as the only hope of unity for China against Japanese encroachment. By 1939, about the time of the Hitler-Stalin Pact, they had switched to criticism of Chiang Kai-shek as corrupt, fascist, feudal, and reactionary; and they played up the Communists as the democratic agrarian reformers who were the hope of the future for China.

"This continued until June 22, 1941, when Hitler broke the Hitler-Stalin Pact by his invasion of Russia. All of a sudden, again, the two Communist organs and the IPR switched completely to praise of Chiang Kai-shek as the hope of liberty in China. This praise of Chiang by both the Communist and the IPR continued until the spring of 1943 when suddenly the old attacks on Chiang were renewed and dusted off and brought to the fore again after the Soviet victories at Stalingrad."

Thoroughly convinced by this time that Dr. William was right and that a subversive element was operating in the IPR and manipulating it, Alfred Kohlberg methodically set down on paper the material that would later start his famous controversy with that organization.

Dr. William obviously approved of the way his protégé tackled the job. In a letter to Kohlberg dated January 16, 1946, he said:

"If only more Americans had your knowledge and your understanding of the meaning of Stalin's moves, how utterly helpless they could render him! His entire power consists of *our* ignorance. What a terrifying realization!"

Now living in Los Angeles, Dr. William made this comment to the writer:

"Alfred was ready, but he demanded that I produce proof in support of my charges against the IPR. Once satisfied that I had established my case, he went to work —and how he worked! The American people owe Alfred a debt of gratitude for opening the eyes of all who would see."

Unfortunately though, there were many who had eyes but they saw not. Worse, they not only did not want to be shown, but they turned their fury on the man who tried to teach them.

CHAPTER SEVEN

"The Truth Is Not in Them"

WHEN ALFRED KOHLBERG STARTED STUDYING THE publications of the Institute of Pacific Relations, as Dr. Maurice William had suggested, he was admittedly not well informed about Communism. He had seen its manifestations all about him for years but their significance had escaped him. In this connection a story he told about himself is revealing. In 1932 he made a trip to the Orient, and on that occasion he traveled from Berlin to Moscow by air, and then took the Trans-Siberian Railway across Russia and Siberia to Harbin in Manchuria.

"Russia," he said, "was being socialized regardless of cost. The trip was made in June and the weather was comfortably warm. The sight of deserted villages along the railway in Siberia, and railway freight cars standing on the side-tracks full of human beings, men, women and

79

children, gave me an idea of what was going on. I asked who these people were and what they had done, and was told by the GPU man on the train that they were counter-revolutionaries. They looked just like old Russian peasants to me, but I took his word for it, showing that I was neither smarter nor more stupid than most of the Americans who went to Russia in those days, when one could get in."

By the end of 1944 he was not so gullible. He had learned a great deal about Communism and Communists and the publications of the Institute of Pacific Relations played an important part in his education. Using what he found in them, he prepared an 88-page study (frequently referred to in the McCarran hearings) and sent it with a covering letter to Mr. E. C. Carter. Copies were also sent to each of the trustees of the IPR, and to other persons interested in the Far East.*

Kohlberg said that the specific piece of IPR literature that moved him to make this study was a booklet entitled "War-Time China," by Maxwell S. Stewart which appeared in 1944. This booklet identified Stewart as "Editor of Public Affairs Pamphlets and Associate Editor of *The Nation.*" Later, in the IPR hearings, it was disclosed that he had also been identified with a number of Communist enterprises although he denied that he was a Communist. In any case, in a covering letter that he sent with his 88-page study, Kohlberg described this article of Stewart's as "... a deliberate smear of China, the Chinese and the Chinese Government."

Stewart's pamphlet, he said, repeated lies similar to those he had heard previously in Washington and Chungking, including the myth that the Chinese Communists were in reality only liberals—Chinese New Dealers. Here is how Stewart presented the line in "War-Time China":

"As China is not like any other country, so Chinese

*The complete text of Kohlberg's covering letter to E. C. Carter appears as Appendix C.

Communism has no parallel elsewhere. You can find in it resemblance to Communist movements in other countries and you can also find resemblances to the 'grass-root' Populist movements that have figured in American history. Because there is no other effective opposition party in China, the Communists have attracted the support of many progressive and patriotic Chinese who know little of the doctrines of Karl Marx or Stalin and care less."

However, the statement in Stewart's pamphlet that especially irked Kohlberg was this: "They [the American, British, and Soviet Governments] have, however, limited their economic and military assistance because of fear that any supplies they send might be used in civil strife rather than against the Japanese." This, said Kohlberg, was completely contrary to what President Roosevelt had said repeatedly: that all aid was being given to China and this aid would continue.

Urging Carter to study the clippings reproduced in his document, so he could see for himself how IPR publications echoed the *New Masses* and *The Communist,* Kohlberg made this charge:

> I think you will find that your employees have been putting over on you a not-too-well camouflaged Communist line. Your staff publications follow the *New Masses* line exactly but not so frankly, and the *New Masses* articles are much better documented. . . .
>
> This study poses the question: What are the Soviet Union's aims in the Far East? Is there a sinister purpose behind this Communist inspired campaign to discredit China? Only Marshal Stalin can answer this question.
>
> But another question has been bothering me as I made this study. That question is: Is it treason? Does the publication of untruthful statements give "aid and comfort" to our enemy Japan in its attempt to break Chinese unity under Chiang Kai-shek? This question I propound to your Board of Trustees.

Look over these clippings and see if you do not
think it is time for a house-cleaning of the IPR. . . . If
you agree that a housecleaning in the IPR is long
overdue, I will be happy to help. My suggestions
would be:
1. Fire all the Reds, because the truth is not in
them.
2. Adopt a policy of presenting facts rather than
opinions. Identify the sources of your information.
3. Name a responsible body to determine policy.-
This last point is suggested to me by what I missed
in going through your last 7 years' publications. I
found:
1. No criticism of Japan in those 7 years, except of
her rural land system;
2. No single criticism of Communist China; and
3. No single criticism of the Soviet Union: whereas
I found:
4. Severe criticism of the Chinese Government,
alternating with praise, closely following the alternations of the Soviet Union's foreign policy and of the
Communist press.
A responsible committee controlling and vouching
for your policy would be very reassuring to the members of, and contributors to your Institute.
I am sending a copy of this letter and the accompanying extracts to other members of, and contributors to the Institute, in the hope that many will read
through the material and form their own conclusions.

In a postscript Kohlberg told Carter he was not taking
this matter up with him privately because of the cavalier
treatment he had received at his hands in the Edwards
matter. "I am still waiting for your reply," he said.

The document that accompanied this letter was indeed
impressive. To provide historical background, the first
three pages were taken up with agreements between the
Nationalist Government and the Chinese Communists.
Pages 4 to 37 contained extracts from IPR publications

Far Eastern Survey and *Pacific Affairs,* written by Owen Lattimore, Anna Louise Strong, Harriet C. Moore, Guenther Stein, Edgar Snow, T. A. Bisson, Frederick V. Field, and other IPR luminaries. From pages 37 to 77 Kohlberg presented matching statements from Communist publications, and the remaining pages were given over to "assorted extracts" to bolster further his contention that the IPR was spreading the Communist Party Line. Throughout, he annotated the various items with pointed and sometimes highly sarcastic remarks.

From his previous experience with Carter, Kohlberg was sure that his present complaint would be ignored if it were sent only to him. So this time he gave it wide circulation, sending it to people in the IPR and to others outside the organization. This was a tactic he was to use extensively, whenever he wanted to drive home a point and impale someone publicly while doing so. This public disclosure obviously stung Carter as a form of lese majesty. When he answered Kohlberg a month later he completely ignored the charges and petulantly protested that Kohlberg had circulated the letter without discussing it with him first. Then he devoted most of his letter to an explanation of why he had not replied to Kohlberg's query about Edwards almost a year before, in the course of the AB-MAC controversy.

"I did not reply to it because it seemed to be a matter calling for the formal action of the UCR Board of Directors, not for the expression of a personal view by the individuals." He then went on to say that anyway Edwards had been exonerated of Kohlberg's charges.

Never one to back away from an argument, Kohlberg replied, reminding Carter that he, Carter, had promised to look over his letter but nothing had come of this. He also quoted the report of the Board of Directors of UCR, which stated: "Due to the fact that Mr. Edwards was not present, your Committee freely admits its inability to pass judgment on all the details in the charges made by Mr. Kohlberg." Even so, Carter continued to insist that Edwards had been cleared.

It would probably be incorrect to say that Edward C. Carter was a confused individual but he had a genius for creating confusion. Some of this befuddlement crept into the reply that the IPR circulated in response to Kohlberg's charges. This clearly showed Carter's hand, though it was signed by others.

The two-page letter could be divided into two parts. One described the makeup of the American Council of IPR and its policies, lauded the high caliber of its personnel, and told what a fine job they were doing. The second part of the letter was entirely taken up with an attempt to justify Carter's action in the *Edwards* matter, though this had nothing do to with the charges Kohlberg was then making. The Board of Directors of UCR, it said, had taken action "completely exonerating their representative."

The letter did not entirely ignore Kohlberg's charges against the IPR but it wasted few words in dismissing them:

"The Executive Committee and the responsible officers of the American Council find no reason to consider seriously the charge of bias. The character of the personnel associated with the Institute, the long history of its research activities, and the demonstrated value of its research testify to the fact that it has properly fulfilled its function to conduct impartial research on important issues even though they are controversial. The Committee believes a full presentation and discussion of such issues is desirable, even in wartime."

And that was all about *that.*

The signatures of four very distinguished gentlemen appeared at the end of this statement:

Robert G. Sproul, President of the University of California.

Robert D. Calkins, Dean of the School of Business, Columbia University.

G. Ellsworth Huggins, President of Catlin Farish Company, Inc.

Philip C. Jessup, then Professor of International Law, Columbia University, and now the United States Justice on the World Court.

By their action in signing this statement these men gave Kohlberg an excellent opening for another letter, which he dispatched to the trustees on December 28th:

"I am puzzled by your letter of Dec. 19, signed (among others) by Chairman Robert G. Sproul, who was not in New York on Dec. 11, the date of your meeting, but who wrote me from California on Dec. 14 stating that he would carefully study the matter. I am also puzzled by the contents of your letter, which contains a statement of the circumstances surrounding my meeting with Mr. Carter in Chungking in August 1943. These circumstances could not, by any stretch of the imagination, be known to the four signers of the letter and are, in fact, inaccurately stated. . . . What these circumstances have to do with the issues presented in my letter of November 9 is another puzzler to me."

In this letter he took the opportunity to repeat his previous charges of pro-Communism in IPR publications, and then he made some new ones, among them the following:

"As a member, I would be interested to know who elected or appointed to your Board and to your Executive Committee, Mr. Frederick V. Field, Generalissimo of the White House pickets until their liquidation, June 22, 1941, [this was the day Hitler turned on Stalin, when the Communist line made an abrupt switch] and now featured writer on China for the *Daily Worker, The Communist,* and *New Masses.* I would also be interested to know what makes him an 'expert' on China."

Later it was disclosed that Frederick Vanderbilt Field,

sometimes called "the millionaire Communist," had contributed $60,000 to the IPR to make up its operating deficits. Meanwhile not many people took Kohlberg's charges very seriously.

Some time later the IPR got around to preparing an answer to these charges. It was fifty-two pages long and was circulated on a very restricted basis. Kohlberg did not receive a copy, and when his request for one was turned down he had to get a court order forcing the IPR to give him one. However, all this took time and he was unable to read their answers until October 1946.

The genesis of this IPR document was disclosed long afterwards during the IPR investigation by the Senate Internal Security Subcommittee. The following exchange between Robert Morris, Subcommittee Counsel, and Raymond Dennett is enlightening:

> Mr. Morris: Mr. Dennett, were you secretary of the American Council of the IPR when Alfred Kohlberg brought his charges that there was communist influence in the Institute?
>
> Mr. Dennett: I was.
>
> Mr. Morris: Mr. Dennett, was there ever any thorough investigation made of the so-called Kohlberg charges?
>
> Mr. Dennett: I would say "no." I would say an answer was prepared, which is somewhat different.
>
> Mr. Morris: Who prepared the answer?
>
> Mr. Dennett: Marguerite Ann Stewart.
>
> Mr. Morris: Did she make an objective investigation of the so-called charges?
>
> Mr. Dennett: I am not really in a position to judge that, Mr. Morris. I would be inclined to think not.

By another of those coincidences that kept cropping up in IPR's small world, this Marguerite Ann Stewart was the wife of Maxwell S. Stewart, the author of "War-Time China," which Kohlberg had singled out for special attention when he first attacked the IPR.

If Edward C. Carter, the Executive Committee, or any other officials of the IPR thought that their dismissal of his charges was going to discourage Alfred Kohlberg from taking further action, they soon found out they were mistaken. Nor was he content to let the matter rest with an exchange of correspondence, much of it made public as an important part of his strategy.

Probably more important, he started to make an intensive study of Communism. "I came to learn more," he said, "not only about the workings of the Institute of Pacific Relations and the Communist line in China, but about Communism in general. This came about partly from the study of the Communist press, which I had originally started in the library to check on the IPR, and partly through meeting people who were authorities on the matter. Among others were Nelson Frank, of the New York *World-Telegram;* Max Eastman, who came to me early in 1945 for material on the Communist Chinese for an article for the *Reader's Digest*; some of the staff and Congressional members of the Un-American Activities Committee of the House of Representatives; Felix Morley and Frank Hanighen of the publication *Human Events*; Freda Utley, who was then working for the Chinese Ministry of Information; and Father Mark Tsai, who was then editing the *China Monthly,* a journal of China articles which were in some way, I believe, sponsored by the Catholic Mission group. In addition to the letters with which I bombarded the IPR group during 1945 and 1946, I began to try writing articles for the *China Monthly* and had a number accepted. One was a biography of Owen Lattimore; the other an analysis of the Agreements between China and the Soviet Union, made in August 1945. It was not then known that they were based on the still secret pact of Yalta."

The letters with which he "bombarded" the IPR group were interesting in that they showed he was getting irrefutable information. In them he exposed the highly questionable backgrounds of certain of the IPR personnel, citing their affinity for Communist causes. Discussing the line of IPR writers to the effect that Chinese Communists were not really Communists, he was able to quote such bona fide Reds as Mao Tse-tung to the contrary. Now and then, to assist in the educational process of those on his mailing list, which eventually was stabilized at approximately 800, he would mail out reproductions of material appearing in Communist and non-Communist publications, explaining the significance of the material.

Sometimes the barbs he aimed were sharp. In a letter to Frederick V. Field he said: "I remember on June 21, 1941, you were marching up and down in front of the White House carrying a placard reading: 'The Yanks Are Not Coming,' 'Roosevelt Is Tricking Us Into the Second Imperialist War,' while on June 23 you were demanding an immediate second front in Europe. Your Institute of Pacific Relations made a similar switch, although not so quickly. . . ."

Armed with the facts provided by his research, Kohlberg often aimed at other targets. In a letter to Raymond Gram Swing, a liberal radio commentator who was heard on the American Broadcasting Company's network, he called his attention to "a long list of embarrassing errors in your broadcasts and suggest that you take steps to inform yourself about China from first-hand sources instead of relying on the pro-Communist cabal in the Institute of Pacific Relations and the Foreign Policy Association. The qualifications of their China experts seem to consist chiefly of either never having been to China, or at least since Pearl Harbor; a slavish repetition of the Chinese Communist propaganda, inability to read or speak Chinese; and an awe-inspiring admiration of the Soviet Union."

Kohlberg then cited Swing's "embarrassing errors," that "the Chinese Communists are not Communists; that their armies were the only ones fighting the Japs; that the National armies were hoarding U.S. equipment to fight the Communists instead of using it against the Japs; that China's armies wouldn't fight, and, because they were half-starved, couldn't if they would; that the National Government is feudal and fascist; that the censorship is the worst in the world, etc., etc."

Mr. Swing ignored the letter.

One of Kohlberg's best known pieces dealing with the IPR was called "A Red Dream." Written in satirical vein, it purported to be a view of world history as set down by Earl Browder, the Communist leader. Kohlberg took great pride in this, and every year he sent copies of it to members of Congress. The following is an excerpt from this classic of Kohlbergiana:

> As the Soviet liberators advanced with the Chinese Communist brothers-in-arms . . . the scholarly non-Communist research organizations such as the Institute of Pacific Relations and the Foreign Policy Association, together with the Communist press, exposed the true character of the National Government of China as reactionary, pro-fascist, and pro-Japanese. They exposed the false claim that they had been fighting the Japanese for 8 years. In disabusing the American public of the idea that China was its friend and proving that the true meaning of cooperation was acceding to Communist demands, many famous non-Communist Chinese experts and scholars were outstanding, particularly Agnes Smedley, Edgar Snow, Theodore White, Mark Gayn, Maxwell Stewart, L. K. Rosinger, T. A. Bisson, and Frederick V. Field. Thus the American government insisted that the Chungking Government negotiate directly with Moscow, and the United States of America refused to intervene in the internal affairs of China.
>
> "During the years 1946-49, the Chinese Soviet Republic gradually extended its territories to include

all of China and restore order throughout its realm by liquidating all traitors to the people. . . .

Which was pretty good forecasting for 1945—immeasurably better than that of many politicians and diplomats, columnists, commentators, professors, and theologians.

Naturally, Prophet Kohlberg was not held in high esteem by such people. As he put it:

"Although the untruthfulness of the Communist line was apparent by the switches . . . and although the Institute of Pacific Relations had dutifully followed each of the switches in the Communist line, the result of my publication of this material was mostly to bring down on my head abuse from almost all quarters with few exceptions. For the most part the exceptions wrote me privately and not for publication in support of my position. So thoroughly had the Communists' propaganda captured American minds that the intellectual community was almost an appendage of the Kremlin."

Meanwhile he continued his efforts to get a hearing by the Trustees of the IPR or by a special committee empowered to consider his charges.

"This time," he said, "I avoided being booby-trapped as I had been with United China Relief, and insisted that any hearings had to be full and complete, with plenty of days for the presentation of the case. Negotiations for such were entered into but produced nothing but attempts on the part of the IPR people to get me to present my case to a packed jury of leftists. Although I was not well-informed, they picked out such leftists that I found [their] public records sufficient to warn me. . . ."

His next step, according to his affidavit, previously mentioned in this chapter, was to ask for permission to circularize his fellow members.

"This was granted by letter from Mr. Raymond Dennett. But when I sent a secretary by appointment to copy the names, they withdrew permission. I filed suit for the membership list which after various court vicissitudes was settled by agreement by the IPR to address on their machines under my inspection any one mailing I might choose to send their members.

"In said mailing, dated March 18, 1947 [more than two years later], I included a printed resolution calling for the appointment of an impartial committee of investigation and a proxy to vote for same."

Also included was an article from the *New Leader* and one from *Plain Talk,* both dealing with the IPR, together with a letter in which Kohlberg set forth the reasons why he thought the IPR was an integral part of the Communist conspiracy. (This letter appears as part of Kohlberg's affidavit in the Appendix of this book.)

The IPR, however, took steps to counter this move. On March 17 it sent a letter to all its members and pointed out that, "In many countries as wartorn as China, there may well develop honest differences of opinion," and it related this to the request for proxies that Kohlberg was sending out. However, there was no mention of the fact that the IPR had done its utmost to try to stifle Kohlberg's "honest differences of opinion," and that it had taken a lengthy court battle to force the issue. Rather, the members were told that "as one of the many efforts to meet Mr. Kohlberg's demands he has been offered the privilege of mailing his accusations. . . ." But to make it easy for the members to make up their minds, the letter stated:

"The Executive Committee of the Board of Trustees has investigated Mr. Kohlberg's charges and found them inaccurate and irresponsible."

This letter was signed by Joseph C. Chamberlain, Arthur H. Dean, Walter F. Dillingham, Brooks Emeny, Huntington Gilchrist, W. R. Herod, and Philip C. Jessup. It is interesting to note that Jessup joined in this action against Kohlberg even though he had by that time retired from all IPR offices.

On April 22, 1947, according to Kohlberg's affidavit, at a court-ordered meeting of the IPR, "the tellers advised me that they had over 1,000 proxies against the resolution for an investigating committee. I presented 88 but they disqualified about 20, though they refused to show me their proxies." The actual vote against him was 1163 to 66.

Kohlberg then read his resolution to the group and explained why he thought an investigation was imperative. Apparently his argument fell on deaf ears. Again referring to the affidavit:

"Mr. Arthur H. Dean, Vice Chairman of the IPR, presided in the absence of the Chairman, Robert G. Sproul. He answered my statement, saying that the IPR was lily-white (not Red) and he could vouch for it. The vote cast by the nearly 100 present was unanimous against the resolution. A few days later, by letter, I resigned from the IPR, since which time I have devoted little time to it."

In the minutes of that meeting, the acting Chairman, Arthur H. Dean is quoted as follows:

"I would like to say on behalf of the Board of Trustees, if there is anyone, whether a member of the Institute or not, who has any evidence that the Institute through any members of its staff or through its publications or staff or any manner whatsoever is following Communist party line or not following a strictly scholarly line, or is in any way subversive of the high purpose of the American Government, the Trustees would welcome such evidence, and I promise you we will appoint an impartial committee to investigate."

Further on Mr. Dean declared: "If Mr. Kohlberg or anyone else has any evidence that anyone on the staff of the

Institute of Pacific Relations is connected with any Communist-front organizations, I shall assure you he will be properly disciplined."

At this point Alfred Kohlberg probably realized he was fighting a lost cause in trying to do some housecleaning within the organization. He did, however, keep Philip C. Jessup and Arthur H. Dean in mind, and now and then he addressed letters to them or made references to them and their activities. He was obviously intrigued by the fact that Philip C. Jessup ended up on the World Court and that Arthur H. Dean represented the United State in dealing with the Communists in Korea, at the Panmunjom meetings.

It might be pointed out that Kohlberg did weaken his case in one respect. He did an outstanding job in compiling evidence to show the parallels between what appeared in IPR publications and what the Communist press published. Unfortunately, the way in which he made his presentation left much to be desired. Here is where he could have made good use of professional help. He was submitting this material in many cases to business executives and professional people who were accustomed to slick presentations that combine the talents of advertising copywriters, public relations experts, and art directors. Many of the people who received his 88-page document doubtless formed their opinions of its contents on the basis of its mediocre physical appearance.

A better grade of paper could have been used, and the reproduction of printed matter could have been improved. The comments that Kohlberg made about the various items were crudely hand-lettered, some in the form of gibes and many of them were confusing. While there is no doubt that the inner circle of the IPR knew exactly what Kohlberg was driving at in these comments, many others must have been completely baffled by them.

This undoubtedly included many if not most of the Trustees—innocents—who may have thought they were dealing with a crank and cast their ballots accordingly.

After all, how could a little businessman possibly know
as much about these matters as all those distinguished
scholars and renowned authors who did such a marvelous
job for the Institute of Pacific Relations?

CHAPTER EIGHT

His Good Friend Joe

THE STORY OF SENATOR JOSEPH R. McCARTHY'S "NUM-bers game" that made him an international figure has often been told. However, so fanciful are some of the versions that a few facts may be in order here, as a reminder of what actually happened.

First, it is important to remember that a lot of strange and puzzling things had been taking place in this country prior to and at the time the Senator made his famous February 9, 1950, speech in Wheeling, West Virginia. People were still talking about the *Amerasia* case involving many hundreds of top-secret documents which were found in the possession of people with strange backgrounds, including ties to the Institute of Pacific Relations. The Judith Coplon spy case was going on in New York, after hearings in Washington which had brought out some lurid details concerning the former employee of the Justice Department.

Alger Hiss, a one-time official of the Institute of Pacific Relations, had been found guilty just two weeks before, on January 24, after a sensational second trial. People had been shocked at this, and were stunned to hear their Secretary of State, Dean Acheson, say, "I will not turn my back on Alger Hiss" on the very day that Hiss was sentenced to five years in prison. They recalled that two Justices of the United States Supreme Court, Felix Frankfurter and Stanley Reed, had appeared in court to testify to Hiss's good character. The spirited defense that Eleanor Roosevelt had put up in behalf of Hiss was fresh in mind, as was President Truman's famous remark that the trial was only a "red herring."

Probably most important of all, Americans had seen China fall to the Communists, and these were indeed Communists and not the "agrarian reformers" they had been called by so many of our diplomats and so-called molders of public opinion. Something, obviously, was wrong, and when a United States Senator declared that the State Department harbored Communists, millions of Americans were inclined to take him at his word.

Unfortunately, McCarthy got off to a bad start in that famous Wheeling speech. He later maintained that he had said, "I have in my hand 57 cases of individuals who would appear to be either card-carrying members or certainly loyal to the Communist Party, but who nevertheless are still helping to shape our foreign policy." His opponents, led at that time by Senator William Benton, gave a different version. According to Benton, McCarthy had said, "I have here in my hand a list of 205—a list of names that were made known to the Secretary of State as being members of the Communist Party and who nevertheless are still working and shaping policy in the State Department."

On this point controversy continues to this day. Then, to complicate matters further, the following night McCarthy made another statement—this time on a Salt Lake City radio station—in which he elaborated on his original statement by saying, "Last night I discussed the Communists in the State Department. I stated that I had the names of 57 card-carrying members of the Communist Party. . . ."

If this proved anything at all, it showed that Senator McCarthy at that time was no expert on Communism. The Communist Party never did go in for passing out cards to all its members, and certainly not to people operating in strategic spots. A membership card could have been the most damning kind of evidence against them.

From the reaction he got, the Senator probably realized that he was getting into trouble. On February 20 he must have been certain of it as he spoke to the Senate in a rough session that lasted six hours. On this occasion the number he mentioned was 81, which included the original 57, but there was a significant difference. He made no attempt to make a case that these were all Communist Party members, but said they were loyalty risks anyway. His fellow senators, however, made it virtually impossible for him to state his case. Senators Lucas, McMahon, Lehman, and Withers interrupted him repeatedly, a total of 123 times. He was obviously treading on ground that the Administration had posted as "verboten" and a more prudent man would have turned back. But of course that was not the McCarthy way.

Two days after this, on February 22, Senator Scott Lucas introduced Senate Resolution 231 authorizing an investigation of the State Department to find out whether disloyal persons were employed there or had been employed there. These hearings of the Tydings Committee opened on March 8, 1950, and it soon became apparent that McCarthy was to be the prime subject of the hearings. Senator Tydings set the tone at the outset when, charging McCarthy with having instigated the hearings, he said, "... and so far as I'm concerned in this Committee you are going to get one of the most complete investigations ever given in the history of the Republic, so far as my abilities permit."

Unaware of the full implications of this statement at the time, Senator McCarthy ran into another booby trap when, testifying in executive session on March 21, he declared that a top Russian espionage agent, whom he privately identified as Owen Lattimore, was an employee or consultant of the State Department.

It is apparent that McCarthy's early advisers soon corrected him on some of the technicalities that so often trip up people who try to fight Communism. McCarthy's reference to "card-carrying members" was not his only error. Calling Lattimore "a top Russian espionage agent" was another, and he modified this a few days later when he referred to Lattimore as the "architect" of our disastrous Far Eastern policy.

By this time McCarthy had become a front-page sensation and there was much speculation as to where he was getting his information. "The China Lobby" offered a plausible explanation, and out of this grew the myth that it was Alfred Kohlberg who had prodded Senator McCarthy into making his charges in the first place. As has been told in the opening chapter of this book, Kohlberg had no connection whatever with McCarthy until the Senator's crusade against the State Department was under way, and then it was by request. Here is Kohlberg's comment on their first meeting:

"I first heard from Senator McCarthy, whom I had not previously met, on March 15th [1950] in a letter in which he asked I contact him if I had personal knowledge of Lattimore's activities or knew anyone who did. In response, I met him on my next visit to Washington about

March 23rd or 24th and promised to give him such data as I had, which I did a few days later. Most, but not all, of this material had previously been published by me, beginning in November 1944. Copies of it, as published, were sent to Lattimore's last known mail address and other copies to the Institute of Pacific Relations."

When Lattimore returned from Afghanistan in a blaze of publicity, to appear before the Tydings Committee, Senator McCarthy may well have been wary for he was indeed up against a formidable team of opponents. In his best-selling book, *Ordeal by Slander,* Lattimore tells how the stage was set to counter the charges that he was sure would be made against him. Aiding him as "rewrite man and tough guy" was Joseph Barnes, former Foreign Editor of the *New York Herald Tribune* and then editor of the leftist *New York Star.* Barnes was subsequently identified as a member of the Communist Party and as one who had collaborated with agents of the Soviet intelligence apparatus, both of which charges he denied. Another member of the team was Stanley Salmen, executive vice-president of the book publishing firm of Little, Brown and Company, who flew down from Boston to serve as "editor." Rounding out this impressive trio was Abe Fortas, partner in the powerful law firm of Arnold, Fortas & Porter (later a Justice of the United States Supreme Court). No second team this, from the standpoint of public relations or legal counsel!

With such forces arrayed against them, Joe McCarthy and Alfred Kohlberg took a merciless beating. Indeed, the manner in which the Tydings Committee did its job should be kept in mind by all those liberals who continue to deplore the way in which Senator McCarthy "persecuted" those who appeared before him. The tone set by Tydings at the start of the hearings was maintained throughout the four months that the proceedings lasted. The Democratic majority made little attempt to conceal the fact that they were out to discredit McCarthy and clear the State Department of the charges McCarthy had made against it. Indeed, the Committee paid little attention to the actual charges or to the laxity of State Department security that allowed subversives to operate in this vital agency.

Three names that figured prominently in IPR doings were brought into the Tydings hearings—Owen Lattimore, Philip C. Jessup, and John Stewart Service.

McCarthy's most important charges against Jessup pertained to the IPR, the people Jessup had worked with in that organization, and the part he had played in implementing the party line, particularly through the IPR publication *Far Eastern Survey.* McCarthy also charged that Jessup had been affiliated with five Communist fronts, had appeared as a character witness for Alger Hiss, and had urged that the United States stop all work on atom bomb production.

However, McCarthy's charges were given scant attention, while Jessup was treated as a celebrity honoring the Committee by his presence. He made a speech in which he declared he was not a Communist, that the Red press of the Soviet Union had repeatedly attacked him, and he had letters from Generals Marshall and Eisenhower supporting him.

Senator Hickenlooper, of the Republican minority, asked the Chairman if Senator McCarthy could ask Jessup some questions. As an indication of the topsy-turvy nature of the proceedings, Senator Tydings replied that this would have to be passed on by the Committee. However, he expressed the opinion that Mr. Jessup "might be entitled to interrogate Senator McCarthy."

When McCarthy said he'd be glad to allow Jessup to ask him any questions he wanted to, Tydings curtly shut him up, saying, "Just a minute. We haven't asked you as yet, Senator McCarthy."

No questions were asked by Senator McCarthy and the ordeal of Philip C. Jessup came to a happy ending as the majority members of the Committee rushed to shake his hand. It came as no great surprise when the Tydings Committee later reported: "This subcommittee feels that the accusations made against Philip C. Jessup are completely unfounded and unjustified and have done irreparable harm to the prestige of the United States."

The press carried the glad tidings to the public, not neglecting to mention that Jessup had the backing of Truman, Acheson, Marshall, and Eisenhower.

With regard to John Stewart Service, Senator McCarthy charged that he had been a top policy maker in the Far Eastern Division of the State Department, part of the "pro-Soviet group" which had worked for the overthrow of Chiang Kai-shek and for the establishment of a unified China with Communists in the government. As proof of this, McCarthy offered reports that Service had sent from China. Then, too, there was the notorious *Amerasia* case in which Service had been involved.

Here again the Tydings Committee found that McCarthy was more to be censured than the man he had named. The Committee concluded that Service was neither disloyal nor pro-Communist. Nor was he a security risk. His was a case of "complete innocence."

The Owen Lattimore case took a lot more time than those of Service and Jessup. Indeed the Committee permitted the renowned Far Eastern expert to expound on a wide range of subjects, to the extent of 191 pages of printed testimony. And at the end of this, Tydings and his majority used 26 more pages to absolve him of any wrongdoing.

In those 191 pages of testimony Lattimore made excellent use of his forum to establish certain points. He scored a propaganda bull's-eye on May 3 when he came up with a brand new word to describe the charges against him as

"McCarthyism." The next day Lattimore's smear word was prominently featured in a lead article in the *Daily Worker.* The author of the piece was Gus Hall, who now heads the Communist Party in the United States. Said the commissar:

"We Communist fully share the alarm and indignation which Senator McCarthy's Goebbel-like articles have aroused in all democratic circles. McCarthyism is but one manifestation of the chain reaction set off by the President himself. . . ."

The word McCarthyism soon became a part of the language, used in the same sense that Lattimore and Hall employed it. It is hardly necessary to point out that it is still being used in the original sense.

In the course of his testimony and later on, in his book, *Ordeal by Slander,* Lattimore gave wide circulation to another term which, till then, had not been generally known. He used the term "China Lobby" to describe people who were "persecuting" him—agents of a "discredited, corrupt and tottering foreign government," Nationalist China. Kohlberg was portrayed as an occidental Fu Manchu who was trying to destroy him and through him strike a devastating blow at the kind of objective scholarship Lattimore represented.

In the course of the hearings, Lattimore was asked about some of his associates in the Institute of Pacific Relations—Philip Jaffe, Agnes Smedly, Nym Wales, T. A. Bisson, Frederick Vanderbilt Field. Not one, in his opinion, was a Communist. Liberal, yes, but certainly not Communist.

Throughout the questioning, Lattimore was treated with the greatest deference by Senator Tydings and the majority members of the Committee. Earl Browder also received treatment that bordered on the obsequious, even though he snarled at the senators when they asked too many questions to suit him. And Frederick Vanderbilt

Field, too, was treated with fitting consideration. On the other hand, witnesses whose testimony appeared to uphold McCarthy's charges were treated contemptuously. Louis Budenz, for example, was ridiculed when he told the Committee that Lattimore and Haldore Hanson were Communists. The aged Senator Green asked Budenz if he knew Lattimore and Hanson personally. When Budenz said he did not, Green sarcastically remarked, "But you are not reasoning that everyone you have never seen and never heard may be a Communist. Is that your argument?" Budenz's testimony was dismissed as hearsay.

Freda Utley, who had known Lattimore personally for years, and who was a bona fide expert on China, was cut short churlishly by Tydings when she tried to show how Lattimore's writings followed the party line. Tydings told her, "We want facts, f-a-c-t-s . . . we are getting mostly opinion." Tydings' associates then belabored her with personal questions. Was she being subsidized by Chiang Kai-shek's Nationalist Government? Was she appearing on behalf of Alfred Kohlberg? Was she a Nazi sympathizer?

Owen Lattimore of course received a clean bill of health. As for Kohlberg, the Committee smeared his motives as follows:

"It has been shown that this reference [the charge made by McCarthy that Jessup opposed Kohlberg's attempts to investigate the IPR] is to an attempt made by Alfred Kohlberg to wrest control of the Institute. The dispute was primarily a private feud between the controlling group and the group supporting Kohlberg which resulted in overwhelming defeat for Kohlberg and his faction. While we do not pass on the merits of the contest, it is apparent that this is a correct explanation in contradiction of the erroneous interpretation given by Senator McCarthy."

As though that wasn't enough, the Committee delivered itself of another smear by stating that Kohlberg's wealth "appears to have stemmed from contracts with representatives of the Nationalist Government in China." This was an unmitigated falsehood. Kohlberg never had any financial dealings with the Chinese Government, but conducted a private business in that country.

The press by and large accepted at face value the line put out by the Tydings Committee, and what might be called the Lattimore Lobby. McCarthy and Kohlberg were maneuvered into the role of defendants, and they were portrayed in much of the news coverage of that time as partners in crime, and guilty of trying to ruin the reputations of gentlemen and scholars.

The hearings had scarcely ended, however, when McCarthy and Kohlberg received unexpected confirmation of their contention that the country was being badly misled by a lot of false prophets. On June 25, 1950, Communist armies from the Soviet Zone in Korea poured across the 38th parallel and invaded South Korea. Later that year the Chinese Communists, no longer the "agrarian reformers" they had been depicted by people in the IPR and our State Department, joined their Korean comrades in the battle against American GIs.

It was at this time that someone remembered a piece that Owen Lattimore had written for the pro-Communist *New York Compass* on July 17, 1949. This strange statement by the sage of Johns Hopkins University was so blatant that it was widely reprinted:

"As it became more and more obvious that Chiang Kai-shek and the Kuomintang were doomed, the conduct of American policy became increasingly delicate. The problem was how to allow them to fall without making it look as if the United States had pushed them. . . . Korea is another chapter in the same unhappy story. I have yet to meet an American who knows all the facts and believes that Syngman Rhee is either a popular or a competent president of Korea. In spite of high-pressure elections, his legislature is more badly split against him than China's was against Chiang Kai-shek. *The thing to do, therefore, is to let South Korea fall, but not to let it look as though we pushed it.* Hence the recommendations of a parting grant of $150,000,000." (Italics added.)

The Lattimore statement had found an echo of sorts in a speech Secretary Acheson made on January 12, 1950, and this too was recalled and widely circulated. Korea, said Acheson, was outside the "defense perimeter" of the United States, and so was Formosa. The Communists apparently took note of what appeared to them to be an invitation to aggression and acted accordingly.

With the Korean War as tragic evidence of the kind of leadership they had been getting, the American people reacted strongly. One of the early casualties of the conflict was Millard Tydings, whose "whitewash committee" had become a symbol. Considered unbeatable, the formidable Senator from Maryland was toppled in the next election by John Marshall Butler, a young man who was relatively unknown but whose politics were unlike those of Tydings. Another casualty was Tydings' strong right arm on the Committee, Scott Lucas of Illinois, one of McCarthy's most persistent hecklers. He too was voted out of office, even though he had been the Democratic Majority Leader of the Senate. And in 1951 the Senate refused to confirm Philip C. Jessup as Ambassador to the United Nations.

Kohlberg took note of this in a letter to his sister:

"Four years ago, when Jessup was appointed Deputy Delegate to the United Nations I wrote every member of Congress something about him and I believe there was not a single vote cast against him for confirmation. Now, four years later, when he is appointed delegate, it looks as though the administration can't even get him confirmed by the Senate. That, at least, shows that things are improving, as far as the Senate of the United States goes."

During this period and until McCarthy's death in 1957,

Alfred Kohlberg remained a fast friend of the Senator's. After all, they had many things in common, not the least of which was a similar lineup of enemies, including more than a few who were willing to stoop to any chicanery to destroy them. This friendship lasted through several troubled years, described by Kohlberg as follows:

With the election of Eisenhower in 1952, the Republicans had regained control of the Congress so that Senator Joseph R. McCarthy, ranking Republican on the Senate Subcommittee on Investigations, became the new Chairman. In that position he engaged Roy M. Cohn of New York, a young lawyer of exceptional ability but only 27 years old, to be his chief counsel. Then he began to investigate infiltration of government by Communists and pro-Communists. The uproar . . . was deafening, and continued through 1953 and into 1954, when finally McCarthy was charged with improper activities as Chairman of the Subcommittee on Investigations. The charges were apparently made by the Army. These were the so-called Army-McCarthy hearings of May and June 1954. I took a position of unwavering support of Joe McCarthy and all his activities in this matter, and what has come out bit by bit since convinces me that McCarthy was actually understating the situation in his charges.

The uproar against McCarthy in the spring of 1954, which led to the charges against him and the hearings of May and June of that year, is hard to explain. The ostensible charge that he had sought an Army commission for his assistant David Schine was too unimportant to take seriously. The charge of impolite handling of an Army General [Zwicker] likewise does not hold water. The hearings ended inconclusively, but immediately new charges were filed to the effect that he had treated a Senate Committee with scorn in 1952.

These charges were filed by Senator Ralph E. Flanders. . . . They were heard by a Committee under Senator Arthur V. Watkins. [Both Senator Watkins and Senator Flanders were Republicans, as was Senator McCarthy.] The Committee recommended censure of McCarthy, which was carried out by a unanimous vote of Democrats and almost half of the Republicans. The Committee he had "scorned" had been investigating his income tax returns and he refused to dignify their proceedings by even appearing. Strangely, an official Treasury investigation of Senator McCarthy's income tax returns, concluded before his death in 1957, found he had overpaid his taxes and refunded about $1,000 to him. Washington rumors attributed the whole plot against McCarthy to Presidential Assistant Sherman Adams with President Eisenhower's blessing.

And it all happened the year after his wedding to beautiful Jean Kerr. Ida and I attended the wedding in Saint Matthew's Cathedral in Washington. All Washington that counted, except only the President, was there. . . .

After the incident of the $500 check which Senator McCarthy returned, Alfred Kohlberg was circumspect about gifts to his friend. Apart from a wedding present, the only time he spent money in McCarthy's behalf was to buy a hundred copies of the Senator's book, *America's Retreat from Victory,* which he distributed. This buying and circulating of books he liked was a common practice of Kohlberg's.

He did, however, give McCarthy something more valuable, his loyalty, at a time when many were turning away from him. A cliché of the time (which is still heard) was, "I approve of the Senator's aims but I disapprove of his methods." Alfred Kohlberg was more forthright. Writing in *The American Legion Magazine* for January 1954 he said, "Constantly we hear people say they approve McCarthy's goals but not his methods. I have known the

Senator for some time, and have watched him closely from the beginning. My judgment is that I approve of his methods but not his goals. Personally I think his goals are too restricted. I would like to see him spread out and follow the trail from the Reds in government into all other fields."

The point made here by Kohlberg was not generally understood. In a speech made in 1951 he had said much the same thing in defining "McCarthyism." Kohlberg's definition was considerably different from that of the liberal element:

"Very simply put, it consists of exposing disloyalty, dishonesty, and actual treason in government, and demanding that something be done about it, now, before it's too late.

"McCarthyism is a very old American custom. It is an age-old American determination to get rid of traitors and grafters and disloyal public servants."

The Communists and those who somehow take their cues from Communists, spread the idea that McCarthyism was something quite different—that the Senator from Wisconsin was a rising Hitler who was using his dangerous power to sight in on college professors, clergymen, people in show business, or anyone else he didn't like. Many of these people joined in a united front against McCarthy. The country started to hear a chorus of mournful cries that thought control was being exercised on our campuses, that witch-hunters and hate merchants were loose in the land, and other hysterical poppycock.

To fight the "Joe Must Go" propaganda that soon went into high gear after having been launched by the *Daily Worker*, Kohlberg spared no effort. He made public appearances wherever he could find a forum. In a letter to Senator McCarthy dated July 24, 1953, he told him, "I have agreed to appear on WOR-TV Saturday night, 10:30 to 11:00 August 15th on the question 'Is McCarthyism a Menace?' To set you straight I shall take the negative ... I hope you do not watch the program as I am going to have to criticize you severely as a master of understatement."

On another occasion he debated James Wechsler, the very liberal editor of the *New York Post,* on the subject: "Resolved: That Senator McCarthy's activities are in accord with the principles of true Americanism." The debate was held in the auditorium of the William Howard Taft High School in the Bronx on December 11, 1953, under the auspices of an American Legion Post.

Two weeks before the meeting it became apparent that there was likely to be trouble. In a letter to a Legionnaire friend, James F. O'Neil, Kohlberg stated, "I have been called up by people I do not know, who tell me that the neighborhood is very leftist and they warn me that I will not get a fair hearing or fair handling. I do not believe this. ... Nevertheless, I thought that possibly somebody from the office of the County Commander, or the Chairman of the Americanism Committee of the Bronx County Legion might wish to be on hand to observe. . . ."

The people who warned Kohlberg were right. Outside the auditorium an unruly mob of anti-McCarthyites kept up a refrain of "Hitler! Hitler! Hitler!" Inside there were frequent catcalls and interruptions when Kohlberg was speaking. But for the police, who were there in force, there might have been a riot.

Wechsler pointedly turned his back when Kohlberg offered to shake hands, and he refused to pose with him for pictures.

In a letter to his sister, Alfred Kohlberg explained very simply why he believed so strongly in the McCarthy cause:

"The proof of the fundamental soundness of McCarthy's charge lies in the fact that we have lost all of the objectives for which we fought the war. They were the Atlantic Charter and the Four Freedoms, sunk without a trace these many years, also the independence of China, the demand for which called forth the attack on Pearl Harbor.... Now everybody knows that our Army, Navy, and Air Force did not lose the war, that our objectives in the war have been completely lost since the job was taken away from the Army, Navy, and Air Force and handled by two Presidents and five Secretaries of State...."

In another letter to his sister he discussed an article in the *Daily Worker* which denounced McCarthy. Said Kohlberg, "McCarthy's attacks on labor . . . I do not know about. Do you? Nor do I know about anybody whose civil rights have been interfered with by McCarthy. Do you? But I do know all about the money behind McCarthy because, according to the press back here, it's all mine. The amount I've contributed to him is exactly zero from beginning to end. He seems to have done a very good job on so little money."

Some of Kohlberg's most amusing letters were those he sent to McCarthy. One, dated March 8, 1953, told him, "I enclose the *Daily Worker* for last Monday because it was an especially good issue. . . . In this issue you are denounced on page 1, in three different articles on page 4, in one article on page 6, in one article on page 7. Pages 2, 3 and 8 seem to have gotten along without you.... Now I understand what some of my dopey friends mean when they tell me that Joe McCarthy is doing more good than harm to the Communists. They mean that if you weren't around the *Daily Worker* would have to close up for lack of news, and then what would I do for daily reading?"

On another occasion he wrote McCarthy concerning the theater critic of *The New York Times*, Brooks Atkinson, who had also done a stint in China. "I enclose correspondence with Brooks Atkinson," said Kohlberg. "You see, he and the *Daily Worker* agree that you are the cause of the low level of plays on Broadway. Maybe he will now advise me that you caused bad business in the handkerchief field also. Maybe you are also the cause of bad business for the Democratic Party. Aren't you ashamed?"

There were letters in more serious vein, too, bits of information that were passed along for consideration and possible action. One of these was a lengthy report of a trip the Kohlbergs had made through Europe. It told how Europeans were being given the idea that McCarthy was the head of a neo-Nazi group that was planning to seize power in America. In the course of this report Kohlberg said: "It was only as day after day went by and everyone to whom we spoke, with one exception, asked us about the neo-Nazi movement which was extremely powerful in the United States, that we began to realize that the campaign of calumny directed at you was being used in Europe to destroy the reputation and prestige of the United States."

By this time Kohlberg was well aware of the difficulty of trying to explain anything about Communism and Communists to many people—even to such sophisticated people as United States Senators. He once discussed this subject at a dinner whose guest of honor was Roy M. Cohn, counsel to the McCarthy Committee:

"Some of my best friends are Senators. But beware of them, Roy. They are just too mixed up. To them it seems perfectly okay for the Senior Senator from Vermont to call the Senator from Wisconsin a rising Hitler and an anti-Semite; but it's all wrong for the Junior Senator from Wisconsin to say a few unkind words about Fifth Amendment Communists. It's much too confusing for a simple country boy from New York. In fact, poor Senator Lehman seems to think that loyalty to the Constitution is fulfilled by invoking the Fifth Amendment.

"Let me illustrate by the sad case of Senator Flanders. Four years ago I called on him to inquire about a farm in Vermont, jointly owned by Owen Lattimore and Vilhjalmur Stefansson [the latter had a lengthy pro-Communist record]. As soon as I mentioned their names Senator Flanders told me they were friends of his, and that anybody who called Stefansson a communist was cockeyed. He knew him intimately, he said, and his ardent anti-Communism was proven by his attempt to start moose culture in Northern Vermont. If it had succeeded, he said, it would have put the Soviet Union out of the moose culture business and knocked old Joe Stalin for a loop."

Joe McCarthy and Alfred Kohlberg met on frequent occasions in New York and Washington. The meetings were sometimes held in the New York apartment of the late Dr. J. B. Matthews, an authority on Communism who helped coach the Senator in the early 1950's. The last time Alfred and Ida Kohlberg saw the Senator was in the spring of 1957. On their way to a convention in Miami they stopped off in Washington for a visit with their old friend. That was in April and the Senator died the following month. Not long afterward Kohlberg expressed this opinion:

"Although in the end McCarthy was apparently defeated, and ill health, which led to his death in May 1957, took its toll, part of the furor he aroused was permanent and the chance of Soviet appeasement was ended."

This was one prediction of Kohlberg's which proved wrong. McCarthy's crusade may have made it impossible for the Administration to acquiesce in the conquest of Korea by the Reds as Alfred Kohlberg pointed out. But U.S. appeasement of the Soviet Union has continued to the present day. Even as we fight Communism on many fronts, and spend billions on defense against possible Communist aggression, we are told with growing insistence that it is up to us to learn how to coexist with these enemies by giving them what they want. And, we are told, the only thing we really ought to fear is a resurgence of McCarthyism.

CHAPTER NINE

That China Lobby

THERE IS AN OLD COMMUNIST DODGE THAT AMERICANS have fallen for repeatedly—the "stop thief" tactic. This is the ruse that a pickpocket employs when he thinks he is being viewed with suspicion. Hoping that no one will discover the bulging wallet in his own pocket he will point to someone else and scream, "Stop thief!" Then, as gullible bystanders take out after the innocent party, the crook disappears into the shadows.

The term "China Lobby" was coined as a catch phrase for just such a swindle. The Communist apparatus in this country had done an outstanding job as a lobby for a Red China, conditioning Americans to accept the overthrow of Nationalist China in favor of Mao Tse-tung's Red regime. However, when Alfred Kohlberg and others started making some headway in showing how this had

113

been done, the "stop thief" tactic was employed. It took the form of charging that there was an evil China Lobby at work in the United States trying to get billions of U.S. dollars for a corrupt and discredited Nationalist Government that was on its way to oblivion.

It is interesting to note how the term China Lobby came into use. The procedure is an object lesson in the wondrous ways in which Communist projects are carried to fruition, quite often with the help of people who are not Communists and who would indignantly deny any sympathy for Communism. The fact is that many if not most Communist projects would fail dismally if such dupes did not promote them.

The first use of the term China Lobby in print* was in a "Program for Action on China Policy" issued by the Communist Party of New York State on March 1, 1949, and sent out to the "Dear Comrades" with a covering letter signed by "May Miller, Asst. Org. Secretary." However, the term had been used prior to this. In a letter to Stanley Hornbeck, a former State Department official who had inquired about it, Alfred Kohlberg said he recalled having heard it used at a Communist-front meeting he had attended in January 1949 at the Roosevelt Hotel in New York.

This incident was memorable because Agnes Smedley, one of the speakers, had pointed him out and denounced him as "a spy." This constituted another use of the "stop thief" tactic, since the Smedley woman was an identified espionage agent who had worked for the notorious Sorge spy ring that had operated for the Kremlin in Japan and China.

The March 1 directive to the comrades gave top priority to what it called "the Chinese lobby," and demanded an investigation of its finances—a directive that was to be followed from that time on, not only by the

*The complete letter telling how Communists were to work to attain Party objectives concerning China appears as Appendix D.

comrades themselves but by many others who somehow absorb ideas from Communist sources and are motivated by them. The result has been a flood of millions of words, written and spoken, dealing with the Chinese lobby that "May Miller, Asst. Org Secretary" of the Communist Party wanted investigated.

According to Louis F. Budenz, the term "China Lobby" next showed up in two newspaper articles in September 1949. "Thereafter," he wrote, "the term began to appear regularly in the Communist paper, *Jewish Life,* and in the *Daily Worker.* Then, in April 1950, the words 'China Lobby' burst into the headlines when Owen Lattimore charged before the Tydings Senate Committee that he was a 'victim' of that group. From that time, as if this 'China Lobby' with Kohlberg at its head really existed, the phrase was bandied about by many columnists and commentators. . . ."

To use a word he seemed to favor, Owen Lattimore was extremely "cagey" in the strategy he employed before the Tydings Committee. Aware that the Committee was sympathetic to him, as was much of the press, he went on the offensive and charged that he was being persecuted by the China Lobby because he refused to conform to its line in support of Chiang Kai-shek. This became a dominant issue, possibly *the* dominant issue of the hearings. It was made to appear that because of his scholarly objectivity and independence the China Lobby was out to destroy him. With McCarthy as its mouthpiece the Lobby was even accusing him of being a Communist, and saying he persuaded the State Department to follow policies helpful to Communism, while using his position at the IPR to propagandize along the same lines!

He made it plain that, while it was Senator McCarthy who was making these accusations, the actual source of his troubles was Alfred Kohlberg, who personified the sinister China Lobby. As he explained it in his book, *Ordeal by*

Slander, which deals with the Tydings hearings, ". . .all but one of McCarthy's charges were duplicates of those made by Alfred Kohlberg in his attack on the Institute of Pacific Relations in 1947. Kohlberg had been completely discredited at that time, and I was exasperated to have to go to so much trouble to look up the data all over again to answer his really silly charges. . . ."

This was a highly distorted version of what had actually taken place. It will be recalled that in 1944 Kohlberg made an analysis of the pro-Communist propaganda in IPR publications and called for an investigation. The IPR reacted by trying to discourage him in every possible manner. Kohlberg circularized the board of trustees and his charges were rejected. He asked for an impartial committee to investigate the matter and his request was refused. He sought permission to circularize the membership and the membership lists were denied him. He went to court and after two long legal battles the IPR directors agreed to let him bring his charges before the members. At the showdown only 78 members showed up for the meeting in the IPR's New York offices but meanwhile IPR officials had been circularizing the members calling for proxies. Using these, they voted down Kohlberg's request for an impartial study. The fight lasted almost three years because of the IPR's delaying tactics. Far from disproving Kohlberg's charges it showed only that the inner circle of the IPR, consisting of Carter, Lattimore, Jessup, Field, and a few others, held an impregnable position.

To support his contention that McCarthy was merely acting as an instrument of the China Lobby, Lattimore presented charts which he said had been drawn up by some of his students at Johns Hopkins University to show parallels between Kohlberg's charges and those being made by Senator McCarthy.

It is strange indeed that these charts were taken seriously by the press. In assembling material for the hearings

Senator McCarthy followed the same procedure that a competent newspaperman does. If John Doe is arrested for murder it is the reporter's job to get as much background about the suspect as possible. Police records are checked and the newspaper's "morgue" is consulted. If the records show that John Doe has an unsavory past, the reporter is likely to give that fact more credence than Doe's assertion that he's an innocent man who is being framed.

When it appeared that Owen Lattimore was going to be the star performer of the Tydings hearings it could not have taken Senator McCarthy long to learn that Alfred Kohlberg was his best source of information concerning him. This was a fact well known in anti-Communist circles. In the course of his long battle with the IPR, Kohlberg had done considerable research on the Johns Hopkins professor, and by 1950 he was probably as much an expert on Lattimore as Lattimore was an expert on, say, Outer Mongolia or Inner Tibet.

Proof of this can be found in an article Kohlberg wrote about Lattimore in 1945, when the latter was relatively unknown. At the time of the Tydings hearings many magazine articles appeared concerning the professor, but none was nearly as penetrating as "Owen Lattimore: Expert's Expert" which Kohlberg wrote for *China Monthly* and which appeared in that magazine's October 1945 issue.

It stated that Lattimore had been born in Washington, D.C., in 1900. Taken to China as a child, he was sent to an English prep school, St. Bee's, when he was 15 years old. (This, plus some work at the Harvard Graduate School in 1929, was Dr. Lattimore's only formal education.) He returned to China, worked on a newspaper for a year then got a job with a British import-export firm. He left this to go to Turkestan and then wrote a book. This brought him scholarships and research assignments which made possible trips to other remote parts of Asia.

"During this period," Kohlberg wrote, "he became aware of the vast role in Asiatic affairs to be played by the Soviet Union and a great admirer of the Communist system. In 1934 he was appointed editor of *Pacific Affairs,* the quarterly publication of the Institute of Pacific Relations, and accompanied Mr. E. C. Carter, its Director-General, to Moscow. This trip apparently completed his converion to an admiration of the Soviet Union's system of government and role as world remaker."

In the article Kohlberg set forth some significant facts. He told how, as editor of *Pacific Affairs,* Lattimore had asked the well-known writer William Henry Chamberlin to prepare an article for the publication, but subsequently informed him the article would not be published "because the Soviet branch of the Institute of Pacific Relations objected." He told of Lattimore's service on the editorial board of *Amerasia,* which became involved in a notorious espionage case. He told how, under Lattimore's editorship, *Pacific Affairs* opened its pages to many known pro-Soviet and Communist writers, and he listed them.

Then he explained how Lattimore had operated at policy-making levels of government. He told, among other things, how he had been sent by President Roosevelt to Chungking in 1941 to serve as adviser to Chiang Kai-shek, and how in 1944 he had accompanied Vice-President Wallace to Siberia and China. Providing a disturbing counterpoint to all this activity were quotations from Lattimore's writings. These obviously disturbed Alfred Kohlberg, who concluded, "Mr. Lattimore would apparently use this key to lock China into the Communist World System. . . ."

Lattimore did not like the piece. His reaction, which seems characteristic, may be gauged from a letter Kohlberg wrote him almost a year after the article appeared:

"Last Fall I wrote a short study of your career for the

China Monthly. Prior to its publication the editor showed me a letter from you denouncing anything I might write as malicious and demanding the right to reply in lieu of legal action. Of course I invited him to invite your reply, which he then published in full. You corrected certain errors as to date of return to China, schooling, etc., which you stated showed lack of care, as they were ascertainable from *Who's Who.* That's just where I found those dates; apparently *Who's Who* for different years carries the dates differently. . . ."

Owen Lattimore's intense dislike of Alfred Kohlberg was reflected in the leftward-leaning segment of the press. One leading newspaper accused him of having had ten letters-to-the-editor published in a newspaper called *The Tablet,* which happens to be a large and highly regarded Catholic newspaper serving the Brooklyn diocese. At the time it was staunchly anti-Communist.

Another niggling charge repeatedly made against Kohlberg was that he had once made a campaign contribution of a thousand dollars to Senator Styles Bridges. Still another was that he had served as vice-chairman of a dinner in honor of a Chinese Archbishop, Paul Yu-pin, formerly of Nanking. Senator McCarran, and Patrick J. Hurley were speakers at this eminently respectable affair, but the entire function was compromised in the eyes of the liberal press because the treasurer was alleged to have served years before as financial adviser to Father Coughlin, an anti-New Dealer who used to broadcast from Detroit.

One might point out that this carried "guilt by association" to a ludicrous extreme by the very people who complained most about it. It must be remembered, though, that Kohlberg's opponents could find little in the way of ammunition for their smear guns, so they had to use every bit they could get, even if it made them look silly.

The *Daily Worker* probably displayed more initiative

than any other paper in its coverage of the Tydings hearings, exposing Kohlberg as "The Man Behind McCarthy" and describing the devious doings of the China Lobby. Indeed, it is strange that this highly influential newspaper has never received a Pulitzer Prize for its enterprising journalism—with other big papers playing follow-the-leader. Not only did the *Daily Worker* provide some outstanding examples of interpretive journalism in its coverage of the hearings; it was first to give prominence to the word "McCarthyism," after Lattimore sprung it on the Tydings Committee on May 3, 1950.

Many others, of course, helped the cause, and in *Ordeal by Slander* Owen Lattimore paid high tribute to the fine treatment he was accorded by much of the nation's press. Drew Pearson earned special kudos. The professor told how deeply touched he was when Pearson testified, "I happen to know Owen Lattimore personally and I only wish this country had more patriots like him."

Alfred Friendly, of the *Washington Post,* earned Lattimore's thanks for his efforts in his behalf, as did Edward Harris, of the *St. Louis Post-Dispatch.* Elmer Davis, Lattimore's old boss at the Office of War Information, received well-earned thanks, as did I. F. Stone, Martin Agronsky, and Eric Sevareid. Edward R. Murrow, probably the most influential of the newscasters of that time, performed over and above the call of duty by providing recordings of the Professor's testimony for his use, presumably on non-network stations. Lattimore was also touched by the manner in which various reporters covering the Tydings hearings showed they were definitely in his corner.

Ordeal by Slander certainly does not rate high as a literary achievement, probably because it was dashed off in such a hurry. However, as a public-relations project it rates very high indeed. Indicating the high priority Little, Brown & Company gave the book, its publication set some kind of speed record. The trial ended on June 20, and the book was out and receiving front-page rave reviews in the Sunday book sections of the *New York Times* and the *New York Herald Tribune* of July 30. Emphasizing how much they liked what they found in Lattimore's book, these newspapers again reviewed it the following day. Incidentally, the *Herald Tribune* plug was written by Professor John K. Fairbank, one of Lattimore's old IPR associates. It was not surprising that Fairbank liked it because, as Lattimore gratefully noted, during the hearings he had sent out telegrams "to a long list of Far Eastern experts" calling on them to write to Tydings in support of the man undergoing the ordeal. And all but one obliged, according to Lattimore. Anyway, thanks to hard-hitting, hard-selling book reviews, plus a lot of smart promotion, *Ordeal by Slander* became a best seller. Which was probably some compensation for the ordeal itself.

And what was the ordeal? Lattimore took 236 pages to describe it, but Eugene Lyons, in an article he wrote for the *New Leader* for September 2, 1950, tells the story better in a couple of paragraphs:

"The 'ordeal' part of the book peters out in unconscious comedy. Rarely, it develops, has a Job gotten off so lightly. 'No more cruel or unusual punishment can be devised,' Dr. Lattimore exclaims, 'than allowing a Senator to make charges against individuals that he has not even attempted to substantiate with proof.' But the nearest he comes to pointing to social or economic sanctions against himself is the decision of a Southern college to return 20 copies of one of his books.

"For the rest, everyone seems to have rallied to his banner. Tydings smiles on him. Senator Connally reassures him. Even a uniformed Senate guard whispers encouragement in his ear. Taxi drivers cheer him on. Drew Pearson goes all-out in his defense on the radio. His university faculty stages a triumphal reception for him. The

Afghans (as he solemnly records) voice faith in his loyalty. Editorial writers and reporters are on his side. The National Academy of Political and Social Sciences insists that he lecture to them, and the pressure of new lecture and writing assignments grows heavier. Presumably he has put it on a bit thick, but if the half-hearted attempt to look into his record has damaged him irreparably, this book fails to prove it."

Kohlberg took a dim view of these antics and sarcastically commented, "My heart bled for Lattimore until I noticed that he charged me with being an agent of a foreign government, right in the book. . . ."

Understandably, Kohlberg was annoyed. In his attempt to portray himself as a martyr Lattimore was making some pretty wild charges and making no attempt to substantiate them. In his *New Leader* article, Eugene Lyons made this point in criticizing such people as William L. Shirer and Edgar Snow who had endorsed Lattimore's book.

"These eulogies," said Lyons, "are all full of righteous indignation. They cry out against accusation without adequate proof. But they fail to notice that in crediting Lattimore's version at face value they make themselves a party to the slanders throughout the book—without a shred of proof—against Louis Budenz, Freda Utley, Alfred Kohlberg, and other who claim that the author has been playing a pernicious Communist game.

"Surely they command enough logic to realize that in unreservedly approving this book they are accusing others of the heinous crime of framing an innocent man."

The outbreak of war in Korea created an embarrassing situation for those who had been backing the architects of our Far Eastern policy, and for a time there was a lull in denunciations of the China Lobby. Then, with the opening of the Russell Committee's MacArthur hearings, the subject broke into the open again.

These hearings started soon after General MacArthur was relieved of his command by President Truman on April 11, 1951. Truman's arbitrary dismissal of Douglas MacArthur worried a lot of people, but there were other reasons for concern. As in the Vietnam War today, the war in Korea was being fought in a curious way. Our airmen were restricted in their bombing. There were charges of ammunition shortages. And there were recurrent rumors of diplomacy more attuned to the wishes of Britain, India, and the United Nations than to American interests.

In the course of the Russell Committee hearings, General MacArthur was interrogated only briefly. Considerable attention, however, was given to Secretary of State Acheson, General George C. Marshall, Patrick J. Hurley, Lieutenant General Albert C. Wedemeyer, Major General Emmett O'Donnell, and Vice Admiral Oscar Charles Badger. Partisan politics more than once raised its head in the course of the hearings.

The China Lobby came up for discussion early in June, with Senator Wayne Morse initiating a call for an investigation. Following this, on June 8, Secretary Acheson remarked that President Truman had started to investigate the China Lobby and this news was seized on gleefully by that part of the press which had been calling for such an investigation. The predictable *New York Post* was ecstatic, reporting: "News of this inquiry almost completely overshadowed the appearance today of Lt. Gen. Albert C. Wedemeyer, the author of the famous Wedemeyer report on China."

A person reading the *Post* could not help getting the impression that President Truman was leaving no pebble unturned in his efforts to get to the bottom of things. To expose the nefarious doings of the China Lobby, according to the *Post,* he had ordered into action the Treasury Department, the Federal Reserve Board, the Department of Agriculture, the Justice Department, and the Department of State. The *Post* said nothing about the Army, Navy, Air Force, and Marine Corps being ordered into action, but this may have been because they were tied up in Korea at the time.

In a follow-up to this piece the *New York Post* strongly hinted that, ere long, the country would be set on its ear by disclosures of vast Chinese hoards in this country—the Treasury Department was looking into the matter. And in this and other papers there were dark hints about financial finagling on the part of the anti-Communist Chinese. Sources of this disquieting information were not divulged but the *Post* assured its readers that the reports were authentic.

One of the *Post's* stories, incidentally, described some of Alfred Kohlberg's many activities in opposition to Communism when it commented: "It is doubtful if Kohlberg, a shrewd businessman, has financed all this activity for philanthropic reasons." Apparently the *Post* mentality was such that it could not conceive of anyone fighting Communism unless there was money to be made out of it.

Kohlberg was naturally annoyed at such nonsense, and he became especially irked at some of Senator Wayne Morse's free-wheeling oratory which supplied grist for the mills of writers who were not overly discriminating about the charges they made or where the charges originated.

"Morse," he commented in one letter, "even went so far as to charge that Chiang had sent $654,000,000 over to pay for the Lobby. The only one identified with the Lobby by name at that time was myself."

In a letter to Senator Bridges, dated June 8, Kohlberg commented at some length on charges being made before the Russell Committee:

"The denunciation of the China Lobby yesterday by Senator Morse and the double-talk about it by Secretary

Acheson carefully omitted my name, although bringing in the name of Bill Goodwin. [William J. Goodwin, a public relations man, worked for the Nationalist Government in 1948-1949 and was registered under the Foreign Agents Registration Act.] I, of course, have never been in any way connected with Goodwin, except that he got copies of my public material. There was once a near financial transaction. I asked him to pay three dollars to join the American China Policy Association, which he said he would. He forgot to do it and I forgot to remind him again. That was the nearest we came to it. This letter is to suggest that General Wedemeyer be asked something about the China Lobby and particularly whether I ever called on him during the couple of years that he was supposedly in charge of military supplies in China. The truth is, I did not. . . ."

At the height of the controversy an interesting story was published in *The New York Times* of June 11, 1951, telling that a top Chinese diplomat in this country had been asked by an important but unidentified U.S. government official to persuade Alfred Kohlberg to moderate his attacks on the administration's Far Eastern policy. The diplomat in question was Dr. T. F. Tsiang, chief of the Nationalist Chinese delegation to the United Nations. Tsiang made it clear that Kohlberg had never asked for or received any money from the Nationalist Government.

"I assumed that the Mr. X who approached me believed that Mr. Kohlberg, whom I had known for eight years, respected my opinion and that I could do something to change his attitude," Dr. Tsiang said. He had not interpreted the request as an indication of a belief on the part of the U.S. official that the Nationalist Government exercised any form of control over Mr. Kohlberg, he added.

"I did suggest to Mr. Kohlberg that he tone down his attacks," the Chinese diplomat continued. Kohlberg's response to this suggestion was emphatically negative. The

Times quoted Dr. Tsiang as saying, "He gave me hell. He
called me an ignoramus, said I didn't know American politics."

Alfred Kohlberg sent a letter to Secretary Acheson saying there was a rumor that he was the man who had
approached Dr. Tsiang and was it true? Subsequently
Kohlberg learned he had been mistaken about Acheson,
in this case at least. He later wrote that it was John Foster
Dulles who had made the approah to Dr. Tsiang. Dulles
at the time was one of our delegates to the United Nations.
According to Kohlberg he invited Dr. Tsiang to his home
in Cold Spring Harbor, Long Island, where he told the
Chinese diplomat that he was trying to get the State Department to modify its policies more in favor of the Nationalist Government. However, because of Kohlberg's
attacks on the State Department he was having trouble,
and couldn't Tsiang use his influence to get Kohlberg to
moderate his attacks?

At the time the Tsiang story appeared in print Kohlberg
was in Europe, on a trip that could have proved embarrassing. Senator Morse had made his call for an investigation of the China Lobby, and this was getting its biggest
news play when Kohlberg was about to leave to join his
wife and her sisters in Europe where they were vacation-
ing.

"For convenience sake," he said, "I moved in from
Bronxville to the Commodore Hotel the morning of June
9th, [1951] as I had to be at the airport at 10 A.M., June
10th for my flight. I had told the help I would be at the
Commodore but later Saturday morning when one of the
newspapers called Bronxville for an interview, they forgot
that detail and said I was leaving for Europe and they
didn't know where I was. That started the rumor that I
was running away. That story appeared in the early afternoon editions, so I telephoned the press and called a conference for later in the afternoon. At this press conference

I explained that my trip to Europe had been arranged long since and showed them my ticket, which had been bought weeks earlier. That stopped the rumor in its tracks."

Once the Senators of the Russell Committee started discussing the China Lobby, they filled more than 50 pages of their report with testimony on this subject. Unfortunately not enough public attention was ever focussed on the following exchange between Senator Styles Bridges and Secretary Acheson on June 9, 1951:

> Senator Bridges: Mr. Secretary, you have stated that the United States has given some $2,000,000,-000 worth of aid to this anti-communist Nationalist Government of China, in addition to some intangible military advice, is that correct?
>
> Secretary Acheson: I think that was since VJ-Day, Senator.
>
> Senator Bridges: Are we today sending to the anti-Communist Nationalistic Government of China some military and economic aid?
>
> Secretary Acheson: Yes, sir.
>
> Senator Bridges: Do we support the anti-communist National Government of China today?
>
> Secretary Acheson: Yes, sir.
>
> Senator Bridges: When Mr. Rusk stated that the anti-Communist National Government of China is more representative of the Chinese people than the Communist government of China. Was he correct?
>
> Secretary Acheson: It won that recognition and we recognize it for that reason.
>
> Senator Bridges: And Mr. Rusk, in voicing that policy, is he speaking for the administration?
>
> Secretary Acheson: He was voicing the policy which the administration has consistently followed.
>
> Senator Bridges: Then if we do have a China lobby in this country, which I know nothing about, in reality it is supporting the policy of the United States, is it not?

Secretary Acheson: If that is what it was doing it would be supporting the policy, yes.

Senator Bridges: And we recognize that the anti-Communist Nationalist Government headed by Chiang Kai-shek is strongly anti-Communist, do we not?

Secretary Acheson: Yes, sir.

Senator Bridges: And we recognize that the so-called People's Government of China is strongly pro-Communist, and is killing Americans, and is our foremost enemy in a limited war today?

Secretary Acheson: Yes, sir.

Senator Bridges: Now would it be true that anyone who attacked the anti-Communist Nationalist Government headed by Chiang Kai-shek, whose support is our firm, consistent policy, and in turn supported or advocated the anti-Communist Chinese Government, would be advocating and supporting a policy entirely different from a policy of the United States of America?

Secretary Acheson: I don't know what you mean by "attacked." It depends upon what you mean by "attacking" them. If they were advocating that we should support the Communist Government, and not support the Nationalist Government, they would be advocating policies which are contrary to those of the Government.

Senator Bridges: And if we have a lobby today, in this country, or a group of individuals who are doing that, they could be readily called the Communist China lobby, could they not?

Secretary Acheson: They can be called a great many things, Senator. That might be a description.

Senator Bridges: And if we find that there are members of the China Communist lobby in this country who have been using their various powers and operations, and if we find some of them are within the American Government, inasmuch as we fired General MacArthur, or General MacArthur was fired because he differed with the policy of the American Government, should they not be fired immediately?

Secretary Acheson: I presume that would be the proper action.

When Senator Morse was in the midst of his campaign for an investigation of the China Lobby he received support from a surprising quarter—Alfred Kohlberg. In a letter written as he was leaving for Europe, Kohlberg said:

"I desire to congratulate you and Senator McMahon for bringing before the Russell Committee the question of the 'China Lobby.' The State Department and the anti-Nationalist and pro-Chinese Communist press and columnists have been having a holiday with these charges since the fall of 1949 when, I believe, the first series of articles appeared in the *Washington Post* and the *St. Louis Post-Dispatch.* [Kohlberg then cited specific instances of publications and writers who had disseminated the charges.] In all the vast amount of published words I have seen, only two men were generally named. One was William J. Goodwin, whose name you mentioned and who was, I am informed, a foreign agent registered with the Department of Justice.

"The other name mentioned was mine. I am neither a lobbyist nor a foreign agent and am not registered as such, nor ever have been. Therefore, so far as I am concerned, either all the charges of the papers and the ladies and gentlemen above are untruthful or I am guilty of evading registration under the lobbying or foreign agents acts, and your call for an investigation is past due. It might even be contended that the Department of Justice is lax in not having long since investigated the charges against me by the above left-wing newspapers and columnists."

The lengthy letter cited further instances of how the

State Department had worked with the "kept press" to smear him. Then, calling for an investigation, he said:

> "Last year I three times asked the Lobbying Committee of the House to call me for questioning but did not even receive an answer. I wrote the Secretary of the Treasury as per the enclosed letter. So that of the 'Soong-Jung-Kohlberg-Knowland axis" all but Senator Knowland have called for public revealment. I am sure that Senator Knowland would join you in requesting an invitation. But you will have to fight for it, because the Administration likes the present situation of unsupported smears and no investigation.
>
> "A thorough investigation would reveal the real 'China Lobby' to be the 'China Communist Lobby' in the press, in the State Department and even in the Central Intelligence Agency."

This may have stung Senator Morse into action. On July 6, 1951, on behalf of himself and Senator Brien McMahon, who had previously starred in the Tydings Committee hearings, he introduced Senate Resolution 170. This authorized the Foreign Relations Committee to investigate what attempts, if any, had been made by individuals or groups of individuals representing the Chinese Nationalist Government, the Chinese Communist Government, or any other foreign government, to influence the foreign policy of the United States since September 2, 1945, and the extent and means, including methods of financing, of such attempts.

In a lengthy speech dealing with the China Lobby, delivered in the Senate, Republican Senator Harry P. Cain of Washington, on June 6, 1952, told what subsequently happened:

"So far as I know, Mr. President, silence thereafter rested upon the scene. What the chairman of the Foreign Relations Committee, the Senior Senator from Texas

[Senator Tom Connally] thought or did about the resolution, I do not know. Despite Secretary Acheson's voluble assurance that the Executive was going to cooperate eagerly, nothing more was heard.

"When we reflect upon this resolution, Mr. President, it must occur to us that if a thoroughgoing investigation were carried out . . . it might cause profound embarrassment in administration circles."

Among those who might be embarrassed, said Senator Cain, was the Secretary of State himself, whose old law firm had as their clients, "lush clients indeed," the Governments of Denmark, Greece, Iran, Colombia, Sweden, Pakistan, Finland, and Communist Poland. Since there was certainly no dishonesty, why shouldn't the matter be investigated?

Senator Cain then cited other reasons why an investigation would be considered out of order by the administration. Certainly the administration wanted to see no more investigations. Especially since the resolution as drafted also called for looking into "groups of individuals representing the Chinese Communist Government.

"With the memory of the Tydings whitewash all too vividly in mind," he said, "the Administration must have shuddered at the thought." As for an investigation of efforts of the Chinese Nationalist Government to influence public opinion, that had its dangers too. Maybe, he pointed out, the anti-Communist Chinese had seen how lobbyists get things done. Maybe they had done what so many others did, and hired themselves "numerous noble administration officials or former officials." Why it might even be revealed that Chinese Nationalists had contributed to Mr. Truman's 1948 campaign fund! It obviously had risks. Senator Cain concluded, "And that, I judge, is why the Morse-McMahon resolution now gathers dust in Senator Connally's capacious pigeonhole."

A somewhat similar tone crept into Alfred Kohlberg's

remarks concerning Senator Wayne Morse when, in a speech made before the Commonwealth Club of San Francisco, he referred to the Senator's charge that the China Lobby had received $654,000,000 from Chiang Kai-shek:

"As a matter of fact," he said, "I have never bribed anyone in Washington, until last month. My briberies prior to that have never gone higher than to the head porter at the St. Francis. But last month I wrote a letter to that sterling Republican statesman from your neighboring state, Senator Wayne Morse. Some of you might recall that last summer, in the MacArthur hearings, he charged me with being the China Lobby, and said I'd received $653,-000,936, from the Chinese Nationalist Government. Well, I wrote him and said: 'How about the investigation that you were going to have? I am looking forward to it, and to show you my good faith, I hereby attach $1,000, a one-thousand-dollar bill, to this letter.' I then sent a copy to seventy-nine other Senators, each with a thousand-dollar bill attached. Well, they all kept the bills, except Senator Morse. He sent his back with a letter, putting it on the line that he wouldn't take the money from me. Oh, I forgot to say that was Chinese money that I sent them. But still no investigation of the China Lobby."

In a column of Westbrook Pegler's, published in the *New York Journal-American* on October 3, 1952, a Kohlberg telegram to President Truman is quoted which even took the Chief Executive to task on the China Lobby issue, and his failure to investigate it:

> *Times* and *Herald-Tribune* both report you as saying quote the special privilege groups from the oil lobby to the China lobby have joined together behind the Republican Party unquote.
>
> When you refer to the China Lobby that's my baby. I'm supposed to be it. Under oath before the Senate MacArthur Committee [The Russell Commit-

tee] last year Acheson swore he instructed other executive agencies to investigate the China Lobby.

I am not registered as a lobbyist or as a foreign agent. It is therefore apparent that investigation by Executive Department either proved there was no China Lobby and your speech writers involved you in false charges, making you guilty of what you call McCarthyism, or else Executive Department found evidence making me guilty of failing to register legally yet have failed to act.

Suggest you either apologize to me or fire Attorney General for neglect of duty.

Still there was no investigation, then or ever. Vainly Kohlberg called on the Buchanan House Lobbying Committee, on the McCarran Committee, on Senator Morse, on Senator Connally and others for an investigation. Indeed, he was still trying in 1956 when he solicited the help of Senator Lyndon B. Johnson to look into the China Lobby. Nothing was done and he remained the prime target of the uninformed and those who were well informed indeed.

"My reaction to all this," he commented, "was to contend that I was not a lobbyist, and there was no China Lobby that I knew of in the legal sense. After contending that for a while I realized that I was playing into the hands of the propagandists who could argue that indefinitely. So I changed and said, 'Yes, I am the China Lobby. I am not paid, I do this because I think America's interests are involved, and so what?' "

He once wrote an article about the China Lobby as he saw it, for a Catholic magazine, *The Sign,* which he concluded as follows:

"I am still the China Lobby. If there are any contenders for the title, my answer to them is a quote from former World's Heavyweight Champion, Gentleman Jim Corbett: 'Go get a reputation.' "

CHAPTER TEN

Max's Big Bomb

THE MOST HIGHLY PUBLICIZED OF THE ATTACKS MADE against the China Lobby undoubtedly were those that appeared in two issues of *The Reporter.* This now-defunct liberal magazine, whose editorial policies and positions in some respects were highly commendable, took such an extreme position on this matter that a charge was made on the Senate floor by the Hon. Harry P. Cain, of Washington, that the publisher and his associates "have been 'suckered' by the Communists from start to finish, or they have deliberately participated in a Communist maneuver."[*] The sensational *Reporter* articles were extensively promoted. Kohlberg estimated that an incredible $400,000 was used to buy newspaper advertising, spot radio com-

*June 6, 1952. Reference to this speech appears in Chapter 9.

mercials, and direct-mail advertising to plug this "exposé" of the China Lobby.

However, the big bomb that Max Ascoli, the publisher, had prepared went off like a soggy firecracker. Apart from the visibility obtained from the advertising expenditure and from publicity in likeminded publications, the articles contributed little in the way of newsworthy controversy. A press release that purported to tell "the story behind the story" set the tone. With unconscious humor it opened with this queer rhetorical fanfare: "It was one mild April day last year that we had the idea of *doing a job on the China Lobby...*"(Italics added.) What brought this on, the release explained, was Truman's firing of MacArthur, the "popular passions" aroused by this, and the possibility that this might give the China Lobby a new lease on life. That is IF the China Lobby really did exist. There was some questions about this. It was a mysterious thing, and the editors had been hearing about it in a very strange way:

"Like most readers, we knew just enough—the gleanings of cocktail gossip, syndicated columns, and a few indignant editorials—to suspect it would be difficult to know much more. But it was worth a few week's [sic] exploration. The preliminary inquest resulted in a decision to go ahead."

After this ingenuous preamble the release went on to tell how the "inquest" convinced them that there really was a dragon on the prowl in America, an appalling thing indeed, a foreign government which had even succeeded in discrediting our fearless leaders in Washington. So the intrepid editors of *The Reporter* decided to charge through the alcoholic fumes of the cocktail circuit and face up to the Chinese dragon lurking in the shadows.

With a flourish of typewriter keys the composer of "the story behind the story" proclaimed:

"Finally, to make our decision stick there was the fact

that if *The Reporter* did not undertake to expose the
Lobby no one would. Only *The Reporter,* we felt, had the
courage *and* the independence to do the job. And so,
feeling like David outside the camp of the Philistines, we
picked up our sling. . . ."

In view of what resulted from a year of whatever little
David did during that time, he might just as well have
gone back to the cocktail circuit. Or have picked up a few
good books on China instead of a sling. For both highly
touted issues of *The Reporter* read like a continuation of
the fatuous press release which heralded their advent.

The procedure followed by one of the participating
writers was described thus by Kohlberg, writing later
about the incident:

"When on August 2, 1951, Mr. Charles Wertenbaker
called on me for a long interview, all had again been quiet
for many weeks on the China Lobby front. Mr. Wertenbaker told me he had been engaged by an obscure fortnightly, *The Reporter,* to do an article on the China scene
or China Lobby. After some discussion it was apparent
that he knew almost nothing about the China situation,
which he was frank to admit. He expected to learn as he
went along, he said. Because of his almost complete ignorance I invited him to return for more questions after he
had better informed himself. That time never came, nor
did Mr. Wertenbaker return.

"He asked if he might take notes during our discussion.
I of course assented and am happy now that I did. I recoil
with horror at what might have happened if he had not
taken notes. For even with this precaution Wertenbaker
was so confused that I was able to count 36 factual errors
in the articles as published.

"It must be evident that if there is a China Lobby,
which has written and spoken over the years for military
aid to the anti-Communist Government of the Republic of
China, there must be some opposition, which might, with

at least equal justice, be called the anti-China or Red China Lobby. In my desire to be of help I told Mr. Wertenbaker of both lobbies, using the term very broadly. I gave him the names of the most effective on each side. Apparently the spelling must have confused him for not a single name of the Red China Lobby, nor even mention of its existence, appeared in his articles."

The basic points covered in the April 15th issue were (a) China was not really a first-rate power and should never have been so considered, (b) hints of corruption had been rife since 1943 (which was true enough because that is when the Communists turned against the Nationalist Government), (c) much of $500 million in U.S. aid had been divided among the Soong and Kung families, (d) attacks began in 1945 on all those who had attacked Chiang, and Kohlberg was one of the attackers, (e) General Marshall conceded failure and as Chiang's armies retreated the China Lobby grew bolder, (f) Truman's re-election in 1948 was a blow to the lobbyists but they started looking ahead and hired a new public relations firm.

This synopsis was developed so that it read like a Sax Rohmer thriller, with inscrutable Orientals slinking around with satchels of money, shopping for Senators and Congressmen willing to go to bat for Chiang Kai-shek and his family—or, better yet, willing to start World War III, to put Chiang back on the mainland of China.

There were human interest touches too. Such as the following: "Americans have been impressed by Soong's flair for exotic, expensive gestures. In the spring of 1946 his wife, to whom he is deeply devoted, fell ill. Soong chartered a private plane in Nanking to go to Connecticut to pick up a cargo of dogwood, of which Mme. Soong is particularly fond. The bouquet must have cost between twenty and thirty thousand dollars."

This was indignantly denied as untrue by T. V. Soong.

The April 29th issue featured more of the same. The tone for the contents was set in an editorial note that appeared on the first page:

"On Friday, April 4, a man who was described as 'of Asiatic appearance' approached a Washington newsdealer at the corner of Vermont Avenue and H Street, N.W., and offered to buy all copies of *The Reporter's* last issue at fifty cents apiece [twice the going rate]. The eager buyer then said he would give a $500 check for a thousand copies. The newsdealer said no, thanks, and the man drove away in a large black car with diplomatic license plates.

"This is just one more example of how the Chinese Nationalists spend their American money to buy things on a big scale and well above the market price."

This fable of the extravagant Asiatic diplomat and the newsstand dealer who could not be corrupted with U.S. money was about as credible as the rest of the issue's contents, particularly when it dealt with financial matters.

Money, it seemed, was the root of the evil being perpetrated by the China Lobby, and the lobbyists were tossing it around madly for wicked purposes. For instance, they were trying to make the American people dump Secretary of State Acheson, and to strip our State Department of such noble and experienced Far East experts as John Paton Davies, Oliver Edmund Clubb, John Stewart Service, and John Carter Vincent.

The Reporter made it clear that there was plenty of money at hand for this dirty work:

"It is everywhere. In a massive stream it flowed from the United States to China. It has returned in large amounts to the United States via numberless channels to create more millions, more propaganda, more aid, more private corruption, and more public confusion."

Indeed there was so much of this filthy lucre floating

around that a few paragraphs earlier in the piece quoted above, the author stated:

"On one occasion a Nationalist official begged this reporter to help him devise some means of safely destroying several million dollars of Nationalist funds. . . . 'I would rather die than return that money to Chiang Kai-shek,' he declared."

The Reporter's reporter did not disclose whether he lent the overburdened Chinese his cigarette lighter to help him out of his awful predicament, though that would have seemed the humane thing to do.

In any case *The Reporter* soon heard from some of the people mentioned in the articles. One letter, dated April 18, came from T. S. Tsiang, Permanent Representative of China to the United Nations:

"On page 7 you state: 'The first lump sum in support of the Lobby's work, according to former Nationalist officials in a position to know, did not follow the customary route. In the summer of that year (1949) $800,000 was transferred from Mr. Wang Shih-chieh, Chiang's chief secretary on Formosa, to Dr. Tsiang openly via the Bank of China in New York.'

"I have since the fall of 1947, when I assumed my post as the representative of China in the United Nations, disbursed not US $800,000 but US $6,000,000. The recipients of this money have been Mr. Trygve Lie and Mr. Byron Price [Assistant Secretary-General of the UN]. What these gentlemen have done with the money and what service they have rendered to China is no secret; at least Messrs. Lie, Price, and myself do not wish this matter to be kept a secret. All information relating to these disbursements is available in the records of the UN Secretariat.

"As to the $800,000 which you say that Dr. Wang Shih-chieh transferred to me in the summer of 1949 via the

Bank of China, the figure and the transaction are both
fictions. I would be glad to give any member of your research staff such legal help as I could to enable him to
make a thorough examination of any transaction with or
through the Bank of China."

Then Dr. Tsiang went on to make a counter-charge:

"If you could name a single American who, during the
past four and a half years, has received any sum of money
from me in remuneration for political services of any kind,
I would gladly acknowledge your article to be truthful. I
would allow you one year's time for this research. If at the
end of the year you fail to produce the name of a single
American, as I am deadly sure you will fail, I think I would
be justified in calling this article dishonest and untruthful."

This letter was published in the magazine's June 10,
1952, issue with the following disingenuous editorial dis-
claimer:

"We appreciate Tsiang's highmindedness and the
handsome tribute he pays his American friends. We
should like to remind him however, that *we did not say
that he had directly and personally paid Americans for
service to the China Lobby* (italics added). He thus chal-
lenges us to prove a point that he himself has raised for the
first time. The challenge interests us. We should be most
happy to explore further the possibility of our examining
the records of the Bank of China, provided Dr. Tsiang will
extend his invitation to include a Chinese financial expert
of our own choice."

A study of *The Reporter* for the balance of the year gave
no indication that any study of the bank records was ever
made. Certainly the editors of *The Reporter* were quib-
bling when they said they would like to examine the records "provided Dr. Tsiang will extend the invitation to
include a Chinese financial expert of our own choice." Dr.
Tsiang had already extended that invitation when he said,

"I would be glad to give any member of your research staff such legal help as I could to enable him to make a thorough examination of any transaction with or through the Bank of China."

Other prime targets of *The Reporter* were T. V. Soong and H. H. Kung, who were presented as ringleaders in the financial finagling that the magazine said was going on. However, here the magazine was dishing up warmed-over charges that had been made before and denied. Indeed, Alfred Kohlberg had prodded the diffident Chinese into making the denials and getting them into the *Congressional Record* for April 10, 1950, a fact that *The Reporter* noted.

Three letters had been published in the *Record.* One, from Kohlberg, was addressed jointly to Dr. H. H. Kung and Dr. T. V. Soong. It told of a story that had appeared in *Newsweek,* one paragraph of which read: "The administration has an ace up its sleeve in case criticism of its Formosa and China Policy becomes too hot. It is ready to disclose how Chinese Nationalist officials sold out their country by transferring personal funds and assets to the United States. The Treasury has the names and figures at its fingertips."

In his letter, Kohlberg asked Soong and Kung if they would be willing to make the facts of their personal finances known to responsible government officials. From Kung came the following: ·

"To your question, although I cannot speak for others, I give the answer that I shall be perfectly agreeable to making public by the State Department or Treasury Department the factual figures on the personal funds and assets I have in this country based on actual accounts, if this action is judged by them to be pertinent and relevant to the discussion."

From Dr. Soong: "Thank you for your letter of May 5 [1950], calling attention to Mr. Constantine Brown's column of May 3 in the *New York Journal-American.* When you originally wrote me on March 3, suggesting that I permit you to quote me as having no objection to official release of the record of my total holdings in the United States, I then replied that I did not choose to dignify the untruthful attacks by pro-Communists in the American press by any notice on my part. However, when a man of Mr. Constantine Brown's reputation for integrity makes the same statements, I feel constrained to have you advise your friends in the United States Government that I have no objection to the publication by the United States Treasury or State Department of my total holdings in the United States."

Constantine Brown's column, referred to, had stated that Soong and Kung had $500,000,000 here and the State Department had a record of it. When questioned about this he declared that actually he had been told by a top State Department official that they had recorded assets of $850,000,000 in this country. Informed of this, Dr. Kung wrote to Constantine Brown and made this offer:

"If the State Department will reveal the $850,000,000 I am willing that 90 percent of it be given to the Nationalist Government of China; that 9 percent be given to any charities that Mr. H. [the State Department official in question] may select; and I will be very happy to keep only the other 1 percent."

There is no record to indicate that Mr. H. or the State Department that employed him ever took Dr. Kung up on this attractive offer.

This writer learned of one inflated figure published by *The Reporter* when talking to General Albert C. Wedemeyer. This, however, was relatively minor since it involved only $5,000,000. A "cable" which the magazine had obtained under odd circumstances said that Chiang Kai-shek had offered General Wedemeyer $5,000,000 to come to China in his service. According to *The Reporter,* this "fact" was verified by Drew Pearson. However, the General told me a different story.

He was approached by a Mr. Reynolds, of the Reynolds Aluminum Company, of Virginia, acting as an intermediary, and an offer was indeed made. However, it was not for $5,000,000. Further, General Wedemeyer did not have a direct offer from the Generalissimo; neither did he ever discuss the matter with the Generalissimo. A few representatives of the Nationalist Chinese Government residing in Washington at the time did not discuss such an arrangement. They seemed to be knowledgeable concerning the offer passed on to him by Mr. Reynolds. However, apparently they did not have the authority necessary to consummate a deal even if he were inclined to accept it.

"Mr. Reynolds," said the General, "stated that I would be paid a million dollars for a five-year contract. I would be given $500,000 immediately, in escrow, in any bank in the world. The other $500,000 would be paid at the rate of $100,000 a year."

He said he turned down the offer since he was then out of touch with Far East matters, at least on a policy level, and he certainly had no influence at that time which would be helpful to the Chinese. His views, set forth in his famous 1947 report, had not been favorably received, and he said he was aware that people in the policy-making sections of the State Department would do everything they could to thwart him in any efforts in behalf of Nationalist China. When Mr. Reynolds broached the subject to General Wedemeyer, he (the General) pointed out that he had never been interested in money per se. He added that he would not have followed the military profession during most of his mature life if the acquisition of money had been an important goal.

Also, General Wedemeyer explained to Mr. Reynolds that if he were to accept such a generous offer of a large sum of money from the Generalissimo, he would use it to build schools which were so sorely needed in China, and also he would support constructive steps in that country in order to create conditions that would help the Generalissimo in his struggle against Communism.

Granted, Chiang's million-dollar offer was generous. However, it might be noted that it was not out of line with salaries being paid top executives in big industries in this country. And at that time General Wedemeyer was executive vice-president of Avco Manufacturing Corporation, an industrial giant. Even so, he said he did not reject the Chiang offer for financial reasons but because he was aware of the odds against being able to do a good job for Chiang in this country.

Although critics of the China Lobby have cited large and impressive figures to imply that a lot of American dollars were flowing to China's fat cats, they had little to show in the way of large and impressive figures when it came to the lobbyists themselves. One fee, of $30,000, was paid to a public relations man, William J. Goodwin, for a year's service. The following year, *The Reporter* noted, Goodwin switched to the Chinese News Service and worked there for $25,000 a year. Also helping out on public relations, according to the magazine, was a firm called Allied Syndicates, which was hired by the Bank of China at a fee of $60,000 a year. Another publicity man, one Norman Paige, was also listed by *The Reporter* as having worked for the Chinese News Service for $30,000 a year.

Be that as it may, official figures compiled by Senator Harry P. Cain, and read into the record during his June 6, 1952 discussion of the China Lobby, presented a different picture of public relations than that set forth by critics. During 1950 the following expenditures were made by various governments:

China News Service	$ 77,972
Israel Information Office	94,821

Netherlands Information Bureau	210,371
Yugoslavia Information Center	187,582
British Information Services	868,343

Indeed, far from being extravagant, as readers of *The Reporter* were led to believe, the Chinese might be regarded as niggardly.

Commenting on public relations expenditures by foreign governments, Senator Cain had this to say:

"First about the hiring of lawyers, public relations people, and the use of publicity generally. Foreign governments by the score do it here in the United States, the custom is recognized, and, by law, all such people must register under the Foreign Agents Registration Act. The people who are hot and bothered about the China Lobby admit that Mr. Goodwin was so registered. On the releases of the Chinese News Service the following statement is prominently displayed:

" 'This material is filed with the Department of Justice, where the required registration statement of Chinese News Service under Fifty-sixth Statute, pages 248-258, as an agency of the National Government of China is available for inspection: Registration does not indicate approval or disapproval of this material by the United States Government'

"As for Mr. Charnay [of Allied Syndicates], I assume that he also was registered as an agent of the Bank of China, and if he was not Senators Morse and McMahon might look into the matter."

In Alfred Kohlberg's files copies of *The Reporter* for April 15 and 29, 1952, there were numerous marginal notations made by him calling attention to errors. Sometimes sections of text would be blocked out and the word "ignorance" written alongside. One notation read, "new degree for me." This referred to a brief biographical sketch of himself. It read:

"However, it is known that he was born and brought up

in San Francisco [correct], that his father was in the wholesale food business [entirely incorrect], and according to San Franciscans, was well off [what is well off?]. Alfred graduated from Lowell High School in 1904 [correct], and from the University of California in 1908 [wrong]."

Any reporter would be accused of sloppy reporting with a 50 percent score like that, but *The Reporter* seemed to take such things in stride.

Kohlberg said that his first reaction was one of anger but he considered the articles so ridiculous that he finally shrugged them off. In fact, he wrote to Ascoli as follows: "I was very intrigued with Mr. Wertenbaker's article, but believe that the cartoon of me on page 9, holding a cigar, is definitely libelous per se as I have never in my life smoked a cigar. If, however, you will retract the cigar, I would be willing to settle the libel for the original of the cartoon—unless you have already promised it to Secretary Acheson for his game room."

The cartoon in question showed Kohlberg as a grotesque and repulsive figure with a web of deep lines all over his face, wearing a gaudy necktie and holding a cigar. In the background was a Chinese flag. He put the caricature to use as a book plate.

He later commented on the articles in a piece which appeared in *The Freeman* for June 30, 1952:

"When as children we played a game called 'Pin the Tail on the Donkey,' the awards included not only a first and second prize but a consolation prize as well. In the field of journalism the Pulitzer people have long been taking care of the first prize, but it seems to have been left to me to award the consolation prize. The Kohlberg Consolation Prize for 1952 goes uncontestedly to Max Ascoli of *The Reporter,* for his China Lobby feature. Mr. Ascoli not only failed to pin the tail on the donkey; he couldn't even find the donkey to pin his tale on."

Some of the distortions presented in *The Reporter's* China Lobby articles are still accepted in some quarters in lieu of the facts. As an example of this, in 1960 Macmillan published a book by Ross Y. Koen, an assistant professor at Humboldt State College in Arcata, California. The blurb for the Koen book, *The China Lobby in American Politics,* read as follows: "While this book will arouse strong reactions, those who disagree with Professor Koen will encounter meticulous documentation for his statements throughout." Repeatedly the professor's "meticulous documentation" was a reference to *The Reporter!*

The general tenor of this book may be ascertained from its final chapter, "Summary and Conclusions," in which Koen sets forth the premise that "the China lobby approach is based on the assumption that no negotiations or agreement with the Communists is possible except on terms which will lead to their aggrandizement and to the defeat of the West. This assumption is not peculiar to the China lobby. It has long been held by Russophobes and extreme anti-communist groups." He makes it plain that we cannot expect to have a *rapprochement* with Red China so long as American policy is "bound fast to the Chiang regime on Formosa."

The evidence that he presents attempts to support that premise. The China lobby, he maintains, created "myths," and these were "supported and reinforced by congressional action." Some of these "myths" dealt with the *Amerasia* case, General Hurley's charges against Foreign Service officers, General Marshall's mission to China, and the U.S. failure to supply arms to Chiang when he was fighting the Communists. Needless to say. Dr. Koen takes issue with the position of "the China lobby" on all these matters.

The Koen book waas withdrawn by the publisher after a few copies had been circulated. Probably in an excess of enthusiasm, the author had accused the Nationalist

Government of China of being involved in the smuggling of narcotics into the United States. He also declared that prominent Americans had participated in these transactions, and said that evidence "indicates further that the narcotics business has been an important factor in the activities and permutations of the China lobby."

H. J. Anslinger, then U.S. Commissioner of Narcotics, branded the charge as false. Writing to the Chinese Ambassador, George C. Yeh, he said:

"I can give you an unqualified statement that this is manufactured out of the whole cloth; that there is no scintilla of evidence that any Chinese officials have engaged in illegal smuggling of narcotics into the United State with the full knowledge and connivance of the Chinese Nationalist Government. This statement is so fantastic that if it is any measuring rod to the rest of the book I assume it can be similarly classified."

As he did with *The Reporter* articles, Alfred Kohlberg made a study of the Koen book and wrote a lengthy critique, citing numerous factual errors. This he did in March 1960, but no use was made of his study since the book was recalled and Kohlberg died a month later, on April 7. However, in liberal circles the withdrawal of the book is not attributed to defects but to some more diabolical activity on the part of Chiang Kai-shek's agents. This kind of thinking was expressed in a letter published in *The Christian Century* for August 3, 1966, which stated: "Shortly after the book came out, strong pressure—reputedly by the China Lobby and the U.S. state department—led the publisher to withdraw the book from circulation." The writer of the letter then made a not very subtle pitch to have the book issued. How, asked the letter writer, can we have "a significant change in U.S. policy toward China unless evidence such as that included in Koen's book is brought into the open?"

How indeed?

A more recent book which purports to tell how the American public has been misinformed about China is *A Curtain of Ignorance,* by Felix Greene. The jacket blurb states that Mr. Greene, "a former senior official of England's BBC, retains his British passport, but has lived in America for many years and is well known as a lecturer on current affairs. He has made three visits to China. Those in 1957 and 1960 resulted in his previously and widely-acclaimed book *Awakened China.* "

In a speech before the Senate on July 21, 1966, Senator Milward L. Simpson, of Wyoming, described Mr. Greene in somewhat different terms:

"Not only is this Britisher, who has lived off our country for more than a quarter century, able to champion the cause of the People's Republic of China without registering as a foreign agent, he is able to travel between the United States and China in violation of our laws, slap the face of our government in his travels, and have re-entry permission handed him on a silver platter. . . . Today, unregistered, he is a most articulate and persuasive advocate of the People's Republic of China."

Senator Simpson cited in some detail Greene's propagandizing efforts in behalf of Red China, then referred to him as "an alien leech in this country's jugular, proselytizing on behalf of our enemy, deprecating our policies, and inveighing against our objectives." He concluded that "it is about time this country took action to boot him back to Peiping."

There is no point in devoting much time to Greene's book telling "how the American public has been misinformed about China." It is exactly what one might expect. The China Lobby—that is, the anti-Communist China Lobby—is presented as a major devil. And here again *The Reporter* provided much of the ammunition for this "advocate of the People's Republic of China," as Senator Simpson called him.

One item picked up from *The Reporter* was the story, branded false by T. V. Soong, that the Chinese had chartered a plane to fly from China to Connecticut and back with a bouquet of dogwood for his ailing wife. Understandably, Greene also thought well of the Koen book which, he pointed out, "has not yet been made available to the public."

In a footnote, Greene gave credit where credit was due: "Both *The Reporter* articles and Dr. Koen's book indicate very careful research and both are profusely documented." Which is high praise indeed from such a scholar. He quotes, without demurrer, Senator Morse's fantastic statement that the China Lobby "had spent in the neighborhood of $654,000,000 to influence American public opinion." Others who serve as references are Drew Pearson, Jack Anderson, Senator J. William Fulbright, Jr., and Richard Rovere.

Rovere is quoted at some length because Greene feels exactly as the former associate editor of *New Masses* does about McCarthy ("this bully and fraud"). Touchingly solicitous about the welfare of his American cousins, the distinguished British author and lecturer deplores what McCarthy did during his "brief and terrible passage across the pages of American history." As for the China Lobby, well, "the China Lobby and McCarthy needed each other." Even this rather labored witticism was not original, having appeared years before in *The Reporter* articles.

Amazingly, neither Greene nor Koen seemed to be aware of the lobbying activities of the most active China agent of all—Frederick Vanderbilt Field. Greene makes no mention at all of "the millionaire Communist," and while Koen sets down a few uncritical references to him, he apparently had no idea he was a big-time operator in the lobbying business. This seems like a serious omission for two scholarly works dealing with the China Lobby, but the omission may have resulted from the absence of any mention of Field's lobbying in *The Reporter* articles. Fortunately, Senator Cain did a better job of reporting than *The Reporter* did, and presented this report on the most important China lobbyist of all:

"Communist China's principal representative in this country is Frederick Vanderbilt Field. He has registered twice as an agent of a variety of governmental and business concerns. Field's first filing listed him as an agent of three corporations of the Chinese Communist State, including the Bank of China and also a Hong Kong bank. He is also listed as President and Director of the American-Chinese Export Corp., a trading agency dealing with 10 other corporations which handle a variety of Chinese products and commodities."

Mr. Field will be recalled as one of Alfred Kohlberg's prime targets in the Institute of Pacific Relations, where he was a very important person indeed.

It is possible that the authors responsible for these studies of the China Lobby did know about Frederick Vanderbilt Field but refused to concede that he was lobbying. After all, in certain situations what some people might decry as lobbying is really in the people's interest.

It's all in the point of view.

CHAPTER ELEVEN

Footnotes to Foreign Policy

IN THE EARLY 1940's THE UNITED STATES HAD BECOME "the arsenal of democracy," and to accomplish the defeat of the fascist powers we provided billions in military and economic aid to nations around the world. After the war was over our foreign aid continued, and this time we included not only allies but former foes and potential enemies in the lineup of beneficiaries. This of course was in the hope that our generosity would provide lasting peace in the postwar world.

More than a hundred billion dollars were given away by us in this way after World War II, and in view of this the American public could well believe that China was getting all those billions its critics hinted at. The fact is that China got relatively little help from the United States either during the war or after, but none of those who condemned the China Lobby for seeking American help ever demanded investigations of far more effective lobbies. There was never a call for an investigation of a Soviet Lobby, though the Soviet Union had obtained eleven billion dollars from the United States, much of it in the form of equipment for postwar use. Nor were there outcries for investigations of a British Lobby, a French Lobby, a Yugoslav Lobby, or an Indian Lobby, to name just a few of the nations that received billions.

It is noteworthy, too, that we sent no bright young men, "experts," from our State Department to those countries to tell them what they had to do to get American aid. Their rulers were not ordered to cut out corruption, fire grafting politicians, hold honest elections, become more efficient, and re-cast their government in a form more to our liking—or else. Yet that is precisely how we tried to bully Nationalist China.

As Alfred Kohlberg repeatedly pointed out in his public statements, it was amazing that Chiang Kai-shek put up with us. Chiang had had an opportunity to make deals with Japan, and also with the Soviet Union, which would have been far better for him than the sort of thing our politicians and diplomats held out to him, but he refused those deals on principle. Is it any wonder that he refused on principle to accept the kind of proposition that Washington demanded—that he establish a coalition government with the Communists? He had seen how such coalitions had worked out in Europe, where the United States had been involved in the same sellout of once independent nations, and he wanted no part of such enforced suicidal togetherness. Which of course made him anathema to the Communists and their camp followers.

These people demonstrated their hatred of Chiang in their propaganda, and a recurring theme of this was that he had stolen or wasted billions of dollars of American aid. As has been mentioned, Nationalist China actually received only a small fraction of the aid that Americans generally thought she was getting, and probably the best evidence of this can be found in the State Department's White Paper of 1949. Secretary of State Dean Acheson stated:

"Since VJ-Day, the United States Government has authorized aid to Nationalist China in the form of grants and credits totaling approximately 2 billion dollars.... In addition to these grants and credits, the United States Government has sold the Chinese Government large quantities of military and civilian war surplus with a total procurement cost of over 1 billion dollars."

This was supposed to prove Secretary Acheson's contention that "Nothing that this country did or could have done, within the reasonable limits of its capabilities, could have changed the result...." The result of course being that China was lost to Communism.

Kohlberg wasted no time in challenging the "self-serving statements of the American officials responsible for our disaster in the Pacific," as he put it. Using the facilities of the American China Policy Association, which he had helped to establish in 1946, he pointed out numerous omissions and errors in the State Department document.

To compensate for one of the omissions, the American China Policy Association undertook a formidable job. It obtained and reproduced by photolithography two Army Intelligence reports, totaling 453 pages, that had been made in 1945. One of these, of 441 pages, was titled "The Chinese Communist Movement—Confidential," and the other, of 12 pages, was titled "The Chinese Communist Movement—Secret." Congressman Walter Judd had complained that these documents should have been included in the White Paper and Secretary Acheson later had had two copies made for inspection by the press. However, the only member of the Washington press corps who showed enough initiative to copy the documents was a representative of Tass, the Soviet news agency. Kohlberg and his associates therefore decided to give American journalists a hand.

These documents made it abundantly clear that in 1945 our military intelligence had an excellent understanding of the China situation. Indeed, the conclusion of the report starts out: "The Chinese Communists *are* Communists. They are the most effectively organized group in China." It went on to state that "The 'democracy' which the Chinese Communists sponsor represents 'Soviet democracy' on the pattern of the Soviet Union rather than democracy in the Anglo-American sense." It told how the Chinese Communists refused to keep their pledges and how they were obviously bent on seizing control of China through a coalition government.

With ideas of its own, the State Department had suppressed this report and recalled copies which were circulating. Then it went ahead with its postwar policy of refusing to support the Nationalists unless they formed a coalition government as the Communists demanded. It was in line with this policy that General Marshall was sent to China to try to force Chiang to take Mao's Communists into his government.

When Chiang balked at this, our government took a step that throws a strange light on the White Paper's argument that the United States had done everything it could to keep China from falling into the hands of the Communists. On Chiang's refusal, an embargo was placed on shipments of aid to China. This lasted from August 1946 to May 1947, which was a crucial period. Prior to this the Chinese Communists had been armed, through Soviet connivance, with vast stocks of war equipment that Soviet troops had seized from surrendering Japanese troops in Manchuria. The obliging Russians gave their Chinese comrades 300,000 rifles, thousands of artillery pieces and machine guns, many thousands of tanks and tractors, 925 planes, and other military supplies.

With this loot that the USSR had grabbed during its five-day war with Japan, Mao's armies moved in force against the Nationalists. Chiang and others pleaded with the United State for help to meet the Red onslaught but Washington was adamant. Among those who called for help was General Albert C. Wedemeyer who had been sent to China in 1947 by President Truman to study the situation. On September 19 he submitted a report to the President. In it he urged the United States to seize the initiative in China "to create and maintain bulwarks of freedom." Our difficulties there, he said, stemmed from the Yalta Conference, where we had agreed to let Russia move into Manchuria, and from our wthholding of aid from the National Government. It was essential, he argued, to stop the spread of Soviet influence in Asia and he pointed out that "China dominated by Chinese Communists would be inimical to the interests of the United States." To bolster opposition to Communist expansion he called for economic and military aid.*

On December 17, 1947, he appeared before the Senate Committee on Appropriations. Asked if he had his report he said that Secretary of State George C. Marshall had told him he should "maintain security" on it. The report was thus suppressed and wasn't published until two years later, at which time the warnings it contained had been justified by the fall of China to the Reds. Marshall was subsequently asked by the Senate Armed Services Committee why he had joined in the suppression of this vital report. Marshall replied curtly, "I did not join in the suppression of the report. I personally suppressed it."

*There was considerable speculation as to the contents of General Wedemeyer's suppressed report. In an attempt to get some clues, the Senate Appropriations Committee asked him testify, which he did on December 17, 1947. This testimony is presented as Appendix E.

Marshall's vindictive attitude towards the Nationalists is hard to understand. Admiral Charles M. Cooke has testified to his boastful statement: "As Chief of Staff I armed 39 anti-Communist divisions, now with a stroke of the pen I disarm them."

President Truman played his part in the Chinese debacle by issuing an executive order on August 18, 1946 that had the effect of keeping the Nationalists from acquiring American weapons that might help them in the civil war then raging. As a result of this, Chiang's troops were forced to rely on what they had left in the way of materiel after years of warfare with the Japanese and with Mao's Communists, who had never ceased to harass the Nationalists when the opportunity presented itself.

Congressional pressure in time forced the Truman Administration to take some action to help China. The President tried to limit this to economic aid but the 80th Congress, so loudly deplored by Truman, added a provision to the Marshall Plan Act which called for military aid to that country in addition to economic aid. This bill, signed by Truman on April 3, 1948, provided for $436,000,000 in aid, of which $125,000,000 was to be for military equipment. Even this much might not have been done had it not been for the fact that a presidential election was coming up and the Truman-Acheson-Marshall policies toward China were coming in for increasing criticism.

As it was, an effective job was done in sabotaging the military aid that was authorized. Months passed before the Defense Department got around to releasing the materiel in its stockpiles, and more time elapsed before the first ship left for China. Then Harry Bridges, whose ties with the Communists were no secret, engineered a shipping strike that caused further delays. By the time the first supplies of arms reached Shanghai the Communists were in control of Manchuria and North China.

In his book *How the Far East Was Lost,* Dr. Anthony Kubek contrasts our actions at that time with the speed shown by us when England was in danger a few years before:

"Roosevelt had ordered a survey taken of the surplus arms and ammunition we had in the United States, to replace what the British had lost at Dunkerque. In eight days they were being loaded into boats at Perth Amboy to go to England. In contrast, the Congress in 1948 passed a law which the President signed on April 3, authorizing economic and military aid to the hard-pressed Republic of China. But it was eight months before a single rifle moved."

Even more outrageous were other actions that had to do with military aid to China during this crisis. The Joint Chiefs of Staff approved a shipment of 20,000 rifles, seized from the Germans after VE-Day, for use by Chiang. This was on its way when it was stopped by an order on White House stationery signed by Lauchlin Currie. Much of the aid that Chiang did receive, and which was charged to him, was useless junk—much of it stuff that had been picked up on Pacific islands where it had been left to rust and rot. Some of the weapons we sent were useless for the kind of warfare going on in China. Essential parts of the weapons were often missing, making the shipments worthless.

As a result of our incredible behavior, Nationalist troops were sometimes required to go into action against the Communists with as few as three or four cartridges per man. In one battle Nationalist soldiers ended up by throwing rocks at the Reds opposing them. Later these poor devils would be reviled by pro-Communist propagandists as cowards who broke and ran when they came up against the inspired Communists.

Probably as hypocritical as any of our actions was some of the bookkeeping employed by our government. In some cases we actually charged China more for the equipment than the amount we had paid to procure it. Capping this monstrous hypocrisy was the fact that we were selling the same stuff to other nations at a fraction of the list price.

On the face of it, the Chinese Nationalists had made themselves extremely unpopular with the Administration because of their refusal to play ball with the Communists as we demanded. However, the futility of a coalition was obvious to those who knew the facts about China. General Wedemeyer, who had such knowledge, tried to explain the situation to General Marshall, at the time Marshall arrived in China in December 1945, as President Truman's representative. General Marshall carried a directive from the President which required him to bring the Nationalists and the Communists together in a coalition government. General Wedemeyer told him there was as much chance of getting them together as there was of mixing oil and water.*

The Nationalists, he explained, who still had most of the power, were determined not to relinquish one iota of it. The Communists, for their part, were equally determined to seize all power, with the help of the Soviet Union.

General Marshall angrily told him, "I am going to accomplish my mission and you are going to help me."

The sort of thinking that guided our moves in the Far East is illustrated by a proposal made to President Truman at a White House Conference by Secretary Acheson and Ambassador at Large Philip C. Jessup, on February 5, 1949. This pair suggested that "supplies which were then being loaded in ships in Hawaii and San Francisco for the Chiang Kai-shek government be dramatically stopped as a move toward world peace." Fortunately, we did not go quite that far.

One of the most questionable of all the items in

---

*In time General Marshall was to realize the truth of this, after long and fruitless negotiations. His disillusionment is expressed in a statement he gave President Truman on January 7, 1947, which appears as Appendix F.

Acheson's 1949 White Paper was a charge of $335,817,-910 made against Chiang for disarming and repatriating Japanese troops after VJ-Day. This was something that had to be done, but why the charge for doing it was levied against the Chinese Government is not quite clear. Incidentally, this figure is three times greater than the amount of our entire postwar military aid to China, which the Chinese Government insisted came to only $110,000,000. The State Department's much higher figure included UNRRA grants of almost a half-billion dollars (which were shared with the Communists) and nonmilitary ECA aid.

But even if one accepts the White Paper figure, it still does not support the impression that it tried to create, that we had gone all-out to aid China. Whereas this staunch ally was supposed to have received approximately $2 billion in grants and credits, we had provided as much or more aid to countries which had fought *against* us. Germany in the postwar years received more than $3 billion, Italy more than $2 billion, and Japan $1,720,000,000.

A recurring theme of criticism against the so-called China Lobby was that its primary purpose was to get the greatest possible amount of American money for China. In this connection it is worth noting the following, which appeared in a memorandum that Alfred Kohlberg sent to Mr. Paul Lockwood, Secretary to Governor Thomas E. Dewey, for the Governor's attention. The year was 1947 and Alfred Kohlberg was looking ahead to the 1948 Presidential campaign, as was New York State's Governor. The memorandum dealt with China, described Communist plans for the seizure of China and told how they might be foiled. The following part of the Kohlberg memorandum discusses proposals that had been made by William C. Bullitt and published in *Life* magazine:

> Mr. Bullitt then proposes:
> (1) $600,000,000 for credits.
> (2) $150,000,000 for a monetary fund; and

(3) $600,000,000 for a military aid.

With regard to No. 3, I favor military aid, but am not competent to judge the amount, which seems too high.

With regard to No. 2, I think it would be pure waste as the Chinese monetary system must be made over and reformed from within and not from without. The history of attempts to bolster unsound currencies in China and elsewhere proves this point.

As to No. 1, I question the necessity for so large a figure, particularly if China would release controls on imports and exports and permit Chinese funds abroad to be freely used. Furthermore, Mr. Bullitt does not state who should get these loans. I would suggest that the Export-Import Bank make these loans very largely to private industry and not to the Chinese Government. I have had experience in aid to Chinese Government institutions and, in addition, I know a little of the experience of UNRRA, and without going into details, it is sufficient to say that a large part of such intergovernmental advance will be inefficiently and wastefully handled exactly as it was in the past, whereas sound loans to private industry in much smaller amounts would probably accomplish much more in toto and certainly much more per dollar . . .

If Alfred Kohlberg was working for the Chinese Government to get money for it, as charged, it would appear from this that he was not doing a very good job. The simple fact is, in his crusade to save China from Communism he felt he was working for the American people and the Chinese people. And although he had engaged in this kind of "lobbying" since 1943 he never met Chiang Kaishek until July 1949, after the Generalissimo had been driven off the mainland and was living in the mountains outside Taipei, Formosa.

Kohlberg made a flat declaration concerning his relations with the Chinese in a letter he sent to a Missouri critic (not Harry S Truman) who wrote him in 1954. Said Kohlberg:

"In my case, as a matter of fact, I have never had any connection with the Nationalist Government, or any other government, in China. I have never had any financial transaction, or done any business with them or any other government, or with any Chinese who ever, before, or since, was connected with any government of China. I have, as you say, been twice decorated by the Government of the Republic of China. The first decoration was presented to me in 1941 for my work as a Director and Chairman of the Executive Committee of the American Bureau for Medical Aid to China, the largest of the China aid organizations. The second award was voted me in 1948, apparently for my activities on behalf of the truth with regard to the China situation."

Another charge made repeatedly against Kohlberg was that he had a vast financial stake in China, based on a business that exploited Chinese workers. The implication was that Kohlberg was anxious to re-establish the status quo, since Mao Tse-tung's agrarian reformers would not permit him to exploit the proletariat.

Kohlberg had a good business but it was not the vast enterprise that it was made out to be. Its "vastness" may be judged from the fact that its *gross* volume of business was between a million and two million dollars a year.

As for being an exploiter of Chinese workers, as charged, a different light is cast on this in an article by Irene Corbally Kuhn that appeared in *The Sign*, a Catholic magazine, in June 1951:

"In China," said Mrs. Kuhn, "he has built a reputation over the years for scrupulous honesty and fair dealing. When he returned to China after the war, when his business had been suspended for the duration of the hostilities, he found that he had been repaid in kind. At the time of Pearl Harbor, Kohlberg's firm had 3,500,000 pieces in work in China. When the Japanese struck, he simply wrote off that shipment as a complete loss. Early in 1946, however, he discovered that his workers had managed to store away nearly 70 percent, secreting it from the Japanese behind false walls, or in underground caches. Some of the Chinese had gone to great lengths, often at great personal expense, to hold up what they considered their end of the bargain. They had salvaged for him more than $100,000 in goods.

"As a matter of course, Kohlberg took over all living expenses for his employees in China for the four years of the war. 'They risked their lives to fulfill their contract and save my goods—even when they could have made a fortune from selling them in black markets,' he says, matter-of-factly. 'I just put them back in business.' "

Kohlberg's British and French friends in China could not understand why his workers had taken risks to keep his merchandise from falling into Japanese hands. He had a simple answer to their questions on this score:

"Don't you have any Chinese friends?"

Usually they did not, but conducted their business with the Chinese through intermediaries. Unlike them, Kohlberg went directly to the people in the countryside, into the cottages of the people who were working for him. Mrs. Kohlberg said he once told her:

"First I am an American, second I feel Chinese, but above all I am a human being."

Another charge, frequently made, that Kohlberg and McCarthy "needed each other," with the implication that they were partners in a sinister plot, does not hold water. They allied themselves informally in a common cause against common enemies but either one could—and usually did—manage without the other. Probably the most noteworthy aspect of this alliance, if one chooses to call it that, is not that both men were making charges against certain individuals but that those individuals obviously wanted no part of any investigation unless the investigation could be made on their terms. To attempt to imply that charges made by McCarthy were without foundation because he was merely repeating Kohlberg's charges is ridiculous since Kohlberg's charges against the IPR were never given the impartial investigation he called for until the McCarran hearings started. Kohlberg was in the position of a person asking that someone be arrested, with the policeman refusing to bring the suspect into court to stand trial.

Kohlberg's big problems stemmed from the strange mentalities he encountered. He could not understand what is sometimes referred to as sophisticated thinking, many examples of which were brought to light in the course of the McCarran Committee hearings. The following document is a fair sampling of what Kohlberg was up against. This letter, entered into evidence, was written by Edward C. Carter on March 11, 1947, to a trustee who had expressed concern about the Kohlberg charges. Said Carter:

> I can well appreciate how the connection of Frederick Field and myself with the IPR have added to your difficulties in the Bay Region. Without doubt an easy, though merely temporary gain, would result from a decision on his part and mine to withdraw from all official connection with the IPR.
>
> But, alas, we are up against a vastly complicated, abundantly financed movement which is employing the classical Nazi methods in attacking liberals, leftists, and middle-of-the-road conservatives.
>
> Mr. Kohlberg is one of the spearheads of this nation-wide intrigue. He has carefully planned his time table and is moving with great skill from objective to objective. To the IPR he has added the FPA [Foreign Policy Association] and to that he has recently added an attack on Alger Hiss, the very able but by no

means leftist successor to President Nicholas Murray
Butler as the new President of the Carnegie Endowment for International Peace.

Reverting to the IPR, Kohlberg's time table is
roughly something like this: (1) the expulsion of
Field, (2) the expulsion of Carter, (3) of Lattimore, (4)
of Salisbury, (5) of Staley (6) Mrs. Stewart, and so on.
Now you may personally feel that Field, Carter, Lattimore and Salisbury should leave, but I am sure you
would regret the loss of Staley. It is because of the
end result rather than the fortunes of Field and myself that I am inclined to stand my ground in adhering to the invitation extended to me by Sproul,
Jessup, Calkins, and others late in 1945: that I accept
a three-year appointment as Executive Officer of
the American IPR beginning in the early part of
1946. . . .

And stand his ground Edward C. Carter did, until 1952,
when the Senate Internal Security Subcommittee cut the
ground out from under his feet in the kind of investigation
that Alfred Kohlberg had tried to institute eight years
earlier.

But by 1952 the damage had been done. As Alfred
Kohlberg had predicted, hundreds of millions of Chinese,
once our friends, were now facing us as enemies.

CHAPTER TWELVE

Propagandists and Promoters

OWEN LATTIMORE MADE HIS FIRST PUBLIC APPEAR-
ance before the Senate Internal Security Subcommittee,
better known as the McCarran Committee, on February
26, 1952. As when he had appeared before the Tydings
Committee, he had Abe Fortas as his legal counsel, and
the press was duly primed for his appearance with a 50-
page statement prepared by Eleanor Lattimore.

There was, however, a new element, a mass of evidence
which had been uncovered in an old barn on the Lee,
Massachusetts, farm of Edward C. Carter. Acting on a tip
from a man who had worked on the place, a member of
Senator McCarthy's staff seized secret records stored
there. These were turned over to the Senate Internal
Security Subcommittee and carefully studied for five
months before the hearings got under way.

The very atmosphere of the McCarran Committee hearings was different. For one thing, there was none of the fanfare that had made the Tydings hearings a gala occasion. Joe Barnes was not in evidence as "rewrite man and tough guy," as he had been, possibly because Barnes had earlier been identified before the committee as a Communist and a Soviet agent, charges that he denied. Nor is there any indication that Little, Brown and Company dispatched a vice-president from Boston to help out with editing chores. Even the Lattimores' well-publicized Mongolians were not on hand to pose for the press.

At the start, Lattimore took the offensive. After giving his name he lashed out at the committee:

"Senators, I have asked for this public hearing because your proceedings have resulted in serious damage to my reputation as an objective scholar and patriotic citizen, to the Institute of Pacific Relations, with which I have been connected, and to our Government's Foreign Service personnel and the conduct of its foreign policy."

Shortly after this he charged, "The impression has been assiduously conveyed in your proceedings that I am a Communist or a Communist sympathizer or dupe . . ."

As was the case when he testified before the Tydings Committee, Lattimore named Alfred Kohlberg and the China Lobby as the source of his woes. However, at this point he started to run into trouble. The Senators asked him to name the people who comprised the China Lobby. Lattimore named Alfred Kohlberg and William Goodwin; then said, "And I believe some Senators may be considered to be a part of the China lobby or occasional allies of the China lobby." As an example he named Senator William Knowland of California, with the observation that he was frequently referred to as "the Senator from Formosa."

This stirred up a hornets' nest. Knowland's fellow Senators obviously resented the slur and insisted on knowing where Lattimore had picked up this "Communist line."

Lattimore's memory failed him but he denied having seen
it in any Communist paper. Senator Homer Ferguson then
read into the record an editorial from the Communist
People's World of San Francisco, which repeatedly referred to Knowland as "the Senator from Formosa."

Pressed for names of other China Lobby members, Lattimore was able to mention only three—Freda Utley, the
China expert who had testified against him two years
before; George Sokolsky, the columnist; and Victor Lasky,
a newspaperman and writer. Following this, Senator Wil-
lis Smith expressed annoyance at the witness. He said he
would continue to listen to him, "But when such flimsy
statements as this are made, and then he cannot back it
up, I think it is something we should consider as to
whether or not we should throw this whole statement of
his out. . . ."

The questioning of Lattimore continued for thirteen
days and the testimony covered 776 pages of the Committee's printed report. However, Lattimore did not leave in
a blaze of glory. When he finished on March 21, he was
castigated by Senator McCarran:

> Mr. Lattimore came here at his own request to
> appear and testify. He came with a 50-page state-
> ment which was no casual document. It bore obvious
> indicia of careful preparation, and the witness tes-
> tified he had been working on it for months, and had
> been assisted by his counsel. It was released to the
> press before delivery, and Mr. Lattimore's invective
> was scattered to all parts of the country. Many times
> when asked if he had facts to support his insulting
> conclusions the witness replied that he did not.
>
> The committee has been confronted here with an
> individual so flagrantly defiant of the United States
> Senate, so outspoken in his discourtesy, and so per-
> sistent in his efforts to confuse and obscure the facts,
> that the committee feels constrained to take due no-
> tice of his conduct. . . .

The committee might have had a right to expect that a witness who claimed to be an objective scholar and a patriotic citizen would first objectively analyze the past policy of the United States in the Far East and help point the way to a determination of what has been wrong, and what corrective measures might be required. The committee might have had a right to expect that he would lend eager aid in exposing whatever Communist infiltration there may have been in the Institute of Pacific Relations. . . .

Instead, the committee was confronted with an initial fusillade of invective, and a consistently evasive, contentious, and belligerent attitude. . . .

Senator McCarran then cited certain aspects of Lattimore's testimony, including untruths of a serious nature, and concluded his remarks about the witness as follows:

The shaping of United States policy with respect to China was a factor in the success of Communism in that land, in the establishment of firm roots for Soviet influence in all Asia, and in the subsequent ordeal through which United States boys are being taken in Korea. If this policy in its initial stages or at any time was affected by acts or stratagems on the part of anyone having any slightest purpose except the welfare of this Nation, it would be a matter not to be lightly dealt with, nor one which the American people should easily overlook or forget. The intimate knowledge which this witness had of Asia and of Asiatic affairs, coupled with his deliberate and adroit attempts to mold American thinking with respect to those affairs, including his efforts to establish certain concepts in the mind of the Chief Executive of the United States, necessarily bring this witness within the orbit of any realistic appraisal of this whole situation. When, in the face of the record, he undertook before this committee a deliberate attempt to deny or cover up pertinent facts, this witness placed himself in a most unenviable position.

All things considered, Owen Lattimore probably decided there was no point in writing a sequel to *Ordeal by Slander,* even though this had indeed been an ordeal.

The IPR fared even worse than Lattimore.

Repeatedly, officials of the IPR testified that theirs was an organization devoted to objective, scholarly research, and participating in this were some of the world's greatest scholars and gentlemen. While this argument had some plausibility, since over the years the IPR had attracted many scholars and had made some valuable contributions, there was another side to the story and this was anything but pleasant. Working behind a facade of respectability, largely provided by distinguished people who innocently lent their names to it, propagandists, promoters, and imposters, it was shown, had manipulated the IPR. These elements used the organization "to serve international Communist interests and to affect adversely the intersts of the United States."*

The Institute of Pacific Relations was started in 1925 at a conference in Honolulu of religious leaders, scholars, and businessmen from various countries in the Pacific area "who realized the need for greater knowledge and frank discussion of the problems of Asia and the relations of Asia and the West. To permit this a research program was inaugurated, and over the years the major contributors to the IPR were the Rockefeller and Carnegie Foundations. These organizations provided 48 percent of the IPR's total receipts of $2,569,000 during the years from 1926 to 1951. The IPR at the time of the McCarran hearings was made up of national councils in ten countries, but of these the American Council was by far the most important, and it was this branch that figured most prominently in the hearings.

Anyone could join the IPR, merely by filling out an application blank and sending it with a check for $10, or

* A roster of people affiliated with the IPR who also had Communist affiliations, was compiled by the McCarran Committee. It appears as Appendix G.

more, to IPR headquarters at 1 East 54th Street, New York City. Many joined to get IPR publications, notably the magazines *Pacific Affairs* and *Far Eastern Survey.* IPR literature often listed the people who served as trustees and many of these were of national prominence. Among the well-known people who served in this capacity were General George C. Marshall, Gerard Swope, Sumner Welles, Paul G. Hoffman, Henry Wallace, as well as others who certainly could not have been aware of the kind of outfit the IPR really was. Indeed, Henry Wallace testified that he served as a trustee for two years without knowing of it.

"I was informed," he said, "by Alfred Kohlberg. He had written me in August 1950, that I had been a trustee of the Board of the Institute of Pacific Relations for at least 2 years."

However, there were other IPR trustees who had a bit more than an inkling of what was going on, among them Owen Lattimore, Frederick Vanderbilt Field, Alger Hiss, Lauchlin Currie, Edward C. Carter, Harriet Lucy Moore, and John Carter Vincent. These people took an active part in the intramural and extracurricular affairs of the IPR. Unfortunately, not all of these activities had to do with scholarly pursuits, despite the testimony of various witness that the IPR was nothing but a research center.

This concept was sharply challenged. Raymond Dennett, who had served the IPR as secretary of the American Council, said, "I do not think it was an objective research organization." Professor Kenneth Colegrove of Northwestern University, who had joined the IPR in the early thirties, went even further, saying, "Behind the front, the Institute of Pacific Relations was nothing else than a propaganda organization, supporting a [Communistic] line."

However, the most eloquent testimony of this nature came from Owen Lattimore himself, in the form of a letter which was introduced into evidence, the famous "cagey" letter he sent to Carter in 1938, two paragraphs of which follow:

"I think you are pretty cagey in turning over so much of the China section of the inquiry to Asiaticus, Han-seng and Chi. They will bring out the absolutely essential radical aspects but can be depended on to do it with the right touch. [All three of these were important Communists. Asiaticus was Hans Moeller, a Comintern agent. Chi and Han-seng are now in Communist China.]

"For the general purpose of this inquiry it seems to me that the good scoring position, for the IPR, differs with different countries. For China, my hunch is that it will pay to keep behind the official Chinese Communist position— far enough not to be covered by the same label—but enough ahead of the active Chinese liberals to be noticeable For Japan, on the other hand, hang back so as not to be inconveniently ahead of the Japanese liberals, who can not keep up, whereas the Chinese liberals can. So the chief thing is to oppose the military wing of Japanese aggression in China, counting on a check there to take care of both the military and civilian components of aggression in Japan. For the British—scare the hell out of them, always in a polite way, but usually in a way that looks as if it might turn impolite. The British liberal groups are badly flustered; but being British, the way to encourage them to pull themselves together is to fluster the Tories. For the U.S.S.R.—back their international policy in general, but without using their slogans and above all without giving them or anybody else the impression of subservience. . . ."

This kind of special pleading hardly seems like a scholarly approach, but a remark once made by Lattimore shows that he understood his place in the IPR scheme of things:

"I am making a practice of submitting everything I write to Carter so that he can reprove me when I say anything unbecoming a propagandist and a gentleman."

The testimony provided some humorous touches when it came to the promotional activities of some of the people who ran the IPR. Indeed, Edward C. Carter had a high tribute paid to his talents in this area by Professor John K. Fairbank, who said, "Mr. Carter has been associated with the IPR and has been so useful partly because he is a promoter by temperament."

There were frequent references in the testimony to fund-raising gimmicks and getting people to open their purse-strings; to various kinds of public relations pitches and free-loading (the Russians were rated as excellent hosts); to getting scholarships, grants, and strategic jobs for the right kind of people. It told of windfalls in the way of lucrative orders from the government and from schools for IPR material, and it discussed various kinds of log-rolling operations for the benefit of IPR projects and personnel.

Probably the most impressive achievement in the log-rolling department was the manner in which IPR people exercised tremendous influence in book publishing circles. This came about because these "experts" virtually monopolized the reviewing of books dealing with the Far East. This would have been all right if they had reviewed books honestly and objectively, but their bias was unmistakable. And to make matters worse, the same IPR people who reviewed books were prolific authors of books dealing with the Far East. The result was one of the strangest literary performances of our time. Indeed it was a veritable burlesque. A book written by an IPR luminary or by a writer who comformed to the IPR line was certain to get a glowing review in the most influential media. If the book was by an "outsider," particularly by a person who did not go along with IPR thinking, the book was either ignored or it was worked over with an axe.

The Report of the McCarran Committee told how this brazen book promotion operated:

"Owen Lattimore's *Solution in Asia,* for example, was reviewed by Edgar Snow in the *New York Times,* by Richard Watts, Jr., in the *New Republic,* and by T. A. Bisson in the *Saturday Review of Literature.* L. K. Rosinger's *China Crisis* got its send-off from Owen Lattimore in the *New York Herald Tribune,* Richard Watts, Jr., in the *New Republic,* and T. A. Bisson in the *New York Times.* Messrs. Watts, Pfeffer and Lattimore polished up Guenther Stein's *Challenge of Red China;* Rosinger, Fairbank, Snow, and Watts took care of Annalee Jacoby and Theodore White's *Thunder Out of China.* Messrs. Rosinger, Lattimore, Watts, and Miss Jacoby assessed for the reading public the worth of their IPR colleague John K. Fairbank's *The United States and China;* while Owen Lattimore's book, *Pivot of Asia,* was in 1950 entrusted to Theodore H. White, John K. Fairbank, and T. A. Bisson."

Books that tried to explain that the Chinese Communists were really Communists, and that Chiang Kai-shek was not corrupt and deserved our help were either ignored or got rough treatment. It is still a mystery how these people were able to get away with this blatant propaganda in some of our largest and most influential newspapers, but they did.*

Publishers, of course, got the message that there was little profit in bringing out books that were likely to get nowhere.

After taking due note of the activities of the IPR and the go-getters who made up its inner core of activists, the report of the McCarran Committee stated:

"The subcommittee noted throughout all the testimony and all the exhibits that so great a portion of the IPR energies went into public relations, lobbying, propaganda, and other activities that it is not correct or adequate to describe the IPR as a scholarly and research

---

*The thought control practiced by the IPR in the writing and reviewing of books is dramatized in a study published in the Congressional Record of June 6, 1952, presented as Appendix H,

organization. Its chief function was rather that of a crucible of United States public opinion in the Far East."

Then, thoroughly confirming the point that Alfred Kohlberg had tried to make, the report stated:

"The subcommittee concludes . . . that the IPR has been, in general, neither objective nor nonpartisan; and concludes further that, at least since the mid-1930's, the net effect of the IPR activities on United States public opinion has been pro-Communist and pro-Soviet, and has frequently and repeatedly been such as to serve international Communist, Chinese Communist, and Soviet interests, and to subvert the interests of the United States."

How was the IPR able to do so much? The most complete record of IPR achievements can be found in the Report of the McCarran Committee, which summarizes 6,000 pages of testimony compiled in eleven months of hearings, despite "equivocation, evasion, hostility and efforts to mislead" on the part of leading IPR officials.

Part of this report tells of Soviet ties with the Soviet Union, and how Soviet intelligence utilized IPR facilities as a "two-way track," to secure information and to influence U.S. policy. In this connection it was shown how the Russians made IPR officials toe the mark and do things as they wanted them done. And as usual this mighty power received tremendous value for the money it spent. W. L. Holland, testifying, pointed out that the frugal Russians "contributed no more than 2 or 3 percent of the IPR annual budget" from 1935 to 1939. For this modest outlay the Russians were even able to get the IPR to go to bat for them to try to justify the infamous 1936-1938 Moscow purge trials.

However, the report concerned itself primarily with the IPR's activities in the propaganda and promotional field, and what follows is a summary of these as presented in the Report:

Among the first of the IPR leaders to play a vital role in

government affairs was Owen Lattimore. This was in 1941. On June 18, while the Hitler-Stalin Pact and the Japanese-Soviet Alliance were still in force, Lattimore and Edward C. Carter had a two-hour luncheon in Washington with Constantine Oumansky, Soviet Ambassador to the United States. At this time two important events were about to take place. The Hitler-Stalin Pact would be broken three days later, on June 22, and Lattimore was being sent to Chiang Kai-Shek as his adviser. This nomination had been suggested to President Roosevelt by Lauchlin Currie. No publicity had been given to the appointment at the time of the Lattimore-Carter-Oumansky luncheon, and the report stated that "Lattimore could give no reasonable explanation as to why he should confer with the Ambassador of a country that had an alliance with both Germany and China's enemy, Japan, and was at political war with the United States." As Roosevelt's personal representative in China, Lattimore was in a strategic position, which he used to oppose any settlement with Japan while there was still some possibility of a compromise. Negotiations were broken off, as told in an earlier chapter, and we found ourselves at war with Japan.

Lattimore returned from China in February, 1942 and used a desk in Lauchlin Currie's office in the State Department Building. Since Currie was then Roosevelt's special adviser on Far Eastern affairs, this put Lattimore in a pivotal spot. He spent four days a week in Currie's office for a period of "three, four, or five months," had a White House telephone extension, took care of Currie's mail, and used White House stationery. Meanwhile he was also serving as an adviser to the IPR.

This setup was helpful in many ways. When Frederick Field wanted to get a commission as an intelligence officer in the Army, Lattimore took up the matter with Currie. Currie was also responsible for setting up a conference with Under Secretary of State Sumner Welles, Earl

Browder, and Robert Minor. Browder and Minor, of course, were top Communist officials. The fruit of this meeting was a State Department document about Chinese "unity" that the Communist Party looked upon as an official policy document upholding their viewpoint. This was printed in the October 16, 1942, *Daily Worker* and was used all over the world to enhance the prestige of the Chinese Communists.

Much of the testimony told how the IPR ground out propaganda pamphlets undermining the Chinese Government and how IPR personnel in strategic spots promoted them. Even the Army was using vast quantities of this slanted material to indoctrinate troops fighting in the Pacific, while bales of their pamphlets were going to the nation's schools and colleges.

One such IPR pamphlet was Maxwell S. Stewart's "War-Time China" which had so aroused Alfred Kohlberg that he cited it in the letter that opened his fight with the organization. However, Kohlberg was not the only one who considered this propaganda piece important. The IPR had the manuscript checked by John Carter Vincent, John K. Fairbank, and others. Vincent said it was "good and well worth publishing. Fairbank thought these things should be said but in a more subtle manner."

Although our official policy during 1941–1945 was to aid the Government of China and keep Chiang's armies in the field, this policy was being undermined. Efforts were being made to apply pressure on the Nationalists by the U.S. Government to change the policies of China. Three different approaches were used: The efforts of Foreign Service officers in the field during 1943–1944; the Henry A. Wallace mission; and the directive to General Marshall and its implementation.

This part of the testimony told how on November 20, 1942, John Carter Vincent and John Stewart Service met with the Communist leaders Chou En-lai and Lin Piao. At this meeting the Communist told Vincent and Service what the United States should do about China. What they wanted done, obviously, was to have the United States help the Red cause in every possible way. Somehow the Red cause was interpreted as "democracy," and the Foreign Service officers stressed the democratic origins of the Chinese Communist movement, and worked to encourage such "democracy."

The actions of these men brought the following comment from General Chennault: "Since it was still official American policy in the summer of 1944 to support the Chungking Government, it was a common joke that Stilwell's headquarters [where John S. Stewart and John Paton Davies were advisers] were definitely operating a private foreign policy with John Davies as Secretary of State." Reports by this pair advocated interference with the Chinese Government, undermined Chiang, and plugged for the "democratic" element that opposed him.[*] They exaggerated the weaknesses of the Nationalists, stressed the economic instability of the Government and tried to promote the idea that there was no connection between the Chinese Communists and the Soviet Union.

The mission of Vice-President Henry Wallace to China brought new pressure on the Chinese Government "and this pressure also coincided with the recommendations of the Chinese Communists." Accompanying Wallace on this mission were John Carter Vincent, Owen Lattimore, and John N. Hazard. As an indication of the wheels within wheels, Vincent testified that he first heard of the mission from Lauchlin Currie in June 1944, and that he first met the Vice-President in connection with it in Currie's office. Vincent admitted that he did influence Wallace and that

[*]An example of the way in which this was done can be found in a report from John S. Stewart to General Stilwell, dated October 10, 1944, in which Stewart suggested that Stilwell take a strong line against Chiang Kai-shek and the Kuomintang. Such prompting may have been responsible for the poor relations between the two men. Service's presumptuous Report No. 40 appears as Appendix I.

this influence had as its end result insistence by Wallace on a settlement between Chiang and the Communists.

Following his return from China, Wallace made a report to President Truman concerning which there was considerable mystery. It was not publicized and it did not appear in the State Department's White Paper. Attempting to get a copy of this report or at least some idea of what it contained, Kohlberg carried on correspondence with Wallace. This proved to be an exercise in futility as his queries were met with vagueness. Possibly some idea of what the report contained may be ascertained from this quotation, said to be from it, published in a Communist publication, *Far East Spotlight:*

"Chiang, at best, is a short-term investment. It is not believed that he has the intelligence or political strength to run postwar China. The leaders of postwar China will be brought forward by evolution or revolution, and it now seems more likely the latter."

More widely publicized was a book that Wallace published after his return, *Soviet Asia Mission.* This was actually written by one Andrew J. Steiger, identified before the Committee as a Communist and a writer for the *Daily Worker.* A draft of the book was sent to Lattimore before it was finished. A further glimpse of the wheels within wheels at the IPR was provided by testimony concerning another Wallace literary effort. This was a pamphlet which the IPR published under the Vice-President's name, "Our Job in the Pacific." Eleanor Lattimore did much of the writing, Frederick Field had it approved by the trustees of the IPR, and when it came out it was praised in the *Daily Worker* in a column written by Field.

Much testimony concerned the ubitiquous Owen Lattimore—as Roosevelt's free-will offering to Chiang in the role of adviser, as an associate of Currie and traveling companion to Wallace, and as an official of the Office of War Information under another friend, Elmer Davis. It was shown that in 1945 John Carter Vincent tried to make Lattimore a consultant to the China Division, and while this effort did not succeed, Lattimore soon afterwards turned up on the State Department payroll as a member of the Pauley Reparations Mission to Japan.

Looking ahead to the postwar world, the IPR set up an important international conference at Hot Springs in January 1945. This served as a curtain-raiser to the San Francisco founding conference of the United Nations. According to Raymond Dennett, who testified on this, as well as to correspondence in the record, recommendations for delegates to the Hot Springs conference came from Philip Jessup and Lauchlin Currie.

Before the conference, the American delegation caucused to determine what positions it should take. "A report of the caucus showed that it considered the question of taking a position in intervention in the internal affairs of the Chinese Government. Jessup presided at the caucus and Lattimore was the most vocal and dominant conferee. The conferees, who also included Frederick V. Field, Len De Caux, Frank Coe, and Miriam S. Farley, agreed that their position should be one of pressing for changes in the internal situation of the Chinese Government." Field, De Caux, and Coe were all identified as Communists. The Farley woman was shown to have written extensively for official publications of the Communist Party.

Lattimore went beyond the China situation during the conference and aroused resentment on the part of British, French, and Dutch delegates by his attacks on colonialism. He also urged that postwar plans for Japan ignore the Japanese emperor, a Communist position that had been strongly stressed in IPR publications. Two months after the conference Alger Hiss recommended that copies of its report be made available to each of the delegations to the UN conference.

IPR influence on postwar planning did not end with just this conference. A member of the Postwar Planning Staff of the State Department testified to the type and volume of IPR publications that were circulated there and said they were "almost the only publications on the Far East coming into the State Department."

The fine hand of Alger Hiss, who was head of postwar planning for the State Department, was shown in the cooperation between the IPR and the Department of State. And in this portion of the testimony the interlocking of IPR and State is evident from the names of those involved—Alger Hiss, Edward C. Carter, Harry Dexter White, John Carter Vincent, W. W. Lockwood, Lauchlin Currie, Philip C. Jessup, Esther Brunauer, V. Frank Coe, and others.

The stage was being set for intervention in China, in favor of the Communists, and a major move in this direction was taken on June 10, 1945 when Owen Lattimore wrote to President Truman and urged a revision of our policy toward China. His argument was that by aiding Chiang we were setting a precedent which the Soviet Union could use as a pretext to come to the aid of the Chinese Communists. This he followed up with a visit to the White House on July 3, 1945, at which time he left a memorandum with Truman calling for a coalition government in China, with the Communists having power in the government. This followed by only two weeks the promulgation of an official resolution of the National Committee of the Communist Party of the United States, dated June 20, 1945, which denounced the dangerous policy reactionaries were following in bolstering "the reactionary incompetent Chiang Kai-shek regime," and preventing a "strong, united and democratic China." A significant part of the Communist resolution was a call to "remove from the State Department all pro-Fascist and reactionary officials."

Testimony showed that these demands of the Communist Party in this country came shortly after the Seventh National Congress of the Chinese Communist Party, meeting in Yenan earlier that year, had called for a coalition government. This set the course followed by American Communists, a course which, by one of those coincidences, was set forth in the memorandum presented to Truman by Lattimore.

In view of what happened later, it would appear that the President bought the package that Lattimore handed him. It is therefore interesting to speculate on some remarks made by Mr. Truman, years later, in a speech before the National Convention of The American Legion, meeting in Las Vegas in 1962:

"I believe that one of the most important things that you of The American Legion can do is to give support to the President of the United States in his foreign policy.

"The President has available to him information from many sources so that he can make those decisions which —in his judgment—will maintain the security of this country.

"This is no time for politicians to embarrass the President when they do not have and cannot have all the facts."

This speech was made at a time when Americans were worrying about another Communist threat, this time in Cuba, and wondering again about the people who were dealing in "facts" for presidential decisions.

At the time that Lattimore called on the President, the people in the State Department who had most to do with our Far Eastern policy were Joseph Grew, Joseph W. Ballantine, and Eugene Dooman. Within four months all three were out of the State Department. John Carter Vincent, an intimate friend of Lattimore, went in as head of the Far Eastern Office. On November 28, 1945, Vincent recommended a course of action in China which called for having the Nationalist Government include other political elements. It was pointed out that the Nationalist Government was a one-party government and the United States could not support it by "military intervention in an internecine struggle." There was a call for a truce between the armies of the Nationalists and the Communists. As the IPR report states:

"An analysis of the President's declaration of policy dated December 15, 1945 [which became the cornerstone of United States policy toward China until June 1950], shows that it was in most of its substance the same as this draft of Vincent's and Vincent acknowledged that it was."

Vincent made another contribution in the form of a memorandum for the War Department, which was signed by Secretary of State Byrnes on December 10, 1945. This set forth a policy and prescribed operations to be taken in furtherance of the policy. It called on the "Central" Government of China to compromise with the "dissident elements" and expressed the belief that Chiang Kai-shek should "broaden the base" of his government to give those elements a voice. To this end the United States would exert its influence.

Stated in non-diplomatic language, Vincent's memorandum was a demand that Chiang give the Communists a share in the government—or else. Chosen to present this harsh program to Chiang Kai-shek was General George C. Marshall, whose prestige was such that no one would dare to charge that he was being used to carry out what was essentially a Communist objective. Also called on to help out in this project was General Wedemeyer. It is noteworthy that the substance of the instructions which the Department of State called on the War Department to convey to General Wedemeyer was—in the words of the IPR report—"directly contrary to the recommendations which General Wedemeyer himself had submitted. Mr.

Vincent in his testimony recognized this."

The McCarran Report thus summarizes the chain of events:

"Thus the demand for support of the idea of a coalition government in China, made in May 1945 by Mao Tse-tung, taken up by the American Communist Party, and recommended to the President by Owen Lattimore in his memorandum of July 3, 1945, was adopted and sponsored by Vincent; memoranda elaborating upon that idea were drafted by Vincent and were affirmed by the Secretary of State; these became the basis of the policy in relation to China which was announced by President Truman on December 15, 1945, and in pursuance of that policy General Marshall was sent to China to bring to bear upon the Chinese National Government the pressure of United States influence."*At the time that General Marshall began his mission to China at the end of 1945, the Chinese Nationalists had the upper hand. Chiang's divisions were chasing the Communists north. However, Marshall's demands for a coalition government eventually changed the situation. One plan actually approved by General Marshall called for the reduction of the Chinese Nationalist Army to 50 divisions and the incorporation into that army of 10 Communist divisions, all of which were to be armed by the United States. This plan failed when no coalition could be arranged.

Marshall was empowered to grant a loan of $500,000,-000 to the Chinese, but there was a string attached—Chiang had to establish a coalition government. The loan was withheld and never granted. Marshall set up truce teams, each one made up of one Nationalist, one Communist and one American, for the purpose of enforcing truces between the then winning Nationalists and the losing Communists The Reds used the truce teams, characteris-

*Three key documents which describe General Marshall's fateful mission to China to force Chiang Kai-shek to form a coalition government appear as Appendix J.

tically, to gain advantages. When the going got tough they would call for a truce. But instead of coming to terms they would regroup, recover their strength, and then go on the offensive.

When the Chinese Government did not bow to our dictates and form a coalition government by the summer of 1946, U.S. military assistance was halted, as has been described in the previous chapter. And, as has been told in that chapter, the Chinese Communists were armed by the Soviet Union from Japanese war supplies seized by the Russians in Manchuria.

While we were thus making it impossible for Chiang to win his war against the Communists in China, here at home the American people were being conditioned to accept this betrayal as inevitable and the fault of Chiang Kai-shek. Of course the IPR played a key role in this propagandizing, as has been told.

Nor were the propagandists of the IPR satisfied when Chiang was finally forced off the mainland and onto Formosa. The next objective was to get the United States to recognize the Red regime. The Soviet Union, naturally, took the lead in recognition, quickly followed by Bulgaria, Romania, Soviet Poland, and Czechoslovakia. American moves to follow suit were soon instituted.

The State Department set up a 3-day conference attended by 25 persons selected by the State Department. Of these, 17 were active in the IPR and here again Owen Lattimore starred, with Lawrence K. Rosinger in a supporting role. (During the course of the IPR hearings Rosinger was identified as a Communist but he refused to affirm or deny it on the grounds of self-incrimination.) The prevailing view of the conference was that "Nationalist China was defeated and that all recommendations should recognize this as a fact."

Also expressed were positions favoring the seating of Red China in the United Nations, withholding aid from

Formosa, looking upon Ho Chi Minh as a revolutionary patriot "with only a color of loyalty to Moscow," withholding of approval of the Chinese embargo against supplies to the Communists.

Philip C. Jessup presided over the conference. Harold Stassen, who was one of the delegates, conferred with Jessup off-the-record. According to Stassen's testimony, "Jessup asserted that greater logic lay with the findings of the majority present who expressed their views."

The McCarran Committee obtained the memoranda submitted in advance of the conference by the two dominant conferees, Lattimore and Rosinger.

"Basically," the IPR Report stated, "the Rosinger memorandum called for withholding aid to the Chinese Nationalist Government and Chiang Kai-shek, avoiding economic and military intervention in Formosa, returning Formosa to the Chinese Communist Government, imposing no impediments to normal trade with China with the exception of outright materials of war, etc."

Lattimore's recommendations coincided with Rosinger's in almost every respect: support had to be withdrawn from Chiang and from "the scattering of little Chiang Kai-sheks in Asia;" we should not cut off trade with Communist China; we should give up our efforts to keep South Korea alive; and should accept a list of countries for admission to the United Nations. Naturally, Communist China was on Lattimore's list, as was the Mongolian People's Republic.

"At the conference," the Report continued, "the three points which received the greatest stress were the recognition of the Chinese Communist Government, the establishment of normal trade relations between Communist China and the United States, and the breaking of what the conference called the Nationalist blockade."

Obviously when a group of such experts spoke, the administration listened—and lost no time before acting. Just six weeks after the conference, on November 16, 1949, Secretary of State Acheson protested Nationalist China's action in firing on the *Flying Cloud,* an American ship trying to run the blockade by taking supplies to the Communists. On December 3rd Acheson said that this country did not recognize the legality of the blockade. On December 23rd the State Department sent a memorandum to Foreign Service personnel minimizing the importance of Formosa, clearly paving the way for the surrender of that stronghold. On January 5, 1950, President Truman announced that the United States had no intention of providing military aid to the Nationalists on Formosa, and that Formosa should be returned to "China," in accordance with the Cairo Agreement. Testimony was introduced to show that our State Department was preparing to recognize Red China.

But the Chinese Communists crossed up their friends and allies in the IPR and in our government. On June 25 1950, the North Korean communists crossed the 38th parallel, spearheaded by 100 Russian tanks and bearing Russian arms. On November 26, 1950, 200,000 of those Chinese "agrarian reformers" that Americans had been hearing so much about joined in a war that was to kill more than 50,000 Americans and wound more than 100,000.

The experts of the IPR fell silent. In the next presidential election the administration which had followed the advice of the IPR experts was turned out of office. Which of course was small solace for the families of 157,530 Americans killed and wounded in a war that need never have been fought.

Robert Morris, who served as Special Counsel to the McCarran Committee, told the writer of the role Alfred Kohlberg played in the hearings:

"He volunteered information, which was always helpful, but he always remained in the background. Even when he was denounced publicly by Lattimore he did not demand the right to testify. He submitted an affidavit telling how he had become involved with the IPR and how he had been unable to get the investigation he wanted, and he rested his case on that.*

"My most vivid recollection of Alfred Kohlberg was, one day, I believe in 1952, he showed up with a whole trunkful of documents. He said he had been receiving these things for the past several weeks. Not knowing what else to do with them, he decided they ought to be turned over to a branch of Congress, and then maybe given to the FBI.

"He took out an envelope and handed it to me. It was a classified report about Communists in government, and one item was a letter written by two CIA agents, Lyle H. Munson and Ed Hunter. It told how John Paton Davies [with the State Department] had made a recommendation that six people, some of them unabashed Soviet agents, though not demonstrably so at the time, should be in charge of a propaganda unit of the United States Government. Obviously someone was using Kohlberg as a conduit to expose these things. I know he acted in a most responsible manner in turning the material over as he did. What else could he do? Congress has a right to know these things."

Alfred Kohlberg's comments on the IPR hearings were brief and charitable.

"It conclusively proved," he said, "that the Institute of Pacific Relations was actually a Communist-operated propaganda and espionage organization. Charges that I had made against it were not only proven but over-proven.**

"When the facts were all brought out, the non-Commu-

---

*Alfred Kohlberg's affidavit is presented in full as Appendix K.

**Vindication of Kohlberg's position can be found in the Conclusions of the Report of the Committee on the Judiciary which investigated the IPR. These are presented as Appendix L.

nist trustees of the IPR for the most part quietly resigned and disappeared into the woodwork. It seems too bad they could not have looked into my charges in 1944. They could have avoided not only eight years of further involvement with it, but eight years of lending aid to a semi-respectable front to a Communist espionage and propaganda operation which, as the Report of the Senate Committee shows, diverted American policy from our best interests and made it a tool of Communist world conquest in China."

As for the IPR, it languished and finally closed up shop in the United States.

CHAPTER THIRTEEN

Venture Into Journalism

THE WAY IN WHICH NEWS ABOUT THE FAR EAST WAS handled by an important segment of the press in this country was a constant source of annoyance to Alfred Kohlberg. Well aware of what was happening in China, he frequently complained about the way the press distorted news concerning that country.

He made a flat charge of pro-Communist bias in a release he sent to opinion-molding editors in November 1947. This opened with two questions: "What is wrong with American correspondents in China?" and "Why are most of them sympathetic to Chinese Communism and to Soviet Russia?" Citing examples of how reporters seemed to rely on propaganda and rumors, and how they presented Communist handouts as authentic news, he accused them of open hostility to the Nationalist Government.

He told of the failure of correspondents to report a massacre by Chinese Reds of at least 200 civilians and 300 Nationalist soldiers at Siwantze, in North China, a few months earlier. Only one American correspondent, Waldo Drake, even bothered to go to the scene, he said.

"If the Nationalists had destroyed a village and massacred its inhabitants we may be sure it would have been fully covered," he charged.

As exceptions to the rule, he cited some reporters who provided good coverage—Tillman Durdin of the *New York Times,* Arch Steele of the *New York Herald Tribune,* William H. Newton of the Scripps-Howard papers, and Waldo Drake of the *Los Angeles Times.* Pointing out that distorted news coming out of China had a by-product in distorted editorials, he said:

"We suggest that the editors urge the press agencies to replace the fellow-travelers and dupes in the Far East with Americans who have at least some knowledge of the history and the culture of the countries to which they are assigned."

As Kohlberg said, ignorance was often at the bottom of the poor news coverage. Indeed, it could have been simply ignorance that caused some correspondents to accept at face value Communist propaganda, whether it came from Mao Tse-tung, Chou En-lai, key American diplomats at Chungking, or fellow correspondents with leftist leanings. Nor was this sort of thing restricted to news coverage in China. Kohlberg told of a press conference held in New York by General Claire Chennault of the famed Flying Tigers.

"I went," he said, "and was horrified to find the people the New York press had sent to interview him were young ignoramuses more accustomed to police news or sports than to China. They scarcely knew who Chennault was, and asked such foolish things as, 'How do you spell Shanghai?' and, 'How do you spell Canton?' and so forth. This was not because the New York press didn't have men who knew about China, they simply didn't send them, as they didn't want to give Chennault the chance to really be understood and explained to the public."

This dim view of the powerful metropolitan press was strengthened by the incredible manner, described earlier, in which the press promoted books that plugged the Chinese Communists. This, incidentally, had a very valuable journalistic by-product that few people realized. When a pro-Communist book was logrolled into the bestseller column its author was immediately in demand by magazine editors. A look at the leading magazines of that period will show that the same authors who wrote books glorifying Mao's agrarian reformers were telling American readers the same thing in leading periodicals. In addition there was another kind of literary promotion, indicated in the following letter written by Edward C. Carter and introduced into evidence in the IPR hearings:

"At long last our friend Joe Barnes persuaded the Ogden Reids to appoint Edgar Snow as a *Herald Tribune* correspondent in China. Edgar Snow is, therefore, giving the American people a more accurate picture of the serious state of affairs in China than any correspondent has given in cabled stories since the war began."

It was, of course, the kind of picture that the IPR wanted the American people to get.

Annoyed at some of these manifestations, Kohlberg once circulated a letter which was not exactly complimentary toward the *Herald Tribune*. The paper's attorneys wrote saying the letter was libelous and called for a retraction.

This incident was recalled by Edna Lonigan, who was associated with Kohlberg in the American China Policy Association. "Alfred phoned his lawyer and said, 'I'd like to have your legal advice about this, but in all fairness I must warn you that if you tell me to retract I intend to get another lawyer.' " There is no record of any further action.

Discussing Kohlberg's relations with the press, Miss Lonigan said, "He would have made a marvelous reporter. He insisted on getting all the details, the complete picture. He had a phenomenal memory and retained the information he got. As a result, everything he had was complete. One reason his opponents were so furious with him was because they could never find flaws in his material. He had intellectual precision."

Always a realist, Kohlberg had no illusions about the odds against him. One day he told Miss Lonigan, "I'm discouraged. I keep sending this stuff out and I get no response to it. I wonder if it's doing any good." She said she had told him, "They get it and they read it, and eventually they will see that you were right."

At that time his basic weapon was a mimeograph machine which ground out a constant stream of letters (usually of the "open" variety) to officials, press releases, letters to editors, and reports and statements backing up his arguments. Among the latter he often included official Communist documents and items reproduced from the *Daily Worker* and other Communist papers. His usual procedure was to get out a mailing at least once a week to a list of approximately 800, and this was supplemented by other mailings to special lists of congressmen and others.

It is significant that Kohlberg subscribed to no clipping bureaus. This was no vanity operation he was conducting, to provide material for personal scrapbooks. His sole interest was in trying to alert the American people to the disaster that was building up in the Far East. And arrayed against him were mammoth presses capable of turning out material by the ton, much of it contradicting his puny output.

He was also handicapped by certain intangibles. First, he had no impressive credentials. He was just a businessman, so unimportant that no president or governor had ever even appointed him to a board or a commission, to be photographed at a desk and interviewed to tell the public what his commission was supposed to do. He had written no books, nor had he commissioned any to be ghost-written for him. He was not listed in *Who's Who in America,* nor had he ever received an honorary degree from Harvard or Siwash U. In fact he had never even earned a B.A., and while this put him in the same class with Owen Lattimore, the newspapers never referred to him as Dr. Kohlberg.

Because of the way he was portrayed in the press, people could not help getting the impression that he was a publicity-seeker and a sorehead who was trying to get back at the IPR because he had been kicked out. This image doubtless caused many of his mimeographed releases and letters to be discarded; but many were printed, usually outside the big metropolitan centers.

Alfred Kohlberg failed to get one other kind of treatment usually given to controversial figures. Ordinarily our great national magazines show remarkable enterprise in telling their readers about men and women who play a significant part in life at home and abroad. Kohlberg, who certainly rated attention on this score, was almost completely ignored. The only national publication that ever presented a biographical piece about him was *The American Legion Magazine,* of which I was then the editor. It also published a piece by him in which he presented his ideas on brainwashing as it was being practiced in this country. He criticized editors whose "editorial pages have become collections of current political dogma," and went on to say, "Such editors do not seem to understand that a newspaper must find its justification in the honest portrayal of news, else it will fail."

Kohlberg contributed fairly regularly to two magazines, *The New Leader* and *China Monthly*. The first he described as "an obscure magazine of opinion on the non-communist left, the official organ of the Social Democratic movement in America." He said it appealed to him as "the only magazine in America that was willing at that time to present an anti-Soviet viewpoint." At one time, to help out the publication, he attempted to raise $8,500 to cover the cost of a supplement for a year. This supplement, to be called *Alert*, was to arouse America to the dangers of ill-conceived agreements with the Soviet Union. This, he felt, was a worthy cause indeed.

"I agreed to underwrite the $8,500," he explained, "and gave a small dinner at the Waldorf-Astoria to which I invited a few prospective contributors. As I knew few people with money I had to invite those I knew and who I thought might give. Unfortunately, out of the group I had there, only Mrs. Jolles and Charlie Noyes contributed, each about $500, I believe, and I was left to make good almost all of the balance of $7,500."

Kohlberg's experience, it might be mentioned, was typical. People of great wealth are often generous with their money, but not when it comes to anti-Communist causes. Contrary to the general notion that rich conservatives back anti-Communists with extravagant contributions, the fact is that in this area they are usually miserly. Indeed, Alfred Kohlberg, whose resources were relatively modest, was noted among anti-Communists as the outstanding exception to this rule.

Over the years *The New Leader* published a number of letters he wrote. The *China Monthly*, however, was more important to him since it published articles he wrote on subjects dealing with the Far East. This magazine was supported by a Catholic mission group and was edited by Father Mark Tsai, whom he knew. All told he wrote seventeen articles for *China Monthly* over a period of five years.

The first of these, incidentally, was "Owen Lattimore: Expert's Expert," described in Chapter 9.

By 1946 he had decided that there was need for a publication that would concentrate on fighting Communism, and this idea was brought to a head by the Reverend John Cronin, Secretary of the Catholic Welfare Conference in Washington. Father Cronin invited Kohlberg to attend a meeting with a group of ex-FBI men and Ben Mandel, who was at that time with the House Committee on Un-American Activities. At this meeting it was decided that Isaac Don Levine would be an ideal man to edit the magazine if he could be persuaded to accept the position. Mr. Levine, a well-known writer, had been a foreign correspondent and was an expert on Communism.

Mr. Mandel arranged to bring Mr. Kohlberg and Father Cronin to the Levine home in Norwalk, Connecticut, in June 1946, where they outlined their plan. This was to establish a publication and a research service in the area of Communism.

"It was not completely clear to me what such a research service would be," Mr. Levine said, "but I knew no publication of the type we discussed could function without a research staff.

"I took the matter under consideration and after I thought the matter over for a few weeks I said I would undertake the assignment, with the understanding that I would draw no salary for the first year or two. I said I would try to work out some kind of deal for reprint rights and whatever accrued to the magazine from the *Reader's Digest* would go to me, but I would not be a burden on the payroll which Mr. Kohlberg generously undertook to maintain."

It was estimated that $25,000 would be needed to get the magazine started and keep it going for a year. It was to be published monthly in a pocket-size format, about the size of *Reader's Digest,* and to consist of some 48 to 64 pages. Another $25,000 was allocated for the research organization which Kohlberg described as "a sort of Un-American Activities Committee or FBI file system for the use of the magazine and for others interested." This was to be run by the former FBI men. The entire $50,000 was pledged by Alfred Kohlberg, who also provided office space in a building at 240 Madison Avenue, New York, which belonged in part to him. The magazine, called *Plain Talk,* set up shop in the front half of the second floor of the building, and the research department was installed in the rear wing of the building on the 12th floor, reachable only by the freight elevators through the 38th Street entrance.

In a matter of weeks the research service led to a break in the organization, one that was precipitated by Isaac Don Levine.

"I was responsible for it," he explained. "I discovered that this research service was being made available to industrial concerns, merchants, unions, and others who wanted information about Communists. I had no objection to this kind of a service but I had objections to an independent journal being connected with it. So we parted and out of the group severed from *Plain Talk* came a publication called *Counterattack.*" Mr. Kohlberg had no connection with this newsletter.

As editor, Isaac Don Levine insisted on running *Plain Talk* as he saw fit, and his aim was to put out a magazine that would "carry the message on a factual exposé basis to the elite, the thinking people, the leaders—editors, clergy, educators, librarians, people on the hill, our policy makers." The editor and the publisher did not always see eye to eye on how this should be done.

"There developed a humorous kind of war between Kohlberg and me very early," he said, "I think he felt, with some justification, and so did Father Cronin, that I

was ungovernable, that I had my own standards and that
I was overriding and overconfident in my judgments. A
humorous tug-of-war developed on the subject of libel.
Kohlberg, who was financially liable for the enterprise,
felt that the risk of libel, the gamble of libel, was worth it
and would make for publicity, and publicity would help
the magazine. I thought we had enough publicity, but
above all I felt that libel should be avoided at all costs.
That even if you knew something to be a fact, if you didn't
have the evidence you should not rush into print with it.

"I think that is one of the keys to his character. Kohlberg felt that if it's the truth bring it out and let the devil
take the hindmost. So more than once and more than
twice we had semi-humorous and semi-serious differences. If we agreed it was a fact, we disagreed as to the
available proof of the fact. In the field of Communism
everything is subject to that issue.

"There was another element of friction that developed.
A silent sort. Kohlberg would dash off a piece of copy of
six or seven pages that I considered poor composition and
I would reduce it to a page or two and send it back to Miss
Murray, his secretary, and ask her to have him make such
changes as to facts which he alone could make. Still I
cannot recall a single strident argument with him or a
strong session. I think we had too much mutual respect,
and he recognized that I had to be the boss in my shop."

Alfred Kohlberg obviously enjoyed his role as a publisher. From the time he had worked as a campus correspondent at Berkeley he liked to write for publication.
And even though Levine was critical of his writing, saying, "he was not sufficiently disciplined in the copy he
turned out," this did not discourage Kohlberg. Too, he
liked to associate with writers, and as a magazine publisher he was able to meet more of them. And there was
another asset. Levine told how, as *Plain Talk* gained in
influence, Kohlberg found doors being opened to him.
Senators and people of prominence who had been diffi-

cult to see were more gracious toward Kohlberg the publisher of an influential magazine. For while *Plain Talk*
never had a paid circulation of more than 12,000, it had
a great deal of influence. It reached the kind of audience
that Isaac Don Levine had in mind and it made an impact
on them.

The very first issue, that of October 1946, carried an
article which had repercussions almost four years later,
during the Tydings hearings. Titled "The State Department Espionage Case," it was written by Emmanuel S.
Larsen, a State Department official who had been involved in the *Amerasia* case. In this article Larsen told the
inside story of his involvement with Philip Jaffe, Kate
Mitchell, Mark Gayn, Andrew Roth, and John Stewart
Service, who were all arrested when *Amerasia's* offices
yielded more than a hundred files containing top-secret
and highly confidential papers stolen from the State Department, War Department, Navy Department, and other
strategic places.

When he testified before the Tydings Committee in
1950, Larsen repudiated this article. He said Isaac Don
Levine and Ralph de Toledano, then managing editor of
Plain Talk, had completely rewritten the piece he had
drafted and then coerced him into agreeing to allow it to
be published. Without making any check of this with Mr.
Levine or Mr. de Toledano, the Committee presented this
version, although it pointed out that Larsen's "credibility
generally is open to serious doubt." Had Senator Tydings
or any of his associates checked with Mr. Levine he could
have been shown Larsen's revised manuscript with his
initials on every page. He could also have seen a letter
from Larsen lauding the revised article and requesting
copies for his friends. Months later Larsen wrote another
article for *Plain Talk*, which would indicate that he was
not unhappy at that time over the treatment the editors
had given him.

The magazine carried a succession of hard-hitting articles. In the issue after that which presented the sensational *Amerasia* story, was one titled "Stalin's Hand In the Panama Canal." This dealt with the United Public Workers Union of America, an outfit that was subsequently fired out of the CIO. The following month *Plain Talk* exposed the IPR in an article titled "IPR-Tokyo Axis," which dealt with many of the people who later starred in Senate hearings. During a life span of less than four years *Plain Talk* was first to expose the barbarities of the North Korean Communists (in 1947); first to expose the A-bomb spies, long before the Rosenbergs were arrested; and anticipated the Korean War. It broke the story of the slave-labor camps in the USSR, exposed the curious background of the publication *In Fact,* and in an article titled "Red Star Over Independence Square," by Freda Utley, it discussed the strange case of Edgar Snow, then on the editorial staff of *The Saturday Evening Post.* In addition it took the lead in discussing the devious doings of such notables as Alger Hiss, Harry Bridges, and Mrs. Earl Browder. Among its contributors were Clare Booth Luce, Eugene Lyons, John Chamberlain, Rodney Gilbert, George Creel, Freda Utley, and Victor Lasky.

In the course of publishing *Plain Talk* Kohlberg made an interesting discovery—that it was not a good idea to tell the whole truth or at least as much as was known, because if you did people wouldn't believe you. This may seem like an extreme statement but it must be kept in mind that *Plain Talk* devoted itself exclusively to Communism and many people could not bring themselves to believe some of its incredible aspects.

In fact, Kohlberg maintained that "The truth, the whole truth, and nothing but the truth should have been our motto, but it was not. If we told more than 15 percent of the truth nobody would believe us and the magazine would not be useful."

Two years after *Plain Talk* folded he made a speech in

which he cited a specific case to prove his thesis—the matter of Whittaker Chambers vs. Alger Hiss.

"The editor of the magazine was Isaac Don Levine, the man who took Whittaker Chambers to Adolf Berle on September 3, 1939, and sat that evening until one o'clock in the morning while Chambers made his confession to Berle. And when he went back to his hotel Levine made notes from memory, and he still had those notes. And we decided—that was back in 1946—that we could not publish those notes. That was one of the 85 percent that we skipped because, of course, we couldn't prove it in court. Whittaker Chambers was senior editor of *Time* magazine by that time. Alger Hiss had gone up to be Secretary General of the UN, and then on to the Carnegie Foundation [Carnegie Endowment for International Peace] and we couldn't tell the truth."

One of the most interesting of all the *Plain Talk* articles was contributed by the publisher himself. Entitled "Soviet-American Spy Prodigies," it dealt with the Richard Sorge spy ring and appeared in the May 1948 issue.

Actually Sorge's nest of spies, which had done so much for the Soviet Union, had been broken by October 18, 1941, by which time most of the principals were in jail. Sorge himself was hanged in Tokyo's Sugamo Prison on November 7, 1944. When Japan surrendered, the facts about this sensational ring became known and Major General Charles A. Willoughby, MacArthur's Chief of Intelligence, amassed a vast amount of information about Sorge and his associates. According to General Willoughby, "the documentation was complete, incontestable, checked by the best talent available to MacArthur's Headquarters." But there seemed to be a reluctance on the part of Washington to publicize the case, known to the press since 1946.

Kohlberg tried to stimulate some action on October 16, 1947, when he mailed to editors a reprint of a story about the Sorge case from the *China Weekly Review* of Shanghai. To confirm that story he again circularized editors, on February 12, 1948, with a reprint of "the same story in more detail as published in the *Chicago Tribune* and based on Japanese Government records found by our G-2." The *Tribune* story and Kohlberg's covering letter referred to two members of the Sorge ring, Agnes Smedley and Guenther Stein. Miss Smedley, who had written several pro-Communist books and who had served as adviser to General Stilwell, was at the time teaching at Skidmore College, in Saratoga Springs, New York. Stein was identified as Chungking correspondent for the IPR as well as for the *Christian Science Monitor* and other dailies.

Despite Kohlberg's efforts to stir up interest in the sensational case it remained dormant. Then—whether by design or by chance is not clear—he made a trip to Japan early in 1948. This is what happened there, as he tells it in his memoirs:

"At that time no American could enter Japan without the permission of SCAP, that is, the Supreme Commander Armed Forces in the Pacific—in other words, General MacArthur. General MacArthur was a subscriber to *Plain Talk* and his Chief of Intelligence was Major General Charles A. Willoughby. So when I applied for admission I was not only granted permission to go to Japan but Willoughby invited me to be his guest while I was there. I naturally put up in a house which the Intelligence Services used as headquarters. There I ate breakfast every morning with Army Intelligence operatives and sometimes had dinner with them, although generally I was out elsewhere for dinner. I remained about a week.

"One night I came back to my room in this Intelligence house at about 11 P.M. The room had twin beds in it although I had the room to myself. On the night table between the two beds I saw a large document. It was stamped in big letters 'Confidential.' I looked at it and discovered the entire document was the report of a spy ring that had operated for the Soviet Union in Japan prior to Pearl Harbor. . . . Not knowing how it got there, but knowing that it was there for me to look at, I sat up until 2 A.M. reading this report and making notes. When I finished I put it back right where I had found it and went to bed and to sleep. The next morning I got up and went downstairs to breakfast as usual. When I returned to my room after breakfast the room had been made up and the 'Confidential' report was no longer there. I asked nobody about it but when I returned to America I wrote it for *Plain Talk* and published it with a little fanfare." It appeared in the May 1948 issue.

Kohlberg's article minced no words in discussing the people who worked with master-spy Sorge, particularly Agnes Smedley and Guenther Stein. He told how the Smedley woman organized a ring in Shanghai in 1929 and served as a recruiting officer for Sorge there. Stein was portrayed as a courier for the ring, and his home was used to store the secret radio transmitter that flashed vital information which ended up in the Kremlin.

This article doubtless prodded the War Department into taking action that was long overdue. In his book *Shanghai Conspiracy*, General Willoughby tells how on December 8, 1948, the Secretary of the Army queried Tokyo on the matter, with a reminder that a summary had been published in *Plain Talk*. The reaction, he said, was "like a string of Chinese firecrackers."

After preparing to release the story, which G-2 Tokyo was ready to furnish, Washington made an astonishing about-face. The Army Public Relations officer stated, "We have no proof to back up the charges against Miss Smedley. No names should have been used."

Going even further, Secretary of War Kenneth C. Royall appeared on "Meet the Press" on February 27, 1949, and said, "The spy release was made inadvertently. The Army should run for cover." However, the incident could not be covered up, as the Secretary seemed to hope it would be. In his *Foreign Intelligence Digest*, General Willoughby told of subsequent actions:

"We challenged the Secretary at once in an open broadcast. Miss Smedley, whom the Communist Party used as a 'feminine front,' was sufficiently encouraged to sue for libel; when we accepted promptly she lapsed into prudent silence. Then Harold Ickes got into the act. This crafty politician (who hated MacArthur for some obscure reason) published a syndicated column at the time. He orated: '. . . No one who knows Miss Smedley would ever accuse this courageous, intelligent American citizen to stoop to spy for any country—not even her own, to which she is so deeply attached.'

"All these alarms were sufficient to scare the press away from a story that Washington itself apparently repudiated. By these maneuvers, the early exposure of international Communism, involving the American Communist Party, was discouraged, stopped, emasculated!"

General Willoughby added that when the House Committee on Un-American Activities issued a supboena for Smedley they found she had skipped the country. She was traced to England. Guenther Stein vanished at the same time. Those who had championed Agnes Smedley as the victim of a vicious smear attack were made to look ridiculous not long afterwards. She was in England writing a biography of her friend General Chu-teh, the commander of the Chinese Communist "volunteers" in Korea, when she died, "under mysterious circumstances," as General Willoughby pointed out. She left her estate to General Chu-teh, and her will ordered that her body be cremated and her ashes flown to China, to the Red General, "there to be laid to rest at any place designated by him."

The success of *Plain Talk* as a forum for ideas that seemed to be taboo in so many other places gave the editor, Isaac Don Levine, ideas for expansion. Toward the end of 1948 he approached Kohlberg with the thought of enlarging the publication, to make it a full-scale magazine that would deal with politics, the arts, literature, the theater, book reviews, and current events other than those concerned with Communist issues. As editors, part or full time, Levine had in mind John Chamberlain, then with *Life*, Henry Hazlitt, who had just gone with *Newsweek* as their economist, and himself.

Former President Hoover had previously been approached by Levine and had expressed interest to the extent of trying to raise the $250,000 that Levine thought would be necessary for such a magazine. A dinner was arranged at the Waldorf-Astoria for shortly after the 1948 elections. Mr. Hoover sent out invitations but was unable to attend himself because President Truman called him to Washington to make his final report on the Hoover Study of Government Operations. In his place he sent Will Hays, former chairman of the National Republican Committee and "czar" of the motion picture industry.

"There were 25 or 30 men present," Kohlberg recalled, "including some of great wealth, such as J. Howard Pew, of the Sun Oil Company, Lammot du Pont of du Pont & Company, Ernest Weir, the steel magnate, and a few others. Don Levine, John Chamberlain, Henry Hazlitt, and Eugene Lyons made the presentation. I made a brief statement from a businessman's point of view and as the publisher of *Plain Talk*. I told them I preferred *Plain Talk* as it was to what they were proposing but as a businessman I deferred to their judgment."

By the beginning of 1950 most of the necessary money had been raised, about $200,000, of which Kohlberg had pledged $15,000. Then troubles started. Levine insisted on a strictly hands-off policy in the running of the new magazine (*The Freeman*) and agreement was about to be reached on this when he wrote an article for *Plain Talk* which accused Mervin K. Hart, of the National Economic Council, of anti-Semitism. This caused an uproar and Levine withdrew from the operation. Plans for the new magazine, however, went ahead. *The Freeman* made its appearance in September 1950. *Plain Talk*, meanwhile, expired with the May 1950 issue. Editors of the new magazine were John Chamberlain, Henry Hazlitt, and Suzanne LaFollette. Kohlberg became Treasurer.

"However," he explained, "as *The Freeman* developed I saw it operating on an expensive scale that frightened me, and so, being able to do nothing about it as the management was firmly in the Board of Editors, I resigned as Treasurer but remained as Director."

In the October 2, 1950, issue, *The Freeman* set forth its editorial policy: "It will be one of the foremost aims of *The Freeman* to clarify the concept of individual freedom and apply it to the problems of our time. . . ."

Unfortunately, friction developed among supporters of the magazine as *The Freeman* became increasingly political. In 1952 this came to a head when it openly took the side of Senator Robert A. Taft for the presidential nomination. This involved the editorial board too, and by the time the elections were over the rift was serious.

"It was my opinion," said Kohlberg, "that the differences in viewpoint were not irreconcilable, that the principal differences were personal disputes between the editors which could be smoothed over. I failed to sell this idea to the Board of Directors and a vote was taken. I sided with the pro-Taft forces, who were also the ones who were opposed to too conservative a viewpoint on economics. The other group, backed by Mr. J. Howard Pew, Mr. du Pont, and some of the other larger money people, had the majority vote. They voted to dismiss the editors who would not agree with their viewpoint. I then resigned as a Director, ending my connection with *The*

Freeman. A year or so later the magazine folded up."

As a by-product of his early writings Alfred Kohlberg was instrumental in getting a book published which remains a classic in the field of literature exposing the Communist conspiracy. Called *Blueprint for World Conquest,* it came about through a chance remark made by Max Eastman in 1945 when he read Kohlberg's pamphlet *Red Dream,* which portrayed a Soviet world of the future.

"He told me," said Kohlberg, "that *Red Dream* must surely have been based on communist documents of which he had heard but which he had never seen. This aroused my interest in those documents. I learned from Nelson Frank, of the *World-Telegram* that he knew about them and could probably find them, which he did in a second-hand book store. One was called 'The Theses and Statutes of the Communist International,' and the other 'The Program of the Communist International.' After studying them I had them published as the *Blueprint for World Conquest.*" This book appeared in 1946 with an introduction by William Henry Chamberlin, "to give the American public the opportunity to become acquainted with a summary of the philosophy which dominates Stalin and other Russian readers."

He saw to it that the book was circulated where it conceivably would do some good. Hundreds of people on his mailing list received copies, and later on it was issued commercially by the Henry Regnery Company. Now out of print, it has become virtually a collector's item. It is interesting to note that even though this could be considered his book his name appears nowhere in it.

Alfred Kohlberg contributed to the anti-Communist literature of our time in still another way, through the assistance and encouragement he gave to people who fought the menace.

As a rule the anti-Communist writer has a hard time of it. Usually he is looked upon by the liberal element that dominates the communications media as a reactionary or an extremist whose ideas must be kept from the public. This is not to say that no anti-Communist material is ever published. A Whittaker Chambers, a George Orwell, a J. Edgar Hoover, and others of this stature can get a hearing, but most anti-Communists get little encouragement from major publishers. Nor can the publishers be blamed too much in view of the treatment that can be expected at the hands of "liberal" reviewers and in the trade itself. What happened to the books about China is a case in point.

More than one anti-Communists writer found Alfred Kohlberg a friend in need, willing to help out with money to pay the rent or buy food or clothes. While he did not have the vast resources of the great foundations which were supporting the IPR and other projects, he did what he could with the money he had made in his importing business.

He helped many authors in another way, as explained by Edward Hunter, the author who made the word "brainwashing" a part of our language. When Hunter's book *Brainwashing in Red China* was published he was pleasantly surprised to learn that Kohlberg had purchased and was distributing a hundred copies of it.

"This obviously did not mean a great deal to me financially," he told me, "but it meant a lot to know that he liked my work enough to circulate it in this way."

One person who was helped by Kohlberg was a Vienna-born journalist, Julius Epstein, who had an explosive story to tell but needed assistance to break through the indifference he encountered. Kohlberg could sympathize with him because Epstein's story, too, ran counter to what Washington wanted the American public to believe.

His was the true story of the Katyn Forest massacre in which 15,000 Polish officers had been slaughtered by the Russians in 1940 to make sure they would never lead an army against the Soviet Union. When the mass graves were uncovered by German troops in 1943, Communist propaganda charged that the Germans were responsible. The Germans countered by having the bodies examined by an international medical group. Despite the findings of these experts, that the Poles had been killed three years before, when the Russians controlled that area, Communist propaganda continued its Big Lie. And our own propaganda machine, Elmer Davis's left-of-liberal Office of War Information (where Owen Lattimore had run the Far Eastern division) echoed the Kremlin line faithfully.

It was against this kind of opposition that Julius Epstein was pitted in trying to present the evidence he had compiled showing that the Russians had perpetrated this genocide. In the course of his fight Epstein had rough going, but Kohlberg helped him over the financial hurdles and in the end he too was vindicated. A Congressional investigating committee was set up which was finally able to exert enough pressure on the Pentagon to release classified reports that had concealed this monstrous Soviet atrocity.

An American, Lieutenant Colonel Donald Stewart, who, as a prisoner of war of the Germans, was called on to witness the exhumations testified before the congressional committee:

"I left Katyn convinced that the Russians had executed those men . . . that massacre just could not have been falsified or planted. . . . We did not like the Germans. But these men had been executed by the Russians!"

Certainly neither Julius Epstein nor Alfred Kohlberg had any reason to attempt to justify claims by the Nazis. But it is probably a measure of their integrity that they did not allow their personal feelings to interfere with their passion for the truth.

CHAPTER FOURTEEN

Advisers to Presidents

ALTHOUGH ALFRED KOHLBERG CAST HIS FIRST VOTE—
for William Howard Taft—as soon as he reached voting
age in 1908, there is no indication that he took much
interest in politics at that time. The only reference he
made to anything of a political nature appeared in a report
of a business trip from New York to San Francisco. He
stopped in Indianapolis in October 1916 and told of seeing a tremendous banner stretched across a square in the
center of town. More than a block long, it carried this
message:

THE COUNTRY IS OUT OF WAR AND THE STATE
IS OUT OF DEBT. THE DEMOCRATS DID IT.

Six months later, he pointed out, we were at war with
Germany. The facts were set down without comment, so

presumably his reaction was a normal American cynicism concerning the promises and performances of politicians.

It was not until November 1928 that politics played any part in his life and at that time he was directly involved, though in a minor capacity. In a letter sent from New York he said: "Election Day will be my busy day. I shall be at the polls at 187 Broome Street (under the Williamsburg Bridge) at 5:30 A.M. and will be relieved at 3 P.M. I expect considerable dissension as the usual Tammany practice of accompanying the voters into the booth must be stopped."

He went on to say that in the evening he planned to go to Hoover-Curtis headquarters, adding, "I feel confident it will be Hoover and I think New York is in doubt, though the chances here favor Smith."

Some years later the Munich Pact, the Hitler-Stalin Pact, and the outbreak of war in Europe caused Kohlberg to address letters to government officials, interpreting what was happening in the light of his global travels. He also had some personal dealings with people in the State Department. One expression he heard there troubled him because of the thinking that prompted it. He was told that "the foreign policy of the United States is not made by the State Department. It is made by public opinion and the State Department only recognizes it." He quoted this on several occasions as a possible explanation of foreign policy moves that seemed to be dictated by political expediency rather than principle.

It was a logical step for Kohlberg to go from diplomats to legislators, and it was understandable that the opinions he expressed to them concerned the subject that interested him most, China. One such letter, dated February 9, 1940 and addressed to members of the U.S. Senate, contained a statement expressing his concern over the Sino-Japanese War then raging and he suggested a way to end it. He called for a peace conference to be arranged by the

United States at which the differences between Japan and China might be worked out. If either country refused to participate, he proposed that the United States place an embargo against the recalcitrant country.

A different note crept into a letter he sent a few weeks afterward to John Lord O'Brian, who was then with the Republican National Committee. This was in the peppery style that was to become familiar later to the hundreds of recipients of his famous mimeographed letters. Commenting on the presidential nominating convention soon to begin, he said, "The party's leaders have been so consistently wrong in their judgment of foreign affairs and so wrong in their judgment of American public opinion that an unbiased observer must conclude that they will be wrong again next week." Discussing possible candidates, notably Henry L. Stimson and Frank Knox, he said, "We should nominate a Churchill and not a Chamberlain and in November with war already declared or imminent, we must not present a man or platform of Munich to the American people."

The man chosen, Wendell Willkie, apparently pleased him. At least he circulated a six-page letter supporting him, and while most of the letter was a slashing attack on Roosevelt the last paragraph was a strong plug for the Republican candidate. Kohlberg condemned the third-term candidate for his foreign and domestic policies and heaped scorn on the President's professed concern for the poor. Pointing out that all Roosevelt's friends were very rich people, he said that until he became Governor of New York at the age of 47, "nobody ever heard of him doing anything to improve the condition of the poor. Since then he has spoken on behalf of the poor morning, noon and night because he knows there are a great many more poor voters than rich ones."

Pearl Harbor caused Kohlberg to moderate his criticism of the President, but he renewed his attack when he saw

Roosevelt making deals that he knew could only result in the ascendancy of Communism in Eastern Europe and the Far East.

Kohlberg in time became an adviser to presidents and presidential candidates—though it must be admitted that his advice was not often solicited and seldom followed. The first one to whom he offered an idea was Wendell Willkie, but since this happened after Willkie had been defeated in the 1940 campaign, Kohlberg cannot be blamed for *that.*

In May 1941 Willkie was the featured speaker at a dinner held in New York for the benefit of United China Relief. He spoke about the importance of a free China market and the value of 400,000,000 Chinese customers. Afterwards Kohlberg, who had met him in Canada, took his daughter Roberta and some friends backstage to meet him.

"The next day," said Kohlberg, "I called on him and told him I thought he had made a very poor speech. I congratulated him on being there but could not say much for what he had said. He seemed somewhat shocked to hear that and invited me down to his office to discuss it further."

At this meeting Kohlberg told him that the people at that dinner were not the least bit interested in our commercial relations with China; their interest was humanitarian and patriotic. Therefore he had failed in his appeal to them. Kohlberg then explained that China was important to America for other reasons, and Willkie asked him to set down his ideas in a memorandum.

This he did. He presented a brief history of American relations with China, stressing that "America's vital interest in the Far East is the maintenance of the balance of power. To prevent the conquest of the Far East by any one power which would confront us across the Pacific with an empire of 800,000,000 people has been the object of American diplomacy for nearly one hundred years."

Telling about this incident, Kohlberg added, "I was greatly pleased in 1943 when his book *One World* was published to find that he had used this argument to explain our interest in the war on China. This item is to be found on pages 106 and 107 of the cloth bound edition."

This incident may have suggested the procedure he afterwards followed of working through political figures, presenting them with information and ideas and letting them disseminate and otherwise use them. Of course in doing so he was following the same basic procedure as an Owen Lattimore did in offering President Truman certain "facts" on which the President could make his decisions. Or a John Carter Vincent drafting a policy paper that would send General Marshall off to present an unacceptable set of conditions to Chiang Kai-shek. Unfortunately, Alfred Kohlberg's recommendations did not carry similar weight in quarters where the big decisions were then being made.

The 1944 presidential campaign presented a new opportunity to do something about an administration that Kohlberg now thoroughly distrusted. In a letter of June 28, 1944, to Herbert Brownell, Jr., who was associated with Governor Dewey as his campaign manager, he argued that the coming campaign should be fought on the issue of foreign policy, not on domestic issues. As evidences of failures in that field he said:

"Now in the 7th year of the war in China, the 5th year of the war in Europe and our 3rd year in the war, Roosevelt's only pronouncement (3 weeks ago) is to re-establish the proven failure of the bankrupt League of Nations, practically without change.

"Meantime, he has bypassed his Secretary of State to sell out Poland, and maybe France, and maybe China to the U.S.S.R. There is circumstantial evidence. (There may be leaks from China as to Wallace's demands) . . . Our fundamental interest is clear and simple. It is to prevent the establishment of any super-state anywhere in the world so big and powerful that we would always have to be armed to the teeth in fear of it."

Kohlberg urged that the United States proclaim "an extension of the Monroe Doctrine to the world" to prevent the development of such a super-state, and he set down a suggested "proclamation" for future use. It started:

"I, Thomas E. Dewey, President of the U.S.A., mindful of the sacrifices, the efforts and the hopes and aspirations of the armed forces and of the entire population of the United States . . ."

Mr. Dewey, of course, never had occasion to use this proclamation, but Kohlberg was reconciled in advance to the defeat of his candidate. Writing to Herbert Brownell the night before the election, he said:

"If Mr. Dewey should, as I do not expect, be elected tomorrow, he will inherit from Mr. Roosevelt an American foreign policy already sold out to a dictator possibly more ruthless and cruel than Hitler, certainly more powerful, and with a stronger fifth-column in every country in the world. Mr. Dewey, in inheriting this black situation and in attempting to save some of the high principles of the Atlantic Charter and the Declaration of Cairo from the wreck, would be made by the opposition to appear to have caused the mess and would, undoubtedly, be blamed for it by the mass of the people."Kohlberg was more optimistic about Republican chances in 1948. In the same letter he pointed out that Mr. Dewey had the opportunity, as leader of the opposition, of being "as eternally right as was Mr. Churchill when he was an opposition of one and of being the only available man when the Democratic Party busts wide open and the country turns Republican, as it certainly will in 1948."

Kohlberg did not, however, wait until 1948 to offer

further advice. In letters to Brownell he kept urging a forthright position.

"Recent Republican pronouncements on foreign affairs," he said in one letter, "have been timid evasions of the truth . . . Therefore I appeal to you for a strong, fearless and honest Republican position on the dangers that face the Republic, an abandonment of the 'me-too' approval of Democratic appeasement and the Coué diplomacy of proclaiming everything is better in the world every day, while we sell out the liberties of hundreds of millions of people in nations which were independent before World War II."

In another letter he argued, "It seems to me the job that Mr. Dewey and the Republicans owe the country is to be right two years from now and not necessarily seem either popular or correct today."

Some of Kohlberg's messages obviously got through to the Governor because in 1947 there was correspondence between the two men, with Kohlberg offering more advice. One suggestion was that "our Party could properly demand a complete exposure of all secret agreements entered into, prior to its agreement to support the President in implementing a policy the essentials of which he still conceals. No niceties of consideration for the memory of the former President should permit the continued concealment of his acts from the American public . . ."

This call for a "complete exposure of all secret agreements" coincided with a campaign, critical of U.S. foreign policy, that Kohlberg was carrying on himself, personally and through the American China Policy Association. Letters of a highly critical nature were addressed to President Truman and to George C. Marshall, then serving as Secretary of State. These were also released to the press, to keep their contents from being completely overlooked.

In one of these letters he bluntly told Truman: "It took genius to lose the cold war. It took hundreds of wrong decisions to reduce you to the necessity of calling for help to challenge a scarcely fifth-rate Soviet satellite [North Korea]. It took scores of wrong decisions to bring about the conquest of one-third of the world in the last 5 years, without the shedding of a drop of Russian blood. And all by a punch-drunk Soviet Union which had seen half its European territory ravaged, 20,000,000 of its sons and daughters slain, and 1,000,000 of its army in revolt at the end of World War II.

The President ignored all of Kohlberg's letters but one. On January 14, 1948, Kohlberg wrote protesting the appointment of Dr. Frank P. Graham as U.S. Representative on the UN Security Council Committee on Indonesia. Dr. Graham was much too liberal to suit Kohlberg and in his letter to the President he cited some of Graham's recent activities. On January 17 the President replied: "I read your letter of the fourteenth about Dr. Frank Porter Graham with considerable surprise. I consider Dr. Graham a very able and patriotic citizen. He made a wonderful contribution to the war effort and he has made a contribution in the Far Eastern situation which is now nearing a solution, I hope."

Kohlberg made many efforts to persuade Governor Dewey to take a strong stand on China, and the most noteworthy was in the form of a lengthy memorandum sent to the Governor's secretary, Paul Lockwood, on November 11, 1947. This was submitted to the Governor at his request following a meeting that Kohlberg had with him and Mr. Lockwood. Part of this, containing Kohlberg's recommendations for scaling down William C. Bullitt's proposals for financial aid to China, was referred to in an earlier chapter. However, there was more to the memorandum. Kohlberg made some pointed references to certain State Department personnel and their "treasonable actions" with the notation that "Corroboration is available for all statements in this memo." One of the most

interesting parts of the memorandum was the suggestion
that a demand be made for publication of certain reports
and documents that were being kept secret by the Administration. Eight items were listed:

1. Henry Wallace's report of 1944.
2. Telegrams, reports, etc., concerning Stilwell.
3. Report on Chinese Communists made by Army
   Intelligence in 1945.
4. *Full* text of Yalta agreements and conversations
   leading to same.
5. Text of Potsdam agreements, with understandings
   on China, none of which had been released.
6. Recommendations of Far Eastern Division of State
   Department made in 1946 recommending abandonment of China.
7. Release of Wedemeyer Report.
8. Release of OSS and FBI reports on present and
   past personnel of Far Eastern Division of State
   Department.

It is entirely possible that some of Kohlberg's ideas
struck fire because two weeks later Governor Dewey, in
a speech at a dinner of the alumni of Columbia University
Law School, demanded that the United States help China.
He also expressed strong criticism of Administration policies in the Far East. He described "the strange spectacle
of our own President, publicly ordering our Chinese allies,
under pain of losing American support, to accept into
their government the very Communists who seek to destroy it."

More than two years later, on July 13, 1950, Kohlberg
had occasion to refer to this speech in a letter he sent to
Governor Dewey, again on the subject of foreign policy.
"I trust you will pardon me as an older Republican," he
wrote, "for saying that under your leadership the Republican Party has been remiss in its duty to the country. It has

failed to explain and denounce the combination of treason and incompetence that has brought us to the verge of disaster, now becoming so apparent in the hills and rice paddies of Korea. Your speech of November 23, 1947, on China and Korea was a classic and predicted exactly the very disaster that has now befallen us in both countries, But neither you nor the Party carried through."

Kohlberg was not content to tell his story to just one Republican leader. The same arguments were advanced "through friends" to Senator Taft, Senator Bridges, Alf Landon, and Governor Stassen. Indeed, he made a trip to Topeka late in November 1947 to see Mr. Landon personally, but, according to Mrs. Kohlberg, the former Presidential candidate showed little interest in what Kohlberg had to say.

Although Kohlberg scoffed at our bipartisan policy of the time, in which Republican leaders usually acquiesced in Democratic decisions and actions, he employed a bipartisan approach himself in offering a plank on China for the platforms of both parties. In letters sent on June 12, 1948, to the Chairman of the Resolutions Committee of the Democratic National Convention, and to his opposite number in the Republican Party, Kohlberg offered this plank for consideration: "The _____ Party reaffirms the principles of the Open Door Policy and pledges support to the National Government of China in its efforts to regain sovereignty over all China, including Manchuria with its ports of Dairen and Port Arthur. To attain these objectives we promise to that Government adequate financial aid, military supplies, advice and training."

The Republican Party's 1948 platform put Alfred's suggestion somewhat differently: "We will foster and cherish our historic policy of friendship with China and assert our deep interest in the maintenance of its dignity and freedom." The Democratic Party platform talked at some length about foreign policy but managed to ignore China entirely while considering the problems of Italy, Hungary, Israel, Poland, Bulgaria, Romania, and, of course, the United Nations.

As further contributions to the Republican campaign, Kohlberg sent Herbert Brownell a slogan and a check. The slogan was "Thomas E. Dewey is the man to get the government out of the red and the Reds out of government." The check was for $5,000. Shortly after this he expressed these misgivings to Brownell:

"If Mr. Dewey is going to repeat his 1944 role of acquiescent dupe of the Russian agents and the assorted confused liberals, pacifists, and career yes-men in the White House and State Department, I shall lose some enthusiasm for him."

In an attempt to persuade Governor Dewey to take a strong stand on the Communist issue, particularly as it concerned foreign policy, a committee was set up to compile factual material that he could use. Presumably, the Governor had expressed interest in getting such material. In a memorandum Kohlberg wrote on September 7, 1948 he said:

"Mr. Dewey gave us two long range tasks in addition to campaign aid as the occasion might arise. The first of these was to discuss, develop and propose a long range foreign policy . . ."

The memorandum was addressed to "Messrs. Loeb, Humphreys, Lyons, Schuyler & Woltman."

One of them, George S. Schuyler, in his recent book *Black and Conservative* tells about this operation:

"When Thomas E. Dewey won the Republican nomination for President, a group of outstanding anti-Communists arranged to confer with him in Albany, New York, in the hope that we might be able to prevail upon him to make two or three speeches dealing exclusively with the Communist menace in government. The Truman Administration was very vulnerable on this point and we felt that if Dewey made a head-on attack on the Red issue, he would win the election.

"The delegation was led by Senator Styles Bridges of New Hampshire and included Alfred Kohlberg, William Loeb, publisher of the *Manchester Union Leader,* Isaac Don Levine, Louis Waldman, and myself. We first met for lunch, and afterwards went to the Governor's office.

"Mr. Dewey seemed super-confident about being elected. We conversed for some time but we were unable to bring him around to our viewpoint. He would only say he would touch upon the subject of Communism in some of his speeches but not devote any speech exclusively to the subject. We felt that would be a mistake, and said so. Dewey lost by a narrow margin."

Kohlberg was convinced that Dewey's defeat was the result of the Republican Party's equivocal stand on foreign policy and he made this clear in a letter to the Chairman of the New York State Republican Committee who had invited him to attend a fund-raising dinner at $100 a plate. Kohlberg refused the invitation.

"My reason," he said, "is because I feel the Republican Party has failed in its duty to the Republic."

In a three-page letter he told of "Democratic betrayal of America's traditional foreign policies; of American principles; of America's wartime pledges; and of the cause of freedom everywhere." He said the Republican Party had gone along with these things, making no effective protest, and had even given approval to certain reprehensible actions.

"Because there is nowhere else to go," he concluded, "I shall have to remain a Republican. I cannot, however, support the present timid leadership of the Party, subservient as it is to Democratic initiative in foreign affairs."

He did not, however, stop corresponding with Governor Dewey. When the occasion warranted he would write to Albany, usually with information that Kohlberg thought might be helpful.

The re-election of Robert A. Taft to the Senate caused Kohlberg to visit him in Washington to offer his congratulations, and a memorandum of the visit is interesting in showing the thinking of the two men:

"I took the liberty of saying to Senator Taft that great numbers of his fellow citizens were looking to him to give the leadership in world affairs for which they had looked to President Truman in vain. And I said to the Senator, 'But they look to you in vain, also.'

" 'You are quite right.' he said, 'but how can I give leadership in world affairs when the President keeps all the information brought to him by the State Department and the Intelligence services secret from me? Think how cockeyed I could prove, shooting off my mouth without that information.'

"I begged to differ with the Senator. 'You do not have day to day dope,' I said, 'but that is of minor importance compared to full knowledge of the enemy's long-time strategy and tactics which are not secret."

Probably the best proof of Kohlberg's contention that Communism's moves are predictable can be found in the way he was able to call the turn on Communist actions that completely confused many others. To Kohlberg it was very simple. Communists had to go by the book, and if you knew what was in the book you knew what they would do.

Kohlberg's constant jibes at the Administration finally produced one result. "The Treasury Department," he explained, "put me on their special list for full investigation and sent one of their specialists to my office in August 1950. After six weeks of investigation of my personal returns, he found that I had overpaid my income tax in two of the years which were not outlawed, and I received a refund of a few hundred dollars."

Most people would have been satisfied with this, but

Kohlberg sent a sharp letter to the Secretary of the Treasury in which he deplored the waste of time and money represented by the investigation. The same investigator was sent back to Kohlberg's offices for further study.

"He found nothing wrong," said Kohlberg, "except that beginning with 1948 he disallowed a great number of expenses which had been allowed previously. The disallowed items ran as much as $20,000 to $30,000 of tax per annum, beginning with 1948 and running to 1949 and 1950 . . ."

Glad to get a chance to fight this in court he paid the tax under protest, but the Treasury did nothing about his protests. In 1955, unable to go into court because of a second coronary attack, he instructed his lawyers to make a settlement, and he got back half the additional tax he had paid.

Later on there was further government harassment involving his business.

"After consulting with the Foreign Assets Control Section of the Treasury in 1952," he wrote, "I sent linens to Hong Kong to make handkerchiefs. At each stage of the operation I consulted with the Treasury and they encouraged me to go ahead. When, however, the handkerchiefs were finished they refused to license the import. This also meant a lawsuit, which I had to carry through and finally won against the Treasury."

Involved were handkerchiefs worth $90,000 which Kohlberg maintained had been made in Hong Kong. The weakness of the government's contention that they had been made in Red China is indicated by a Treasury Department spokesman who was quoted as having said that the department was not accusing Kohlberg of having had the handkerchiefs made in Red China but that "we are only saying he has not proved they were not."

The incident was made to order for the left-wing press. The *New Republic,* for example, told that "the voluble

New York propagandist who seven years ago led the China Lobby's attack on the State Department's now-exiled China hands," had been "hoist with his own petard." Even though Kohlberg won his case against the bureaucrats, the story of his alleged commercial dealings with Red China has now become a stock item of left-wing folklore, offered as fact.

In 1952 Alfred and Ida Kohlberg made a trip to Chicago to attend the Republican National Convention. Kohlberg was a staunch Taft supporter and fully expected that "Mr. Republican" would get the nomination. However, he may have been instrumental in making Dwight D. Eisenhower the candidate. As Mrs. Kohlberg told the story, when General Eisenhower was at Columbia University he confided to a friend that he was anxious to be briefed on certain aspects of Communism, and this person spoke to Alfred Kohlberg who suggested Louis F. Budenz or Richard M. Nixon for the job. Nixon was called in and later wrote to Kohlberg, speaking of the General in the most enthusiastic terms.

The aftermath of this came at the convention. Mrs. Kohlberg said that when they talked to Richard Nixon at the convention they were surprised to learn that he intended to support Eisenhower, not their favorite, Bob Taft.

This did not, however, disrupt their friendship. Kohlberg strongly supported Eisenhower over Adlai Stevenson, and exerted special effort in Nixon's behalf. Later on friendly notes passed between the two men, with Kohlberg often pssing along information or calling attention to something that he thought would interest the Vice President. The letters were informal, on a "My dear Dick," and a "Dear Alfred" basis. That Mr. Nixon appreciated the correspondence is indicated by a letter dated March 26, 1958:

"This is just a note to thank you for taking the trouble

to send me your memorandum of February 20. You have a rare ability to state broad general principles in simple, understandable language. I am going to take the liberty of plagiarizing some of your comments in speeches I will be making in the next few months."

Kohlberg's relations with President Eisenhower were on a different plane. There was never a meeting of the two men and letters addressed to him were infrequent and formal. One such letter, which the President said he found interesting, had a personal touch and was written in 1953:

"While I was on Quemoy Island last week," Kohlberg wrote President Eisenhower, "two Nationalist Chinese spies returned from the mainland. They reported that the people of the village where they had hidden were called to an indoctrination meeting by the Communist cadres. At this meeting they were told by the Communist lecturers that Chiang Kai-shek was no longer War Criminal #1, but had been promoted to War Criminal #2. The new War Criminal #1, they were told, was a man named Ai Sheng How Wei Erh, of whom, of course, they had never heard.

"So the lecturers explained that Ai Sheng How Wei Erh was dictator of the Imperialist United States, a warmonger and intent on conquering the world and turning it over to the enslavery of the American capitalists, to whom the proletariat of that unhappy country were already enslaved. The village people asked the Nationalist spies if this was true and whether Ai Sheng How Wei Erh was actually on his way with a large army to liberate them."

In the early part of Eisenhower's administration, Kohlberg was inclined to be tolerant of the new President. He wrote him, for example, on June 3, 1953, as follows:

"Last March, when I was in Formosa at the same time as Adlai Stevenson, I told my Chinese friends that I had worked hard to make Governor Stevenson's trip possible by helping defeat him for President . . . Since my return I have been greatly disturbed by a growing dissatisfaction with you and your administration—especially among rank and file Americans. They seem to feel that you have succumbed to the wiles of the same ill-advisers who led President Truman from the unconditional victories of 1945 to the near-disaster that confronts us now.

"Although I am not well-informed on Washington, I do not accept this viewpoint. I think your acceptance of virtual defeat in Korea is enjoined on you by the disastrous state of the world, the overwhelming power of the Soviets, and the weaknesses of our possible allies, and is to be blamed on the previous Administration."

Two years later he was apparently disenchanted, and wrote the President as follows:

"My first vote was cast for William Howard Taft in 1908. In 1910 I was a charter member of the Lincoln-Roosevelt League (in California), forerunner of the Progressive Party of 1912. That was my only venture into revolt; I've been a Republican ever since. But now, at 68, I'm revolting again and, if a mouse may challenge a lion, here, sir, is my card. I have no seconds.

"This time, as in 1910, I am not leaving the Republican Party, just challenging the control which I believe to be in bad hands. Yours, I mean. For I have learned at last that the U.S.I.A. boys were right and I was just plain stupid. It is apparent to me, as it was not then, that in spite of the anti-Communist, anti-containment and pro-liberation planks of the 1952 platform, you have joined the neutralists . . ."

Alfred Kohlberg's "revolt" was the result of an extensive trip through Europe the previous year where, he said, he had found U.S.I.A. people "playing ball with the neutralists." When Kohlberg asked why, they told him that "the climate of intellectual opinion was so leftist that they could not be openly anti-Communist." Kohlberg was also annoyed because these people were doing nothing to discourage the idea that the United States was on the verge of a fascist putsch led by Senator McCarthy.

Although Alfred Kohlberg could be bitter in his criticism of a person's public actions, an entirely different note could be found in personal letters to the same person. Certainly he was no admirer of Henry Wallace as a public figure, but a series of letters he wrote him, starting in 1950, he introduced himself as the "persistent critic" of the IPR and said: "By your resignation from the Progressive Party, you and I are now both free of party entanglements and hoping to find a road for world peace. Your road and mine, of course, are different, but the goal is the same . . ."

Kohlberg suggested a meeting at Wallace's home in South Salem, New York, but Wallace replied that he was so busy with correspondence and "duties around the farm" that a meeting was out of the question. The correspondence, however, continued. In a letter dated September 9, 1952, Wallace made a revealing statement. Thanking Kohlberg for some information he had sent him he said: "It confirms me in my view that the extremists, knowing my objectives, never wanted me to build a strong middle-of-the-road progressive movement. They came out for me in 1948 to cut down my vote. I recognized this at Sandwich Center, N.H., in the fall of 1948 when I said that if they would run a ticket of their own I would gain three million votes. My mistake was in not repeating this again and again."

To which Kohlberg replied: "I quite agree that you would have done better had you divorced yourself from the Communists in '48, but the trouble was that they turned up all around you. . . . Why not come out and admit the Commies completely fooled you, as they formerly did me and many better men, and then tell what they put over on you, so as to warn your fellow Americans who are still naive and lack experience. . . ?"

Kohlberg showed little interest in the 1956 campaign. In 1954 he suffered the first of several heart attacks and these curtailed his activities. Most of his available energies were concentrated on "A Program to Govern Our Foreign Relations," which was announced in full-page newspaper advertisements in 1955.

He did not, however, stop writing letters, and on January 9, 1958, he addressed himself to Sherman Adams, President Eisenhower's assistant at the White House. For "Dear Sherm" he had a suggestion. Quoting *The Worker,* he pointed out that the Chinese Communists had sent 800,000 bureaucrats out to work on the farms. According to the Communists, this was not only good for their health, it made them more efficient in their government jobs. Why not a similar project for American bureaucrats?

"Sherm" took it in stride, and countered with an interesting proposition to "Dear Alfred." After a cordial greeting to the "sole proprietor of the China Lobby," he wrote:

"Why should you continue to burden yourself with sole responsibility for the China Lobby? Surely it is high time to let the public in on this magnificent enterprise. I shall be happy if you will allow me to consult a number of eminent persons in Wall Street and the National Press Club, who will join with me in forming a syndicate to take the China Lobby off your hands. Incorporated either in Delaware or the Dominican Republic, it could be organized and expanded and diversified in a number of scientific ways, with stock ownership both common and preferred and also interstitial and peripheral, to say nothing of all those debentures.

"At this moment, I need go no further in suggesting the financial possibilities. What is far more important, of course, is the immense vista of opinion-molding potentialities. Remembering, as I do, how often Drew Pearson and Elmer Davis expressed themselves on the subject of the China Lobby (who could forget Elmer's pet phrase, 'Alfred Kohlberg, the China Lobby Man'?) it seems to me that both Drew and Elmer would be eager to join with me in forming the Syndicate. . . . What is your asking price? Let's begin haggling."

In a somewhat different vein was an exchange of correspondence with President Gamal Abdel Nasser, of the United Arab Republic. This took place in 1959, and it was Kohlberg's last correspondence with a head of state. He wrote to Nasser warning him of the dangers of collaborating with Communists. These are Nasser's words of explanation:

"National movement in Asia and Africa are directed against liberation from exploiting foreign dominion in the interest of national sovereignty and economy. It is calculated with a view to emancipating the African and Asiatic citizen, long subjected to bondage and exploitation at the hands of colonialists . . .

"We believe that the battle waged by liberty against colonialism and dominion is one integrated and unified battle despite different battlefields and no possible guarantee for the future security of the Afro-Asiatic States, so long as foreign dominion is closely and tightly on the scene.

"That is why we are determined to give ourselves devotedly to the role, we are destined to fulfil in the battle for the liberation of Africa and Asia from the exploiting forces, which deny us our liberty, independence and equality.

"But in doing so we are not passing from one yoke into another. This is evidenced by the fact explicably and repeatedly stated that our policy is one of positive neutrality emerging from our free conscience weaving our web of international relations on the basis of equality and mutual benefit . . .

"As regards the U.S.S.R., it has always backed resurgent nationalities and liberation movements morally and materially in the latter respect almost unconditionally. Would not this a nobler attitude commendable enough? But in no sense do we allow the U.S.S.R. the least shadow in the exercise of our national sovereignty. Russia is even conscious of our further reaches—that Communism is banned in our country, imprisons to the essential of our social structure."

Many things could be read into President Nasser's letter. Alfred Kohlberg was impressed by Nasser's statement that he had banned the Communist Party in the U.A.R., even though the Soviet was extending aid. In circulating Nasser's letter to members of the 86th Congress he suggested that we follow Nasser's example in this country "by making overt activity on behalf of World Communism constitutionally treasonable, as we all know it to be."

As for Kohlberg's warning of the dangers of collaboration with Communists, this obviously did not trouble Nasser. The Communists might pose a threat to some people but *he* knew how to handle them. Which seems to prove that politicians all over the world speak the same language and keep repeating the same nonsense.

CHAPTER FIFTEEN

The Organization Man

THE AVERAGE PERSON HAS A STEREOTYPE CONCEPT OF Communists and the duties they perform for the party. He looks upon most of them as dedicated troublemakers who go in for picketing and demonstrating, while a few in the upper brackets specialize in stealing military secrets and engaging in sabotage for the Soviet Union.

Certainly there is some truth to this. One can see Red judas goats leading docile followers in all sorts of protest marches and engaging in other activities that are definitely not in this nation's interest. As for upper-echelon activities, there is ample testimony concerning such people as the Rosenbergs, Morton Sobell, Rudolf Abel, Philip Jaffe, Steve Nelson, and a host of others who made themselves useful to the Soviet Union. However, even the best, or worst, of these characters don't rate with the Russiafirsters who are in a position to make or influence foreign policy. Here we get to the big-time operators, such people as Alger Hiss, participating in the Yalta Conference or helping to set up the United Nations; or a Harry Dexter White, drafting a plan for Henry Morgenthau's signature, the infamous Morgenthau Plan, designed to turn Germany into a helpless pawn of the USSR.

Indeed, it is in this area that the Communists have made their most spectacular gains. As far back as 1933 they infiltrated the Department of Agriculture, and the cell there divided and formed other Red organisms that, cancer-like, moved into other and more strategic branches of government.

The State Department, naturally, was a prime target and the story of Communist successes there has been spelled out in millions of words of testimony. Even so, there has never been a concerted move on the part of top officials to clean up this situation or even admit officially that it ever existed to a dangerous extent. Moves to force a cleanup have invariably met with violent reaction. Senator McCarthy's experience is an excellent case in point.

A major reason is that any attack on an Alger Hiss, a William Remington, or a Harry Dexter White is interpreted by their political superiors as an attack on them, and a threat to their position. So, regardless of the facts and heedless of the nation's security, the protective association goes into action. We have seen important people turning up as character witnesses even for an Alger Hiss, and we have seen other types of aid and comfort extended to such people. All this is in strange contrast to the treatment accorded those who have tried to present the facts about these people and their peculiar projects. Indeed, it is as though a doctor were sued for malpractice because he discovered a cancer and said it had to be removed to save a patient's life.

Alfred Kohlberg was in the position of such a hapless

doctor and he realized his position would be stronger if he had an organization to back his efforts. This idea may have been suggested by the IPR's success in getting things done. By themselves, such people as Frederick Vanderbilt Field, Owen Lattimore, Lawrence K. Rosinger, and others had limited effectiveness. But working through the Institute of Pacific Relations with its awe-inspiring roster of trustees, and with publications at hand to disseminate their ideas, these people were able to accomplish a great deal indeed.

Kohlberg set up an organization called the American China Policy Association. This followed an unsuccessful attempt made by Christopher Emmet, Jr., late in 1945, to set up a similar organization.

"Shortly thereafter," said Kohlberg, "early in 1946 a meeting was called at the apartment of Edna Lonigan, a professor at Brooklyn College. Among those present was J. B. Powell, who had been the dean of American newspaper correspondents in China and editor of the *China Weekly Review*. Powell had been seized by the Japanese at the time of Pearl Harbor and so badly beaten and mistreated in prison in Shanghai that, when he was finally repatriated on the *Gripsholm* exchange ship, his feet were beyond saving. . . . Out of that meeting came other meetings which resulted in the formation of the American China Policy Association, Inc., with J. B. Powell as President and a number of moderately well known Americans as officers and directors. I was elected Vice President and Chairman of the Board."

It has been charged that in setting up the ACPA Kohlberg was motivated by spite, to get back at the IPR. The fact is that he never looked upon the ACPA as a competitive organization. This is implicit in a letter he wrote to his sister in 1947, long after the organization was functioning:

"I have not thought of either attempting to reorganize

the IPR or start a counter organization for several reasons: (1) such an organization cannot be born full grown but must develop over the years; (2) before such a new organization could be effective the IPR will, I am sure, be either blown up or taken over by the government as an enemy organization . . . I regret this because the IPR could be a useful organization."

Indeed at the time he started the ACPA in 1946, he was still a member of the IPR and was fighting in the courts for the right to circularize the membership to ask their help in his call for an investigation. For that matter, the two organizations were essentially different in approach. Theoretically, at least, the IPR was supposed to be scholarly and objective, representing many nations and varying points of view. Kohlberg's ACPA had entirely different aims.

"When we first discussed the organization," Miss Lonigan told the writer, "Kohlberg made it clear that ours was to be an all-American policy. There were to be no Chinese associated with it, only Americans. We were to operate not with the idea of what was good for China but what was good for America."

Which was a remarkably strange attitude for a man who was supposed to be the China Lobby incarnate.

In Miss Lonigan the ACPA had an associate who not only had excellent academic credentials but considerable Washington experience. She had served as an adviser to Secretary of the Treasury Morgenthau and had seen the pattern of Communist infiltration in government, from the time it started in 1933.

Helen M. Loomis, who joined the ACPA as secretary, had a different background. She had been a missionary in China and was sent back to this country by missionary groups to tell what was happening in that country under Japanese rule. The story of Japanese atrocities was not getting through in this country because newspapers here still recalled how they had been hoodwinked during World War I. Editors were still leery of reports that reminded them of propaganda stories that had told of the boche cutting off the hands of women and children and other bestialities.

Miss Loomis had convinced the press of the authenticity of her material by releasing, without comment, reports that came to her from mission stations all over China. Miss Loomis, incidentally, remained with the ACPA until 1949 when she returned to Singapore to teach.

As for Kohlberg, according to Edna Lonigan he contributed four very important things: "He had a vast amount of information, a printing press, a mailing list, and stamps." She noted that he had something else, too—a certain invulnerability. "They couldn't destroy him. They couldn't get at him through his job, his income, or his reputation."

For his Board of Directors, Kohlberg was able to enlist a group of Americans every bit as distinguished as those the IPR boasted. One was Clare Booth Luce, who succeeded to the Presidency of the ACPA when Powell died in 1947. Sharing Vice Presidential honors with Kohlberg were Irene Corbally Kuhn and Dr. Maurice William.

At the time the ACPA started there was an urgent need for information to balance the sort of material that was emanating from official channels and from the liberal and left-wing segment of the press. General Marshall was in China and the State Department's big drive was on to force Chiang to accept Communists into a coalition government. As Kohlberg explained the situation:

"Much of what he [Marshall] was doing was kept secret; and, on top of that, most of the press was represented in China by leftists of different varieties. Some were out-and-out Communists . . . and most of the rest were what might be called naive fellow travelers. As a result, American understanding of what was going on was very confused."

The first effort of the ACPA to correct this was in a document called the Manchurian Manifesto, issued July 24, 1946. This was a protest to Secretary of State Byrnes concerning a statement made by Under Secretary Dean Acheson promising American training and supplies to Chinese Communist armies prior to their incorporation in the National Army of China. The Manifesto strongly opposed this and in so doing it presented some recent Chinese history and Communist documents which made it clear that the Communists intended to seize control of China, and General Marshall's actions were helping them in this effort. Among the signers of the Manchurian Manifesto were such distinguished Americans as Sidney Hook, Norman Thomas, Max Eastman, Christopher Emmet, Jr., John Earl Baker, Felix Morley, Major General David O. Barrows, Clarence Streit, and others of this caliber.

It is doubtful that the signers of the Manifesto, as realists, seriously expected that this would bring the State Department up short. That probably was not the idea. Thanks to Kohlberg's printing facilities, his mailing list, and those stamps mentioned by Miss Lonigan, the Manifesto landed on city desks across the nation. And in view of the prominence of the signers it could not be brushed off as a crackpot contribution. At the very least it may have done some good by arousing doubts concerning the Marshall Mission in China.

The ACPA did not limit its efforts to keeping the press informed of things that otherwise might have escaped attention. On September 6, 1946, for example, it sent President Truman a document which it felt might interest him—with Alfred Kohlberg serving as messenger. This was "a translation from the Chinese of Notice #16 of the Central Political Bureau of the Communist Party of China." This document purported to reveal "the continuance of Russian control of the Chinese Communist Party. ... Notice #16 also states the negotiations carried on with

General Marshall by the Chinese Communist negotiators headed by Chou En-lai, are deceitful and without intention of agreement."

There was more in this vein, and the covering letter to Mr. Truman urged that Russia be told to keep hands off China and "the perfidy of the Chinese Communists be denounced and all support of them and their causes be completely abandoned."

In a memo to directors and members of the ACPA, Kohlberg reported that this document had been "delivered to Charles Ross, press secretary to the President, by me last Friday." He also mentioned that it was later released to the press and was carried in summary by the three major wire services. As a postscript he added: "Tass News Agency telephoned me and asked if they could have the complete text of the above if they sent a messenger. A complete copy was given to them."

In the fourteen years of its existence, until Kohlberg's death in 1960, the American China Policy Association maintained a constant flow of releases, supplementing those sent out by Alfred Kohlberg as an individual. These provided editors and others with information that quite often was not made available to them through other channels. Occasionally the releases would be accompanied by reprints of material that had appeared elsewhere, and in many cases factual errors and distortions in this material were sharply pointed out. Very often the releases were in the form of open letters to high government officials, and these frequently asked questions that must have made the recipients wince.

Through the ACPA releases one can follow fairly closely what was happening in China, as well as events in the United States that were bound to have an effect on China's destiny. For example, during 1946 and in the early part of 1947, emphasis was placed on General Marshall's activities in China, with little of the reverence that was customarily shown the General. One release quoted Marshall's naive remark of January 7, 1947, that "on the side of the Chinese Communist Party there are, I believe, liberals as well as radicals ..." This was not done to poke fun at the General but rather to show how little understanding he had of the problem he had been sent to solve.

Released with this item, as a double feature, was a reproduction of a news story from a Shanghai paper telling how the General had placed his plane at the service of Chou En-lai, the wily Communist negotiator. There was another reference to this in a report Kohlberg made to the American China Policy Association. He was in China at the time Chou borrowed Marshall's plane and he quoted a story in the *Shanghai Evening Post and Mercury* which told that Chou had loaded the plane "with several hundredweight of clothing and foodstuffs" for his use in Yenan. Kohlberg sarcastically commented that this planeload of stuff was "no doubt purchased out of savings from his pay which is presumed to be the same as that of a private."

One of the Big Lies of the late 1940's was the allegation that the United States had given Chiang Kai-shek billions of dollars which he had either wasted or allowed to be stolen by a favored few insiders. This was the line used by apologists for the State Department and it was generally accepted as official. Actually the figures were highly inflated and distorted, and the ACPA repeatedly tried to call attention to the facts. Subsequently the State Department in its 1949 White Paper admitted that only $2 billion had been given to Chiang since VJ-Day, and even here Kohlberg through the ACPA was able to show this was an inflated figure arrived at in devious fashion.

The White Paper itself became a major issue with the ACPA. Said to have been prepared under the direction of Philip C. Jessup, Kohlberg's old adversary in the IPR, this verbose document of 1054 pages set out to prove certain things, as set forth thus in the conclusion:

"The unfortunate but inescapable fact is that the ominous result of the civil war in China was beyond the control of the government of the United States. Nothing that this country did or could have done within the reasonable limits of its capabilities could have changed that result; nothing that was left undone by this country contributed to it. It was the product of internal Chinese forces, forces which this country tried to influence but could not. A decision was arrived at within China, if only a decision by default."

As soon as Kohlberg could get a copy of the White Paper he went to work on it. Helping on this project was Edna Lonigan, who said, "I sat down with him at his home and we went over the entire thing in a few hours. He knew all the details and so within 48 hours we had our answer circulated through the ACPA." Kohlberg made this comment on the White Paper: "[in] August 1949 our State Department issued the White Paper on China, 409 pages of self-serving statement, which has already become full of holes. And 605 pages of Appendix. Now we can skip the 409 pages but the 605 pages are a strange assortment of documents. In it there are sections by John S. Service, John K. Emmerson, John Paton Davies, and others of our diplomats out there. But none of the reports of Pat Hurley, of General Wedemeyer and some of the other top men we had out there. For the purpose of these pages, whether they knew it or not, was to make clear in official documents the fact that while China was our fighting ally we were preparing its betrayal . . ."

Another caustic comment on the White Paper was made by General Pat Hurley in a release sent to newspapers and radio on August 7:

"Nearly all the officials relieved by me in China because they were pro-Communist are now in the State Department—presumably writing alibi White Papers."

A few months after our State Department issued its White Paper the Republic of China also issued one and presented it before the United Nations. This set forth shocking particulars of Soviet duplicity in the fall of China to Communism, and provided details of Russian thievery of property in Manchuria, property valued at $800,000,-000. No words were minced in the references to the Communist criminals. Certain that few newspapers were likely to get more than a highly condensed version of this story, or possibly a highly distorted one, the ACPA saw to it that editors got a copy of the Chinese White Paper in its entirety.

When Chiang Kai-shek and the remnants of his army fled to Formosa, the ACPA fought moves that were being made to allow the Chinese Communists to seize that sanctuary. It also strongly opposed strenuous diplomatic efforts that were being exerted to recognize Red China, welcome it into the United Nations, and even extend aid to it. When Mao Tse-tung's legions entered the Korean War it argued that Chiang should be allowed to help us in that conflict.

The last ACPA release, dated March 17, 1960, was addressed to the attention of the "Chief Editorial Writer." It discussed a letter, a copy of which was attached, from Secretary of State Christian Herter. This letter, received in reply to one sent by Kohlberg, emphatically denied a current report that this country was planning to recognize Red China. The ACPA statement contained the following paragraph:

"How any other policy could be even considered, in view of our Treaty of Military Alliance with the Republic of China, it would be difficult to understand, but there seems to be a Red China Lobby pressing for a change of policy and negotiations with the Red Chinese. This Lobby calls for 'negotiations' with Red China, in which they suggest that only we might compromise."

Which sounds strangely like the pitch of what might be called the North Vietnam Lobby that is so active in the United States today.

Alfred Kohlberg received some valuable assistance at a crucial period when it appeared that the liberal element calling for recognition of Red China would get its way. This support came from the Reverend James Keller of The Christophers. Kohlberg was friendly with Father Keller who had discussed The Christophers with him at the time he was starting the organization.

"I couldn't quite understand what he had in mind," Kohlberg later admitted, "and advised against the attempt, but he went on with it and was extremely successful."

At that time there were 115,000 Christophers, people opposed to Communism and other evils, and Kohlberg pointed out to Father Keller that recognition of Red China would mean a great gain for world Communism. The priest offered to help.

"We jointly wrote out a postcard," said Kohlberg, "calling on members to write the President, the Secretary of State and their Senators and Congressmen, opposing the recognition of Red China. I agreed to pay for the postal cards and we decided to try 50,000 and see if they actually responded. I paid him for that, and then a couple of weeks later I went to Washington to see what had happened.

"I discovered that a great many letters were being received in all Congressional offices, and I presumed in the White House and the State Department, against recognition of the Reds. When I returned to New York I got in touch with Father Keller and told him I would like to send out the other 65,000 cards, but he told me he had thought so well of it that he had done so at the expense of the organization. This flood of mail scared the State Department into delaying recognition."

It is worth noting that the motto of The Christophers is, "Better to light one candle than to curse the darkness." This action on the part of the organization proved the truth of its motto because the delay it caused was extended and Red China was not recognized. The Scripps-Howard newspapers then started crusading against the Chinese Reds for their brutal treatment of Angus Ward, the American Consul General in Mukden who had been thrown into jail there. Even though India and Britain recognized Red China on January 5, 1950, our State Department held back and American action was not taken.

Although much of Kohlberg's organizational work was of a negative nature, expressing opposition to official actions, in 1955 he became involved in something that was unquestionably positive. In view of repeated diplomatic failures that had made hundreds of millions of human beings subject to Communism, he became convinced that we had no foreign policy. Instead, whenever the Communists made a move we merely reacted in whatever way seemed expedient at the time. Confirming him in his belief that the United States had no foreign policy was his failure to get answers to questions he constantly asked as to what our foreign policy really was.

To fill this void, in 1955 he set up a Committee of Endorsers which prepared a statement on foreign policy which was extensively promoted through advertisements in leading newspapers. Among the signers of this statement were three former ambassadors, nine general officers of the Army and Air Force, six of equivalent rank in the Navy, and other distinguished Americans. He himself appeared before the House Foreign Affairs Committee and the Senate Foreign Relations Committee to present this program. Since the eleven proposals in "A Program to Govern Our Foreign Relations" summarize Kohlberg's thinking in this area, they are presented herewith as they were set forth in the advertisement:

1. Mobilize the strongest possible deterrents to war —military, psychological, political and economic.
2. Return to those traditional American policies which sustained us in the past, especially:
   (a) The policies recommended by President George Washington in his Farewell Address.
   (b) The Monroe Doctrine.
   (c) The Open Door Policy as defined in the Nine Power Treaty of 1922.
3. Exterminate the Communist conspiracy in the United States.
4. Withdraw recognition from the Soviet Union and its satellites.
5. Employ all measures to sap the economic strength of the Communist World.
6. Scrupulously observe present military alliances (where such alliances are in truth honored by our contracting allies), and form new alliances only for the period of the emergency.
7. Extend military and economic aid only to cooperating allies.
8. Wage unremitting psychological warfare against Communist regimes, including aid to effective anti-Communist exile, underground, and resistance groups, based on the principle of the Golden Rule.
9. Return to Open Diplomacy, except where military security imposes secrecy.
10. Oppose all activities which tend towards a world state, super-government, or the transfer of decisions for American security and welfare to foreign powers and/or foreign nationals. To this end, press for the expulsion of Communist member-states from the U.N. Reform the U.N. by removing all semblance of a permanent military alliance and separate it from its specialized agencies.

Amend our Constitution to provide that neither the U.N. Charter, nor treaties, nor covenants, shall supersede it.

11. Base American Foreign Policy solidly on Moral Law, Patriotism, Enlightened Nationalism, and the Teachings of Christ.

There is a note of disappointment in Alfred Kohlberg's comments on this project. In the expectation that there would be some sort of response to the advertisements, he set up an office in Washington and arranged with a friend, Nicholas Nonnenmacher, to help out on a part-time basis.

"Under his direction and with my approval," Kohlberg noted, "about 200,000 copies of the *New York Times* advertisement were sent out to many different organizations, such as posts of The American Legion, chapters of patriotic organizations, even such organizations as Parent-Teacher groups. What may have been accomplished by this I really was never able to find out, although we do know that a few, such as the Colorado Department of The American Legion passed resolutions in favor of it, as did a number of posts."

A new group called the "Citizens Foreign Relations Committee" was set up late in 1956 to continue to press for the adoption of the program, but although it continued in existence for two or three years there is nothing to indicate that it made any headway.

Recently many Americans were shocked to learn that our Central Intelligence Agency had subsidized the left-wing National Student Association to the extent of $3,-000,000, and that some of this money had been used to send American college students to international student gatherings. An interesting footnote to this is provided by another of Alfred Kohlberg's ventures into international relations this time by means of an informal organization informally established.

In 1959 he was approached by Herbert Romerstein,

who had done some work for him previously. A huge international Communist rally called the Seventh World Youth Festival was scheduled to be held in Vienna in the summer of that year and Romerstein got the idea of attending with a small group. The gathering was the first of its kind ever to be held outside the Iron Curtain and this gave non-Communists a chance to participate.

Kohlberg liked the idea and took the initiative in raising a fund of approximately $10,000 to send Romerstein and seven others to Vienna. When the festival opened, approximately 17,000 people were present. Of these roughly 400 were Americans, and of the American group approximately a hundred were "sponsored" by the U.S. Government, presumably by the CIA. However, it is doubtful that the entire delegation of government-sponsored U.S. students provided as much anti-Communist propaganda as the handful subsidized by Kohlberg.

One of Romerstein's projects was to have 2,000 pamphlets printed en route in Germany, addressed to the youths attending the festival. These pamphlets, printed in German, English, Chinese, and Russian, contained a heavy charge of the usual Communist clichés, as camouflage. But in addition they stressed something that was anathema to the Reds—freedom. The pamphlets exhorted the youths attending the festival to fight for freedom for all peoples, including Hungarians and Tibetans. When the commisars running the festival learned of the hoax they were furious. Indignantly the hand-picked "United States delegation" (not those sponsored by the U.S. Government) condemned the pamphlets in a statement to the press. One revealing sentence of this declared: "From whom and with what authority do the authors and deseminators [*sic*] of this particular piece of ill-meaning literature speak?"

A small riot took place when the big parade of August 2nd was about to begin. Kohlberg's delagates at that point

unfurled banners reading "Remember Hungary,"
"Remember Tibet," and "What About Soviet Imperialism?" This was too much for the comrades. The *New York
Times* of August 3rd told how the small group was beaten
up. Charles W. Wiley, one of them, was knocked to the
ground by Communist "enforcers" and his wife Katina,
seven months pregnant, was cut and bruised. Thanks to
the prompt action of Austrian policemen there were no
serious injuries, and the little band was rescued from the
furious Reds.

As for the larger group from America, present under
government auspices, their activities were considerably
more genteel and refined, as befitted ladies and gentlemen of liberal persuasion. They caused the Communists
no trouble at all. One of the Kohlberg group told me with
amusement of their attitude.

"They made it plain that they deplored our actions,
which they insisted were undignified and not the proper
way to build friendship and understanding."

The Communist leaders made a more realistic appraisal
of the propaganda deficit that had been incurred. In a
New York Times story dated October 26, 1959, under the
headline "Reds Displeased With Red Fete," several reasons were given for their failure. A special eleven-member
evaluating committee, comprised of top Communist Party
officials, leveled strong criticism at the festival committee
for their "underestimation of the effectiveness of opposition groups and individuals, both in their influence on
delegates and in their criticism of the Communist aims of
the festival." The Commie bigwigs then declared there
would be no more festivals for the time being.

One aspect of the various investigations of Communism
that troubled Alfred Kohlberg was the manner in which
Jewish names were sometimes brought to the fore. As he
put it:

"The stains upon the good name of Jewry left by the

activities of the Rosenbergs and the Glassers, the Harry Dexter Whites and Irving Potashes, the John Howard Lawsons and Howard Fasts, to mention a few, are deep and corroding. They are being exploited by twisted minds and conscienceless bigotry to fashion an anti-Semitic legend."

The crackpots and anti-Semites who raised the cry that "all Jews are Communists" conveniently overlooked the fact that a great many Jews had distinguished themselves in anti-Communist activities. Alfred Kohlberg was only one of a group that included Eugene Lyons, George Sokolsky, Dr. Maurice William, Victor Riesel, Ben Mandel, Louis Waldman, Isaac Don Levine, Bela Fabian, Lawrence Fertig, Ben Gitlow, Morrie Ryskind, Victor Lasky, Ralph De Toledano, J. A. Marcus, Frank Chodorov.

Kohlberg was aware that the anti-Semites were not the only ones who were trying to show that Jews were Communists. The Communists were saying the same thing. It was good strategy. Kohlberg pointed out that while Earl Browder was head of the Communist Party he repeatedly said, "Anti-communism and anti-Semitism are two different names for the same thing." In furtherance of this argument Communists proclaimed, "Hitler rose to power by denouncing the Communists, so everyone in America who denounces the Communists is an American Hitler—hence an anti-Semite."

There was an answer to this, of course, in such facts as the Hitler-Stalin alliance, the anti-Semitic purge trials behind the Iron Curtain, and the suppression of all Jewish community life in the Soviet Union. And there was an answer in the violent anti-Semitism of Karl Marx himself. Though he was of Jewish background he hated the Jews and the Jewish religion with a rabid fanaticism, and expressed his hatred in vicious terms: "What is the secular cult of the Jew? Huckstering. What is his secular God? Money. . . ."

There was still another answer to the slur that "Jews are Communists." As Kohlberg put it, "no Communists are Jews in the religious sense because all Communists are atheists."

In an attempt to do something about the anti-Semitic propaganda which served Communist purposes by pitting group against group, and in which Gerald L. K. Smith and Earl Browder joined hands, Kohlberg was instrumental in forming an organization called the American Jewish League Against Communism. This was established in 1948 and its first meetings were held in the home of Eugene Lyons who had for years advocated the creation of such a group. Among those who took part in those sessions were Louis Waldman, Lawrence Fertig, Isaac Don Levine, George Sokolsky, and of course Alfred Kohlberg.

To head the organization, Isaac Don Levine suggested a young rabbi, Benjamin Schultz. Rabbi Schultz exemplified a problem that existed in the Jewish community, the extent to which many Jews had been influenced by the propaganda that "anti-Communism and anti-Semitism are the same thing." He had served a congregation in Yonkers, New York, for several years and was popular there. However, his services were abruptly terminated in 1947 when he publicly condemned the left-wing activities of a few well known Jewish clergyman.

"We were exploring the ground, feeling our way," Levine explained to the writer, "and Rabbi Schultz seemed to be the logical one to head such an organization. But I for one wanted this organization to function in the synagogues, among Jews. I was not in favor of an organization that would tell the country that there is a handful of Jews fighting Communism, or which would use a public occasion to honor J. Edgar Hoover. I wanted one that would go from synagogue to synagogue, to carry the message.

"But before a decision was made I discovered that Mr. Kohlberg had taken the ball and had run with it. He installed Rabbi Schultz in a building he owned on 42nd Street, put a shingle up, and the organization was launched. I made it clear that I considered this action a little bit hasty, and I got out when I felt that the committee had gotten off the track by neglecting the education of many Jewish people in the facts about Communism. But in setting up the AJLAC as he did, Kohlberg was being his impetuous self. He was given to impetuous actions. When an idea hit him he called in his secretary and started dictating."

George Sokolsky in a column published in 1956 presented another view of the part Kohlberg played in the League:

"He and I organized, with others, the American Jewish League Against Communism and there must be a jinx about it because my coronary came during my presidency of this organization as his did. This is a good operation because it states categorically what so many of my coreligionists are now discovering, namely, that Soviet Russia and the Communists are universally the enemies, as they must be, of the Jews and of everything Jewish. This must be so because they hate God.

Sooner or later those Moslems who, for political profit, are now playing footsies with the Kremlin will discover that it does not pay, because those who hate God must bring misery in their wake. They must be brutal and cruel and deceitful.

We, who organized the American Jewish League Against Communism, set out to establish beyond doubt that every Communist, even if born of Jewish parents, must be regarded as an enemy of all Jews and of everything Jewish.

So we fought a tough battle with little support but with sureness in the righteousness of our case. And today, after Khrushchev's exhibition of hatred for the Jews, it is impossible not to recognize that we were

right, although a bit early. At any rate, if our worries
over all this helped to give Kohlberg and myself our
coronaries, it was done in a good cause and that is
something of a compensation.

A pamphlet issued by the League explained its aims.
"Like every other American racial and social group," it
stated, "the Jewish community has been infiltrated by
open and disguised Communists. The first and most vital
job of our League is to expose and combat that infiltration.

"In line with this purpose, it turns the spotlight of publicity on Communist efforts to exploit real Jewish griev-
ances for sinister ends. It exposes and tries to stop the
capture of legitimate Jewish causes and organizations by
Communist agents.

"It unfolds the long-suppressed truth about persecution
of Jewish religion, education, and culture in Soviet Russia.
It cooperates with other principled anti-Communist
groups in the struggle against the Red totalitarian danger
to America and the world."

Communist infiltration into various Jewish organizations was exposed by the League, and financial support
and sponsorship of Communist fronts was ended when
Jewish leaders were told how they had been duped. Communist propaganda which had been circulated through
Jewish organizations was countered, and anti-Communist
literature was prepared and distributed.

One of the League's most noteworthy achievements
was its work showing how Jews were being persecuted
behind the Iron Curtain. Communists in this country had
been able to enlist a certain amount of sympathy by telling
the Jewish community here that Jews were well treated in
the USSR and its satellites. The facts were quite different,
and these were made known by the League. The organization aroused considerable interest when it protested to
the United Nations against the deportation of Jews in

Russia to Siberia, a fact that was later confirmed by the Jewish Telegraphic Agency.

Through its activities the Jewish community was alerted to Communist machinations and Communist hypocrisy, but equally important, non-Jews were reminded of the simple truth that "The overwhelming majority of Jews are not only non-Communists but non-Communists They know that despotism, whether, Black, Brown, or Red, is the foe of Judaism, a faith which rests on the sanctity of the individual . . ."

The League staged a number of large and impressive gatherings where fighters against Communism were honored or where forums were conducted. But here the League took a stand that antagonized many liberal Jews. Among those singled out for honors were such men as Senator McCarthy and Senator Goldwater. Such powerful organizations as the American Jewish Congress and the American Jewish Committee not only refused to support the League but opposed it.

While the AJLAC continued to function and is still in being, Alfred Kohlberg in 1958 came to the conclusion that it had so little influence on the Jewish community at that time that there was little point in continuing with it. He was overruled on this by George Sokolsky and Roy Cohn, and while the League continued in existence he took little further active interest in it. George Sokolsky took over the running of its affairs and on his death in 1962 Roy Cohn succeeded him.

CHAPTER SIXTEEN

Man at Work

MOST PEOPLE ARE UNAWARE THAT A MAN NAMED
Alfred Kohlberg ever lived. They may have been aware of
him at one time, when his name was in the headlines, but
that covered only a brief span of time and, in any case,
headlines are soon forgotten. However, this relatively obscure little businessman had an impact on our times that
cannot be measured by the number of times his name
appeared in print.

Probably the most eloquent testimonial to Alfred Kohlberg is the report of the Senate Internal Security Subcommittee confirming his warnings about the machinations of
the Institute of Pacific Relations. Shortly after the report
appeared, the *New York World-Telegram* of July 23, 1952,
published an editorial which stated:

"The committee report on the IPR unfolds a story of

intrigue with few parallels in recent history. It also shows what one citizen can do to set things right when a majority of his associates are deaf, dumb, and blind, and whenever the government itself has been deluded. If there were medals for citizenship, Alfred Kohlberg would merit one for his successful fight to unmask this instance of Soviet penetration."

As the editorial indicated, it is possible for an individual to do a great deal "to set things right," even when he is opposed by powerful forces. Unfortunately, not many citizens are qualified to become involved in foreign intrigue of the sort that preoccupied Kohlberg. One of his qualifications was the fact that he was a merchant who had done business in China over a long period. No less an authority than the master spy Richard Sorge explained the importance of this:

"I believe that in Japan and China," said Sorge, "the best thing an agent can do is to become a big merchant. A man clever enough to take up espionage work as a career in the first place would not forsake his career for business, and, even if he did, the chances are he would not succeed. Generally speaking, the mercantile class is made up of men of average or less intelligence, and the agent who assumes such a cover would be quite safe from detection by the police. Moreover, as a merchant with extensive business connections (which he would utilize as a source of information), he could associate with people of various classes without arousing suspicion."

Kohlberg, of course, was not operating in China as a spy. But as Sorge pointed out, as a merchant he was able to learn what was going on through his extensive connections in that country. Indeed, it was because he was so well informed about China that he was able to question the Communist propaganda that was being disseminated wholesale by the IPR. Nor was his interest in Far Eastern political affairs something that developed after he became embroiled with the IPR. Consider this forecast which he made in 1939:

"If we help China openly the Japanese will secretly retaliate on Americans and particularly American property in China and I will lose my investment there. But I and all other Americans have realized this for a long time and we cannot complain when it happens. We have gambled and we must be good losers.

"If we try to remain neutral I am confident that we will be at war with Japan within two years. We are very likely in the reasonably near future to shut off war supplies to Japan. When we do the Japanese Army in China (not the Japanese Government) will retaliate on Americans there and they will do it less suavely and secretly than the Japanese Government would have directed, and American opinion, realizing its attempted neutrality, will become more resentful, and then another *Panay* incident will be like the blowing up of the *Maine* years ago . . ."

That other *Panay* incident came in the form of Japan's attack on Pearl Harbor two years later.

Because of his business interests, Kohlberg traveled frequently to China until Pearl Harbor erupted, and he was one of the first American civilians to enter the country at the end of hostilities. The first-hand knowledge he acquired in his travels made him scornful of the IPR's "experts," many of whom had little actual knowledge of the country. And supplementing the information he picked up on his travels were reports from people working in various parts of China. A typical communication of this sort, found in his files, came from a Protestant missionary in Shantung in 1946. This clergyman described the Chinese Communists in terms that were far different from those set forth in best-sellers produced by such authors as Edgar Snow, Owen Lattimore, Theodore H. White, Agnes Smedley, John K. Fairbank, and others. Two paragraphs of the minister's letter will give the general idea:

"Nearly all Shantung Province is in the hands of the Communists. In less than one year they have destroyed more property and terrorized the people more than the Japanese in eight years. Most people in America don't understand the present internal trouble we are having in China. The Communists here are sponsored by Moscow; the leaders are of the lowest strata of society. In sections where they rule everything that is right has been upset. Home life, virtue of womanhood, filial piety, religion, etc., etc., have all been done away with as far as the communists are concerned. Any person having more than 2 acres of land is considered 'capitalist,' is arrested, publicly humiliated, everything taken from him and he is driven out to beg. In some places churches have been closed and Christians scattered. I'm glad to say that in spite of the persecutions and suspense not one of our co-workers has deserted his post.

"The Communists in China have their own separate government, not recognizing the Central Government of China. They have their own army, postal system, etc., that is responsible to Yenan, their capital in northwest China—and to Russia. I have not found one good thing in the kind of Communism we have in China. The people are fed up. There can never be any cooperation between the Nationalists and Communists. The only way to settle this thing is by armed force; driving the Communist leaders clear out of China into Russia. We may have to deal with Russia later, but the sooner Communism is eradicated from the earth, the sooner we shall have peace. You may think this doesn't sound Christian; it is, and it comes from one who knows China and loves the soul of every one of her 450 million people. The sooner America gets her eyes open to facts and uses every effort to save China from Communism, the sooner she'll prove her real interest and friendship for the people here . . ."

Because of such intelligence, Alfred Kohlberg was familiar with the tragedy that was taking place in China. But he was handicapped in getting this story across to the American people since the major communications media in general reflected the IPR-State Department line on China. Alfred Kohlberg was in truth a voice crying in the wilderness.

Even so, he managed to make his points, and one of his most effective techniques was to make them by proxy. Senators and congressmen, newspapermen and others who had access to public forums were given the benefit of his research while he remained in the background. The files which provided such information are revealing, reflecting his wide range of interests. For the most part they deal with individuals and organizations, with an interesting dossier on Alfred Kohlberg himself. This contained material of a derogatory nature which was being circulated, and in one case Kohlberg obviously employed someone to purchase a rundown on himself from one organization. The bill of particulars bought from this oufit contained many of the same smears, mentioned in an earlier chapter, that were used in certain newspapers. Including the ridiculous charge that some of Kohlberg's letters had been printed in the Catholic newspaper *The Tablet.*

One of the smear sheets, which originated with a bizarre Los Angeles organization, purported to show that Kohlberg was a key man in a sinister Jewish plot, and his anti-Communism was really a sham. Why did he support Chiang Kai-shek? The answer, according to this bit of fantasy, was that Chiang Kai-shek was in reality a traitor who had sold out to the Communists. Hadn't he failed to keep China from becoming Communists? As for Kohlberg's fight with the IPR, that too was phony. After all, he had been active in the organization prior to 1944 and there were Communists in it then. Charging that he was actually a secret agent for Bernard Baruch, this lengthy paper concluded:

"The depths of Kohlberg's guilt, his subversive activities, may never be known, but enough of the pattern is apparent to the astute observer to prove conclusively that if he cannot be exposed, at least he can be avoided like the Red Plague."

One organization that Kohlberg actually did belong to, although it can hardly be called subversive, was the Masons. Proof of this was a bulletin issued by Fidelity Lodge No 120 F. & A.M., of San Francisco, dated November 1959, which stated that Kohlberg was to receive his Fifty-Year Button that year. However, the announcement contained a rebuke:

"Brother Kohlberg was raised in our Lodge on February 11, 1909, and has not been in lodge for nearly forty years."

People who knew Kohlberg and worked with him describe him as an excellent reporter who spared no effort to dig out information. But he was also a first-rate public relations man, with a rare ability to get his views across in spite of handicaps. I was privileged to watch him in action on more than one occasion, and one incident is noteworthy because it cast him in a dual role, as reporter *and* public relations man.

On this occasion he phoned me and asked if I could have lunch with him and a third party. This man, he said, would probably have an interesting story to tell. He mentioned his name, one that had figured prominently in the Army-MCarthy hearings, adding that he himself had never met him. I was invited because I was then a magazine editor and Alfred thought I might be able to get an article out of the meeting. As it turned out the story was of such a nature that it could not be used and even now it is necessary to protect the identity of the person involved.

At the time of the luncheon the Army-McCarthy hearings of 1954 had long since ended but it was obvious that our friend was still unable to understand certain aspects of the case in which he had been involved. This was understandable in view of the way in which the hearings had been aborted when they were turned into a public spectacle which starred a Communist dentist, Dr. Irving E. Peress; Maj. Gen. Ralph Zwicker, who had signed the papers promoting him; and a New England attorney, Joseph Welch, whose theatrical performance before the subcommittee later won him a Hollywood contract—not to mention innumerable television appearances where he was lionized.

The story we heard from the Army man made clear the fact that the investigation was badly needed, that our military had been caught with its security down. It also told of the operations made behind the scenes to keep the lid on. Probably most interesting of all, proving that Washington had succeeded admirably in diverting attention from what McCarthy was trying to uncover, was the fact that this top Army official himself was still puzzled over the way in which a group of Communists had wormed themselves into the most strategic part of a vital military base.

"We had thousands of civilians employed there," he told us, "but most of them were engaged in routine tasks. They drove trucks, washed windows, cut the grass and handled supplies. When it was learned that communists were working there we found none of them doing jobs like these. We also employed a lot of people at routine desk jobs. None of the Commies turned up in those jobs either. Ours was an important research center, and we had a great many people developing equipment for military use. But most of the work was not original, just adaptations of known principles of communication. None of the Communists were found in that area either.

"However, we also did a great deal of research and

development of an original nature. We had made some important advances on projects that we felt would give our country a military edge in certain fields. It was all top secret work, naturally, but when we started looking into the situation that is where all the Communists were concentrated.

"Now you tell me how it was that those people managed to colonize just that one vital sector."

Kohlberg explained that this was the usual pattern. The Party did not have manpower to waste on unprofitable chores. It was therefore necessary to concentrate the comrades where they would be most effective. As for how they did it, that was a familiar story to Kohlberg. He told how the same pattern had been followed in IPR operations, and he quoted Elizabeth Bentley's reply to Senator Ferguson's question about this during the IPR hearings:

"Once we got one person in he got others, and the whole process continued like that."

Kohlberg mentioned another familiar tactic of the Communists: once they moved in on a situation they were utterly ruthless in forcing out those who stood in their way. This, incidentally, is never mentioned when people talk about Communists being "persecuted for their beliefs."

In the course of the discussion the official was asked if he knew anything about the present situation at the base. He did. The situation, he replied, was far worse than it had been previously. Couldn't anything be done about it? He shrugged and shook his head. The lid had been clamped down tightly on further embarrassing disclosures and heaven help anyone who tried to pry it loose again. He certainly did not care to risk it.

If one may call a luncheon such as this a social occasion, much of Alfred Kohlberg's work was done in a social manner. He rarely ate by himself but used the opportunity to meet people and talk to them in a relaxed atmosphere.

Now and then when he came across someone with an interesting message he would provide a forum for him, inviting a group to a private luncheon at a club.

Quite often the Kohlberg home at Bronxville was the scene of gatherings where important messages were presented by people of prominence, and on such occasions guests were usually present who were in a position to pass the word along if they considered it sufficiently important. The following excerpts from Kohlberg's personal letters will give some idea of this:

"Sunday we had a party at our house, last night I was the guest of the Chinese Ambassador at a dinner to American industry, and tonight I am giving a small dinner to twelve men in honor of Lt. Gen. Al Wedemeyer, who is speaking later at an off-the-cuff meeting."

"We had refreshments for 40 men on Monday night, and on the following Sunday, that was May 27th, we had about 120 people here for cocktails and food, for our Congressman, Ralph Gwinn. . . . The funniest part of this was that with Ida's approval I fired the cook, Japanese, about two hours before the cocktail party for 120. We didn't miss him."

"We had a party Sunday in honor of Nikolai Khokhlov, of the cigarette case which contained poisoned bullets. The George Sokolskys and Victor Riesel and Eugene Lyons and Frank Barnett and a Chinese couple out of Red China and the UN representative of the Sumatran rebel government were there. Also Ruth Alexander. . . ."

At these gatherings, which in pleasant weather were usually held outdoors close to the swimming pool near the big stone house, one could see many nationally known figures. A partial listing would include Senator McCarthy, Robert Morris, Ayn Rand, Suzanne Labin, Roy Cohn, Roy Howard, Dr. and Mrs. J. B. Matthews, Archbishop Yu-pin, Louis Budenz, William F. Buckley, Jr., Irene Corbally Kuhn, General Willoughby, Admiral Cooke, Archibald

Roosevelt, Eugene Lyons, Clarence Manion, Freda Utley, Dr. Walter Judd, and various Chinese diplomats and military officials. On one occasion I was introduced to a candy manufacturer, an unassuming individual by the name of Robert Welch.

It should not be inferred from this that Kohlberg's life was a round of social activities. Actually these cocktail parties and dinners were social only in a secondary sense. Primarily they were a means to an end, another aspect of the host's incessant efforts to acquire useful information and get it in circulation. There would be, for example, a party in honor of Morrie Ryskind, who was spending a few days away from Hollywood. This guaranteed that there would be some significant, and amusing, news about the proletariat of the movie colony and their latest plans for manning the barricades. Or one might hear Mme. Suzanne Labin, just back from Saigon, tell with no amusement of the problems besetting the Diem regime. In all these programs Alfred usually stayed in the background. If he made speeches they were short, to introduce others, and that was unfortunate because he had a sharp wit and, as the saying goes, "he was quick on his feet."

While the Kohlbergs never lacked for company, few of their Bronxville neighbors showed much friendship after he became known as "the China Lobby man." Prior to that he participated in various community activities, by invitation, and was in fact president of a neighborhood association. But once his controversy with the IPR broke into the open, with the facts embellished by interpretive journalism, he was snubbed by many of his neighbors. Meeting these people on the street or at the New York Central station, he would see them turn their backs as he approached. They stopped coming to his home and of course there were no more invitations to their social or community activities.

In this case the issue was not entirely the China Lobby.

A local controversy had developed over ultra-liberal Sarah Lawrence College, in the Bronxville section of Yonkers. Kohlberg had joined the Westchester County American Legion in its criticism of some of the faculty and certain teaching practices, and of the fact that Communist leaders were permitted to speak on campus and that Sarah Lawrence students had marched in the Communist May Day parade in New York City.

This controversy was prominently featured in the metropolitan press and caused a division in the community. Liberals living in the area were called on to sign petitions defending the college—and many prominent people did. Kohlberg and his Legionnaire friends were looked upon as pariahs who were trying to give the college a bad reputation. In the midst of this, Kohlberg offered his services, free, to teach a course on Communism at Sarah Lawrence. The highly liberal president, Harold Taylor (no longer employed there) rejected the offer saying, "Our curriculum in social science is already complete . . ." Which of course it was. The way Taylor wanted it.

"Politically," Ida Kohlberg commented, "we lived on the wrong side of the tracks."

Kohlberg's neighbors were not the only ones who snubbed him. On several occasions when he was introduced to well known people his outstretched hand was pointedly ignored.

"He suffered the worst frustrations," Mrs. Kohlberg recalled, "but it neither crushed him, nor diminished his efforts, nor changed his mind. He knew he was right and he fought right to the end—that was the essence of his life —and there was no compromise. But throughout all this there was no hatred on his part. He had understanding of human weaknesses and he knew that most of these people were ignorant of what was going on."

There was one exception, a person who could not claim ignorance in excuse of his actions, and Kohlberg was shocked and pained by a snub received from him. This was a college professor who had done some research for him and who of course had been paid for it. One day Alfred Kohlberg and his wife visited the campus of the college where the professor taught and saw him talking to some of his colleagues. Kohlberg approached and greeted him. The professor looked at him coldly and said, "You must be mistaken; I don't know you." Later on he sought out Kohlberg and explained that he could not admit that he knew him in front of other faculty members. Then he asked if Kohlberg could let him have some money for a new project he was starting.

The building that Kohlberg used for his business, at 1 West 37th Street, in New York, became the headquarters of his fight to keep China from going Communist. From the outside it was not much different from many other buildings that stretched westward from Fifth Avenue into the garment district. It had a large plate glass window, painted black, with the Kohlberg trademark, the capitals AK in a diamond. Inside, the place was much different from other business establishments along the street. Here one found striking reminders of the China that Kohlberg knew and loved. The walls were adorned with priceless tapestries. Staggered glass cases showed off superb examples of Chinese needlecraft. Pretty Chinese girls busied themselves with the stock, which included handkerchiefs that sold for as much as $200 a dozen.

Alfred Kohlberg's office was near the front of the showroom and his door was always open. Through it passed some very important people, American and Chinese, not to mention customers. But in time, as China was lost, there were fewer customers, and there was even less reason for maintaining a large establishment when Kohlberg's health became troublesome. So in 1957 he moved his offices to an upstairs suite in the same building.

As headquarters for Kohlberg's China Lobby, the building achieved a certain fame because of the steady flow of letters and statements that issued from it. Many of these were marked by a dry humor that was characteristic of Kohlberg. An example was his famous telegram to President Truman suggesting that the Chief Executive either apologize for calling him a lobbyist or fire the Attorney General for not doing his duty and prosecuting him.

Kohlberg's writing took many forms. He once wrote a book review in the form of a Chinese fairy tale. The book in question was Elliott Roosevelt's *As He Saw It*, which purported to tell the inside story of the big conferences in which his father had starred. Kohlberg treated the book and its illustrious subjects with no reverence whatsoever. In this fairy tale review President Roosevelt was referred to as "the Emperor" in this vein:

"And the Emperor, who had a big heart and a great fatherly feeling, did take the unfilial one with him to many strange places where were gathered rulers from far and near. And the unfilial son was permitted to be bottle bearer to the Great One on Whose Kingdom Never Sets the Sun, and to the Great Leader of the Middle Kingdom, and to the Great Dictator of All the Proletariat of the Seven Seas, and he did listen to many words of wisdom, or otherwise . . ."

As for what Elliott said in his book, here is how Kohlberg saw it:

"He sang of the Great Dictator who wished only for friendly neighbors and who made all his neighbors into friends, or else. He sang of their tourneys and their meetings and their courtiers, and of how his father, the Great Emperor, in his truly impartial generosity gave away the small countries of his minor allied princes, and the lands of his enemies, and his own arms and machines and bread and spam and tractors and what not to the Great Dictator of the Proletariat of the Seven Seas . . ."

In another review, this one of Henry Wallace's *Soviet*

Asia Mission, Kohlberg quoted Wallace's figures which were supposed to show how the Communists had increased production by 2,000 percent in the industrial city of Novo-Sibersk in only four years. At the same time the Vice President called on the United States to send some industrial experts to Russia to help the Communists out. Kohlberg had another idea:

"If his statements are correct his Department of Commerce would do well to borrow a few of Russia's miracle workers to get Detroit turning out some cars, Pittsburgh some bathtubs, Rochester some suits and other cities all the various articles our returning veterans complain they cannot find."

Usually he was highly critical of General Marshall's moves in diplomatic fields but on one occasion he was a bit charitable. Broadcasting over a small New York City radio station, he likened General Marshall's mission to China to the Lindbergh case. Reminding listeners of the way in which Jafsie Condon had been given $50,000 to hand over to persons unknown in a graveyard, in a vain attempt to recover the kidnaped Lindbergh baby, he said that Marshall's function was similar to Jafsie's. State Department advisers, he declared, had authorized the General to give the Chinese Communists everything they wanted, at the expense of the legitimate Chinese Government.

"General Marshall," he concluded, "carried out his mission superbly; it wasn't his fault that the baby was dead before he started."

Some of Kohlberg's humor was deplored by friends who argued that he was dealing with people utterly devoid of humor. Something said in jest, they pointed out, might be taken seriously by these humorless people and used against him. There is no indication that this ever happened but Kohlberg's friends were right about one thing. Some of his adversaries had little to show in the way of a sense of humor. This was proved by a practical joke he once employed, mentioned by William F. Buckley, Jr. in the Introduction to this book.

In the early 1950's, when investigations were showing the extent of Communist infiltration into government, education, the communications media and other strategic areas, a tremendous outcry swelled up from the ranks of self-proclaimed liberals. It was almost impossible to pick up a newspaper or turn on one's television or radio without being assailed by loud laments that freedom of speech had become a victim of McCarthyism and it was no longer possible for liberals to express their views.

This ludicrous situation inspired Kohlberg to draft a speech which he dubbed "The Black Silence of Fear."* Into it he loaded all the clichés that were being uttered incessantly, and to make it all the more pointed he used actual quotations from the most vocal of the wailers. Among those who unwittingly contributed to Kohlberg's effort were Justice William O. Douglas, Robert M. Hutchins, Eleanor Roosevelt, Henry Steele Commager, Senator Herbert H. Lehman, Adlai Stevenson, and W. Averell Harriman.

Among the clichés that Kohlberg borrowed from these people and worked into his satire were "reaction is on the march," "the Communists and the reactionaries find common ground in their opposition to the cause of freedom," "there is a reign of terror abroad in the land," "vigilante groups are being formed, suspicion, mistrust and fear stalk the land," "good and honest men are being pilloried," "this is the Black Silence of Fear," "the black evil of McCarthyism has captured the imagination of the American people," and so on ad nauseam.

This nosegay of nonsense was then mimeographed by Kohlberg and sent to colleges and universities with an offer to deliver it as a commencement address. Much to his

*Kohlberg's burlesque of a Commencement Address, with most of the liberal cliches of the time is presented as Appendix M.

amazement he received a number of letters seriously complimenting him. These literal-minded liberal college officials hastened to point out that they had already made arrangements for that year's commencement speakers— one mentioned he had booked Walter Reuther—but they'd certainly like to keep him in mind for the coming year.

"No wonder it's so easy to hoodwink such people," Kohlberg commented.

One of the most amusing letters of all came from a highly publicized liberal clergyman in New York City. This man, still as active as ever in liberal causes, gushed:

"I want to thank you for your good letter of January 17th enclosing your excellent Commencement Address on the subject of anti-intellectualism. May I give you my warmest commendation. More power to you!" The reverend gentleman added a postscript saying he'd like to have Kohlberg address one of his forums. This was too much for Kohlberg. He responded by telling the minister what he thought of him and his foolishness, in unmistakable terms.

If there was a "black silence of fear" in the country at that time it was a fear of the Kohlberg point of view, and he rarely got the opportunity to speak to a large audience. Despite all the attention he received in the left-wing press and in certain columns as the embodiment of the China Lobby, he received few invitations to appear on major networks. Shut off from large, ready-made audiences he addressed any groups he could find. An account of a trip he made to the west coast early in 1951 indicates this:

"On this trip, instead of speaking privately to publishers and men of some importance, I spoke to public gatherings of various kinds. The most important of the speeches was delivered on a Sunday night in the First Congregational Church of Los Angeles. My friend, the Reverend James W. Fifield, Jr., was pastor of that church, the largest Protes-

tant church in Los Angeles. I also spoke to the Long Beach
Rotary Club and to a large woman's club, the name of
which I've forgotten. And on a Friday night I spoke from
the pulpit of an orthodox synagogue in Los Angeles, and
on Sunday morning in the assembly room of another orthodox synagogue in another part of Los Angeles. Also I
spoke to a luncheon club of about 50 or 60 prominent
citizens at a private luncheon given by Dr. Fifield at the
California Club in downtown Los Angeles. Also to a dinner meeting of the Los Angeles Chapter of the American
Jewish League Against Communism, of which I was at
that time National Chairman."

Kohlberg of course paid all the expenses of his speech-
making tours and accepted no money for his appearances.

He spoke on numerous occasions before Catholic organizations such as the Knights of Columbus, and before
American Legion groups. I was present at one American
Legion function, a Westchester County convention held
in Mamaroneck in June 1957, when Alfred Kohlberg, as
guest of honor, came on the scene accompanied by his
wife and his old friend Archibald Roosevelt. He had just
taken his seat when he suffered a heart attack and had to
be assisted out.

This was not his first seizure. That had come three years
before, in September 1954, and had put him in the hospital for six weeks. Two months after this there was another
and more severe attack. The Kohlbergs then took an
apartment in New York City, for convenience.

A year later he had almost recovered from these attacks
but in attempting to escape the cold New York weather
he had an experience that almost brought on another attack. En route from California to Hawaii his plane was
almost midway across the Pacific when an engine failed.
The plane returned to San Francisco and a substitute
plane got him safely to Honolulu, but the trip was too
much for him and he was sick throughout his stay there.

A few weeks after his attack at Mamaroneck in 1957 he had to undergo an operation and he had hardly recovered when he and Mrs. Kohlberg were involved in an automobile accident. This brought on another coronary.

The time had come for him to curtail his activities, but somehow situations developed which made it necessary for him to reach for his nitroglycerin tablets. Repeatedly he mentioned occasions when he had recourse to them. One of these occurred when Robert Welch of the John Birch Society called on him. The two men got into a discussion, and finally in exasperation Welch said, "If I didn't know you so well, Alfred, I'd suspect you were a double agent."

Over the years Alfred Kohlberg became known for his generosity. Although he was not very rich, in the sense that the Rockefellers, the Kennedys, and the Harrimans are rich, he could be counted on to help individuals or organizations needing assistance in fighting Communism. Nor was this merely a matter of advancing needed funds. He was unsparing of time and effort, too, if he considered the person or the cause a deserving one.

Because of this, and as a token of appreciation for it, it was decided to give a dinner in Kohlberg's honor. The idea for this originated with Charles W. Wiley, a free-lance journalist who had become an active anti-Communist nist with Alfred Kohlberg's help. Wiley, incidentally, was one of the pro-Americans who attended the Youth Festival in Vienna in 1959, and later he was to achieve more fame when he spent some time in one of Fidel Castro's Havana jails.

Wiley set up a meeting to make plans for the dinner but immediately a question arose. Would it be advisable to try to surprise Kohlberg with an affair like this? The shock might be too much. There was a consultation with Ida Kohlberg and with Alfred's doctor, and the decision was that the guest of honor should be notified beforehand.

He probably had no idea that the dinner would be as impressive as it was. His pleasure was obvious as he was escorted to the dais of the Waldorf-Astoria's Starlight Roof the night of January 26, 1960. Sharing the dais with him were distinguished people indeed, and the huge room was filled with more than 650 people, most of them of national prominence. But more important to Alfred Kohlberg was the knowledge that these people were his friends.

It was a light-hearted occasion. There were no impassioned speeches deploring anything or denouncing anyone. There were references to "the enemy," but on this happy evening he was laughed at. Bill Buckley, in a talk that dealt with some of the more amusing aspects of Kohlberg's crusades, set the tone. Throughout, Alfred resembled nothing so much as a benign oriental idol radiating happiness.

The dinner was the last big event of Alfred Kohlberg's life. Less than three months later he was dead. On April 6, 1960, he had a visitor at his East 64th Street apartment, Louis F. Budenz. They had become good friends from the time in 1946 when Kohlberg had paid a call at his home in Crestwood—and had been turned away by Mrs. Budenz. Her husband had just returned from Notre Dame and was still in seclusion after his break with the Party. Subsequently Kohlberg and Budenz had played roles in both the Tydings and McCarran hearings and they met frequently.

"We went to lunch together at least once a week," Budenz told me, "and oftener if something interesting was happening. On this occasion we drank our respective healths, both stating that our 'health' might be our demise very soon."

The following evening Alfred Kohlberg was playing cards at home with Ida and some friends when the phone rang. The call was from his old friends, J. B. and Ruth

Matthews, inviting the Kohlbergs to visit them the following Saturday. They accepted and went back to their cards. But not for long. The game came to an abrupt end moments later when Alfred had another heart attack and died at once.

Ten years before, on July 18, 1950, his good friend Styles Bridges had made a speech on the Senate floor in which he had said: "When an Army officer loses a battalion, he is relieved of his command, in disgrace. When a naval officer loses his ship or runs it aground, in the mud, he is court-martialed. But when foreign policy advisers lose a whole continent they are applauded or even promoted."

Today many of these same advisers are still around. Despite their past failures they continue to offer advice, over the air, in print, and from the lecture platform. Meanwhile, to repeat what was said at the start of this chapter, most people are unaware that Kohlberg (who tried to present the truth to Americans) ever lived. From this it might be inferred that he was a failure. True, he failed to prevent a Communist takeover of China. But the fact that some of Asia is still free is proof that his was not entirely a lost cause.

CHAPTER SEVENTEEN

Repeat Performances

EARLY IN 1951, WHILE AMERICAN SOLDIERS AND marines were fighting in Korea, Alfred Kohlberg made a speech in Los Angeles in which he expressed certain reservations about the United States:

"I doubt an America," he said, "that permits its home grown traitors... in the Communist press and in meetings in New York and San Francisco and Los Angeles to rant against the heroes fighting its battles in Korea; while these vile Communist, calling themselves Americans, praise our mortal enemies ..."

What was happening at that time had happened before and the performance was to be repeated during the war in Vietnam. At the time Kohlberg made his speech the Communist Party line, being echoed by the usual gullibles, was "Bring our boys back from Korea!" but only five years earlier the same kind of people were demanding that the United States get out of China, to make way for Mao's agrarian reformers. And only a few years before that they were performing for the benefit of Stalin, assisting him in his European aggressions.

Invariably the kind of people who participate in such performances pride themselves on being avant-garde. They profess to be interested only in new and original ideas, and the newer the better. Yet, amusingly, the gold bricks they get from the Commie con-men are shabby from use, without even a fresh coat of gilt to disguise their antiquity. And the ingenuous intellectuals who accept them prove only that they are utterly incapable of learning anything from experience.

Undoubtedly the greatest of all such swindles, one that exposed the people who lent themselves to it as worse than fools, was perpetrated at the time Hitler and Stalin went into partnership through the Soviet-Nazi Pact. Till then the comrades and their dupes had been insisting that the United States should end its isolation and oppose fascism. But immediately after the infamous pact was signed the demonstrators started warning the United States to keep hands off while Hitler and Stalin grabbed what they could of Eastern Europe. Meanwhile Communist-run strikes and sabotage in the United States hampered the production of war materiel for Britain and France.

During World War II, when American aid made it possible for the Soviet Union to survive, the Communists tolerated us and greedily accepted the billions in economic and military assistance we gave them. However, the war had hardly ended when the Reds were making it plain that the United States was no longer wanted in Europe and Asia. Since China was so important to the success of world Communism the United States was particularly unwelcome there, and Kohlberg obtained a copy of a Party memorandum which he circulated to show what the comrades were up to in that part of the world. The key paragraph follows:

"Today, American imperialism, by armed force, is intervening in the struggle of the Chinese people to establish a democratic Chinese Republic. Victory in China for the American monopolists, defeat for the Chinese people, will set back the anti-imperialist struggle of all colonial and semi-colonial peoples. It will strengthen American imperialism in its drive for domination of the world, and will intensify their attacks against the working class at home. It will sharpen the contradictions between the United States on one hand, and Great Britain, Holland and other imperialist countries with Far Eastern interests, on the other. It brings much closer the possibility of war against the Soviet Union."

The memorandum went on to order picket line demonstrations, mass meetings, shop gate meetings, visits to congressmen by delegations, and other pressures that the Communists use time and again to make it appear as though they represent an irresistible force—the will of the people.

Proving that we Americans are not quite as bright as we think we are, and fully deserve the contempt that the Communists have for us, we fell for their propaganda and pressures and permitted China to fall to Communism.

At the time Kohlberg made his speech in 1951 the Communists were exerting similar pressures to force us out of Korea, and again they were getting the help of a great many people who were either not quite bright or, in Kohlberg's words, "home grown traitors."

Looking back on what happened during the Korean War and how it started, it is hard to understand how any rational American could have fallen for the crude propaganda of the Communists. The aggression was obvious. On June 25, 1950, a thin line of North Korean troops had moved across the 38th parallel, the boundary between

North and South Korea. This screened a powerful force armed with heavy weapons and tanks, which charged through the screening force which opened up to let it through. The arms for this unprovoked aggression, it should surprise no one to know, were supplied by the Soviet Union.

Yet despite the facts, Communists all over the world soon started screaming that the Americans had committed "aggression against the Korean people." They charged that "American aircraft are bombing Korean towns and villages," and later on they were to accuse this country of germ warfare in Korea. That strange "American," Gus Hall, the gauleiter of the Communist conspiracy in this country, fulfilled his role by charging the United States with "open military intervention in the internal affairs of other peoples and nations."

Incidentally, implementing the Communist propaganda drive in the United States was an outfit called the Peace Information Center, in which the late W.E.B. DuBois took an active part. This is the same DuBois that today's New Left holds in such veneration—with reason. One of his outstanding contributions to the Communist cause was through the so-called Stockholm Peace Appeal, which he helped to engineer. This Communist swindle is said to have been signed by 11,350,000 "peace-loving Americans." On July 21, 1950, *Pravda* showed how the Kremlin looked upon these soft-headed people when it called on them to turn traitor by sabotaging assistance to South Korea, as proof of their desire for peace.

Then, as now, there were some who were willing to assist actively the people who were killing American men. The *New York World-Telegram and Sun* of January 31, 1951 told of a fund-raising drive being conducted in New York for a "1951 Friendship Fund" to buy medical supplies for the Reds. Among the Communists brazenly running this was Kohlberg's old adversary of the Institute of

Pacific Relations, Frederick Vanderbilt Field.

Joining in the chorus demanding that the United States should "Get Out of Korea," as Commissar Hall and other Reds wanted, was a large and motley crew. Howard Fast, the novelist, writing in the Communist publication *People's China,* was able to report, "How it would cheer your friends in China if they could see, as I have seen, the literally thousands of committees and voices for peace forming everywhere in America. It is much as if all the decency and good heart of the American people had broken through this hellish wall of deceit and lies woven around them and voices itself in the single sentence, 'Bring our boys back from Korea and give us peace'."

The time came when the "peace" that these characters wanted came in the form of negotiations at Panmunjom. Those who insist that we negotiate with Communist overlook or are ignorant of the fact that Communist do not look upon negotiations as a means of securing peace but rather as a continuation of a shooting war, a way of securing their objectives "by other means." What happened at Panmunjom is an excellent example of that.

Characteristically, the Communists showed no interest in negotiations until it was apparent they would never win a military victory. But once having called for a truce they made it appear that they were the victors. Negotiators for our side had to ride in jeeps bearing white flags, and they made their way to the negotiating table through a gauntlet of bayonets pointed threateningly at them. These humiliations were filmed by Communist photographers for propaganda purposes. In the meetings there were other humiliations, and this continued for two years. Meanwhile the fighting continued and the United States sustained heavy losses. The peace that finally came has been ephemeral. Large forces of American troops are still tied down in Korea, and murderous border incidents frequently erupt.

One of those who learned about Communists the hard way, as a negotiator, was Arthur H. Dean, who had opposed Alfred Kohlberg in the IPR. Writing about his experiences at Panmunjom he plaintively described how the Communists exploited the meetings for propaganda. He told of the vulgarity of the Red representatives and the utter futility of trying to deal with them. The irony of this is that had Dean heeded Kohlberg he might have been spared such abuse from the Communists.

Further light on the kind of negotiations fancied by Walter Lippmann, Senators Fulbright, McCarthy, MGovern, and other "doves" of today is shed by another American who participated at Panmunjom, Admiral Turner Joy, who headed the UN Command Delegation for ten months. Here is how he described his experiences:

"Communists have two techniques with which to deal with the truth. One: they deny it. Two: they distort it. Throughout the long arguments over the exchange of prisoners of war, the Communists engaged in every nefarious practice known to them. They lied; they blustered; they became vindictive; they welshed; they twisted, distorted and denied truth; they delayed; they threatened."

General Mark Clark, who concluded the negotiations, said, "I gained the unenviable distinction of being the first United States commander in history to sign an armistice without victory."

Which is precisely what some of our "home grown traitors" want to see repeated every time we negotiate with the Communists.

Kohlberg was mercifully spared the sight of subsequent negotiations and the pressures that led up to them, but he was sure there would be other performances after Panmunjom. In the same speech quoted earlier in this chapter he said:

"I do not doubt the courage and patriotism of our young men who fight for us in Korea; and who will fight in the months and years to come, in strange lands and seas, the names of which we scarcely know today. But for what do we ask them to fight? For moral principles, for liberty, for the right? Or for unworthy objectives that may be negotiated—or is it appeased?—next week or the week after in the UN or in some secret meeting with our enemies? Can we compromise all our principles if only Joe Stalin or Mao Tse-tung would be willing to talk to us and not make the price too high?"

He ended his speech with these words:

"No more betrayals of those who fight on our side. No more appeasement of the evil men who seek to enslave the world. No more abandonment of those who fight beside us. . . ."

If one considers these words too strong, too dramatic, it is only necessary to look at the record. As Kohlberg repeatedly pointed out, the United States since the time of Teheran, Yalta, and Potsdam had acquired an unenviable record for surrenders and betrayals which had turned entire nations over to Communism. The list is long— Yugoslavia, Poland, Czechoslovakia, China, Cuba, and others. Plus 400,000 prisoners of war who surrendered to our armies and who were turned over to Stalin, plus a million more, Russian escapees, also returned to Stalin to be killed or enslaved.

Since World War II we have repeatedly appeased the Soviet Union in the fatuous hope that our "gestures" of goodwill would cause the Communists to "mellow." Unfortunately there has been little indication of mellowing. On the contrary there has been continuing Russian belligerence, dramatized most recently by that country's invasion of Czechoslovakia. Because of the weakness we have shown in the face of continuing Communist aggression we find ourselves pretty much alone in the world today, untrusted, facing a conspiracy that is openly dedicated to our destruction, set on a course that permits no deviation.

This is what Kohlberg was trying to explain to Senator Taft, that the Communists have set down their plan for world conquest, just as Hitler had spelled out his in *Mein Kampf,* and all one has to do is read it and act accordingly, without being diverted by tactical maneuvers. Indeed, everything that has happened in Asia for the past few decades, which so troubled Kohlberg, may be understood in the light of Lenin's words, set down in 1923 in *Better Fewer, But Better.* (Selected Works, International Publishers, N.Y., 1943, vol. IX, p. 400.)

"In the last analysis, the outcome of the struggle will be determined by the fact that Russia, India and China, etc., constitute the overwhelming majority of the population of the globe. And it is precisely the majority of the population that during the past few years has been drawn into the struggle for its emancipation with extraordinary rapidity, so that in this respect there cannot be the slightest shadow of doubt what the final outcome of the world struggle will be. In this sense, the final victory of socialism is fully and absolutely assured."

Those who hope for a détente with the Soviets seem to overlook this basic premise and as a result they are sometimes baffled at Soviet actions that should be perfectly obvious. In an earlier chapter mention was made of the way in which Kohlberg distributed the White Paper issued by the Republic of China and presented before the United Nations in 1949. Some idea of the way in which the USSR provided arms for the seizure of that country by Mao Tse-tung may be gained from the following excerpts from that document:

"Soviet active assistance to the Chinese Communists took a variety of forms. One of them was to facilitate their infiltration into Manchuria from North China, there to receive the arms and ammunition captured by or surrendered to the Soviet authorities by the Japanese. Another was for the Soviet authorities to permit the Chinese Communists to recruit locally large numbers of Japanese-sponsored puppet troops as well as bandits to augment their military power. Many of these units of puppet troops and bandits were well armed.

"According to Chinese Government reports, in the one-month period between August 9 to September 9, 1945, the Soviet Army in Manchuria captured 594,000 prisoners of war, 925 airplanes, 369 tanks, 35 armored cars, 1,226 pieces of field artillery, 4,836 machine guns, 300,000 rifles, 133 radio sets, 2,300 motor vehicles, 125 tractors, 17,497 horses and mules, and 742 depots with supplies. In addition, at the time of its surrender, the Japanese Kwantung Army had on its hands 1,436 pieces of field artillery, 8,989 machine guns, 11,052 grenade throwers, 3,078 trucks, 104,777 horses, 21,084 supply cars, 815 special vehicles, and 287 commanding cars. These captured equipment and supplies were not transferred to the Chinese Government. Neither were the surrendered items.

"Shortly after V-J Day the Chinese Communists under the command of Lin Piao infiltrated into Manchuria in large numbers, amounting to about 200,000 men. All of them were unarmed. A short time afterwards, these 200,-000 men were all fully armed with Japanese equipment and supplied with Japanese munitions. Since all the equipment and supplies of the Japanese forces in Manchuria were either captured by or surrendered to the Soviet forces, the Chinese Communist forces at that time could have only one source of supply—namely, the Soviet Army."

Since our administration's policy at that time was to withhold military assistance from Chiang Kai-shek unless he accepted the Communists into his government, this assured the eventual overthrow of this long-time ally. Much of the responsibility for this can be attributed to incredible gullibility on the part of people who should have known better. An example of this is provided by

Vice President Henry Wallace, whose counterparts are still in evidence today. In a 56-page pamphlet issued by the IPR and written in large part by Eleanor Lattimore, the Vice President of the United States went on record with this remarkable statement:

"The Russians have demonstrated their friendly attitude toward China by their willingness to refrain from intervening in China's internal affairs." Seven years later Wallace had second thoughts on this. Testifying before the McCarran Committee on October 17, 1951, he admitted, "It begins to look, for the time being at any rate, that my size-up as made in 1944 was incorrect." But by 1951 the damage had been done, and another nation had been lost to Communism.

Soviet arms again entered the picture when the Koreans swept across the 38th parallel into South Korea in 1950. Not only had the 200,000 North Koreans been armed with Russian tanks, artillery and other ordnance; they had also been trained by the Russians. Opposing them was a lightly armed constabulary of 100,000. And here too Washington had blundered. In his famous report of 1947, General A.C. Wedemeyer had warned of trouble ahead in Korea. Even then Communist agents were, in his words, "creating unrest and fomenting disorder in South Korea," and militarily the Communists were overwhelmingly superior. Their Soviet-equipped and trained North Korean People's Army at that time numbered 125,000 as against a South Korean Constabulary force of only 16,000, and General Wedemeyer urged the creation of a South Korean Scout Force, under U.S. control, "sufficient in strength to cope with the threat from the North."

The report, as we know, was suppressed and its recommendations ignored by the Truman administration.

MacArthur's headquarters had repeatedly warned of danger and one dispatch even predicted that the Communists were likely to cross the 38th parallel in June, as they did. But as Major General Courtney Whitney said, in *MacArthur, His Rendezvous with History,* "The U.S. had seemed to be trying to maneuver us into the diplomatic and military cul-de-sac in which it now found itself."

Later, Communism's relentless drive for all Asia was aimed at Laos, described by Arleigh Burke as "the key to control of the whole of Southeast Asia." Once a part of French Indochina, it was threatened by the Communist Pathet Lao, supported by Ho Chi Minh in North Vietnam, and supplied by the Soviet Union through an airlift. This threatening situation was passively accepted by the Eisenhower administration but it was felt that John F. Kennedy would put an end to the menace when he became President.

This could have been done. In General Phoumi Nosavan the Laotian government of Prince Boun Oum had a competent commander who in December 1960 defeated the Reds and drove them north. U.S. backing seemed assured when on March 23, 1961, President Kennedy made a television address in which he made a strong commitment to Laotian independence. Members of SEATO, the President said, "have undertaken special treaty obligations toward an aggressor in Laos. No one should doubt our resolution on this point." Unfortunately, this was another Kennedy pronouncement which proved to be only an exercise in rhetoric. A few weeks later at Vienna the famous confrontation between Kruschchev and Kennedy took place and the upshot was that Kennedy agreed to the neutralization of Laos.

When the Pathet Lao then became more aggressive Kennedy forced the Laotian government to accept the troika arrangement demanded by Krushchev. Knowing what such a coalition meant, General Phoumi Nosavan and Prince Boun Oum were reluctant to enter it. At this point W. Averell Harriman came onstage. Then Assistant Secretary of State for the Far East, Harriman played the same role that General Marshall had enacted in China when he ordered Chiang to form a coalition government with the Communists—or else. As reported by Joseph Alsop in the New York *Herald Tribune* of April 23, 1962, Harriman attempted to browbeat the Laotian cabinet into a coalition government by reminding them that withdrawal of $3,000,000 a month in foreign aid would be followed by the suspension of military aid. He stated that if the cabinet did not join forces with the Communist and pro-Communist Laotians they would be "responsible for the destruction of their country." Alsop said that General Phoumi Nosavan listened in silence, then replied, "You know, Governor Harriman, we in Laos have many years' experience of colonial rule. But we were never spoken to in quite that fashion in colonial times."

Criticizing Harriman for what he called his "tragic and scabrous views" on this occasion, Nhouy Abhay, education minister in the Boun Oum regime, said, "If we join a coalition under Souvanna Phouma Laos will be lost to the Communists within two years."

The hard-pressed Laotians gave in on June 14, 1962.

Harriman was one of Kohlberg's targets. In a letter to President Truman, dated August 30, 1950, he criticized him as follows:

"As our Ambassador to Moscow, during the latter part of the war, he was either the architect, or at least the chief draftsman, of our Soviet give-away program. He it was who prepared the secret Yalta Agreement giving the Far East to Russia. He brought this to Yalta and had it agreed to by President Roosevelt and Harry Hopkins in a 15-minute session with Stalin and Molotov, according to Secretary Stettinius. When the British learned of it later, it is reported Eden urged Churchill to refuse to sign it, but he said he couldn't fight America and Russia so gave in. I hope Mr. Harriman knows better now, but his education and the development of his judgment are too costly in American lives."

The roving ambassador, as he was often called, again

came to the fore at the time Ngo Dinh Diem's government was in a crisis created by propagandists operating
for the most part in that unfortunate country. Vietnam was
seething because of so-called Buddhist demonstrations
which were being conducted with military precision from
pagodas that were centers of subversion. Headquarters for
the agition was the Xa Loi pagoda where the notorious
left-wing rabble-rouser Thich Tri Quang held forth, incessantly demanding that Diem be eliminated. From the Xa
Loi pagoda went forth not only vast quantities of anti-
government propaganda but unfortunate dupes who had
been persuaded to burn themselves for the cause. The
burnings took place after reporters and photographers
had been given due notice so they could be present for
the spectacles.

The American press, or at least an important part of it,
took a leading role in the outcry against Diem, and this
had a predictable effect on the Kennedy administration,
always sensitive to "world opinion." President Kennedy
named Henry Cabot Lodge as Ambassador to Saigon to
replace Frederic E. Nolting, Jr., who was sympathetic to
the Diem regime. Lodge had no such sympathies. Shortly
after he arrived in Vietnam he reported to the State Department that Diem should be ousted, and he showed his
partiality toward those who were intriguing against the
government. Indeed, the ringleader of the agitators,
Thich Tri Quang, was given asylum in the United States
Embassy when he was being sought for creating disorders
against the government.

The stage was being set for the overthrow of Diem and
in Washington a curious incident took place, described by
the late Marguerite Higgins in her excellent book, *Vietnam Nightmare:*

"The crucial act," said Miss Higgins, "with its overtones
of Greek tragedy, opened with a cable. It was dispatched
to Saigon late in the evening of August 24, 1963, a date

made more significant because it was a Saturday ... The telegram contained spectacular new instructions for the U.S. Embassy in Saigon. It was drawn up at a meeting called by Undersecretary of State Averell Harriman and Roger Hilsman, Assistant Secretary of State for Far Eastern Affairs and head of the Vietnam task force. The President's senior advisers were, for the most part, out of town. C.I.A. Director John McCone was in California. Defense Secretary Robert McNamara was on vacation. Secretary of State Rusk was attending a baseball game in New York. President Kennedy was at Hyannis Port. General Taylor says he knew nothing of the meeting until it was over and the telegram was long on its way.

"The circumstances suggest that the timing of the meeting was not accidental. . . .

"In any case, the cable proved historic. For the first time it gave the signal to 'unleash' the Vietnamese military, flashed a green light for the *coup d'etat* against Diem of which the generals had been talking for so many months."

Miss Higgins quoted Ambassador Nolting that "what the generals were after of course was a flat assurance that if Diem were overthrown the military could continue to have U.S. support—that we would not punish them by withholding aid or recognition."

They got it and went ahead with the dirty business that ended in the assassination of President Diem and Minister Nhu. This threw the country into chaos and the main beneficiaries were the Communists. The military situation deteriorated rapidly as generals fought for political power. The Communists, surprised and pleased at this unexpected break, exploited it to the fullest.

Despite this, and possibly because of his demonstrated talent for forcing compliance on dependent nations, Harriman was named chief negotiator when, just prior to the 1968 elections, President Johnson felt that the time had come to stop the bombing of North Vietnam and negotiate with the North Vietnamese—a course stridently advocated by pacifist and left-wing followers of Senators Eugene McCarthy, George McGovern, and the late Robert Kennedy. Cynics maintain that the President made this move to improve Hubert Humphrey's chances of being elected President, but it is possible that this thought never entered his mind. However, his choice of Harriman to represent the United States at the Paris negotiations indicates that he had hopes that some kind of a deal could be worked out which Ho Chi Minh might not find too distasteful, and possibly before the American people went to the polls.

The Communists, however, demonstrated no spirit of give and take, and Humphrey lost the election. Now more hopeful that they might not be forced into a coalition with the Communists, the South Vietnamese representatives at Paris stalled until the Nixon administration took over. This resulted in a strange performance as administration pressures were openly exerted on the South Vietnamese in an attempt to get them to make concessions. Fortunately the plucky South Vietnamese resisted, and in the midst of their tribulations they probably got a measure of satisfaction when, following the election, W. Averell Harriman glumly announced to the press that his services as a roving ambassador, trouble-shooter and negotiator were being dispensed with as of January 20, 1969. However, a rather ironical note was added when it was subsequently announced that his successor would be none other than Henry Cabot Lodge.

The strange interplay of journalism and diplomacy that had caused the loss of China to Communism and which Alfred Kohlberg repeatedly denounced, was much in evidence at the time of the Diem crisis. Here again influential publications distorted the facts by informing readers that the anti-government demonstrations being staged by Thich Tri Quang were actually battles in a religious war which had been brought on because Diem, a Catholic, was brutally persecuting Buddhists. Among the publications that spread this propaganda were *Newsweek, The New Yorker, Time,* and *The New York Times.* Especially noteworthy were the dispatches of David Halberstam, a youthful reporter of *The New York Times.*

Writing in the magazine *America* about the press coverage of Thich Tri Quang's activities, Fr. Patrick O'Connor, who was in Vietnam at the time, pointed out that not all the foreign correspondents who were there contributed to the drumfire of anti-Diem propaganda. However, he reports that when the regime fell a significant event took place:

"About three weeks after the *coup d'etat* of November 1, the foreign correspondents in Saigon—with some exceptions—were invited by the Buddhist bonzes, as a mark of appreciation, to a dinner. It was given in the premises of Xa Loi pagoda, which had been the bonzes' command post during most of their campaign. The guests were greeted by girl members of Buddhist Youth, who pinned on each a yellow Buddhist ribbon. The nine-course dinner —vegetarian, to be sure—was enjoyed in the jubilant atmosphere of a victory celebration."

Since the public has a notoriously short memory, relatively few Americans at the time of the Diem tragedy recalled how influential publications at the end of World War II had similarly opposed Chiang Kai-shek. Like Diem, Chiang was smeared by the liberal press as corrupt and reactionary, and he was accused of lining his pockets and the pockets of his relatives with American dollars. That all this was untrue was beside the point. The point was that these men were not liberal enough to suit those who try to make foreign policy through the communications media, and so they had to go.

However, the American public certainly should be aware that they are today threatened by a satellite of the

Soviet Union only ninety miles from our shores, thanks in no small measure to the power of the press.

A reminder of the way that particular menace was created may be in order.

In December 1956, Fidel Castro, a relatively unknown rabble-rouser, together with eleven followers, were holed up in the Sierra Maestra mountains of Cuba, the remnant of a group of 83 who had "invaded" the country from Mexico on a leaky boat, the *Granma*. Most of the original invaders had been wiped out or had given up, and the remaining twelve were considered so unimportant that Batista gave up looking for them. Castro himself was thought to be dead.

Ignored and unable to gain recruits, Castro shrewdly decided that he needed publicity. He sent an emissary to Mrs. Ruby Hart Phillips, resident correspondent of the *New York Times* in Havana, telling her that he was available for an interview. Mrs. Phillips reported this to New York and Herbert L. Matthews, the paper's "Latin American expert" was dispatched to meet with the bearded one.

As a result of this meeting the *Times* published three articles which have now become historic. The first appeared on Sunday, February 24, 1957. It was prominently featured on the front page and was widely syndicated throughout the United States and the world. This and the succeeding articles portrayed Fidel Castro in the most effusive terms as a brilliant idealist, a veritable Robin Hood, who was going to overthrow Batista and give the Cuban people a new deal. Matthews categorically denied that Castro was a Communist. According to this "expert" he was strongly anti-Communist.

Following the publicity buildup in the *Times* other representatives of the communications media rushed to get into the act. Television cameras were hauled into the Sierra Maestra by crews working for the big networks, and these image-makers were supplemented by reporters representing numerous newspapers and magazines. Before long Castro was a celebrity, inflated into such heroic proportions that he was a power to be reckoned with. There was no longer any lack of recruits to his cause, and in the United States, our State Department made little if any attempt to interfere with the glamorized Fidelistas who were working in this country to overthrow Cuba's anti-Communist government, one which had always cooperated with Washington.

Reminiscent of the way in which Owen Lattimore had been called on by certain government officials to advise and counsel people who had to be informed about China, Herbert Matthews was used as an official fount of wisdom on Cuba. When Earl T. Smith was being sent to Cuba as our ambassador, the State Department called on Herbert L. Matthews to assist with his briefing.

For a long period of time, after it became painfully apparent that Matthews had been very wrong indeed about Castro, his byline disappeared from the *Times*. However, he was still quietly employed there, in "expert" capacity. He surfaced briefly in August 1967 when the *Times* offered its readers four articles under the Matthews byline on the occasion of his retirement. One of these presented his views on Asia.

It seems that Matthews was also an expert on the mysterious East. "Asia," he explained to *Times* readers, "is so old. The United States is so new." After this profound observation he went on to take issue with Rudyard Kipling's thesis that East is East and West is West and never the twain shall meet. This, said Matthews, "is only partly true," and "wisdom lies in sensing the degree to which Kipling was wrong as well as right."

Following this philosophical foray, Matthews told how he had absorbed much oriental wisdom as a war correspondent in India in 1942–1943, a year which for some reason he described as "chastening." However, the nub of his essay was this: "After all, it was the Communists in their famous 'Hundred Regiments Offensive' who had fought the Japanese. Chiang and the Kuomintang, with American arms and money, did nothing. General 'Vinegar Joe' Stilwell launched into a typical string of expletives when we discussed Chiang, his wealthy family, and his useless army at the time.

"When the mainland went completely Communist in 1949 I agreed with Secretary of State Acheson that nothing the United States could have done would have saved Chiang Kai-shek."

All of which seems to prove that Herbert L. Matthews was every bit as much of an expert on Asia as he was on Cuba. However, it seems strange indeed that the *Times* was willing to advertise the fact.

It would be gratifying indeed to report that the *Times* finally gave up this kind of interpretive reporting. There is no denying that it is outstanding among newspapers, and admirable in many respects. Unfortunately, there has been more of the same. In 1967, its assistant managing editor, Harrison Salisbury, was escorted through sections of North Vietnam hit by U.S. planes trying to cripple Ho Chi Minh's war-making potential. Unfortunately and understandably, some civilians were killed—just as hundreds of thousands of civilians were killed when we bombed Germany and Japan during World War II. Then it was apparently right and proper, but this was somehow different. Salisbury presented—from Communist sources —a lachrymose account of deaths and injuries caused by our bombing of Communist North Vietnam, and it was just what the Vietnik-pacifist set needed to start them off on another crusade to "stop the bombing." And once again the United States took a propaganda beating at home and abroad.

It is interesting to note that Salisbury was once the

subject of a piece written by Alfred Kohlberg in 1951. He was then Moscow correspondent of the *Times* and Kohlberg was highly critical of some of the stuff he was then sending back to his paper. He was especially irked at a dispatch in which Salisbury explained that the Russians were suspicious of us because we had intervened in an attempt to destroy the infant Communist regime after World War I. Kohlberg denounced this as straight Communist propaganda and submitted Salisbury's piece to Major General David F. Barrows, who had commanded American troops in Siberia in 1918–1919. Refuting Salisbury's story in detail, the General concluded:

"Mr. Salisbury has been imposed upon by Communist propaganda which is doubtless effective with the benighted minds of Russians and Chinese but which should not influence any critical mind and especially an American correspondent. His whole dispatch seems to be a plea for American acceptance of untruthful and gross Communist propaganda."

Today the blatant kind of pro-Communist book reviewing that was prevalent during the China crisis is not so much in evidence, but one does not have to look hard to find traces of the same bias that was so obvious two decades ago. On November 13, 1966, the reprehensible "buddy system" of the old IPR days became apparent in a book review by John K. Fairbank, a former IPR functionary. The book being reviewed was *The United States and China in World Affairs.* It was written by Robert Blum and edited by A. Doak Barnett. Professor Fairbank found it good, very good indeed, and was pleased mightily with its theme that "the Peking Government cannot and should not be excluded indefinitely from the normal channels of international contact." Underscoring the importance of this message, *The New York Times Book Review* gave an entire page to the book and Fairbank's laudatory essay plugging it.

The cat was let out of the bag a month later. A *Times* story of December 11, 1966, reported that "4 Critics on China Get Policy Posts." The story told how "four outspoken academic critics of the Johnson Administration's policy toward Communist China have been named to the State Department's new advisory panel on China." Among the four were A. Doak Barnett, who edited the Blum book, and John K. Fairbank who reviewed it.

The same December 11, 1966, issue of the *Times* carried another book review, this one dealing with a volume called *Why Vietnam?* by Frank N. Trager. The reviewer turned thumbs down on this one, and you may be able to figure out why from these quotations from the review:

"Trager's haste to prove Communist villainy leads him to some rather bizarre assertions . . ."

". . . his analytical ability is overcome by his militant anti-Communism, and the book degenerates into a pamphlet for an anti-Communist crusade rather than a dispassionate historical account."

Probably the most damning of all was this: "He heads a group of intellectuals who are attempting to prevent American diplomatic recognition of Communist China and to keep Peking out of the United Nations."

Of course the liberal people who review books for the *Times* cannot permit *that.*

Again and again and again, as we have seen, the Communists repeat the same tactics against us, and again and again and again we fall for them. This is not because the men in the Kremlin are so diabolically clever. It is because so many Americans, preoccupied with the pursuit of happiness in one form or another, permit our foreign policy to be dictated by a relatively small minority. These people control or have access to the powerful communications media, they hold forth in universities, on lecture platforms, in pulpits and in other places where their voices can be amplified out of all proportion to their numbers.

Unfortunately, the din these people create is often taken seriously by politicians who believe that what they are hearing is the voice of the people.

What do these people want? It varies from month to month and from year to year. Get out of Korea! Get out of Vietnam! Negotiate now! Recognize Red China! Ban the bomb! Hands off Cuba! Stop the bombing! Sign this or that treaty! Disarm!

Usually what these people want coincides to a remarkable degree with what Moscow and Peking would like. This certainly is not meant to imply that all those people who buy and sign those expensive advertisements, who march up and down with placards, who address student rallies and church congregations, and who appear on so many television forums are Communists. Very few of them can be so classified. But sometimes it seems as though they are far more interested in promoting the aims of the Soviet Union and Red China than they are in working in the interests of their own country.

People of this stripe incessantly proclaim that it is up to the United States to show good faith to the Soviet Union, despite Russia's record of half a century. They tell us we must get out of Vietnam, where we are trying to prevent another Communist seizure, but the Russian invasion of Czechoslovakia bothers them not a bit. They insist that we must stop interfering in the affairs of other nations, but the fact that the Kremlin is trying to subvert the entire western hemisphere from a base in the Caribbean fails to excite them.

Thanks in large measure to such people, Americans are being subjected to a massive propaganda campaign designed to prove that Communism is "mellowing" and is rapidly becoming many other things, depending on the country in which it holds sway. Certainly, these propagandists tell us, Communism is not the menace it used to be —indeed it is not Communism at all when you come down to it—and with a few concessions and adjustments on our part we can get along just fine with the people behind the Iron Curtain. In an attempt to prove this premise our television screens and printed pages show us Ivan Ivanovich as a very nice person who only wants the good things of life, the same as we do. So why should we not help him achieve the good life by trading with Communist nations, signing a few more treaties, junking our weapons and otherwise "building bridges of understanding between East and West"? Above all, we should stop speaking harshly about Communism and Communists. The danger, we are assured, is not from Communists but from McCarthyism and right-wing extremism which make a détente difficult.

No doubt many Ivan Ivanoviches are very nice persons as individuals, and it appears that changes are taking place in Communism. However, we are not permitted to reach the nice Ivan Ivanoviches and have to deal with the likes of Kosygin, Brezhnev, Gromyko, and others who are not so nice. As for those changes in Communism, they do not encompass any change whatever in the line laid down years ago by the founding fathers of Communism that capitalism and Communism cannot possibly exist side by side. The United States remains enemy number one, and on this point there is no disagreement among Communists, whether they be Russian, Chinese, Bulgarian, East German, or American. Evidence of this can be found in the endless procession of ships, from Communist countries, bearing arms to Vietnam and other nations where American interests and American citizens can be hurt.

This is not the first time we have been subjected to propaganda assuring us that peaceful coexistence is possible. In 1933, when President Roosevelt signed the treaty that recognized the USSR, we were solemnly promised that the Bolsheviks were not going to act like Bolsheviks as far as the United States was concerned. Among other things they swore that they would never meddle in this country's internal affairs. So much for Communist assurances!

We were soon disillusioned but of course we did not learn. Less than a decade later the same kind of propaganda started up again. Good old Joe Stalin desperately needed help, and to get it from us he mellowed amazingly. Even God was tolerated in the Soviet Union—for the duration. Not only did we save Stalin from defeat but we put him on his feet with $11 billion in lend-lease goods, much of which was used to get his post-war industry going. Then, to keep him mellow, our politicians threw in a few countries that of course did not belong to us. Even so, he did not stay mellow very long.

It is interesting to note how the initiative for all this bridge-building between East and West comes from this side of the Atlantic. We make the concessions, we hanker for the opportunity to sign another treaty, we stage the propaganda circuses to prove to ourselves that this time the Russians are going to behave differently. Meanwhile, back at the Kremlin it's the same old monkey business as usual.

There have been some changes in the cast, of course. Some of those who were involved in the tragedy of China have passed to their reward, while others have seen fit to take up residence in other lands. In some cases you will find the offspring of the home-grown traitors of Kohlberg's time leading some of the more gullible youth of today. Frequently you will also see some of the discredited "experts" of yesteryear holding forth on television, seasoning their advice on foreign policy with an overpowering amount of gall. For all too often their recommendations have the same orientation as they had in the past.

Even Owen Lattimore got into the act not long ago.

This "conscious, articulate instrument of the Soviet conspiracy," as he was dubbed by the McCarran Committee, is now teaching in England, and in 1966 an investment publication called *The Value Line Investment Survey* called on him for some words of wisdom about Vietnam. The Professor, of course, obliged.

Any study of Dr. Lattimore's prose makes it necessary to wade through a certain amount of verbal smog, but in this case the message came through loud and clear, like an echo of the good old days when the Professor was articulating at the IPR. Here is a sampling of what *Value Line* readers were told by him:

"There are three basic blunders in the official analysis of Vietnam: (1) that the trouble is of Communist origin; (2) that North and South Vietnam are two quite separate sovereign states, and that the North has wantonly attacked the South; and (3) that if South Vietnam is not shored up the rest of Southeast Asia will go, like falling dominoes."

And how would Lattimore handle this problem? Here is his solution:

"We have committed ourselves to the line that the Vietcong is controlled by Hanoi, and Hanoi by Peking, and that the essence of the quarrel is aggression by North Vietnam against the South. If, however, there is an important movement of Buddhists and others, including some of the military, to negotiate with the Vietcong and work toward neutralism, then we are automatically freed of our commitment because the Buddhist movement is a domestic movement."

All of which shows a singular lack of originality. This sounds just like the cagey Johns Hopkins savant of yesteryear, and it sounds suspiciously like the same kind of advice he dispensed to President Truman and impressionable people in our State Department. Of course in those good old days we were not being called on to deal with Buddhists; they were then called agrarian reformers.

Unfortunately, the Professor overlooked one detail in his *Value Line* composition. He forgot to suggest that we give South Vietnam a parting gift of, say, $150,000,000 and then let it topple without letting it appear that the United States had pushed it. But then we are all becoming old and forgetful.

Asked why this sort of stuff was presented to readers of *Value Line*, an official brightly explained that "Over the years we have, in fact, found that the intelligent exchange of conflicting views is a stimulating and instructive experience."

This kind of rationalization is as good an explanation as any for the sort of stuff that often appears in print. Thanks to those who dote on offering the public "stimulating and instructive" experiences, regardless of the source, people such as Lattimore may be down but they are never out. Certainly they never lack a forum.

It is gratifying to report that some of those who contributed to previous foreign policy disasters have apparently learned from their experience. Notable among these are Dean Acheson and Dean Rusk, who were no heroes to Alfred Kohlberg. At the time of the Cuban missile crisis in October 1962, Acheson was asked to join a Presidential advisory group which became known as the Executive Committee of the National Security Council (Excom). He advocated a hard line in dealing with the Soviets who had brought missiles to Cuba and were building missile sites to launch them. Recognizing that the security of the United States was at stake and that the Russians had no business being in Cuba, he urged that the United States move forcefully. Robert Kennedy, fearful of "world opinion," opposed Acheson who finally stopped attending the meetings. The views of the appeasers prevailed, as we know, and the upshot of the missile crisis was that Communism was given a sanctuary in the Caribbean.

More recently, on December 11, 1966, Dean Acheson

expressed himself on Rhodesia in a now-famous letter which was published in the *Washington Post*. Commenting on an editorial which had appeared in that newspaper, Mr. Acheson pointed out that "Whatever the Rhodesians have done has been done wholly within their own country and contains no element of aggression. But you bother me when you speak of 'the white minority's transgressions.' Transgressions against what? What international obligations have they violated?

"International law does not proclaim the sanctity of British dominion over palm and pine. Certainly we Americans are in no position to declare it—we who conspired to instigate French aggression against British power in America and not only threatened but shattered international peace to achieve our independence."

In this letter not only did Dean Acheson attack the British position on Rhodesia, strongly supported by American liberals. He even criticized the United Nations! Our former Secretary of State accused it of "reasoning worthy of the Red Queen in *Through the Looking Glass*.

"Since Rhodesia by doing what it has always done and with which the United Nations cannot constitutionally interfere, incites less law-abiding members to violate their solemn obligation not to use force or the threat of force in their international relations, Rhodesia becomes a threat to the peace and must be coerced.

"If this reasoning leads the readers to ask with Mr. Chandler, 'Who's loony now?', don't blame Rhodesia, blame the Security Council and Harold Wilson."

During the Kennedy administration Dean Rusk took an ambiguous position. Reflecting this, at the time of the Bay of Pigs and the missile crisis he was neither hawk nor dove but was one of those described as "dawks" and "hoves." Under President Johnson, however, he took a fairly firm stand on Vietnam and this made him anathema to the leftists and liberals who demanded peace with the Communists at any price. Attacks on the Secretary of State became increasingly vicious and personal, and Dean Rusk was well aware of the source of much of the antagonism. In a *New York Times Magazine* article dealing with "The Anti-Vietnam Agitation and the Teach-in Movement," published October 22, 1965, Secretary Rusk is quoted as follows:

"I sometimes wonder at the gullibility of educated men, and the stubborn disregard of plain facts by men who are supposed to be helping our young to learn—especially to learn how to think."

The *Times* staffer who wrote the article accused Rusk of being "uncharitable" for this statement. After all, the Secretary of State was attacking some of *The New York Times'* best advertisers, thousands of them, who regularly buy large-space ads to offer the government their unsolicited advice on how the country and the world should be run. Some of these ad-takers have become more or less notorious over the years for their dalliance with Communists and Communist causes, but most of them are sincere, well-meaning people, much like a Chinese friend of Alfred Kohlberg named Victor Wang.

Kohlberg tells of meeting Wang, an architect and builder, in Swatow in 1949. They entered into a discussion of the Communists who were then taking over China, and Wang took issue with Kohlberg's warnings about the future of China under Mao Tse-tung.

"We know you are an old friend of China, widely traveled in our country," said Wang, "But after all, you are not Chinese and you will never understand us. These Commies may have cockeyed economic ideas, but they are Chinese like us and so we will get along with them somehow."

Other Chinese present agreed with Wang.

Nearly four years later, in British Hong Kong, Kohlberg met some Chinese friends from Swatow, now refugees from the Communist regime.

"What of Victor Wang?" he asked them. They told him that Victor had welcomed the Communists, had taken a contract to lengthen and strengthen the concrete runway at the airport, and had completed the job. But at that point he had been arrested, accused of overcharging the People's Government, and executed.

"Victor Wang," Kohlberg concluded, "died of too much understanding."

The same kind of "understanding," based on a belief that Communists are essentially liberals, though a little extreme in their liberalism, can be fatal not only to those who hold this view but to all of us.

This was an important part of the message that Alfred Kohlberg tried to get across. His basic aim was to show the evil of Communism and the threat it posed to free men everywhere. Once he became aware of this evil his sole aim in life was its destruction. The strategy he employed he may have learned from Lenin himself, who had proclaimed:

"We must train men and women who will devote to the revolution not merely their spare evenings, but the whole of their lives."

To the counter-revolution Kohlberg devoted equal zeal, which made him almost unique among Americans.

APPENDIX A

The following document, "China's New Democracy," appeared in 1940. In it Mao set forth a statement of Communist policy for the conditions presented by the situation in China, and his intention to establish a socialist republic modeled after the USSR. The text originally appeared in the January 15, 1941, issue of *Chinese Culture* and was reprinted in *The Communist Conspiracy*, published on May 29, 1956, by the House Committee on Un-American Activities.

CHINA'S NEW DEMOCRACY
by Mao Tse-Tung
I. WHITHER CHINA?

After the war of resistance began, a cheering and inspiring air prevailed among our countrymen. The former brow-knitted faces were no longer seen, for all believed that our nation had at last found a way out. It is only the recent atmosphere of compromise and the tide of anti-Communism which grows higher daily, that has again created a state of bewilderment. This fact is especially obvious among young students and people of the cultural field whose senses are more acute than those of others. Thus, the question "How to proceed?" or "Whither China?" again stands before us. Because of this, it may be worth while to utilize the opportunity of the publication of the *Chinese Culture* magazine to say a few words about the trend of Chinese politics and Chinese culture. I am a layman in cultural problems. I wish very much to make a study of them, but in such work I have only taken the first step. However, many thoroughgoing articles have been written by our comrades in Yenan on the subject, so this rough sketch of mine may be looked upon as a mere prelude. To the senior cultural workers of the country, our work here serves only as a humble suggestion, through which, we hope, joint discussion can be aroused and a correct conclusion that suits the needs of our nation drawn. A scientific attitude should be one that "searches for the truth from concrete facts," and problems can never be solved with vain, self-assertive and self-important attitudes. The catastrophe of our nation is grave. Only a scientific attitude and a spirit of responsibility can lead us to the road of emancipation. There is but one truth. This truth is determined not by subjective boasting but by objective practice. Only the revolutionary practice of millions of people can be taken as the gauge for measuring truths. Such is our attitude in the publication of the *Chinese Culture*.

II. WE MUST ESTABLISH A NEW CHINA

For the many past years, Communists have struggled not only for the political and economic revolution in China, but also for the cultural revolution, all aiming at the construction of a new society and a new country for the Chinese people, in which not only a new system of politics and economy but also a new culture will prevail. This means that we have not only to change politically oppressed and economically exploited China into a country politically free and economically prosperous, but also to change a country whose people are so ignorant, backward and long ruled by an old culture, into a civilized, progressive one ruled by a new culture. In brief we must construct a New China. And to establish a new culture of the Chinese nation is the aim of our work in the cultural sphere.

III. CHINA'S HISTORICAL CHARACTERISTICS

What is this new culture of the Chinese nation that we are going to establish?

Any given culture (as a form of ideas) is the reflection of a given political and economic system of society, though the former in turn exerts immense influence upon the latter; and politics is the concentrated expression of economy. This is our fundamental point of view toward the relationship of culture, politics and economy. Hence it is the given politics and economy that first determines the given culture, which only subsequently itself exerts influence upon the politics and economy. Marx said: "It is not the ideology of the society that determines its existence, but the existence of the society that determines its ideology." He also added: "Philosophers of former times only explained the world, but the important point is how to change and improve the world." This is the first scientific explanation in the history of mankind, correctly to answer the question of the relation between ideology and existence, and that became the fundamental starting point of Lenin's motive, revolutionary theory of reflection which was developed from this Marxist point of view. In our discussion of China's cultural problems, this starting point should never be neglected.

It is quite clear then that the old culture which we wish to sweep away cannot be isolated from the old politics and old economy of our nation, and the new culture which we aim to establish cannot be isolated from our new politics and new economy. The old politics and old economy are the foundations of the old culture; and the new politics and new economy of the new culture.

What is the content of the so-called old politics and old economy of China? And what is the content of the old culture?

Since the Chow and Chin dynasties, China has been a feudal society. Her politics and economy have been feudal in character. So has her culture—the reflection of her politics and economy.

Nevertheless, since the aggression of foreign capitalism, and since some capitalist elements gradually grew within Chinese society, *i. e.*, in the hundred years from the Opium War to the present anti-Japanese war, China gradually turned into a colonial, semi-colonial and semi-feudal society. At present, in the occupied territories, the society is colonial in character; in the non-occupied areas, it is semi-colonial; while in both of them the feudal system still dominates. This is the character of the present Chinese society, or the "national condition" of China. The dominant politics and economy are therefore colonial, semi-colonial and semi-feudal in character; and so is the culture.

These dominant politics, economy and culture are the objects of our revolution. It is the old colonial, semi-colonial and semi-feudal politics, economy and culture that we aim to sweep away, and it is new politics, economy and culture, something exactly opposite to the old, that we are going to establish.

Then what should be the content of the new politics and new economy of the Chinese nation? And what should be the content of the new culture?

The historical process of the Chinese revolution must be divided into two stages: first the democratic revolution and then the socialist revolution—two revolutionary processes quite different in character.

The democracy mentioned here is not the old democracy of the old type, but the New Democracy of the new type.

Therefore it may be concluded that the new politics, economy and culture of the Chinese nation are nothing other than the politics, economy and culture of the New Democracy.

This is the historical characteristic of the present Chinese revolution. Whoever, while engaging in revolutionary work in China, does not comprehend this historical characteristic will not be able to direct the revolution or carry it on to victory. On the contrary, he will be forsaken by the people and will inevitably become a pitiful failure.

IV. CHINA'S REVOLUTION IS A PART OF THE WORLD REVOLUTION

The historical characteristic of the Chinese revolution is that it is divided into two steps, that of democracy and that of socialism. The democracy of the first step is not democracy in its general sense, but a new, special type of a Chinese style, the New Democracy. How then was this historical characteristic formed? Did it originally exist during these hundred years or was it generated only afterwards?

A superficial study of the historical development of China and the world will reveal that such a historical characteristic did not exist in the days of the Opium War or in the period immediately following it, but took shape after the first imperialist world war and the Russian October Revolution. Let us now stop to study the process of its formation.

It is evident that if the present society of China is colonial, semi-colonial and semi-feudal in character, the process of China's revolution must be divided into two steps. The first step is to change the colonial, semi-colonial and semi-feudal form of society into an independent democratic society, while the second step is to push the revolution forward to establish a socialist society. What we are carrying on now is the first step of the Chinese revolution.

This first step may be said to have begun from the days of the Opium War in 1840, *i. e.*, from the time when the Chinese society commenced to change from its original feudal form to the semi-colonial and semi-feudal form. During this period, we had the Tai Ping Revolution, the Sino-French War, the Sino-Japanese War, the Reform Movement of 1898, the 1911 Revolution, the May 4th Movement, the May 30th Movement, the Northern Expedition, the Agrarian

Revolution, the December 9th Movement, and the present Anti-Japanese War. All the above movements, to speak from a certain point of view, were for the realization of the first step of China's revolution. They were movements of the Chinese people in different periods and in different degrees to realize such a step—to oppose imperialism and feudalism and to struggle for the establishment of an independent democratic society. The 1911 Revolution was only its realization in a more concrete sense. This revolution, in its social character, was a bourgeois-democratic revolution and not a proletarian-socialist revolution. It is not yet consummated, and therefore needs our further effort, because the enemies of this revolution are still extremely strong at present. The word "revolution" in Dr. Sun's famous saying: "The revolution is not yet consummated, and our comrades must still exert their efforts" refers to this bourgeois-democratic revolution.

A change took place in the Chinese bourgeois-democratic revolution after the outbreak of the first imperialist world war and the formation of the socialist state on one-sixth of the earth's surface through the success of the Russian October Revolution in 1917.

Before that, the Chinese bourgeois-democratic revolution belonged to the category of the old bourgeois-democratic revolution of the world, and was a part of it.

Since then, the Chinese bourgeois-democratic revolution has changed its character and belongs to the category of the new bourgeois-democratic revolution. As far as the revolutionary front is concerned, it is a part of the world proletarian-socialist revolution.

Why? Because the first imperialist world war and the victorious socialist October Revolution changed the historical direction of the world, and drew a sharp dividing line between two historical stages.

At a time when world capitalism has collapsed in one part of the earth (a part occupying one-sixth of the earth's surface), while elsewhere it has clearly shown its symptoms of decadence; when the remaining part of the capitalist world cannot go on without relying more than ever on the colonies and semi-colonies; when the Socialist state has been established and declares its willingness to assist the struggle for the liberation movements of all the colonies and semi-colonies; and when the proletariats of the capitalist countries are being freed day by day from the influence of the imperialist social-democratic parties and also declare themselves willing to assist the liberation movement of the colonies and semi-colonies; at a time like this, any revolution of the colonies and semi-colonies against imperialism, or international capitalism, can no longer belong to the category of the old bourgeois-democratic revolution of the world, but to a new category. It is no longer a part of the old bourgeois or capitalist world revolution but a part of the new world revolution—the proletarian-socialist revolution. This kind of revolutionary colonies and semi-colonies should not be considered the allies of the counter-revolutionary front of world capitalism, but allies in the front of the world socialist revolution.

Although according to social character, the first stage of the first step of this colonial and semi-colonial revolution is still fundamentally bourgeois-democratic, and its objective demands are to clear the obstacles in the way of the development of capitalism, yet this kind of revolution is no longer the old type led solely by the bourgeois class and aiming merely at the establishment of a capitalist society or a country under the dictatorship of the bourgeois class, but a new type led wholly or partially by the proletariat and aiming at the establishment of a New-Democratic society or a country ruled by the alliance of several revolutionary classes in its first stage. This kind of revolution, due to the variations in the condition of the enemy and in the conditions of this alliance may be divided into a certain number of stages during its process, but no change will occur in its fundamental character which will be the same until the arrival of the socialist revolution.

This kind of revolution is a great blow to imperialism, and therefore is not permitted but opposed by the imperialists. On the other hand, it is permitted by socialism, and is assisted by the Socialist state and the international socialist proletariat.

Thus, this kind of revolution has become a part of the proletarian-socialist world revolution.

"China's revolution is a part of the world revolution." This correct thesis was proposed as early as 1924-27 during the period of China's Great Revolution. It was advanced by the Communists and was approved by all who participated in the anti-imperialist and anti-feudal struggle of the time. Only the meaning of the theory was not much developed then, and what we mastered was only a dim comprehension of the question. I remember that when Mr. Chiang Kai-shek spoke at Swatow in 1925 during his expedition against Chen Chiung-ming, he also said: "China's revolution is a part of the world revolution."

This "world revolution" is not the old world revolution of the bourgeoisie which has long become a matter of the past, but is the new world revolution, the socialist revolution. In like manner, the "part" means not a part of the old bourgeois revolution but a part of the new socialist revolution. This is an exceedingly great change, a change unprecedented in the world history and the history of China.

It is basing themselves on the correct theory of Stalin that the Chinese Communists advanced this correct thesis.

As early as 1918, Stalin said, in his article commemorating the first anniversary of the October Revolution:

"The following are the three most important points out of the great world significance of the October Revolution. First, it enlarges the scope of the national problem, from the partial problem of opposing national oppression to the general problem of the liberation of oppressed peoples, colonies and semi-colonies from the yoke of imperialism. Secondly, it widens the possibility and opens the true road for this liberation, greatly promotes the liberation work of the Western and Eastern oppressed peoples, and attracts them into the common, victorious anti-imperialist course. Thirdly, it forms a bridge between the socialist West and the enslaved East, *i. e.,* it establishes a new anti-imperialist revolutionary front connecting the Western proletariat and the Eastern oppressed peoples through the Russian Revolution." (Stalin: "The October Revolution and the National Question," *Pravda,* Nov. 6 and 19, 1918.)

Since the publication of that article, Stalin has again and again developed the theory regarding the colonial and semi-colonial revolution, its separation from the old type, and its transformation into a part of the proletarian-socialist revolution. This theory was most clearly and correctly explained in an article published on June 30, 1925, when Stalin carried on a controversy with the Yugoslavian nationalists of that time. The article, entitled "The National Problem Once Again" read in part:

"Comrade Semich refers to a passage in Stalin's pamphlet *Marxism and the National Question,* written at the end of 1912. It says there that 'the national struggle is a struggle of the bourgeois classes among themselves.' By this he seems to hint at the correctness of his own formula for defining the social meaning of the national movement in present historical conditions. But Stalin's pamphlet was written before the imperialist war, at a time when the national question had not yet assumed world-wide significance in the eyes of the Marxists, and when the basic demand of the Marxists concerning the right of self-determination was considered to be, not a part of the proletarian revolution, but a part of the bourgeois-democratic revolution. It would be absurd to ignore the fact that, since then, a fundamental change has taken place in the international situation, that the war, on the one hand, and the October Revolution in Russia, on the other, have converted the national question from a particle of the bourgeois-democratic revolution into a particle of the proletarian-socialist revolution. As early as October 1916, Lenin in his article, 'The Discussion on Self-Determination Summed Up,' said that the main point of the national question concerning the right of self-determination has ceased to be a part of the general democratic movement, that it has become a constituent part of the general proletarian-socialist revolution. I shall not mention the subsequent works on the national question by Lenin and other representatives of Russian Communism. In view of all this, what significance can now be attached to Comrade Semich's reference to a certain passage in Stalin's pamphlet written in the period of the bourgeois-democratic revolution in Russia, since, as a result of the new historical situation, we have entered a new epoch, the epoch of the world proletarian revolution? The only significance that can be attached to it is that Comrade Semich quotes without regard for space and time, without regard for the actual historical condition. By that he violates the most elementary requirements of dialectics and fails to take into account the fact that what is correct in one historical situation may turn out to be incorrect in another historical situation."

From this we know that there exist two kinds of revolutions. The first, belonging to the bourgeois or capitalism category, has become a matter of the past since the outbreak of the first imperialist world war in 1914, and especially since the October Revolution of 1917. From then on, the second kind of world revolution commenced, the proletarian or socialist world revolution, with the proletariat of the capitalist countries as its main force and the oppressed peoples of the colonies and semi-colonies as its allies. No matter to what class or party the oppressed people who participate in the revolution belong, or whether or not they consciously or subjectively understand its significance, so long as they are anti-imperialist, their revolution is a part of the proletarian-socialist world revolution, and they themselves become its allies.

The signifiance of China's revolution is greatly magnified today, because it is happening at a time when the political and economic crises of capitalism have brought the world step by step toward the second imperialist war; when the Soviet Union has reached the transitional period from Socialism to Communism and has the ability to lead and to assist the proletariat, the oppressed peoples and all the revolutionary peoples of the world; when the proletarian forces of the various capitalist countries are growing stronger and stronger; and when the Communist Party, the proletariat, the peasantry, the intelligentsia and the petit-bourgeoisie become a mighty, independent political power. At such a time, should we not estimate that the world significance of China's revolution has been greatly magnified? We should. China's revolution is a magnificent part of the world revolution!

This first stage of China's revolution (which again is divided into many sub-stages) according to its social character, is a new bourgeois-democratic revolution, not the newest proletarian-socialist revolution, though it long ago in the past became a part of the latter, and is a magnificent part, a magnificent ally of it at the present. The first step or stage of this revolution is certainly not to, and certainly cannot, establish a capitalist society dictated by the bourgeoise, but to establish a New Democracy ruled by the alliance of several revolutionary classes. After the accomplishment of this first stage, it will be developed into the second stage—to establish the socialist society of China.

We Communists never repel the revolutionary people (provided they do not capitulate to the enemy or oppose the Communists). We shall persist in the united front with all those classes, strata, political parties, political cliques and individuals who insist on fighting against the Japanese to the end, and shall cooperate for a long term with them. But we shall not allow others to repel us or to split the united front. China must keep on resisting, consolidating and progressing. Whoever wishes to surrender, to split, or to go backward will not be tolerated by us.

VIII. REFUTATION OF "LEFT" DOCTRINAIRISM

If it is impossible for us to go the road of capitalism with a bourgeois dictatorship, would it be possible then for us to go the road of socialism with a proletarian dictatorship? No, it is just as impossible.

Without doubt, the present revolution is only the first step, and a second step—the step of socialism—will be developed in the future. It is only when China arrives at that stage, that she can be called really felicitous. But for the present, it is not the time to practice socialism. The present task of China's revolution is the task of anti-imperialism and anti-feudalism, before the accomplishment of which, it is empty verbiage to talk about the realization of socialism. China's revolution must be divided into two steps, the first being that of New Democracy, the second that of socialism. Moreover, the period of the first step is by no means a short one. It is not a matter that can be achieved overnight. We are not Utopians. We cannot isolate ourselves from the actual conditions right before our eyes.

Some ill-minded propagandists purposely mix up these two revolutionary stages, promoting the theory of "a single revolution," so as to prove that all revolutions are included in the San Min Chu I and that there is no ground for the existence of Communism. Armed with this "theory," they actually oppose Communism and the Communist Party, the Eighth Route and the New Fourth Armies, and the Shensi-Kansu-Ninghsia Border Region. Their aim is to annihilate fundamentally whatever revolution there is, to oppose the thorough realization of the burgeois-democratic revolution and the anti-Japanese war of resistance, and to prepare "public opinion" for their future capitulation to the Japanese robbers.

Such a situation is deliberately created by the Japanese, who, seeing that military force alone could not subjugate China even after the capture of Wu-han, have to resort to the aid of political offensive and economic enticement. Politically, they try to tempt the wavering elements within the anti-Japanese camp, to disrupt the united front, and to ruin the Kuomintang-Communist cooperation, while economically, they plan the intrigue of "industrial cooperation." The Japanese robbers permit the Chinese capitalists to invest 51 percent in Central and South China, and 49 percent in North China, of the capital in the "cooperating" industries, and return to the Chinese capitalists what has been confiscated from them, allowing the confiscated enterprises to be counted as their share of capital. Tempted by such a trick, some conscience-lacking capitalists, represented by Wang Ching-wei, jump at the trap, forgetting justice in front of private benefits, and surrender to the enemy. Others, who have been hiding in the anti-Japanese camp, yearn to go too, but they are timid, afraid that the Communists will stand in their way, and that the people will stigmatize them as traitors. Therefore, they assemble their fellows, and make decisions—to do some preparatory work beforehand in cultural and press circles. With such a plan fixed, they waste no time. Some "metaphysical devils" are mobilized, some Trotskyits are hired to take up their pens and madly bark at the Communists. The result is that a lot of "theories" are invented, such as that of "a single revolution," that Communism is not suitable for China, that there is no necessity for the Communist Party to exist, that the Eighth Route and the New Fourth Armies destroy resistance and sabotage guerrilla warfare, that the Shensi-Kansu-Ninghsia Border Region is a feudal partition, that the Communist Party is not loyal to the Government, disrupts unification, ferments intrigues and tries to make trouble, and so on and so forth, in order to deceive those who do not quite understand the real situation, so that when opportunity ripens, the capitalists may have reasons sound enough to enjoy their 49 percent or 51 percent shares at the expense of the benefit of the whole nation. This trick of theirs is merely the preparation of public thought and "public opinion" before the realization of the capitulation. These gentlemen seem to be serious-minded indeed when promoting the "theory" of "a single revolution" to oppose Communism and the Communist Party, but in their hearts there is nothing other than the sharing of the 49 percent or the 51 percent! How they have racked their brains! The theory of "a single revolution" is the theory of "no revolution." Such is the real nature of the beast.

But certain persons who do not seem to be ill-minded are also fascinated with the theory of "a single revolution" and lend themselves to the subjective thought of "accomplishing both the political revolution and the social revolution by one stroke." They do not understand that a revolution is divided into stages. We can proceed from one revolution to another revolution, but cannot "accomplish everything by one stroke." Their erroneous point of view inevitably confuses the revolutionary steps, decreases effort in realizing the present task, and is therefore very harmful. That the first one is the prerequisite of the second, and that one must follow the other closely, not permitting a bourgeois dictatorship to be inserted between them, that is correct, and is the Marxist theory of revolutionary development. On the contrary, if we say that the democratic revolution has no definite task or definite period of its own, and other tasks that can only be accomplished in other periods, such as the task of social revolution, may be included in those of the democratic revolution, such an empty idea—the so-called "to accomplish all by one stroke policy"—should not be adopted by real revolutionaries.

APPENDIX B*

The Three Principles of the People—or San Min Chu I
(These represent the heart of Sun Yat-sen's doctrines, as followed by the Kuomintang. The first version was promulgated in 1905 —the final and most authoritative in 1924.)
1. Racial nationalism (Min Tsu): That is, the abolition of racial inequality and the unification of the Chinese Nation.
2. People's democracy (Min Ch' üan): This meant the evolution of democracy through, first, national unification, second, a period of tutelage under party control, and, third, constitutional democracy developing from the local level of the county or hsien.
3. The people's livelihood (Min-sheng): This meant a rejection of capitalism and a sort of experimental collectivism or socialism on the purely economic plane. "Historical dialectics," according

* FROM "National and International Movements," *Report on the Strategy and Tactics of World Communism* Supplement III. Country Studies: C. Communism in China. House Document No. 619, Committee on Foreign Affairs, 1948.

to Sun should be based on human fellow-feeling, not on property relationships.

Sun explicitly rejected Marxist Communism, maintaining that Marxian "dialectic materialism" was a false concept of history. Except for this rejection of Communism, the "Three Principles" are easy to twist for Communist purposes, and the Chinese Communists have at all times endorsed them, with, of course, their own interpretation.

APPENDIX C

This is the letter that accompanied Alfred Kohlberg's eighty-eight page document that started the battle he had with the IPR. Note paragraph six; note also the tone of the letter. Kohlberg does not charge the IPR with being Communist, only that it has been infiltrated and a house cleaning is long overdue. Later he modified this opinion considerably and came to the conclusion that the IPR was pro-Communist as a matter of policy.

ALFRED KOHLBERG, INC.
Chinese Textiles
1 West 37th Street, Just Off Fifth Avenue
New York, U.S.A.

November 9, 1944

My dear Mr. Carter:
Institute of Pacific Relations
1 East 54th Street
New York 22, N.Y.
My dear Mr. Carter:

Last June I received from United China Relief a copy of a booklet issued by your IPR entitled "War-Time China" (IPR Pamphlet #10). In a recent advertisement, Rosamund Lee, your Publications Secretary, referring to this pamphlet states "What is the true situation between the Chinese Communists and the Kuomintang as explained by Maxwell S. Stewart in War-Time China."

Frankly, I was shocked at this pamphlet. From start to finish, it seemed to me a deliberate smear of China, the Chinese and the Chinese Government. I was especially shocked by the following:

"They (the American, British and Soviet Governments) have, however, limited their economic and military assistance because of fear that any supplies they send might be used in civil strife rather than against the Japanese."

This statement seems completely at variance with the many statements made by our President to the effect that all possible aid is being given to China and will continue to be given to China.

Three or four years ago, you may recall, I resigned after a dozen years membership in IPR. You asked me the reason for my resignation and I told you frankly that I thought you had too many Communists on your staff. You asked me if I thought you were a Communist, to which I, of course, replied "No." You then told me that you did not question your staff as to their political beliefs: whether they were Democrats, Republicans, Socialists, Communists, or what not; that you investigated their qualifications and judged them by their work. This seemed to me at the time a very business-like attitude and I withdrew my resignation.

After reading the above referred-to booklet, I decided to look into the IPR publications further. Of course, I have received them all these years, but have seldom had time (I thought) to read them. As a result of this reading, I now attach hereto a lot of clippings from your publications, along with clippings from "The Communist" (Official organ of the Communist Party in the U.S.A.) and "New Masses" (another Communist organ), also a few other clippings that seem to bear on the same issues. If you will go through these, I think you will find that your employees have been putting over on you a not-too-well-camouflaged Communist line. Your staff publications follow the "New Masses" line exactly but not quite so frankly and the "New Masses" articles are much better documented. In selecting these, I have had to clip and clip to keep to reasonable length, but I believe that what is left of each article fairly represents the article as a whole, as far as same touches on the subjects covered.

This study poses the question: What are the Soviet Union's aims in the Far East? Is there a sinister purpose behind this Communist inspired campaign to discredit China? Only Marshall Stalin can answer this question.

But another question has been bothering me as I made this study. That question is: Is it treason? Does the publication of untruthful statements give "aid and comfort" to our enemy, Japan, in its attempt to break Chinese unity under Chiang Kai Shek? This question I propound to your Board of Trustees.

Look over these clippings and see if you do not think it is time for a house-cleaning in the IPR. The economic articles (not quoted) sounded to me very much like under-graduate studies, compiled from studies of Chinese economists and lacking any practical business background.

If you agree that a house cleaning in the IPR is long overdue, I will be happy to help. My suggestions would be:

1. Fire all the Reds, because the truth is not in them.
2. Adopt a policy of presenting facts rather than opinions. Identify the sources of your information.
3. Name a responsible body to determine policy.

This last point is suggested to me by what I missed in going through your last 7 years' publications. I found:

1. No criticism of Japan in those 7 years, except of her rural land system;
2. No single criticism of Communist China; and
3. No single criticism of the Soviet Union; whereas I found:
4. Severe criticism of the Chinese Government, alternating with praise, closely following the alternations of the Soviet Union's foreign policy and of the Communist press.

A responsible committee controlling and vouching for your policy would be very re-assuring to the members of, and contributors to your Institute.

I am sending a copy of this letter and the accompanying extracts to other members of, and contributors to the Institute, in the hope that many will read through the material and form their own conclusions.

Very truly yours,

(*Signed*) ALFRED KOHLBERG

P.S. I am not taking this up with you privately because of my sad experience with you last year in Chungking, when I preferred complaints against one of your subordinates in his presence. I referred you to a detailed list previously given him. I am still waiting for your reply.

P.S. 2. In the enclosed booklet, pages
1 to   3—Agreement between Chinese Govt. and Communists
4 to 37—Extracts from Institute of Pacific Relations publications
38 to 77—Extracts from Communist publications
78 to 88—Assorted extracts, including full letter of F.E.A. Administrator Crowley and condensed speech of Clare Boothe Luce

AK:AM
Encl.

APPENDIX D

In its Program for Action on China Policy, the Communist Party of New York called for an investigation of the China Lobby as well as a stop to "all forms of American intervention in China."

COMMUNIST PARTY OF NEW YORK STATE
35 East 12th Street
New York 3, New York

Chairman   Telephone: ALgonquin 4-5705
Robert Thompson

March 1, 1949

To all Sections and Counties
Dear Comrades:

Enclosed please find Program for Action on China Policy, as voted upon by a united front action conference on China, held in New York on January 29, 1949.

We are sure that you will find this material not only informative, but helpful in planning actions on China in your communities.

A special outline has also been issued by the National Education Committee on Communist Policy in China. This can be secured through orders from our District Education Department. The outline can be used as the basis for discussion in your sections and branches.

Any inquiries in relation to further activity can be received by writing to the Committee for a Democratic Far Eastern Policy, at 111 West 42 Street, New York City.

Comradely yours,

May Miller

Asst. Org Secretary

uopwa/16

Program for Action on China Policy
As Suggested by the Action Conference on China Policy
New York City   January 29th 1949

PROGRAM OBJECTIVES

1. Demand a Congressional Investigation
   A. Of the Chinese lobby in Washington—
       One of the largest spending foreign influences in our capital; Not registered as foreign agents.
   B. Of the billions of dollars of private accumulation deposited in American banks and investments by Chinese officials and individuals.
2. Demand a new China policy:
   A. An end to all forms of American intervention in China and of plans to aid any elements and remnants of the Kuomintang.
   B. Preparation by our Government to recognize the government which the people of China are now establishing.
   C. Planning now by our authorities for genuine and self-respecting cooperation with the people's government in China, including normal and friendly trade relations free of any political conditions.
3. Get the facts and implications of the Government's China policy to the American people.

IMMEDIATE STEPS FOR CARRYING OUT THE ACTION PROGRAM

1. Get your organization immediately to pass a resolution on China policy (Use the enclosed January Conference resolution for suggestions).
   Send copies of your organization's resolution to your Senators and your Congressmen; give it publicity in your organization's

publication and elsewhere; send a copy to the Committee for a Democratic Far Eastern Policy.

2. Make use of the "political ammunition" of facts: the American people, if they know, will act.

   A. Make a drive to get readers and subscribers to FAR EAST SPOTLIGHT, the Committee's monthly magazine. This is the indispensable tool for every fighter for a new and friendly policy toward China. Previous sources of reliable information about China and the Far East now have an NAM slant; only FAR EAST SPOTLIGHT gives you the positive and encouraging facts about the Chinese people's great and successful fight against American reaction, and keeps you up-to-date about Washington's evil plans to go on backing reaction in China and the Far East.

   Subscription: $2.00 a year.

   Introductory offer: $1.00 for 8 months.

   Members of the CDFEP get this free.

   B. Push the sale and reading of Anna Louise Strong's TO MORROW'S CHINA—

   Paper bound 65¢; cloth bound $2.00.

   Organizational orders for 5 or more: 25% discount.

   C. Have meetings on the China policy issue.

   a. The Committee can furnish speakers:

   In the *New York City Area:* Telephone the Speaker's Bureau of the Committee any afternoon, BRyant 9-6343
   In California, the *San Francisco Area:* Contact Mr. William Kerner, 1841 Ellis Street, San Francisco.
   Los Angeles Area: Contact Mrs. Jeanette Orel, 362 South Columbia Avenue, Los Angeles.

   b. Send your organization's own speakers to the BRIEFING SESSION ON CHINA. First Session: Friday night February 18th, 7:30 sharp. Telephone the Committee for Registration blanks; Bryant 9-6342. No fee.

YOU CAN'T FIGHT WITHOUT FACTS! FAR EAST SPOTLIGHT IS YOUR BASIC SOURCE OF INFORMATION. MEETINGS ON CHINA WILL BRING FACTS TO HUNDREDS OF OTHERS ° ° ° °

3. See to it that the President and the members of Congress hear

from hundreds of individuals on China policy right now.

Order prepared postcards from the Committee—1¢ each.

Write your own messages.

Make calls—in person and by telephone—on your Senators and Congressmen.

4. Have your organization make an immediate contribution to the work of the Committee or plan to give a regular (monthly, quarterly or yearly) contribution.

5. Support the Committee for a Democratic Far Eastern Policy.

A. By becoming members and by getting your friends to join. Membership includes subscription to FAR EAST SPOTLIGHT.

B. By securing individual contributions for the Committee. Your own; your friends; Throw a party for the Committee.

C. By doing volunteer work at the Committee's office; 111 W. 42 St., Fifth floor—any time; any day.

Every Tuesday night the staff is "At home" to friends who come to help.

THE CHINESE PEOPLE ARE DEFEATING THE AMERICAN REACTIONARIES: SO CAN WE!

CHINA POLICY REVEALS THE OVER-ALL CHARACTER OF WASHINGTON'S FOREIGN POLICY—IT HARMS THE AMERICAN PEOPLE.

CHINA POLICY IS DIRECTLY RELATED TO OUR DOMESTIC STRUGGLE FOR HOMES, FOR MORE CONSUMPTION GOODS, FOR LOWER PRICES FOR INCREASED SOCIAL SECURITY, FOR HEALTHY INTERNATIONAL, TRADE, FOR FREEDOM FROM DEPRESSION AND MILITARISM.

CHINA SHOWS UP THE WEAK SPOT IN OUR REACTIONARIES' PROGRAM. LET'S FIGHT ON CHINA POLICY AND TAKE ADVANTAGE OF THE BLOW THE CHINESE PEOPLE HAVE DEALT THE AMERICAN REACTIONARIES!

Committee for a Democratic Far Eastern Policy—111 W. 42 St., N.Y.C.   BRyant 9-6342

Action Conference on China Policy
New York January 29th 1949
Resolution on China Policy
"This Action Conference on China Policy, meeting in New York City on January 29th 1949, and attended by 182 registered delegates and

observers from 80 organizations and including 48 individual partici-
pants, voted to send to every member of the 81st Congress, through
the Committee for a Democratic Far Eastern Policy under whose
auspices the Conference was held, the following Resolution:

IN VIEW OF THE FOLLOWING FACTS

1. That our Government since V-J Day has violated both the demo-
cratic objective of World War II and the Charter of the United
Nations in giving support to the anti-democratic and dictatorial
Kuomintang regime of Chiang Kai-shek,

2. That our Government since V-J Day has made available to the
Kuomintang regime of Chiang Kai-shek over six billion dollars
($6,000,000,000) worth of the resources of the American people
for use in civil war against the people of China who are our historic friends and allies in the task of building a peaceful, prosperous and democratic world,

3. That American guns, bullets, airplanes, bombs, poison gas, gasoline
jelley, and flame throwers have brought suffering, death and destruction to millions of people in China, thus threatening the aliena-
tion of the billion and a half (1,500,000,000) people of Asia who
are our natural allies in a democratic world,

4. That we Americans whose resources have been wasted and misused
in China are still waiting for adequate and decent housing, for
lower prices on consumption goods and food, for increased social
security, for mutually beneficial trade relations between our two
countries as a factor in preventing a depression, and for freedom
from militarism and for the security which only peaceful and cooperative relations among nations can give,

5. That our Government's policy toward China is causing frictions
and misunderstandings that can easily lead to conflicts and even
to war,

6. That the people of China have decisively demonstrated their purpose and power to rid themselves of the callous, cruel, anti-democratic and outworn feudal regime which for the past years has
existed only with outside (American) support and have shown
their power to negate all the military advice, training and equipment given by the United States to the Kuomintang regime of
Chiang Kai-shek, and are now establishing a functioning government of their own creating,

7. That there are nationally prominent American political, military and publishing figures openly and secretly advocating and working for continued and intensified intervention in the internal affairs of China against the Chinese people,

8. That a strong Chinese lobby is at work in Washington (one of the biggest money spending foreign influences in our capital but not registered as a foreign agent) trying to influence our Government authorities to continue support of the anti-democratic and unpopular Kuomintang elements,

9. That the very Chinese officials and individuals who are urging more pouring out of the American people's money in China are known to have accumulated billions of dollars (wrung from the suffering people of China and stolen from the pockets of the American tax-payers) and now stowed away in American banks and investments.

BE IT THEREFORE RESOLVED THAT WE GO ON RECORD AS DEMANDING:

1. That there be a Congressional investigation
   A. Into the activities of the Chinese lobby in this country   and
   B. Into the private wealth which Chinese officials and individuals have stowed away in American banks and investments.

2. That there be an immediate end to all forms of American intervention in China including an end to any dealings with any elements or remnants of the Kuomintang regime, recognizing the right of the Chinese people to make decisions about their country free of all pressure or interference on the part of our Government.

3. That our Government prepare to recognize the government which the Chinese people are now establishing for themselves and that our authorities begin planning for genuine and self-respecting co-operation with that government, including normal and friendly trade relations free of any political conditions.

APPENDIX E

HEARINGS

BEFORE THE

COMMITTEE ON APPROPRIATIONS

UNITED STATES SENATE

EIGHTIETH CONGRESS

WEDNESDAY, DECEMBER 17, 1947

STATEMENT OF LT. GEN. A. C. WEDEMEYER, FORMER SPECIAL PRESIDENTIAL ENVOY TO CHINA

GENERAL STATEMENT

Chairman BRIDGES. For the moment, gentlemen, if you will step aside, I would like to have General Wedemeyer testify.

General, we asked you up here today because the committee felt that among the Americans, with your experience in China, you would be able to give some valuable information to the committee in determining its position regarding the interim aid bill in which aid to China is authorized. We would like to ask you certain questions and then ask you for any suggestions or opinions.

Will you state to us, first, the capacity in which you have served in China and the period of time.

General WEDEMEYER. Altogether, I have served 10 years in the Far East, including 5 years in the Philippines and East Indian Islands; 2 years (1929-31) with the Infantry regiment in Tientsin, China, during which periods I traveled considerably over China, also visiting Japan and other points of interest in the area.

BACKGROUND AND EXPERIENCE IN CHINA

Immediately after Casablanca Conference, I was sent by the President to indicate to Generalissimo Chiang Kai-shek pertinent parts of the strategy that had been evolved at Casablanca Conference. I spent about 2 weeks in China; that was in January of 1943.

In September of 1944 General Stilwell was relieved and I was assigned to command the China theater and to serve as the Generalissimo's chief of staff. I served in these dual capacities until May of 1946.

ASSIGNED TO SURVEY CHINA AND KOREA

I returned to China recently, that is, in July 1947, when I was designated a Presidential envoy to make a survey in China and Korea, as a matter of urgency, to determine political, economic, psychological, and military conditions in the area.

Although I have had considerable experience in the Far East, I should like to state very frankly to the committee members that I do not presume to be an expert on the Far East, and specifically on China.

Senator REED. Are there any experts, General?

General WEDEMEYER. Yes, sir; there are. However, I would not place myself in that category.

Chairman BRIDGES. General, are you the author of the so-called Wedemeyer Report?

General WEDEMEYER. Subsequent to my observations, investigations, and interrogations in China and Korea, a written report was prepared in consonance with my directive. This report was prepared in collaboration with the members of my mission, representatives of the State, War, Navy, and Treasury Departments. Therefore, I am a coauthor of the report, and certain parts of it were prepared by designated members of my mission. However, I accept full responsibility for the entire report, and agree with the contents, and I believe all of the members of the mission concurred in it. However, that was not their responsibility. I assumed full responsibility for the conclusions and the recommendations in the report.

Chairman BRIDGES. General, do you have the report with you today?

General WEDEMEYER. No, sir; I do not.

Chairman BRIDGES. Are you prepared to make the report available to this committee for consideration in regard to the appropriations being discussed today?

General WEDEMEYER. Mr. Chairman, I have given careful thought to this matter, because as a soldier, my Commander in Chief has directed me to maintain security on the report, and as a temporary special envoy, the Secretary of State and the President admonished me, and asked me to insure that the members of my mission would maintain security with reference to the report. We have tried very carefully to carry out their instructions. Therefore, I would be embarrassed if the committee asked me to reveal the contents of my report, without the authority of the President or the Secretary of State.

I thought, perhaps, I could help you this way, sir. I could give you my observations as a normal observer in that area, and I would try to delineate in my mind between the information, that I received as the result of my special position, as a special envoy, and the information that I would have obtained had I been an ordinary observer going through these areas and talking to businessmen, the intelligentsia, the liberals, and to individuals of various shades of political leanings.

I felt that such information would be helpful to this committee, and yet I would not be embarrassed by disobedience or disregard of instructions given to me by the President and the Secretary of State.

Chairman BRIDGES. Your position is that if the report is to be made public it should be made public by the President of the United States or Secretary Marshall, by whom you were entrusted with the mission?

General WEDEMEYER. That is correct, Mr. Chairman. My directive was top secret. It was indicated as a matter of urgency that I get out to China and return quickly. I was instructed to submit in writing the result of my investigations, my conclusions and recommendations, and to submit a report in writing to the President of the United States. This I did. From there on out I have had no responsibility whatsoever for that report, sir.

Chairman BRIDGES. General Wedemeyer, we, certainly, for the time being will respect your secret, confidential mission, and the fact that you are under orders of the President of the United States and Secretary of State.

However, if the Congress is going to legislate intelligently on the Chinese question, it certainly is entitled to all of the information, and if it is too highly secret for the public, then the Congress or the committee should be presented with that in executive session, and in confidence so that we would have it. In other words, I think that this committee or any committee of the Congress, legislating on a great question on a country like China, is entitled to all the information that we have at our command, and if we cannot have it publicly, if it is not wise for the security of our country or the security of our relations, then I think we should have it in executive session, but we respect your confidential mission from your Commander in Chief.

General WEDEMEYER. Yes, sir.

Senator REED. Mr. Chairman, I am hopeful that you are going to ask the general for an expression of his opinion as far as he can give it.

Chairman BRIDGES. General, what I would like to know, along the line of Senator Reed's suggestion, is your observation of the needs in China and the condition there.

Senator REED. And without any violation of the confidence of what we ought to do here today and tomorrow.

OBSERVATIONS ON THE NEEDS OF CHINA

General WEDEMEYER. Yes, sir. I feel that we should make a world appraisal and consider the requirements of various areas or various nations to insure that our national aims are accomplished. We might give political, economic, psychological aid and assistance to various areas, but it should be in consonance with an over-all plan, not piecemeal, dissipating our resources without supporting data, but following an over-all plan.

The world has been contracted by science, and what goes on in China or in Iran is of the utmost interest to our security and to our well-being.

Therefore, a program for Europe should not be evolved disregarding a program for China or vice versa. The timing and the proportion of aid and assistance that we give to China should be commensurate first, with our ability to meet commitments all over the world, as required by the situation. There is a bottom to our economic barrel.

Second, our aid to any country should be determined by the ability of the government or people to use it effectively. We should exercise the right to supervise, and insure that the American taxpayers' dollars are being employed in China as well as in France or anywhere else, just as we expect them to be employed.

We are confronted throughout the world with the expansion of an incompatible ideological power. I believe our planners should determine the points or areas of greatest danger, and also indicate the steps—that is, United States aid programs—that are necessary to first retard, then block, and, finally, penetrate back into those areas that are being defected or are being drawn within the orbit of that power having world expansion and world aggression in its announced program.

Senator REED. General, is it conceivable that any policy satisfactory to America from a world-wide standpoint can be carried on in Asia without the cooperation of a government in China that, at least, subscribes to something like the same ideology that we hold?

IDEOLOGY OF CHIANG KAI-SHEK

General WEDEMEYER. Well, I do not think it should matter an awful lot, sir. If Chiang Kai-shek is a benevolent despot, which he practically is, or whether he is a Democrat or Republican, that is unimportant. The relevant and important facts are that the man has opposed communism throughout his history, and he also stayed on with us as an ally in the war, containing in China one million and a half Japanese soldiers who might have been employed against our men in the Pacific. It would have made our task more costly in lives and time in the Pacific. But, no, the Generalissimo chose to remain faithful to his allies.

I, personally, think he is a fine character, and that you gentlemen on this committee would admire him and respect him.

Senator REED. Is there anybody else in China with whom we can do business?

General WEDEMEYER. No, sir; I think he is the logical leader of China today. I should like to state, when I speak with so much conviction about him, that I was prepared not to like him when I went over there. I had heard so many conflicting stories about him. I owe him nothing; I conducted myself over there as a theater commander, as you would have me conduct myself. I did not ingratiate myself nor placate the Chinese. I think the Generalissimo is sincere in his desire to help his people, but he needs our help, and he should get our help. He is entitled to it. The degree, the timing, and the scope, the qualitative help that we give him, the gentlemen in the State Department, I think, will, I am sure, determine that.

URGENCY OF ECONOMIC ASSISTANCE TO CHINA

Chairman BRIDGES. Would you consider, in your judgment, that it was urgent that we give military supplies and economic assistance to China at this time?

General WEDEMEYER. Yes, sir; I do.

Chairman BRIDGES. Do you think that, in your judgment, we have kept our promises to China over the years?

General WEDEMEYER. No, sir, I do not. I do not say that in a malicious way. There were conditions, Mr. Chairman, that may have precluded the fulfillment of many of our commitments. I could enumerate some of those difficulties, but I do know of a few instances wherein we have not fulfilled our commitments to China.

USE OF SURPLUS MUNITIONS AND SUPPLIES

Chairman BRIDGES. To your knowledge, are the munitions and supplies belonging to the United States of America which are being destroyed in the Pacific such that could be used in China?

General WEDEMEYER. The bulk of those supplies could not be used in China, sir. It is equipment, a type of equipment, that they would not be able to implement in their country. There are large bombs and heavy cumbersome machinery, of a type that they could not use effectively. They require light equipment.

PROMISES OF CHINA TO THE UNITED STATES

Chairman BRIDGES. I asked you whether we have kept our promises to China. I would like to ask you whether in your judgment Chiang Kai-shek and the National Government have kept their promises to us.

General WEDEMEYER. I think the Generalissimo has endeavored to meet our every requirement, sir. If I were he, I would be quite impatient with America, but he never appeared so.

His parting statement when I left him last August is indicative of his character. He said:

Whether or not your country gives aid or assistance to China, I will continue to use every force at my disposal to combat communism; and I will continue to strive to create a democracy in China but changes in government are going to take a long number of years. I may not be able to accomplish that in my lifetime. It will be contingent upon outside influences, the influence of your country and of Russia, whether or not I am able to create political and economic stability at home.

He made that statement voluntarily, just before I said good-by to him.

Chairman BRIDGES. If there are no further questions, we thank you very much. I know you have another assignment, and we release you from our witness stand.

General WEDEMEYER. Thank you, sir.

APPENDIX F

Even though General Marshall in this statement expresses his disillusionment with the Communists, the Kuomintang still bears the brunt of his crtiicism. And the fact that he still had a poor understanding of the situation is evident from his statement, ". . . it has appeared to me that there is a definite liberal group among the Communists . . ." This naive comment was used by Alfred Kohlberg to show how unfitted Marshall was for his mission to China.

Personal Statement by the Special Representative
of the President (Marshall) January 7, 1947

THE PRESIDENT has recently given a summary of the developments in China during the past year and the position of the American Government toward China. Circumstances now dictate that I should supplement this with impressions gained at first hand.

In this intricate and confused situation, I shall merely endeavor here to touch on some of the more important considerations—as they appeared to me—during my connection with the negotiations to bring about peace in China and a stable democratic form of government.

In the first place, the greatest obstacle to peace has been the complete, almost overwhelming suspicion with which the Chinese Communist Party and the Kuomintang regard each other.

On the one hand, the leaders of the Government are strongly opposed to a communistic form of government. On the other, the Communists frankly state that they are Marxists and intend to work toward establishing a communistic form of government in China, thought first advancing through the medium of a democratic form of government of the American or British type.

The leaders of the Government are convinced in their minds that the Communist-expressed desire to participate in a government of the type endorsed by the Political Consultative Conference last January had for its purpose only a destructive intention. The Communists felt, I believe, that the government was insincere in its apparent acceptance of the PCC resolutions for the formation of the new government and intended by coercion of military force and the action of secret police to obliterate the Communist Party. Combined with this mutual deep distrust was the conspicuous error by both parties of ignoring the effect of the fears and suspicions of the other party in estimating the reason for proposals or opposition regarding the settlement of various matters under negotiation. They each sought only to take counsel of their own fears. They both, therefore, to that extent took a rather lopsided view of each situation and were susceptible to every evil suggestion or possibility. This complication was exaggerated to an explosive degree by the confused reports of fighting on the distant and tremendous fronts of hostile military contact. Patrol clashes were deliberately magnified into large offensive actions. The distortion of the facts was utilized by both sides to heap condemnation on the other. It was only through the reports of American officers in the field teams from Executive Headquarters that I could get even a partial idea of what was actually happening and the incidents were too numerous and the distances too great for the American personnel to cover all of the ground. I must comment here on the superb courage of the officers of our Army and Marines in struggling against almost insurmountable and maddening obstacles to bring some measure of peace to China.

I think the most important factors involved in the recent breakdown of negotiations are these: On the side of the National Government, which is in effect the Kuomintang, there is a dominant group of reactionaries who have been opposed, in my opinion, to almost every effort I have made to influence the formation of a genuine coalition government. This has usually been under the cover of political or party action, but since the Party was the Government, this action, though subtle or indirect, has been devastating in its effect. They were quite frank in publicly stating their belief that cooperation by the Chinese Communist Party in the government was inconceivable and that only a policy of force could definitely settle the issue. This group includes military as well as political leaders.

On the side of the Chinese Communist Party there are, I believe, liberals as well as radicals, though this view is vigorously opposed by many who believe that the Chinese Communist Party discipline is too rigidly enforced to admit of such differences of viewpoint. Nevertheless, it has appeared to me that there is a definite liberal group among the Communists, especially of young men who have turned to the Communists in disgust at the corruption evident in the local governments—men who would put the interest of the Chinese people above ruthless measures to establish a Communist ideology in the immediate future. The dyed-in-the-wool Communists do not hesitate at the most drastic measures to gain their end as, for instance, the destruction of communications in order to wreck the economy of China and produce a situation that would facilitate the overthrow or collapse of the Government, without any regard to the immediate suffering of the people involved. They completely distrust the leaders of the Kuomintang and appear convinced that every Government proposal is designed to crush the Chinese Communist Party. I must say that the quite evidently inspired mob actions of last February and March, some within a few blocks of where I was then engaged in completing negotiations, gave the Communists good excuse for such suspicions.

However, a very harmful and immensely provocative phase of the Chinese Communist Party procedure has been in the character of its propaganda. I wish to state to the American people that in the deliberate misrepresentation and abuse of the action, policies and purposes of our Government this propaganda has been without regard for the truth, without any regard whatsoever for the facts, and has given plain evidence of a determined purpose to mislead the Chinese people and the world and to arouse a bitter hatred of Americans. It has been difficult to remain silent in the midst of such public abuse and wholesale disregard of facts, but a denial would merely lead to the necessity of daily denials; an intolerable course of action for an American official. In the interest of fairness, I must state that the Nationalist Government publicity agency has made numerous misrepresentations, though not of the vicious nature of the Communist propaganda. Incidentally, the Communist statements regarding the Anping incident which resulted in the death of three Marines and the wounding of twelve others were almost pure fabrication, deliberately representing a carefully arranged ambuscade of a Marine convoy with supplies for the maintenance of Executive Headquarters and some UNRRA supplies, as a defence against a Marine assault.

The investigation of this incident was a tortuous procedure of delays and maneuvers to disguise the true and privately admitted facts of the case.

Sincere efforts to achieve settlement have been frustrated time and again by extremist elements of both sides. The agreements reached by the Political Consultative Conference a year ago were a liberal and forward-looking charter which then offered China a basis for peace and reconstruction. However, irreconcilable groups within the Kuomintang, interested in the preservation of their own feudal control of China, evidently had no real intention of implementing them. Though I speak as a soldier, I must here also deplore the dominating influence of the military. Their dominance accentuates the weakness of civil government in China. At the same time, in pondering the situation in China, one must have clearly in mind not the workings of small Communist groups or committees to which we are accustomed in America, but rather of millions of people and an army of more than a million men.

I have never been in a position to be certain of the development of attitudes in the innermost Chinese Communist circles. Most certainly, the course which the Chinese Communist Party has pursued in recent months indicated an unwillingness to make a fair compromise. It has been impossible even to get them to sit down at a conference table with Government representatives to discuss given issues. Now the Communists have broken off negotiations by their last offer which demanded the dissolution of the National Assembly and a return to the military positions of January 13th which the Government could not be expected to accept.

Between this dominant reactionary group in the Government and the irreconcilable Communists who, I must state, did not so appear last February, lies the problem of how peace and well-being are to be brought to the long-suffering and presently inarticulate mass of the people of China. The reactionaries in the Government have evidently counted on substantial American support regardless of their actions. The Communists by their unwillingness to compromise in the national interest are evidently counting on an economic collapse to bring about the fall of the Government, accelerated by extensive guerrilla action against the long lines of rail communications—regardless of the cost in suffering to the Chinese people.

The salvation of the situation, as I see it, would be the assumption of leadership by the liberals in the Government and in the minority parties, a splendid group of men, but who as yet lack the political power to exercise a controlling influence. Successful action on their part under the leadership of Generalissimo Chiang Kai-shek would, I believe, lead to unity through good government.

In fact, the National Assembly has adopted a democratic constitution which in all major respects is in accordance with the principles laid down by the all-party Political Consultative Conference of last January. It is unfortunate that the Communists did not see fit to participate in the Assembly since the constitution that has been adopted seems to include every major point that they wanted.

Soon the Government in China will undergo major reorganization pending the coming into force of the constitution following elections to be completed before Christmas Day 1947. Now that the form for a democratic China has been laid down by the newly adopted constitution, practical measures will be the test. It remains to be seen to what extent the Government will give substance to the form by a genuine welcome of all groups actively to share in the responsibility of government.

The first step will be the reorganization of the State Council and the executive branch of Government to carry on administration pending the enforcement of the constitution. The manner in which this is done and the amount of representation accorded to liberals and to non-Kuomintang members will be significant. It is also to be hoped that during this interim period the door will remain open for Communists or other groups to participate if they see fit to assume their share of responsibility for the future of China.

It has been stated officially and categorically that the period of political tutelage under the Kuomintang is at an end. If the termination of one-party rule is to be a reality, the Kuomintang should cease to receive financial support from the Government.

I have spoken very frankly because in no other way can I hope to bring the people of the United States to even a partial understanding of this complex problem. I have expressed all these views privately in the course of negotiations; they are well known, I think, to most of the individuals concerned. I express them now publicly, as it is my duty, to present my estimate of the situation and its possibilities to the American people who have a deep interest in the development of conditions in the Fast East promising such an enduring peace in the Pacific.

APPENDIX G

The following is reproduced from the Senate Internal Security Subcommittee's report on the Institute of Pacific Relations:

SUMMARY OF COMMUNIST AFFILIATIONS BY INDIVIDUALS WITH THEIR IPR FUNCTIONS

(Missing page references on affiliations are given above)

ADLER, SOLOMON (Schloma Adler), IPR supporter (p. 3594):

Identified as a member of the Communist Part by one or more duly sworn witnesses.

Collaborated with agents of the Soviet intelligence apparatus as shown by sworn testimony.

Out of the country or otherwise unavailable for subpena.

ALLEN, JAMES S. (Sol Auerbach), writer (pp. 245–247, 249, exhibit 1383):

Identified as a member of the Communist Party by one or more duly sworn witnesses.

Refused to answer on the ground of self-incrimination.

Writer for official publications of the Communist Party or the Communist International or for a Communist government or for pro-Communist press services.

Affiliated with: Amerasia (exhibit 1355).

ASIATICUS (Heinz Moeller or Hans Mueller or M. G. Shippe), writer (pp. 47–50):

Identified as a member of the Communist Party by one or more duly sworn witnesses.

Made one or more trips to Communist territory.

Writer for official publications of the Communist Party or the Communist International or for a Communist government or for pro-Communist press services.

Deceased.

Affiliated with: Amerasia (exhibit 1355).

AUSTERN, HILDA, (Mrs. Nat Bretholtz, also Mrs. Jefferson Franklin Ray), assistant treasurer IPR (exhibit 801):

Identified as a member of the Communist Party by one or more duly sworn witnesses. Denied.

Out of the country or otherwise unavailable for subpena.

Affiliated with: Amerasia (exhibit 1355).

BARNES, JOSEPH FELS, secretary, American Council IPR (p. 209):

Identified as a member of the Communist Party by one or more duly sworn witnesses. Denied.

Collaborated with agents of the Soviet intelligence apparatus as shown by sworn testimony. Denied.

Made one or more trips to Communist territory.

BARNES, KATHLEEN (Mrs. Joseph F.), research associate IPR, exhibit 801):

Identified as a member of the Communist Party by one or more duly sworn witnesses.

Refused to answer on the ground of self-incrimination.

Made one or more trips to Communist territory.

Affiliated with: Amerasia (exhibit 1355); American Russian Institute (p. 645).

BARNETT, ROBERT W., research associate; secretary, Washington IPR (exhibit 801):

Affiliated with: Amerasia (exhibit 1355).

BIDIEN, CHARLES, writer (pp. 4610–4611):

Affiliated with: Committee for a Democratic Far Eastern Policy (p. 2789).

Subject of action by agency of American Government or a foreign non-Communist government on grounds involving loyalty or national security (exhibit 1404).

Writer for official publications of the Communist Party or the Communist International or for a Communist government or for pro-Communist press services (exhibit 1405).

BISSON, T. A. (Frederick Spencer), associate editor, Pacific Affairs (p. 4188); research associate (exhibit 801):

Identified as a member of the Communist Party by one or more duly sworn witnesses.

Made one or more trips to Communist territory.

Subject of action by agency of American Government or a

foreign non-Communist government on grounds involving loyalty or national security.

Affiliated with: Amerasia (p. 35); Friends of Chinese Democracy (p. 622); American Committee in Aid of Chinese Industrial Cooperatives, also known as Indusco, Inc. (p. 3793); American Friends of the Chinese People, official organ: China Today (p. 4272); Committee for a Democratic Far Eastern Policy (p. 2789).

Signer of a statement attacking the United States for "supressing the Chinese masses and fomenting civil war among them."

BODDE, DERK, writer (pp. 4610–4611):

Affiliated with: Committee for a Democratic Far Eastern Policy (pp. 4610–4611).

BORG, DOROTHY, staff member (p. 996); education secretary IPR (exhibit 801):

Writer for pro-Communist press services.

Affiliated with: Amerasia (exhibit 1355); Federated Press (p. 2634).

BRANDT, WILLIAM, writer (p. 3254):

Affiliated with: Amerasia (exhibit 1355).

CARLSON, EVANS F., writer (exhibit 1383); lecturer (p. 70):

Identified as a member of the Communist Party by one or more duly sworn witnesses.

Made one or more trips to Communist territory.

Deceased.

Affiliated with: Amerasia (exhibit 1355); Committee for a Democratic Far Eastern Policy (pp. 4610–4611).

CARTER, EDWARD C., secretary, American Council; secretary-general IPR; trustee; executive vice chairman (exhibit 801):

Made one or more trips to Communist territory.

Affiliated with: Amerasia (exhibit 1355); American Russian Institute (p. 296); Russian War Relief (p. 295).

CHAPMAN, ABRAHAM (John Arnold), writer (p. 643); research associate (exhibit 801):

Identified as a member of the Communist Party by one or more duly sworn witnesses.

Writer for official publications of the Communist Party or the

Communist International or for a Communist government or for pro-Communist press services.

Out of the country or otherwise unavailable for subpena.

Affiliated with: Committee for a Democratic Far Eastern Policy (p. 2789).

CHEN, HAN-SENG (Geoffrey) (Raymond D. Brooke), research associate (exhibit 801):

Identified as a member of the Communist Party by one or more duly sworn witnesses.

Made one or more trips to Communist territory.

Writer for official publications of the Communist Party or the Communist International or for a Communist government or for pro-Communist press services.

Out of the country or otherwise unavailable for subpena.

Affiliated with: Amerasia (exhibit 1355); Committee for a Democratic Far Eastern Policy (p. 52); Federated Press (p. 2631).

CHI, CH'AO-TING (Hausu Chan, T. B. Lowe), research associate (exhibit 801) writer (p. 17):

Identified as a member of the Communist Party by one or more duly sworn witnesses.

Made one or more trips to Communist territory.

Out of the country or otherwise unavailable for subpena.

Affiliated with: Amerasia (p. 35); American Friends of the Chinese People, official organ: China Today (p. 14); China Aid Council (p. 410).

CHI, HARRIET LEVINE, assistant to secretary-general (exhibit 801):

Identified as a member of the Communist Party by one or more duly sworn witnesses.

Refused to answer on the ground of self-incrimination.

COE, FRANK V., attended IPR conference (p. 995):

Identified as a member of the Communist Party by one or more duly sworn witnesses.

Collaborated with agents of the Soviet intelligence apparatus as shown by sworn testimony.

CURRIE, LAUCHLIN, attended conferences (p. 114, 133); trustee (p. 133):

Collaborated with agents of the Soviet intelligence apparatus as shown by sworn testimony.

Out of the country or otherwise unavailable for subpena.

DEANE, HUGH, writer (pp. 2780–2781); member (p. 2781):

Refused to answer on ground of self-incrimination (p. 2786).

Made one or more trips to Communist territory.

Writer for official publications of the Communist Party or the Communist International or for a Communist government or for pro-Communist press services.

Affiliated with: Amerasia (exhibit 1355); Committee for a Democratic Far Eastern Policy (p. 2789).

DE CAUX, LEN, trustee (p. 995); attended conferences (p. 995):

Identified as a member of the Communist Party by one or more duly sworn witnesses.

Refused to answer on the ground of self-incrimination.

Writer for official publications of the Communist Party or the Communist International or for a Communist government or for pro-Communist press services.

Affiliated with: Federated Press (p. 2627).

DE JONG, ELLEN VAN ZYLL (Atkinson), research associates (exhibit 801):

Subject of action by agency of American government or a foreign non-Communist government on grounds involving loyalty or national security.

DUGGAN, LAURENCE, supporter (pp. 240, 1218):

Collaborated with agents of the Soviet intelligence apparatus as shown by sworn testimony.

Deceased.

EPSTEIN, ISRAEL, writer (exhibit 1334):

Identified as a member of the Communist Party by one or more duly sworn witnesses.

Collaborated with agents of the Soviet intelligence apparatus as shown by sworn testimony.

Made one or more trips to Communist territory.

Writer for official publications of the Communist Party or the Communist International or for a Communist government or for pro-Communist press services.

Subject of action by agency of American government or a

foreign non-Communist government on grounds involving loyalty or national security.

Out of the country or otherwise unavailable for subpena.

Affiliated with: Allied Labor News (p. 662); Amerasia (exhibit 1355); Friends of Chinese Democracy (p. 622); China Aid Council (p. 1513); Committee for a Democratic Far Eastern Policy (p. 2789).

FAIRBANK, JOHN K., trustee (p. 3742):

Identified as a member of the Communist Party by one or more duly sworn witnesses. Denied.

Affiliated with: Amerasia (exhibit 1335); American Committee in Aid of Chinese Industrial Cooperatives, also known as Indusco, Inc. (p. 3794); China Aid Council (p. 1513).

FAIRFAX-CHOLMELEY, ELSIE (Mrs. Israel Epstein) (pseudonym: Edith Cromwell) (p. 50) writer; assistant to secretary-general (exhibit 801):

Subject of action by agency of American Government or a foreign non-Communist government on grounds involving loyalty or national security.

Out of the country or otherwise unavailable for subpena.

Affiliated with Committee for a Democratic Far Eastern Policy (p. 2789).

FARLEY, MIRIAM S., research associate and pamphlet editor; editor, Far Eastern Survey (exhibit 801):

Writer for official publications of the Communist Party or the Communist International or for a Communist government or for pro-Communist press services.

Affiliated with: Amerasia (exhibit 1355) Federated Press (p. 2628).

FIELD, FREDERICK V., secretary, American Council (p. 995); executive (exhibit 801); trustee (p. 264):

Identified as a member of the Communist Party by one or more duly sworn witnesses.

Collaborated with agents of the Soviet intelligence apparatus as shown by sworn testimony.

Refused to answer on the ground of self-incrimination.

Made one or more trips to Communist territory.

Writer for official publications of the Communist Party or the

Communist International or for a Communist government or for pro-Communist press services.

Subject of action by agency of American Government or a foreign non-Communist government on grounds involving loyalty or national security.

Affiliated with: Amerasia (p. 35); American Friends of the Chinese People, official organ: China Today (p. 116); Federated Press (p. 4152); Friends of Chinese Democracy (p. 622); Russian War Relief (p. 295); Soviet Russia Today (p. 102); Committee for a Democratic Far Eastern Policy (p. 4610–11).

Signer of a statement attacking the United States for "suppressing the Chinese masses and fomenting civil wars among them."

FRIEDMAN, IRVING F., research associate (exhibit 801):

Affiliated with: Amerasia (exhibit 1355).

FRIEDMAN, JULIAN R., participant in conferences (p. 710); writer (p. 711).

Identified as a member of the Communist Party by one or more duly sworn witnesses. Denied.

Affiliated with: China Aid Council (p. 1513); Committee for a Democratic Far Eastern Policy (p. 771).

GERLACH, TALITHA, supporter (exhibit 1334):

Identified as a member of the Communist Party by one or more duly sworn witnesses.

Out of the country or otherwise unavailable for subpena.

Affiliated with: American Committee in Aid of Chinese Industrial Cooperatives, also known as Indusco, Inc. (p. 3793); China Aid Council (p. 1513); Committee for a Democratic Far Eastern Policy (p. 2789); Friends of Chinese Democracy (p. 622).

GOSHAL, KUMAR, writer (exhibit 1334):

Identified as a member of the Communist Party by one or more duly sworn witnesses.

Affiliated with: Amerasia (exhibit 1355); Committee for a Democratic Far Eastern Policy (p. 2789).

GRAVES, MORTIMER, trustee (p. 713):

Affiliated with: Amerasia (exhibit 1355); American Russian Institute (p. 4091).

Signer of a statement defending the Soviet Union as "a consistent bulwark against war and aggression."

GREENBERG, MICHAEL, managing editor, Pacific Affairs (exhibit 801):
Collaborated with agents of the Soviet intelligence apparatus as shown by sworn testimony.

Subject of action by agency of American Government or a foreign non-Communist government on grounds involving loyalty or national security.

Out of the country or otherwise unavailable for subpena.

Affiliated with: Amerasia (exhibit 1355); American Committee in Aid of Chinese Industrial Cooperatives, also known as Indusco, Inc. (p. 3794).

HISS, ALGER, trustee (p. 134):
Identified as a member of the Communist Party by one or more duly sworn witnesses.

Collaborated with agents of the Soviet Intelligence apparatus as shown by sworn testimony.

Subject of action by agency of American government or a foreign non-Communist government on grounds involving loyalty or national security.

HOLLAND, WILLIAM L., research secretary; secretary-general; editor, Pacific Affairs; executive vice-chairman (exhibit 801):
Affiliated with: Amerasia (exhibit 1355); China Aid Council (p. 1513).

HSU, YUNG YING, research associate (exhibit 801):
Made one or more trips to Communist territory.

Affiliated with: Amerasia (exhibit 1355).

JAFFE, PHILIP R. (James W. Philips), conference participant (exhibit 1334); financial contributor (p. 71; exhibit 1383):
Identified as a member of the Communist Party by one or more duly sworn witnesses.

Made one or more trips to Communist territory.

Writer for official publications of the Communist Party or the Communist International or for a Communist government or pro-Communist press services.

Subject of action by agency of American Government or a foreign non-Communist government on grounds involving loyalty or national security.

Affiliated with: Amerasia (p. 374); American Committee in Aid of Chinese Industrial Cooperatives, also known as Indusco, Inc. (p. 3794); American Friends of the Chinese People, official organ: China Today (p. 4170); American Russian Institute (p. 686); China Aid Council (p. 410); Committee for a Democratic Far Eastern Policy (p. 2789).

Signer of a statement attacking the United States for "suppressing the Chinese masses and fomenting civil wars among them."

JENKINSON, ANTHONY, member (p. 71); writer (p. 2642); secretary of British group, IPR conference (p. 662):

Identified as a member of the Communist Party by one or more duly sworn witnesses.

Writer for official publications of the Communist Party or the Communist International or for a Communist government or for pro-Communist press services.

Out of the country or otherwise unavailable for subpena.

Affiliated with: Allied Labor News (p. 658).

JOHNSTONE, WILLIAM C., director, Washington IPR (exhibit 801):

Affiliated with: Amerasia (exhibit 1355); American Committee in Aid of Chinese Industrial Cooperatives, also known as Indusco, Inc. (p. 3794).

KEENEY, MARY J., member Washington IPR (p. 2776):

Refused to answer on the ground of self-incrimination (p. 2774). Indicted.

KEENEY, PHILIP O., writer and speaker (exhibit 1334):

Refused to answer on the ground of self-incrimination. Affiliated with: Committee for a Democratic Far Eastern Policy (p. 2789).

KIZER, BENJAMIN H., trustee (p. 264); vice-chairman, American IPR (p. 264):

Affiliated with: Amerasia (exhibit 1355).

Identified as a member of the Communist Party by one or more duly sworn witnesses. Denied.

LAMONT, CORLISS, supporter (p. 71):

Identified as a member of the Communist Party by one or more duly sworn witnesses. Denied.

Made one or more trips to Communist territory.

Affiliated with: American Friends of the Chinese People (p. 4170).

Signer of a statement defending the Soviet Union as "a consistent bulwark against war and aggression."

Signer of a statement attacking the United States for "suppressing the Chinese masses and fomenting civil war among them."

LANG, OLGA, writer (p. 270):

Identified as a member of the Communist Party by one or more duly sworn witnesses.

Made one or more trips to Communist territory.

Writer for official publications of the Communist Party or the Communist International or for a Communist government or for pro-Communist press services.

Out of country or otherwise unavailable for subpena.

Affiliated with: Amerasia (exhibit 1355); American Committee in Aid of Chinese Industrial Cooperatives, also known as Indusco, Inc. (p. 2793).

LATTIMORE, ELEANOR (Mrs. OWEN), research associate, Washington office (exhibit 801):

Made one or more trips to Communist territory (p. 3315).

Affiliated with: American Committee in Aid of Chinese Industrial Cooperatives, also known as Indusco, Inc. (p. 3793).

LATTIMORE, OWEN, Editor, Pacific Affairs (exhibit 801); trustee; (p. 568); executive committee (p. 1313):

Identified as a member of the Communist Party by one or more duly sworn witnesses. Denied.

Collaborated with agents of the Soviet intelligence apparatus as shown by sworn testimony. Denied.

Made one or more trips to Communist territory.

Affiliated with: Amerasia (p. 35).

LEE, MICHAEL, member ninth conference secretariat, 1945:

Subject of action by agency of American Government or a foreign non-Communist government on grounds involving loyalty or national security (hearings before subcommittee of Committee on Interstate and Foreign Commerce, United States Senate, March 28, 30, and April 4, 1950).

LOCKWOOD, WILLIAM W., research secretary and executive, American Council (exhibit 801):

Affiliated with: Amerasia (exhibit 1355).

MANDEL, WILLIAM MARX, writer (p. 4610–11):

Identified as a member of the Communist Party by one or more duly sworn witnesses.

Refused to answer on the ground of self-incrimination.

Made one or more trips to Communist territory.

Affiliated with: American Russian Institute (p. 663); Committee for a Democratic Far Eastern Policy (p. 4610); Soviet Russia Today (p. 662).

MENEFEE, SELDEN C., proposed IPR conference delegate (p. 2809):

Affiliated with: Committee for a Democratic Far Eastern Policy (p. 4610).

MITCHELL, KATE L., assistant to secretary-general (exhibit 801):

Identified as a member of the Communist Party by one or more duly sworn witnesses. Denied.

Made one or more trips to Communist territory.

Affiliated with: Amerasia (p. 35); Committee for a Democratic Far Eastern Policy (p. 4610).

MOORE, HARRIET L. (GELFAN), research associate; acting executive secretary (exhibit 801); chairman, nominating committee (p. 3858, 3859):

Identified as a member of the Communist Party by one or more duly sworn witnesses.

Refused to answer on the ground of self-incrimination.

Made one or more trips to Communist territory.

Writer for official publications of the Communist Party or the Communist International or for a Communist government or for pro-Communist press services.

Affiliated with: Amerasia (exhibit 1355); American Russian Institute (p. 296); Federated Press (p. 2629); Russian War Relief (p. 295); Soviet Russia Today (p. 297).

NORMAN, E. HERBERT, writer (p. 319):

Identified as a member of the Communist Party by one or more duly sworn witnesses.

Out of the country or otherwise unavailable for subpena.

Affiliated with: Amerasia (exhibit 1355).

Canadian Friends of the Chinese People, affiliate of the American Friends of the Chinese People (p. 4065).

OZAKI, HOTSUMI, conference participant (pp. 363; 505) (exhibit 1383):

> Identified as a member of the Communist Party by one or more duly sworn witnesses.

> Collaborated with agents of the Soviet intelligence apparatus as shown by sworn testimony.

> Subject of action by agency of American Government or a foreign non-Communist government on grounds involving loyalty or national security.

> Deceased.

POLAND, FRED, attended 1945 IPR conference (p. 998):

> Collaborated with agents of the Soviet intelligence apparatus as shown by sworn testimony.

> Subject of action by agency of American Government or a foreign non-Communist government on grounds involving loyalty or national security (acquitted).

> Out of the country or otherwise unavailable for subpena.

PORTER, CATHERINE, research associate; editor, Far Eastern Survey; secretary (exhibit 801):

> Writer for pro-Communist press services.

> Affiliated with: Amerasia (exhibit 1355); Federated Press (p. 2633).

PRICE, MILDRED (COY), member (p. 1246):

> Identified as a member of the Communist Party by one or more duly sworn witnesses.

> Refused to answer on the ground of self-incrimination.

> Affiliated with: China Aid Council (p. 410).

PRESSMAN, LEE, proposed IPR conference delegate (p. 2809):

> Identified as a member of the Communist Party by one or more duly sworn witnesses.

> Collaborated with agents of the Soviet intelligence apparatus as shown by sworn testimony.

PRUITT, IDA, writer (Far Eastern Survey 1945, vol. XIV):

> Affiliated with: American Committee in Aid of Chinese Industrial Cooperatives, also known as Indusco, Inc. (p. 3793).

> Committee for a Democratic Far Eastern Policy (p. 4600).

RAJCHMAN, LUDWIG, proposed observer IPR conference (exhibit 1383):

Made one or more trips to Communist territory.

Subject of action by agency of American Government or a foreign non-Communist government on grounds involving loyalty or national security.

ROSINGER, LAWRENCE K., research associate (exhibit 801):

Identified as a member of the Communist Party by one or more duly sworn witnesses.

Refused to answer on the ground of self-incrimination.

Affiliated with: Amerasia (exhibit 1355); China Aid Council (p. 1513).

ROTH, ANDREW, member conference secretariat (p. 998); writer (p. 670):

Identified as a member of the Communist Party by one or more duly sworn witnesses.

Writer for pro-Communist press services.

Subject of action by agency of American Government or a foreign non-Communist government on grounds involving loyalty or national security.

Out of the country or otherwise unavailable for subpena.

Affiliated with: Amerasia (exhibit 1355); Federated Press (p. 2632); Japanese-American Committee for Democracy (p. 2242).

SAIONJI, KINKAZU, secretary, Japanese IPR (p. 364):

Collaborated with agents of the Soviet intelligence apparatus as shown by sworn testimony.

Subject of action by agency of American Government or a foreign non-Communist government on grounds involving loyalty or national security.

SALISBURY, LAWRENCE, editor, Far Eastern Survey (exhibit 801); American Council IPR (p. 996):

Affiliated with: Committee for a Democratic Far Eastern Policy (pp. 4610–11); Friends of Chinese Democracy (p. 622).

SCHNEIDER, HELEN, business manager, Pacific Affairs (exhibit 801):

Identified as a member of the Communist Party by one or more duly sworn witnesses.

Refused to answer on the ground of self-incrimination.

SERVICE, JOHN S., member and speaker (p. 788):

Subject of action by agency of American Government or a

foreign non-Communist government on grounds involving loyalty or national security.

SMEDLEY, AGNES, member (p. 73):

Identified as a member of the Communist Party by one or more duly sworn witnesses.

Collaborated with agents of the Soviet Intelligence apparatus as shown by sworn testimony.

Made one or more trips to Communist territory.

Affiliated with: Amerasia (exhibit 1355); Committee for a Democratic Far Eastern Policy (p. 2789).

Deceased.

SNOW, EDGAR, member and writer (p. 73, exhibit 1334):

Made one or more trips to Communist territory.

Affiliated with: Amerasia (exhibit 1355); China Aid Council (p. 1514); Committee for a Democratic Far Eastern Policy (p. 2789).

SNOW, MRS. EDGAR (Nym Wales), member and writer (exhibit 1334):

Identified as a member of the Communist Party by one or more duly sworn witnesses.

Made one or more trips to Communist territory.

Writer for official publications of the Communist Party or the Communist International or for a Communist government or for pro-Communist press services.

Affiliated with: American Committee in Aid of Chinese Industrial Cooperatives, also known as Indusco, Inc. (p. 3793); Committee for a Democratic Far Eastern Policy (pp. 4610–4611); Friends of Chinese Democracy (p. 622).

STEIGER, ANDREW, writer (Pacific Affairs, 1941):

Identified as a member of the Communist Party by one or more duly sworn witnesses.

Made one or more trips to Communist territory.

Writer for official publications of the Communist Party or the Communist International or for a Communist government or for pro-Communist press services.

STEIN, GUENTHER, writer (p. 143; exhibit 1334):

Collaborated with agents of the Soviet Intelligence apparatus as shown by sworn testimony.

Made one or more trips to Communist territory.

Subject of action by agency of American Government or a foreign non-Communist government on grounds involving loyalty or national security.

Out of the country or otherwise unavailable for subpena.

Affiliated with: Amerasia (exhibit 1355); Committee for a Democratic Far Eastern Policy (p. 2789).

STEWART, MARGUERITE A. (Mrs. Maxwell Stewart), school secretary; administrative secretary (exhibit 801):

Attended founding meeting of Committee for a Democratic Far Eastern Policy.

STEWART, MAXWELL S., pamphlet editor (exhibit 801):

Identified as a member of the Communist Party by one or more duly sworn witnesses. Denied.

Writer for official publications of the Communist Party or the Communist International or for a Communist government or pro-Communist press services.

Affiliated with: Amerasia (exhibit 1355); American Committee in Aid of Chinese Industrial Cooperatives, also known as Indusco, Inc. (p. 3793); American Friends of the Chinese People—official organ China Today (p. 4272); Committee for a Democratic Far Eastern Policy (pp. 4610–4611).

Signer of a statement defending the Soviet Union as "a consistent bulwark against war and aggression."

Signer of a statement attacking the United States for "suppressing the Chinese masses and fomenting civil wars among them."

STRONG, ANNA LOUISE, writer (exhibit 1334):

Identified as a member of the Communist Party by one or more duly sworn witnesses.

Collaborated with agents of the Soviet Intelligence apparatus as shown by sworn testimony.

Made one or more trips to Communist territory.

Writer for official publications of the Communist Party or the Communist International or for a Communist government or for pro-Communist press services.

Affiliated with: Amerasia (exhibit 1355); Committee for a Democratic Far Eastern Policy (p. 56).

SUES, ILONA RALF, writer (exhibit 1334):

Identified as a member of the Communist Party by one or more duly sworn witnesses.

Affiliated with: Committee for a Democratic Far Eastern Policy (p. 2789); Friends of Chinese Democracy (p. 622).

TERRILL, KATHERINE, executive secretary IPR (p. 295):

Affiliated with: American Friends of the Chinese People, official organ: China Today (p. 4170); China Aid Council (p. 1514); Japanese-American Committee for Democracy (p. 2242); Russian War Relief (p. 295).

Signer of a statement attacking the United States for "suppressing the Chinese masses and fomenting civil war among them."

THOMPSON, VIRGINIA, writer (p. 1222):

Writer for official publications of the Communist Party or the Communist International or for a Communist government or for pro-Communist press services.

Affiliated with: Amerasia (exhibit 1355), Federated Press (p. 2630).

THORNER, DANIEL, writer (p. 3960); member (p. 3957):

Identified as a member of the Communist Party by one or more duly sworn witnesses.

Refused to answer on the ground of self-incrimination.

VAN KLEECK, MARY, member American Council (p. 683); writer (exhibit 1334):

Identified as a member of the Communist Party by one or more duly sworn witnesses.

Out of the country or otherwise unavailable for subpena.

Affiliated with: American Russian Institute (p. 4091); Committee for a Democratic Far Eastern Policy (pp. 4610–4611).

Signer of a statement defending the Soviet Union as "a consistent bulwark against war and aggression."

VINCENT, JOHN CARTER, trustee (p. 713); conference participant (p. 113):

Identified as a member of the Communist Party by one or more duly sworn witnesses. Denied.

WATTS, RICHARD, writer (exhibit 1334):

Affiliated with: American Russian Institute (p. 4091); Committee for a Democratic Far Eastern Policy (pp. 4610–4611); Friends of Chinese Democracy (p. 622); American Committee in Aid of Chinese Industrial Cooperatives, also known as Indusco, Inc. (p. 3793).

WHITE, HARRY DEXTER, proposed conference delegate (p. 444); recommended for conference secretariat (p. 494):

Collaborated with agents of the Soviet Intelligence apparatus as shown by sworn testimony.

Deceased.

WINTER, ELLA, writer (exhibit 1383):

Identified as a member of the Communist Party by one or more duly sworn witnesses.

Writer for official publications of the Communist Party or the Communist International or for a Communist government or for pro-Communist press services.

Out of the country or otherwise unavailable for subpena.

Signer of a statement defending the Soviet Union as "a consistent bulwark against war and aggression."

YARDUMIAN, ROSE, secretary, Washington IPR (exhibit 801); secretary-librarian (exhibit 801):

Made one or more trips to Communist territory.

Writer for official publications of the Communist Party or the Communist International or for a Communist government or for pro-Communist press services.

YAKHONTOFF, VICTOR A., member (p. 73):

Collaborated with agents of the Soviet Intelligence apparatus as shown by sworn testimony.

Made one or more trips to Communist territory.

Affiliated with: American Friends of the Chinese People, official organ: China Today (p. 4182).

Signer of a statement attacking the United States for "suppressing the Chinese masses and fomenting civil war among them."

APPENDIX H

Not only the IPR element have a near monopoly on the writing of books about China in the critical 1940s, but they also did most of the reviewing. Enthusiastically they praised each other's books and condemned those that took issue with the line they were peddling. This scandalous propagandizing finally came to the attention of Congress and this information comes from the *Congressional Record* of June 6, 1952 (page 6808). Here is a graphic picture of shameful literary logrolling:

Nonfiction books on China published in the United States and reviewed in the New York Times Book Review and the New York Herald Tribune Book Review 1945–1950

New York Times Book Review

Book	Author	Reviewer	Review Date
Solution in Asia	Owen Lattimore	Edgar Snow	2/25/45
Report From Red China	Harrison Forman	Edgar Snow	3/11/45
China Among the Powers	David N. Rowe	Edgar Snow	5/20/45
China's Crisis	Laurence R. Rosinger	T. A. Bisson	7/29/45
The Challenge of Red China	Gunther Stein	Nathaniel Peffer	10/28/45
My Twenty-Five Years in China	J. B. Powell	Annalee Jacoby	12/16/45
Thunder Out of China	T. White & A. Jacoby	J. K. Fairbank	10/27/46
China's Destiny	Chiang Kai-shek	J. K. Fairbank	2/9/47
Look South to the Polar Star	Holger Cahill	Annalee Jacoby	2/9/47
No Peace for Asia	Harold Isaacs	Annalee Jacoby	5/17/47
The Unfinished Revolution in China	Israel Epstein	Owen Lattimore	6/22/47
The Revolt of Asia	Robert Payne	Robert Shapiro	9/28/47
China Awake	Robert Payne	J. K. Fairbank	10/19/4
Last Chance in China	Freda Utley	Harold Isaacs	11/23/4
The Stilwell Papers	Ed. by T. White	Ira Wolfert	5/23/48
The United States and China	J. K. Fairbank	Annalee Jacoby	7/11/48
Changing China	Harrison Forman	Annalee Jacoby	11/14/4

Book	Author	Reviewer	Review Date
China the Land and the People	Gerald F. Winfield	J. K. Fairbank	12/12/48
Way of a Fighter	General Chennault	Annalee Jacoby	1/30/49
Russia's Race for Asia	George Creel	Nathaniel Peffer	3/13/49
The Situation in Asia	Owen Lattimore	Stuart Lillico	4/10/49
China Shakes the World	Jack Belden	Nathaniel Peffer	10/23/49
The Chinese Conquer China	Anna Louise Strong	H. R. Lieberman	11/13/49
Pivot of Asia	Owen Lattimore	Stuart Lillico	3/26/50
Dateline: China	H. K. Tong	Robert A. Smith	4/23/50
Ordeal by Slander	Owen Lattimore	R. L. Duffus	7/30/50
Peking Diary	Derk Bodde	Nathaniel Peffer	10/29/50
Mao Tse Tung	Robert Payne	Nathaniel Peffer	10/29/50
Two Kinds of Time	Graham Peck	Nathaniel Peffer	11/5/50
China and the Soviet Union	A. K. Wu	Robert Payne	12/3/50
Blunder in Asia	Harrison Forman	Stuart Lillico	12/10/50

New York Herald Tribune Book Review

Book	Author	Reviewer	Review Date
China Among the Powers	David N. Rowe	E. Lattimore	
Solution in Asia	Owen Lattimore	A. T. Steele	2/28/45
China After Seven Years of War	(Various authors)	Gunther Stein	3/4/45
Report From Red China	Harrison Forman	Floyd Taylor	3/18/45
The Chinese Labor Movement	Nym Wales (Mrs. E. Snow)	E. Lattimore	4/8/45
China's Crisis	Laurence K. Rosinger	Owen Lattimore	7/15/45
The Challenge of Red China	Gunther Stein	Owen Lattimore	10/14/45
My Twenty-Five Years in China	John B. Powell	Owen Lattimore	11/11/45
Earthbound China	Hsiao-Tung Fei & Chih I-Chang	E. Lattimore	11/25/45
China in the Sun	Randall Gould	Richard Watts Jr.	1/27/46

Book	Author	Reviewer	Review Date
Chungking Listening Post	Mark Tennien	E. Lattimore	3/10/46
Our Neighbors, the Chinese	Vaughan White	E. Lattimore	5/5/46
China and America	Foster Rhea Dulles	Owen Lattimore	6/2/46
Sun Yat-Sen	S. Chen & R. Payne	Richard Watts Jr.	7/14/46
Messages of Chiang Kai-shek	Chiang Kai-shek	Owen Lattimore	10/20/46
Thunder Out of China	T. White & A. Jacoby	Richard Watts Jr.	10/27/46
China's Destiny and Chinese Economic Theory	Chiang Kai-shek	Owen Lattimore	2/16/47
The Big Yankee (Carlson)	Michael Blankfort	Richard Watts Jr.	3/2/47
Stalin Must Have Peace	Edgar Snow	Joseph Barnes	5/18/47
No Peace for Asia	Harold Isaacs	Owen Lattimore	6/22/47
The Revolt of Asia	Robert Payne	A. T. Steele	9/28/47
Danger from the East	Richard Lauterbach	Owen Lattimore	11/23/47
Last Chance in China	Freda Utley	Owen Lattimore	11/23/47
Donald of China	E. A. Selle	Owen Lattimore	2/8/48
The Stilwell Papers	Ed. by T. White	Harold Isaacs	5/30/48
The United States and China	J. K. Fairbank	Harold Isaacs	7/11/48
Two Years with the Chinese Communists	Claire & William Band	Owen Lattimore	7/11/48
Way of a Fighter	General Chennault	Harold Isaacs	1/30/49
The Situation in Asia	Owen Lattimore	Edgar Snow	4/10/49
Russia's Race for Asia	George Creel	Christopher Rand	5/8/49
China Shakes the World	Jack Belden	Owen Lattimore	10/23/49
The Chinese Conquer China	Anna Louise Strong	J. K. Fairbank	11/13/49
Pivot of Asia	Owen Lattimore	J. K. Fairbank	3/19/50
Dateline: China	H. K. Tong	A. K. Steele	5/7/50
Ordeal by Slander	Owen Lattimore	J. K. Fairbank	7/30/50
Two Kinds of Time	Graham Peck	Harold Isaacs	10/29/50

APPENDIX I

General Joseph W. Stilwell cordially detested Chiang Kai-shek and made no secret of his hatred for him. This report from John Stewart Service helped to fan the flames, coming as it did just when the General was in the midst of his dispute with Chiang which resulted in an ultimatum from the Generalissimo: Stilwell had to go even if American aid to China was stopped. Stilwell went, but since General Marshall was a close friend, there is reason to believe that Chiang was made to suffer for his dismissal of Vinegar Joe. Service, incidentally, was part of the Vincent-Lattimore-Davies clique. He was also involved in the notorious *Amerasia* Case.

SERVICE'S REPORT TO STILWELL

Report No. 40
U. S. ARMY OBSERVER SECTION, APO 879
October 10, 1944

Subject: The Need for Greater Realism in our Relations with Chiang Kai-shek.

To: General Stilwell, Commanding General, USAF–CBI

1. You have allowed me, as a political officer attached to your staff, to express myself freely in the past regarding the situation in China as I have seen it. Although in Yenan I am only a distant observer of recent developments in Chungking and Washington, I trust you will permit the continued frankness which I have assumed in the attached memorandum regarding the stronger policy which I think it is now time for us to adopt toward Chiang Kai-shek and the Central Government.

2. It is obvious, of course, that you cannot act independently along the lines suggested. The situation in China and the measures necessary to meet it have both military importance and far-reaching political significance; the two aspects cannot be separated. Because of this interrelation, and because of the high level on which action in China

must be taken, there must be agreement and mutual support between our political and military branches. But this will be ineffective without clear decision and forceful implementation by the President.

3. It is requested that copies of this report be transmitted, as usual, to the American Ambassador at Chungking and Headquarters, USAF–CBI, for the information of Mr. Davies.

/s/ JOHN S. SERVICE

Enclosure:
Memorandum, as stated.

MEMORANDUM

Our dealings with Chiang Kai-shek apparently continue on the basis of the unrealistic assumption that he is China and that he is necessary to our cause. It is time, for the sake of the war and also for our future interests in China, that we take a more realistic line.

Kuomintang Government is in crisis. Recent defeats have exposed its military ineffectiveness and will hasten the approaching economic disaster. Passive inability to meet these crises in a constructive way, stubborn unwillingness to submerge selfish power-seeking in democratic unity, and the statements of Chiang himself to the Peoples Political Council and on October 10, are sufficient evidence of the bankruptcy of Kuomintang leadership.

With the glaring exposure of the Kuomintang's failure, dissatisfaction with Chiang is growing rapidly. The prestige of the Party was never lower, and Chiang is losing the respect he once enjoyed as a leader.

In the present circumstances, the Kuomintang is dependent on American support for survival. *But we are in no way dependent on the Kuomintang.*

We do not need it for military reasons. It has lost the southern air-bases and cannot hold any section of the seacoast. Without drastic reforms—which must have a political base—its armies cannot fight the Japanese effectively no matter how many arms we give them. But it will not permit those reforms because its war against Japan is secondary to its desire to maintain its own undemocratic power.

On the other hand, neither the Kuomintang nor any other Chinese regime, because of the sentiment of the people, can refuse American forces the use of Chinese territory against the Japanese. And the Kuomintang's attitude prevents the utilization of other forces, such as the Communist or Provincial troops, who should be more useful than the Kuomintang's demoralized armies.

We need not fear Kuomintang surrender or opposition. The Party and Chiang will stick to us because our victory is certain and it is their only hope for continued power.

But our support of the Kuomintang will not stop its normally traitorous relations with the enemy and will only encourage it to continue sowing the seeds of future civil war by plotting with the present puppets for eventual consolidation of the occupied territories against the Communist-led forces of popular resistance.

We need not fear the collapse of the Kuomintang Government. All the other groups in China want to defend themselves and fight Japan. Any new government under any other than the present reactionary control will be more cooperative and better able to mobilize the country.

Actually, by continued and exclusive support of the Kuomintang, we tend to prevent the reforms and democratic reorganization of the government which are essential for the revitalization of China's war effort. Encouraged by our support the Kuomintang will continue in its present course, progressively losing the confidence of the people and becoming more and more impotent. Ignored by us, and excluded from the Government and joint prosecution of the war, the Communists and other groups will be forced to guard their own interests by more direct opposition.

We need not support the Kuomintang for international political reasons. The day when it was expedient to inflate Chiang's status to one of the "Big Four" is past, because with the obvious certainty of defeat, Japan's Pan-Asia propaganda loses its effectiveness. We cannot hope that China under the present Kuomintang can be an effective balance to Soviet Russia, Japan, or the British Empire in the Far East.

On the contrary, artificial inflation of Chiang's status only adds to his unreasonableness. The example of a democratic, nonimperialist China will be much better counterpropaganda in Asia than the present regime, which, even in books like "China's Destiny," hypnotizes itself with ideas of consolidating minority nations (such as the "Southern Peninsula"), and protecting the "right" and at the same time national ties of its numerous emigrants (to such areas as Thailand, Malaya and the East Indies). Finally, the perpetuation in power of the present Kuomintang can only mean a weak and disunited China —a sure cause of international involvements in the Far East. The key to stability must be a strong, unified China. This can be accomplished only on a democratic foundation.

We need not support Chiang in the belief that he represents pro-American or democratic groups. All the people and all other political groups of importance in China are friendly to the United States and look to it for the salvation of the country, now and after the war.

In fact, Chiang has lost the confidence and respect of most of the American-educated, democratically-minded liberals and intellectuals. The Chen brothers, Military, and Secret police cliques which control the Party and are Chiang's main supports are the most chauvinist elements in the country. The present Party ideology, as shown in Chiang's own books "China's Destiny" and "Chinese Economic Theory," is fundamentally anti-foreign, and anti-democratic, both politically and economically.

Finally, we feel no ties of gratitude to Chiang. The men he has kept around him have proved selfish and corrupt, incapable and obstructive. Chiang's own dealings with us have been an opportunist combination of extravagant demands and unfilled promises, wheedling and bargaining, bluff and blackmail. Chiang did not resist Japan until forced by his own people. He has fought only passively—not daring to mobilize his own people. He has sought to have us save him—so that he can continue his conquest of his own country. In the process, he has "worked" us for all we were worth.

We seem to forget that Chiang is an Oriental; that his background and vision are limited; that his position is built on skill as an extremely adroit political manipulator and a stubborn, shrewd bargainer; that he mistakes kindness and flattery for weakness; and that he listens to his own instrument of force, rather than reason.

Our policy toward China should be guided by two facts. First, we cannot *hope to deal successfully with Chiang without being hard-*

boiled. Second, *we cannot hope to solve China's problems* (which are now our problems) *without consideration of the oppression forces* —Communist, Provincial and liberal.

The parallel with Jugoslavia has been drawn before but is becoming more and more apt. It is as impractical to see Chinese unity, the use of the Communist forces, and the mobilization of the population in the rapidly growing occupied areas by discussion in Chungking with the Kuomintang alone as it was to seek the solution of these problems through Mikhailovitch and King Peter's government in London, ignoring Tito.

We should not be swayed by pleas of the danger of China's collapse. This is an old trick of Chiang's.

There may be a collapse of the Kuomintang government; but it will not be the collapse of China's resistance. There may be a period of some confusion, but the eventual gains of the Kuomintang's collapse will more than make up for this. The crisis itself makes reform more urgent—and at the same time increases the weight to our influence. *The crisis is the time to push—not to relax.*

We should not let Chiang divert us from the important questions by wasting time in futile discussion as to who is to be American commander. This is an obvious subterfuge.

There is only one man qualified by experience for the job. And the fact is that *no one who knows anything about China and is concerned over American rather than Chiang's interests will satisfy Chiang.* [All italics Service's.]

We should end the hollow pretense that China is unified and that we can talk only to Chiang. This puts the trump card in Chiang's hands.

Public announcement that the President's representative had made a visit to the Communist capital at Yenan would have a significance that no Chinese would miss—least of all the Generalissimo. The effect would be great even if it were only a demonstration with no real consultation. But it should be more than a mere demonstration; we must, for instance, plan on eventual use of the Communist armies and this cannot be purely on Kuomintang terms.

Finally, if these steps do not succeed, we should stop veiling our negotiations with China in complete secrecy. This shields Chiang and is the voluntary abandonment of our strongest weapon.

Chinese public opinion would swing violently against Chiang if he were shown obstructive and noncooperative with the United States. We should not be misled by the relatively very few Kuomintang die-hards; they are not the people. The Kuomintang Government could not withstand public belief that the United States was considering withdrawal of military support of recognition of the Kuomintang as the leader of Chinese resistance.

More than ever, we hold all the aces in Chiang's poker game. It is time we started playing them.

JOHN S. SERVICE

October 10, 1944

APPENDIX J

The threat in these three documents is apparent. Chiang Kai-shek was told he had to accept Communists into his government or lose American aid.

The background: On June 10, 1945, Owen Lattimore called on President Truman to have U.S. policy "impartially reviewed." He followed this up with a personal interview with the President on July 3, prior to Truman's departure for the Potsdam Confer-ence. On that occasion he left a memorandum with the President calling for a coalition government in China and urging a change in State Department policy-makers.

Soon after this, Joseph Grew, Joseph W. Ballantine, and Eugene Dooman were let out of the Department of State where they had been responsible for Far Eastern Policy. John Carter Vincent, a close friend of Lattimore, became Director of Far Eastern Affairs.

One of Vincent's first acts was to draft a new U.S. policy for China, one that called for the U.S. to "persuade" China to form a coalition government. The directives here reflect the Lattimore-Vincent thinking and this constituted U.S.-China policy until June 1950, when the Korean War erupted.

DIRECTIVES OF GENERAL MARSHALL'S
MISSION IN CHINA

1. President Truman to the
Special Representative of the President to China (Marshall)

WASHINGTON, *December 15, 1945*

My Dear General Marshall: On the eve of your departure for China I want to repeat to you my appreciation of your willingness to undertake this difficult mission.

I have the utmost confidence in your ability to handle the task before you but, to guide you in so far as you may find it helpful, I will give you some of the thoughts, ideas, and objectives which Secretary Byrnes and I have in mind with regard to your mission.

I attach several documents which I desire should be considered as part of this letter. One is a statement of U. S. policy towards China which was, I understand, prepared after consultation with you and with officials of the Department. The second is a memorandum from the Secretary of State to the War Department in regard to China. And the third is a copy of my press release on policy in China. I understand that these documents have been shown to you and received your approval.

The fact that I have asked you to go to China is the clearest evidence of my very real concern with regard to the situation there. Secretary Byrnes and I are both anxious that the unification of China by peaceful, democratic methods be achieved as soon as possible. It is my desire that you, as my Special Representative, bring to bear in an appropriate and practicable manner the influence of the United States to this end.

Specifically, I desire that you endeavor to persuade the Chinese Government to call a national conference of representatives of the major political elements to bring about the unification of China and, concurrently, to effect a cessation of hostilities, particularly in north China.

It is my understanding that there is now in session in Chungking a Peoples' Consultative Council made up of representatives of the various political elements, including the Chinese Communists. The meeting of this Council should furnish you with a convenient opportunity for discussions with the various political leaders.

Upon the success of your efforts, as outlined above, will depend largely, of course, the success of our plans for evacuating Japanese troops from China, particularly north China, and for the subsequent withdrawal of our own armed· forces from China. I am particularly desirous that both be accomplished as soon as possible.

In your conversations with Chiang Kai-shek and other Chinese leaders you are authorized to speak with the utmost frankness. Particularly, you may state, in connection with the Chinese desire for credits, technical assistance in the economic field, and military assistance (I have in mind the proposed U. S. military advisory group which I have approved in principle), that a China disunited and torn by civil strife could not be considered realistically as a proper place for American assistance along the lines enumerated.

I am anxious that you keep Secretary Byrnes and me currently informed of the progress of your negotiations and of obstacles you may encounter. You will have our full support and we shall endeavor at all times to be as helpful to you as possible.

Sincerely yours,

HARRY TRUMAN

[Enclosure]

2. *Memorandum by Secretary Byrnes*

[WASHINGTON,] *December 9, 1945*

For the War Department

The President and the Secretary of State are both anxious that the unification of China by peaceful democratic methods be achieved as soon as possible.

At a public hearing before the Foreign Relations Committee of the Senate on December 7, the Secretary of State said:

"During the war the immediate goal of the United States in China was to promote a military union of the several political factions in order to bring their combined power to bear upon our common enemy, Japan. Our longer-range goal, then as now, and a goal of at least equal importance, is the development of a strong, united, and democratic China.

"To achieve this longer-range goal, it is essential that the Central Government of China as well as the various dissident elements approach the settlement of their differences with a genuine willingness to compromise. We believe, as we have long believed and consistently demonstrated, that the government of Generalissimo Chiang Kai-shek affords the most satisfactory base for a developing democracy. But we also believe that it must be broadened to include the representatives of those large and well organized groups who are now without any voice in the government of China.

"This problem is not an easy one. It requires tact and discretion, patience and restraint. It will not be solved by the Chinese leaders themselves. To the extent that our influence is a factor, success will depend upon our capacity to exercise that influence in the light of shifting conditions in such a way as to encourage concessions by the Central Government, by the so-called Communists, and by the other factions."

The President has asked General Marshal to go to China as his Special Representative for the purpose of bringing to bear in an appropriate and practicable manner the influence of the United States for the achievement of the ends set forth above. Specifically, General Marshall will endeavor to influence the Chinese Government to call a national conference of representatives of the major political elements to bring about the unification of China and, concurrently, effect a cessation of hostilities, particularly in north China.

In response to General Wedemeyer's recent messages, the State Department requests the War Department to arrange for directions to him stipulating that:

(1) He may put into effect the arrangements to assist the Chinese National Government in transporting Chinese troops to Manchurian ports, including the logistical support of such troops;

(2) He may also proceed to put into effect the stepped-up arrangements for the evacuation of Japanese troops from the China theater;

(3) Pending the outcome of General Marshall's discussions with Chinese leaders in Chungking for the purpose of arranging a national conference of representatives of the major political elements and for a cessation of hostilities, further transportation of Chinese troops to

north China, except as north China ports may be necessary for the movement of troops and supplies into Manchuria, will be held in abeyance;

(4) Arrangements for transportation of Chinese troops into north China may be immediately perfected, but not communicated to the Chinese Government. Such arrangements will be executed when General Marshall determines either (a) that the movement of Chinese troops to north China can be carried out consistently with his negotiations, or (b) that the negotiations between the Chinese groups have failed or show no prospect of success and that the circumstances are such as to make the movement necessary to effectuate the surrender terms and to secure the long-term interests of the United States in the maintenance of international peace.

3. *Statement by President Truman on United States Policy Toward China, December 15, 1945*

The Government of the United States holds that peace and prosperity of the world in this new and unexplored era ahead depend upon the ability of the sovereign nations to combine for collective security in the United Nations organization.

It is the firm belief of this Government that a strong, united and democratic China is of the utmost importance to the success of this United Nations organization and for world peace. A China disorganized and divided either by foreign aggression, such as that undertaken by the Japanese, or by violent internal strife, is an undermining influence to world stability and peace, now and in the future. The United States Government has long subscribed to the principle that the management of internal affairs is the responsibility of the peoples of the sovereign rations. Events of this century, however, would indicate that a breach of peace anywhere in the world threatens the peace of the entire world. It is thus in the most vital interest of the United States and all the United Nations that the people of China overlook no opportunity to adjust their internal differences promptly by means of peaceful negotiation.

The Government of the United States believes it essential:

(1) That a cessation of hostilities be arranged between the armies of the National Government and the Chinese Communists and other dissident Chinese armed forces for the purpose of completing the return of all China to effective Chinese control, including the immediate evacuation of the Japanese forces.

(2) That a national conference of representatives of major political elements be arranged to develop an early solution to the present internal strife—a solution which will bring about the unification of China.

The United States and the other United Nations have recognized the present National Government of the Republic of China as the only legal government in China. It is the proper instrument to achieve the objective of a unified China.

The United States and the United Kingdom by the Cairo Declaration in 1943 and the Union of Soviet Socialist Republics by adhering to the Potsdam Declaration of last July and by the Sino-Soviet Treaty and Agreements of August 1945, are all committed to the liberation of China, including the return of Manchuria to Chinese control. These agreements were made with the National Government of the Republic of China.

In continuation of the constant and close collaboration with the National Government of the Republic of China in the prosecution of this war, in consonance with the Potsdam Declaration, and to remove possibility of Japanese influence remaining in China, the United States has assumed a definite obligation in the disarmament and evacuation of the Japanese troops. Accordingly, the United States has been assisting and will continue to assist the National Government of the Republic of China in effecting the disarmament and evacuation of Japanese troops in the liberated areas. The United States Marines are in North China for that purpose.

The United States recognizes and will continue to recognize the National Government of China and cooperate with it in international affairs and specifically in eliminating Japanese influence from China. The United States is convinced that a prompt arrangement for a cessation of hostilities is essential to the effective achievement of this end. United States support will not extend to United States military intervention to influence the course of any Chinese internal strife.

The United States has already been compelled to pay a great price to restore the peace which was first broken by Japanese aggression in

Manchuria. The maintenance of peace in the Pacific may be jeopardized, if not frustrated, unless Japanese influence in China is wholly removed and unless China takes her place as a unified, democratic and peaceful nation. This is the purpose of the maintenance for the time being of United States military and naval forces in China.

The United States is cognizant that the present National Government of China is a "one-party government" and believes that peace, unity and democratic reform in China will be furthered if the basis of this Government is broadened to include other political elements in the country. Hence, the United States strongly advocates that the national conference of representatives of major political elements in the country agree upon arrangements which would give those elements a fair and effective representation in the Chinese National Government. It is recognized that this would require modification of the one-party "political tutelage" established as an interim arrangement in the progress of the nation toward democracy by the father of the Chinese Republic, Doctor Sun Yat-sen.

The existence of autonomous armies such as that of the Communist army is inconsistent with, and actually makes impossible, political unity in China. With the institution of a broadly representative government, autonomous armies should be eliminated as such and all armed forces in China integrated effectively into the Chinese National Army.

In line with its often expressed views regarding self-determination, the United States Government considers that the detailed steps necessary to the achievement of political unity in China must be worked out by the Chinese themselves and that intervention by any foreign government in these matters would be inappropriate. The United States Government feels, however, that China has a clear responsibility to the other United Nations to eliminate armed conflict within its territory as constituting a threat to world stability and peace—a responsibility which is shared by the National Government and all Chinese political and military groups.

As China moves toward peace and unity along the lines described above, the United States would be prepared to assist the National Government in every reasonable way to rehabilitate the country, improve the agrarian and industrial economy, and establish a military organization capable of discharging China's national and international responsibilities for the maintenance of peace and order. In furtherance of such assistance, it would be prepared to give favorable consideration to Chinese requests for credits and loans under reasonable conditions for projects which would contribute toward the development of a healthy economy throughout China and healthy trade relations between China and the United States.

APPENDIX K

Exhibit No. 1321–A

March 28, 1952.

Senator Pat McCarran,
   Chairman, Committee on the Judiciary,
      United States Senate, Washington, D. C.

My Dear Senator: As proposed in your letter I enclose affidavit for inclusion in the record of your Hearings.

Briefly it states:

1. References to me by witnesses before your Committee as the China Lobby, etc.

2. My background and interest in the Far East.

3. Letters from Air Marshal Bishop and Assistant Secretary of Navy Gates attesting my interest in opposing totalitarianism.

4. Service in Civil Air Patrol.

5. Wartime trip to China and discovery of apparent treasonable activities.

6. Study of IPR and publication of findings November 9, 1944.

7. Answer by four trustees.

8. My answer of December 28, 1944.

9. Special meeting of IPR—my letter to members and defeat of my resolution for investigation.

10. Formation of American China Policy Association in 1946 and letter of Congresswoman Clare Booth Luce, October 11, 1945, revealing attitude of Directors.

11. My appearance before Senate Committees and acquaintance with members of Foreign Relations Committee of Senate.

12. My connection with Senator McCarthy.

13. Admiral Nimitz General Marshall, and IPR.
14. Letter to IPR Trustees, March 13, 1952.
15. Letter to Dr. Roscoe Pound.
16. Closing statement.
    Very sincerely yours,

                          [t] ALFRED KOHLBERG
                          [s] Alfred Kohlberg
           1 West 37th Street, New York, 18, N. Y.

EXHIBIT No. 1321–B

APRIL 9, 1952.

Mr. ALFRED KOHLBERG,
    1 West 37th Street,
        New York 18, N. Y.

DEAR MR. KOHLBERG: I have your affidavit of March 28, 1952, which contains extraneous clippings and supplementary letters.

For inclusion in the record of the Internal Security Subcommittee what you submit should be all in affidavit form.

Kindest regards,
    Sincerely,

                          PAT MCCARRAN, *Chairman.*

EXHIBIT No. 1321–C

(Mr. Alfred Kohlberg's affidavit of April 16, 1952:)

STATE OF NEW YORK,
        County of New York, ss:

Alfred Kohlberg, being duly sworn, deposes and says:

That I reside in New York, my office address being 1 West 37th Street, New York 18, N. Y.

That Professor Owen Lattimore referred to me three times in his statement read to the subcommittee of the Judiciary Committee of the United States Senate, generally referred to as the McCarran Committee. That in addition Professor Lattimore referred to me several times in his verbal testimony; that I was likewise referred to numerous times by other witnesses before the McCarran Committee; also by Professor Lattimore and other witnesses before the Tydings Committee in March, April, May and June 1950; also by Senators Morse and McMahon during the Joint Committee hearings on the dismissal of General MacArthur; and on the floor of the Senate by Senators Lehman, Connally and others.

That beginning in April and May 1950, after Professor Lattimore's statements to the Tydings Committee, articles and editorials appeared in the Washington Post, St. Louis Dispatch, New York Post, New York Compass, New York Daily Worker, New York Times, The Nation (a weekly), the New Republic (a weekly). That I was mentioned 17 times in Owen Lattimore's book "Ordeal by Slander."

That the testimony and articles stated that I was the "China Lobby," that I was the "man behind McCarthy;" that "McCarthy's charges were nothing but a rehash of the irresponsible charges of Kohlberg;" that I was probably secretly in the pay of the Nationalist Government of Chiang Kai-shek; that I had connections with a so-called Christian-front, with fascists, with anti-semites; and an editorial in the Washington Post entitled "Kohlberg's Klan" suggested further disreputable connections.

That I have written evidence that in April 1950 one, Robert W. Barnett, formerly Secretary of the Institute of Pacific Relations, and in 1950 Chief of the Economic Section of the Far Eastern Division of the State Department, advised certain reporters of the above alleged facts about me and further advised them that more details could be obtained from an organization in New York called The Friends of Democracy, headed by Rev. Leon Birkhead; and that Friends of Democracy had prepared a three page statement entitled "The Case Against Alfred Kohlberg."

That the facts concerning my interest and activities in opposing Communism, and opposing the Chinese Communists, are as follows:

I have been engaged in the import textile business for more than 35 years, having offices and agents at various times in China, Japan, Iran, France, Switzerland, and the United Kingdom. At no time have I ever done any business with or had any financial transactions of any character with the Government of the United States or any foreign Government, or any subsidiary thereof (with two exceptions), except for the payment of customs dues and taxes. When I refer to any business or financial transactions, I include myself personally and any and all corporations with which I have been actively connected. The exceptions referred to above were (1) a period of 2 or 3 years during which one of my corporations acted as agent for the Amtorg

Trading Corp. for Russian linens in the late 20's or early 30's; and
(2) the purchase of some surplus navy jackets, after V-J Dày, from
the United States Government.

During these more than 35 years in foreign trade, I came to understand the wisdom of the now-abandoned Monroe Doctrine and the
Open Door Policy. The Monroe Doctrine was designed to prevent
the possibility of the building up of a European empire on this continent, with its resulting constant threat to our security. The Open
Door Policy was designed to prevent any military empire from adding
to its power the resources and manpower of the Chinese Empire,
with a resulting threat to our security in the Pacific.

Therefore when Japan began her all-out war on China in 1937, I
contributed to relief work and addressed some open letters to Congress on America's interest, as I saw it. At the beginning of that war
I learned that the Soviet Union extended aid in military supplies and
a Russian-manned airforce to the Republic of China. Being in China
in the summer of 1938, I learned that the Soviets had ceased their
aid and that Russia had reached agreement with Germany and Japan.
This agreement, which was finally made public as the Hitler-Stalin
Pact of Aug. 23, 1939, I reported in an interview in the New York
Times of Nov. 25, 1938. During the course of said interview I stated,
and the New York Times reported, that Russia, Germany, and Japan
had arrived at an agreement by which Russia "either joined the
German-Japanese alliance, or, if she did not go so far, made peace
with Japan and Germany. The arrangement called for cooperation
with Russia by Japan and Germany rather than antagonism, and provided for withdrawal of Russian support to Chinese forces."

After the war started in Europe the following year, and after the
replacement of Neville Chamberlain by Winston Churchill convinced
me that Britain would really fight the Hitler-Stalin-Japanese alliance,
being a licensed airplane pilot, I went to Canada in May 1940 to
volunteer, but was rejected because of age.

The following month, after the fall of France, I wrote to Wing
Commander Homer Smith of the Royal Canadian Air Force, offering
to volunteer, with my airplane, to fly a suicide mission into any German objective selected by them. On July 2, 1940, Air Marshal W. A.
Bishop wrote me "Wing Commander Smith has shown me your letter
and I wanted to take this opportunity of telling you how much we

appreciate your offer of service, and the offer of your machine. At the moment, however, the age limit makes it impossible for us to accept your services, but should this at a later date change, I will get in touch with you."

Thereafter I volunteered to fly a similar suicide mission for the Australians, the British, and the Chinese; but was refused.

Finally, after Pearl Harbor on December 9, 1941, I wrote Artemus Gates, Assistant Secretary of the Navy for Air, stating in part:

"In May 1940 I volunteered for the R.C.A.F. at Ottawa but was turned down on account of age. In July 1940 I volunteered to fly any old trainer loaded with explosives into a troop transport, warship or any other objective. This offer was refused. In April 1941 I repeated this offer. This last offer is still being considered, but the Air Attaché of the British Embassy in Washington still has no final decision from London, but is not hopeful of a favorable answer, as the regulations provide for no such service."

"I now make this offer to you ° ° ° Can you use me? Rank and pay are no object, but I would like two weeks to wind up my affairs. This letter, of course, is strictly confidential."

On Jan. 8, 1942, Mr. Gates wrote:

"I have your offer very much in mind, in fact, I have not been able to forget it since you wrote me early in December, but to date I just don't know where such 100 percent unselfish services can be used. Perhaps the opportunity will develop but I think our battle on the Pacific is going to be a long war.

"Incidentally, a number of officers in the Bureau of Aeronautics have been acquainted with your sacrifice."

Failing to obtain such a commission, I finally served with the Civil Air Patrol in the antisubmarine patrol in the Gulf of Mexico in the latter part of 1942, and hold Certificate of Honorable Service of the Department of the Air Force.

I refer to this service and attempted service as an answer to charges and implied charges, referred to above, that I was a Fascist or sympathetic to fascist-minded groups, with none of whom have I ever had any association whatsoever.

Meantime I had become a Director and in 1941 Chairman of the Executive Committee of the Board of Directors of the American Bureau for Medical Aid to China. In the Spring of 1943 ABMAC and

United China Relief, of which it had become a part, received unfavorable reports from their staff men in Chungking about graft and incompetency in the Chinese Army medical services, which we were aiding. Mr. E. C. Carter, of the IPR, had become head of the United China Relief Committee that allocated funds to the various agencies in China, and had recommended for appointment most of the employees of United China Relief.

I flew to China in June 1943 at my own expense to investigate. Shortly before leaving for China, Mr. Lauchlin Currie phoned New York and asked me to see him before going, in his offices in the State Department. He told me at considerable length of reports being received from China, of incompetence, corruption and the inability and lack of will on the part of the Chinese to fight. He told me I could check with Americans in Chungking, and that he would be pleased to hear my impressions on returning. On arrival in China Dwight Edwards, head of UCR there, Dr. George Bachman, head of ABMAC, and various other Americans including some in our Embassy confirmed the reports of corruption and incompetence.

As none of them had been in the field, I asked their sources, which they protested were confidential. I therefore felt it necessary to check in the field, which I did against their advice. After traveling through five provinces by truck, ambulance, rail, air and horseback, including 8 days in the 6th War Area, I found the itemized charges either completely untrue or greatly exaggerated.

On returning to America I complained to Dr. Stanley Hornbeck, Political Adviser to the Secretary of State on the Far East, and Joseph Ballantine, Director Far Eastern Division of the State Department, in a lengthy interview. I protested that the untruths were making Chinese-American cooperation difficult, if not impossible, with resultant benefit to the Japanese enemy and unnecessary loss of both Chinese and American lives.

They professed to be unable to do anything about it; Dr. Hornbeck saying: "When I see the people that this Department is sending to China, I shake in my shoes."

It was not until early 1944 that I began to realize that the lies about the Chinese Government and Army were Communist propaganda; and that the main source for spreading them in this country was the Institute of Pacific Relations. Although I had previously been a member of the Finance Committee of the IPR and helped raise funds for them, and had previously recognized that some of the employees were pro-Communist, I had not suspected the scope of the infiltration. As I had foolishly thrown away all back copies of their publications, unread, I went to their offices to rebuy such back copies. They told me that they were out of print.

I therefore went to the public library and from about April to October 1944, read all articles they had published on the Chinese *military and/or political situation* from 1937 to that date. I then read the articles in the New Masses, an official Communist weekly, and The Communist, an official Communist monthly, on the same topics, for the same years.

From these I prepared an 88 page study (frequently referred to in the McCarran hearings) and sent it with a covering letter to Mr. E. C. Carter and to each of the Trustees of the IPR and such members and other persons interested in the Far East as were known to, or suggested to me. (Later the IPR in their so-called analysis which Mr. Dennett testified was prepared by Mrs. Maxwell S. Stewart, and not by the Trustees, and in other testimony, charged that my study contained extracts from only 2 percent of their articles published between 1937 and 1944. This may or may not be literally true, but is irrelevant as I studied and extracted only their articles on the military and/or political situation in China. To the best of my memory my extracts covered all or practically all of their articles in those two fields. I did not attempt to analyze their articles on other countries than China (even including the U. S. and Canada), nor on other topics such as economics, industry, transportation, finance, agriculture, folklore, family life, shipping, missionary activities, fisheries, etc., etc.)

In my covering letter to Mr. Carter, dated Nov. 9, 1944, I said in part:

"Last June I received from United China Relief a copy of a booklet issued by your IPR entitled 'War-Time China' (IPR Pamphlet No. 10). In a recent advertisement, Rosamund Lee, your Publications Secretary, referring to this pamphlet states, 'What is the true situation between the Chinese Communists and the Kuomintang as explained by Maxwell S. Stewart in War-Time China.'

"Frankly, I was shocked at this pamphlet. From start to finish, it seemed to me a deliberate smear of China, the Chinese and the

Chinese Government. I was especially shocked by the following: 'They (the American, British and Soviet Governments) have, however, limited their economic and military assistance because of fear that any supplies they send might be used in civil strife rather than against the Japanese.'

"The statement seems completely at variance with the many statements made by our President to the effect that all possible aid is being given to China and will continue to be given to China.

"Three or four years ago, you may recall, I resigned after a dozen years membership in IPR. You asked me the reason for my resignation and I told you frankly that I thought you had too many Communists on your staff. You asked me if I thought you were a Communist, to which I, of course, replied 'No.' You then told me that you did not question your staff as to their political beliefs: whether they were Democrats, Republicans, Socialists, Communists, or what not; that you investigated their qualifications and judged them by their work. This seemed to me at the time a very businesslike attitude and I withdrew my resignation.

"After reading the above referred-to booklet, I decided to look into the IPR publications further. As a result of this reading, I now attach hereto a lot of clippings from your publications, along with clippings from 'The Communist' (Official organ of the Communist Party in the U. S. A.) and 'New Masses' (another Communist organ), also a few other clippings that seem to bear on the same issues. If you will go through these, I think you will find that your employees have been putting over on you a not-too-well-camouflaged Communist line. Your staff publications follow the 'New Masses' line exactly but not quite so frankly and the 'New Masses' articles are much better documented. In selecting these, I have had to clip and clip to keep to reasonable length, but I believe that what is left of each article fairly represents the article as a whole, as far as same touches on the subjects covered.

"This study poses the question: What are the Soviet Union's aims in the Far East? Is there a sinister purpose behind this Communist inspired campaign to discredit China? Only Marshall Stalin can answer this question.

"But another question has been bothering me as I made this study. This question is: Is it treason? Does the publication of untruthful statements give 'aid and comfort' to our enemy, Japan, in its attempt to break Chinese unity under Chiang Kai-shek? This question I propound to your Board of Trustees.

"Look over these clippings and see if you do not think it is time for a housecleaning in the IPR. The economic articles (not quoted) sounded to me very much like undergraduate studies, compiled from studies of Chinese economists and lacking any practical business background.

"If you agree that a house cleaning in the IPR is long overdue, I will be happy to help. My suggestions would be:

"1. Fire all the Reds, because the truth is not in them.

"2. Adopt a policy of presenting facts rather than opinions. Identify the sources of your information.

"3. Name a responsible body to determine policy.

"This last point is suggested to me by what I missed in going through your last 7 years' publications. I found:

1. No criticism of Japan in those 7 years, except of her rural land system;

2. No single criticism of Communist China; and

3. No single criticism of the Soviet Union; whereas I found:

4. Severe criticism of the Chinese Government, alternating with praise, closely following the alternations of the Soviet Union's foreign policy and of the Communist press.

"A responsible committee controlling and vouching for your policy would be very reassuring to the members of, and contributors to your Institute."

This letter was answered, not by Mr. Carter, but by Messrs. Robert G. Sproul, Chairman; Robert D. Calkins, Dean, Columbia University; G. Ellsworth Huggins, Treasurer, and Philip C. Jessup. In their answer they said:

"At its December 11 meeting the Executive Committee of the American Council reviewed Mr. Kohlberg's charges and demands. It desires to report the following:

"The Executive Committee and the responsible officers of the American Council had no reason to consider seriously the charge of bias. The character of the personnel associated with the Institute, the long history of its research activities, and the demonstrated value of its research testify to the fact that it has properly fulfilled its function to conduct impartial research on important issues even though they are controversial. The Committee believes a full presentation and discussion of such issues is desirable, even in wartime.

"The Institute of Pacific Relations has, and always has had, a responsible body to determine policy. The Pacific Council, with which Mr. Carter is associated, is directed by representatives from the National Councils and that body, made up of these representatives, determines its policies.

"The general policy of the American Council, which is one of the ten constituent bodies in the Institute, is determined by the Board of Trustees. The Executive Committee acts on behalf of the Board of Trustees, when the Board is not in session.

"The research conducted by the American Council is under the direction of its Research Advisory Committee, to which research planning and policy have been delegated by the Executive Committee. This Committee formulates and approves research programs, and it approves the research personnel who are engaged for their competence to undertake the special assignments required in the research program. Having hired competent research workers, it is not the policy of the Committee or of the American Council to censor this findings [sic], but to publish them as the research results of the authors themselves."

This answer of the 4 trustees, I answered Dec. 28, 1944. My answer follows (in part):

"*The issue presented to Mr. Carter* by my letter of Nov. 9 is:

"Have the publications of the I. P. R. (both American Council and Pacific Council) closely followed the Communist line in alternate praise and abuse of the Chinese Government? i. e.

Prior to the Hitler-Stalin pact of Aug. 23, 1939 . . . . . PRAISE.
Then until June 22, 1941 (Hitler invasion of Russia) . ABUSE.
Then until Summer of 1943 . . . . PRAISE.
Since Summer of 1943 . . . . ABUSE.

"*The issue presented to your Board* by my letter of Nov. 9 is: Are these publications treasonable, inasmuch as they are calculated to give 'aid and comfort' to our enemy, Japan, in its attempts by propaganda to break the faith of the Chinese people in the Government of Chiang Kai-shek?

"Neither of these issues is touched on in your letter of Dec. 19. Whether they were discussed at your meeting of Dec. 11 is not stated.

"Your letter states that, having selected competent employees, you let them publish what they wish, without censorship. Do you consider yourselves responsible bodies and if so, do you, or do you not, assume responsibility for those publications by your staff?

"As a member, may I ask your Research Advisory Committee for the qualifications as 'experts' of the following staff members who write your articles on whether, including dates of their visits to China, cities and provinces visited, and whether you feel their impartiality is attested to, or questioned by, their acceptance as authorities by, and contributors to, the American Communist press:

Maxwell S. Stewart

T. A. Bisson

L. K. Rosinger

Y. Y. Hsu

"As a member, I would be interested to know who elected or appointed to your Board and to your Executive Committee, Mr. Frederick V. Field, Generalissimo of the White House pickets until their liquidation, Sunday, June 22, 1941, and now featured writer on China for the 'Daily Worker,' 'The Communist,' and 'New Masses', I would also be interested to know what makes him an 'expert' on China.

"In my letter of November 9, I called attention to the fact that in reading your publications for the past 7 years, I found no criticism of Japan, Communist China, or the Soviet Union, but alternating praise and abuse of the Chinese Government.

"Since that time I have received scores of letters, many from outstanding American authorities on the Far East. None was critical, some were noncommittal, the majority were commendatory of my study. A number were from ex-members of your Institute who resigned because they felt the Institute had become the not-too-well camouflaged agent of a foreign power whose way of life and worldwide fifth column infiltration are antagonistic to the interest of these United States.

"From that correspondence I attach a letter written to you Oct. 8, 1942, by Mr. Miller Freeman, Seattle publisher. Mr. Freeman tells me his letter was neither answered nor acknowledged. Maybe he, too, should have cleared it privately with Mr. Carter.

"Before closing, one more quotation—this from signed statement of Upton Close:

" 'A few days prior to the Pearl Harbor disaster, Mr. Trammell' (head of NBC) 'himself received a letter from E. C. Carter, head of the Institute of Pacific Relations, demanding that I be dropped from the air because I was "anti-Japanese".'

"One of the questions most commonly asked is: 'What are IPR's motives for their current attacks on China.' Possibly your Boards would like to make a statement on this, explaining why all your articles on the current complicated situation are written by staff members, none of whom has been in China for years, while contrary statements by such liberals as Pearl Buck and Lin Yutang are ignored, and articles from your own Chinese Council are rejected. May I also ask Mr. Carter whether he personally presented your public criticisms to Chiang Kai-shek, Ho Ying-chin, Chen Li-fu and Sun-fo in Chungking last year and what were their answers?"

I then asked for permission to circulate my fellow members. This was granted by letter from Mr. Raymond Dennett. But when I sent a secretary by appointment to copy the names, they withdrew permission. I filed suit for the membership list, which after various court vicissitudes was settled by agreement by the IPR to address on their machine under my inspection any one mailing I might choose to send their members.

In said mailing, dated March 18, 1947, I included a printed resolution appointing an impartial committee of investigation and a proxy to vote for same. Also one article from the New Leader and one from Plain Talk, both about the IPR and wrote my fellow members of the IPR in part as follows:

"By order of the supreme court of the State of New York, this letter is being mailed to you by the American Institute of Pacific Relations, Inc.

"Early in July 1943 I was told by several Americans in Chungking that 'the Chinese Government was hoarding tanks and guns given them under lend-lease to use against the Japs.' Late in August, having spent six weeks traveling through Szechuen, Kweichow, Kwangsi, Hunan and Yunnan, I called on Brig. Gen. Arms, U. S. Army, Commander of the Infantry Training School in Kunming. Among other items I asked why he permitted such hoarding. He laughed and said he'd heard some good ones, but this took the cake. He said that up to that date all the arms and ammunition that had come in had gone to him and to the artillery training school; that they were not fully equipped as yet and, until they were, nothing would be flown in (the air route over the hump to Kunming being the only route in) for any other force except the air force whose minimum requirements were the first priority. He explained that nothing but air-force supplies had come in since May, due to the monsoons. After the monsoons ended, he expected the resumption of his equipping; and after that was completed, he explained, General Stilwell was to get full equipment for two of his divisions, and then, after that, 50% was to go to Stilwell and 50% to the Chinese Army—sometime in 1944. At that moment, he said, not one tank or gun or rifle or bazooka or cartridge had been turned over to the Chinese Army under lend-lease—hence none could be hoarded.

"On returning to the United States, I spoke of this and other reports with some heat and was told by friends that the IPR was the chief culprit in the spreading of lies about China, and that the motivation back of it was Communism. I had been a member of the IPR since 1928, but like most businessmen and (as I later learned) like most of their Board of Trustees, I seldom read the literature they sent me, and like most people knew nothing about Communism.

"To check on these charges, I read through the FAR EASTERN SURVEY and our quarterly PACIFIC AFFAIRS from 1937 to that date (summer of 1944). In my reading I read every article on the political and military situation in China and skipped nearly everything else. Then, to learn the Communist line, I read all the articles on the political and military situation in China in the NEW MASSES (weekly) and THE COMMUNIST (monthly), both being Communist Party official publications.

"In the course of this reading I learned that the IPR and the Communist publications had switched their attitude or 'line' on the situation in China several times between 1937 and 1944; both IPR and Communists making the same switches at the same time. Further I noticed that to some extent they interchanged writers and both quoted the same authorities; that they were both lyrical in their reviews of the same books; but that, of the three, the NEW MASSES (possibly because it was franker and more open in taking sides) had the best documented articles. In fact, if the IPR had disregarded whatever information sources it had (if any) and relied only on the NEW

MASSES, it would have omitted little that it published on the Chinese military and political scene.

"After completing my study, I published extracts from the IPR and the Communist press in an 88-page booklet and sent it with a letter to Mr. E. C. Carter and each of our Trustees and to personal acquaintances interested in China. (You may have a copy of this and later correspondence for the asking.)

"At that time I thought that Mr. Carter, who was then President of Russian War Relief, was so busy that he had let some Reds on the staff run off with the Institute. I called on him and the Trustees to fire these Reds and exercise a real control over their publications. (That was November 1944.) The answer of the Executive Committee was to issue a letter stating that they did not think my charges 'merited serious consideration.' (Two of them told me later that they had not read the study.) They then turned the charges and study over to the staff (against whom the charges were filed) to be studied and answered. By April 1945 the staff had prepared a 52-page answer of which I only learned in 1946 and of which even the Chairman of the Trustees couldn't get a copy to give me. I finally obtained a copy by court order in October 1946.

"Since 1944 I have learned much more about the IPR; its apparently completely Communist or pro-Communist staff; that all articles on Far Eastern politics are written by Communists or pro-Communists (some articles on economic, scientific, geographic questions are not); and that it has ties through interlocking directorates or staff with various Communist or pro-Communist organizations.

"Through its influence in the staffing of the State Department, Army and Navy Intelligence, and Far Eastern Divisions; of UNRRA, of OWI, and even General MacArthur's staff, our Institute has put considerable numbers of Communists and pro-Communists where they could and have done the most possible harm and spread the most confusion. How far they have succeeded is strikingly illustrated by comparing the present confusion in our attitude to China with the statement handed to Ambassador Nomura on November 26, 1941, which laid down the terms on which we would restore peaceful relations with Japan (ruptured by the blockade declared July 25, 1941). Hull's essential demand was:

" '4. The Government of the United States and the Government of

Japan will not support—militarily, politically, economically—any Government or regime in China other than the National Government of the Republic of China with capital temporarily at Chungking.'

"To attempt to prove my statements is impossible in this letter. They are proven in part by the study and correspondence referred to above, which will be sent you on request.

"My attempts to arouse Mr. Carter and our Trustees to investigation and action have failed. Several Trustees, including several of the Executive Committee have resigned, claiming that they were worried by the charges of communism, but had no time to look into them so thought they'd better get out. Our Board of Trustees (47) scattered all over the country never meets. The Executive Committee (10) is chairmanned by a Californian who never attends. The connections of the others are as per attached sheet. Most of our Trustees are, of course, not Communists and furthermore don't take Communists very seriously. Their attitude is very similar to that of a witness before the Senate Atomic Committee, as reported in the New York Sun February 22, 1947, as follows:

" 'Cameron said that he roomed with Hart and knew that his roommate held Marxist views, was sympathetic to Russia, and read the Daily Worker, Communist paper, but did not know that he was a Communist.'

"If our Institute is to be saved for the useful work it can and should do in soundly and objectively posting American scholars, teachers, and writers on the Far East, we, the members, will have to do the job. The first step is to appoint a Board of Investigators to listen to my charges and dig out the facts. Some of the gentlemen named in the enclosed proxy are known to me, some are not, but all bear reputations as good Americans informed on the Far East. I have not asked them if they will serve and cannot do so until I hold sufficient proxies. I have no doubt that enough will accept to make up a satisfactory board.

"In order to keep this letter within reasonable length, I have omitted going into the following:

"1. Many of the staff and writers have no real claim to scholarship in the fields they cover.

"2. Much of the material published is plagiarized for the above reasons.

"3. Our staff and officers were instrumental in forming the violently pro-Communist 'Committee for a Far Eastern Democratic Policy.'

"4. Our staff and officers were instrumental in maintaining the pro-Communist 'Japanese American Committee for Democracy.'

"5. Our staff and officers conducted a pressure mail campaign to force NBC to continue the wartime 'Pacific Story'—a Communist-angled dramatic half hour.

"6. Our staff and officers have sponsored and published books and articles by such known Communists as Abraham Chapman, Jos. S. Allen, Harriet L. Moore, Philip Jaffe, Anna Louise Strong, Frederick V. Field.

"7. Members of our Board of Trustees and our staff managed to get control of the Far Eastern Division of the State Department, UNRRA and OWI, where they loaded all three with pro-Communists. Two of them, Owen Lattimore and John Carter Vincent, accompanied Henry Wallace to China in 1944 and talked that adolescent into reporting to Roosevelt that 'we were backing the wrong horse in China' and that 'Chiang Kai-shek's government would collapse within 90 days.' Just prior to that much heralded trip of that great friend of the common man, IPR published a booklet by Henry Wallace, *Our Job in the Pacific*, which they knew he had not written.

"8. Four of the six persons arrested in the Amerasia case were connected with the IPR.

"I no longer believe the officers and Executive Committee can clean up the Institute.

"After such an Investigating Committee has completed its investigation and reported, action will then be up to us. Our Trustees will not act and if we wait until Congressional investigation reaches us, it may be too late to save our institution and even our good reputation."

At the meeting, April 22, 1947, the tellers advised me that they had over 1,100 proxies against the resolution for an investigating committee. I presented 86 but they disqualified about 20, though they refused to show me their proxies. In the meeting I read my proposed resolution and then stated:

"It would be my intention to present first to this Investigating Committee witnesses, and by witnesses I mean more than one, who would testify that the Institute of Pacific Relations is considered by the National Committee of the Communist Party to be one of its organizations and that certain of the Executive Committee of the American Institute are members of the Communist Party.

"In addition to these witnesses who would testify to that effect, I would expect to show that committee that there have been certain misstatements of fact in the publications of the Institute, that these misstatements of fact follow a pattern, that the publications of the Institute have been free of criticism of Japan up to Pearl Harbor except for criticisms of the Japanese rural land system, and that they have been free of criticisms of Russia up to date, both Japan and Russia—that is, Siberia—falling within the area covered by the Pacific Institute.

"I would call attention to the fact that although the Institute has referred to many documents and in books and pamphlets issued by it has published many pertinent documents, four of the most pertinent documents referring to the Far East have always been omitted, and as far as I have been able to find by an examination of the publications, have never been either printed in full or referred to by the Institute.

"Those four documents are the Tanaka Memorial, the Resolutions of the Colonies and Semi-Colonies adopted by the Sixth World Congress of the Comintern, the program of the Comintern adopted by the same Sixth Congress, and the note of Secretary Hull to Ambassador Nomura of November 21, 1941.

"I would also expect to show to that same committee that many of the writers are not qualified and that there are much better qualified people in certain of the fields on, for example, the Philippines, Hawaii, than the writers in the publications of the Institute. They are not qualified, and qualified writers are available, and, in fact, members of the Institute.

"I would also call to the attention of that committee that American policy for the Pacific has been a consistent policy and in a traditional policy. That policy is the policy of the Open Door, proclaimed in 1899 and further confirmed in the Nine-Power Treaty of 1922, and that policy calls for the Open Door, for the independence and the territorial integrity of China, and that the publications of the Institute, although they have published vast amounts of material on China, seldom, if ever, have referred to this policy and its implications.

"I believe that if the opportunity is presented, I can prove each of those statements and also the charges with which you are familiar from the letter sent you March 20."

Mr. Arthur H. Dean, Vice Chairman of the IPR, presided in the absence of the Chairman, Robert G. Sproul. He answered my statement, saying that the IPR was lily-white (not red) and he could vouch for it. The vote cast by the nearly 100 present, was unanimous against the resolution. A few days later, by letter, I resigned from the IPR, since which time I have devoted little attention to it.

Just about a year previous to the above meeting, Mr. J. B. Powell, dean of the American correspondents in China, and Miss Helen Loomis, a former missionary teacher in China, had called a small meeting at Miss Loomis' apartment to form a committee to warn the country of the dangerous policy we were following in China. From this meeting came the American China Policy Association, Inc., of which Mr. Powell was President until his death in 1947, when he was succeeded for one year by former Congresswoman Clare Boothe Luce, and Miss Loomis was Secretary-Treasurer. I was elected Vice President and later Chairman of the Board. By resolution the American China Policy Association, Inc., limited its members to persons of American citizenship and provided that only Americans could be brought as guests to its Board meetings, so that America's interest, only, should be presented for consideration.

Meantime also, I had become publisher and sole financial backer of the magazine Plain Talk, published from October 1946 to May 1950, as a monthly, and now merged with The Freeman, a fortnightly.

During these years, and continuing to the present, I have written numerous open letters to various persons, including Government officials, numerous articles for magazines, and letters to newspapers, on the general topic of our struggle with World Communism. I have also made speeches on numerous occasions. In all cases I have refused to accept monies, from any source, either for articles, speeches or traveling expenses, or as contributions. All expenses have been paid by me personally or by one of the corporations controlled by me and interested in these matters.

I have five times appeared at public hearings before Committees of the Congress—twice on behalf of the American China Policy Association, Inc., and three times as an individual. Three of the hearings were before the Foreign Relations Committee of the Senate and two before the Appropriations Committee of the Senate.

Other than these appearances my visits to Washington have been mostly seeking information as to what was going on in the labyrinth of apparent absence of over-all policy which has led to such disastrous results for America and the Free World. The only members of the Senate Foreign Relations Committee whom I have ever met are Senators Brien McMahon, H. Alexander Smith, Henry Cabot Lodge, and Owen Brewster. These were chance meetings. The only members of that Committee on whom I have ever called are Senators H. Alexander Smith and Owen Brewster. When Senator Smith returned from the Far East in 1949, I sent my card in to the Floor and he came to the Senate Lobby and told me of his impressions. I called on Senator Brewster in New York once when he was en route to Europe and presented him with copies of three important Comintern documents.

Sometime in March 1950 one of Senator McCarthy's assistants got in touch with me and I supplied published material on the Far East and on persons connected with American policy in the Far East. Subsequently, I met the Senator for the first time. Thereafter Drew Pearson broadcast the statement that I was backing Senator McCarthy financially. Up to that moment it had not occurred to me that Senator McCarthy had to pay his staff, as I presumed they were supplied by the Senate. So I wrote Drew Pearson as follows:

"Your broadcast suggested that Senator McCarthy has been put to heavy expense in his patriotic work of exposing the traitors who have controlled our policy in Asia. I think Americans should join in helping pay some of Senator McCarthy's expenses, so I am going to send him a small check today and hope others do likewise."

Some days, or a week later, I sent a check for $500 to Senator McCarthy. He returned it with a polite letter saying that charges that I was the China Lobby made it inadvisable for him to accept the contribution. Since then, Senator McCarthy has not suggested, nor have I offered or made a further contribution; nor had I ever previously offered or made any contribution to Senator McCarthy.

In the course of my studies (which were those of a businessman with some background, but not those of a trained student of international affairs), I learned from persons in a position to know, that at all times for more than 10 years the Communists have maintained control of the Executive Committee of the IPR and of the staff; and that the few changes made, under pressure of public exposure, have not altered this control. About 5 years ago an investigator for the State Department spent two days in my files, and after investigation elsewhere filed a report on the IPR which must have revealed to the State Department the true facts. In spite of which our Far Eastern destiny still lies in the hands of IPR-connected officials.

At about the same time an investigator for ONI called on me, said Admiral Nimitz had been invited to become Chairman of IPR; that he had asked ONI to report, and they were making a routine check. Admiral Nimitz did not become Chairman or a Trustee, but thereafter General Marshall became a Trustee, in spite of the previously filed report of the State Department investigator.

In a speech to the Commonwealth Club of San Francisco, February 29, 1952, I called on those Trustees of the IPR (of whom some were present) who were neither Communist nor pro-Communist to rehabilitate themselves with their fellow Americans by coming forward and publicly revealing who pulled the strings and who had induced them to lend their protection to the Communists. On March 13, 1952, I wrote to the Trustees in part as follows:

"To Messrs. Jos. P. Chamberlain, Arthur H. Dean, W. F. Dillingham, Brooks Emeny, Huntington Gilchrist, W. R. Herold, and Philip C. Jessup:

"In March 1947 I proposed a Resolution for investigation of the Institute of Pacific Relations, to be voted at a special meeting on April 22, 1947.

"In seeking proxies to oppose my Resolution, a public letter (March 17, 1947) issued by all of you, denied that there was any need for investigation of the Institute. Among various inaccurate statements, you said:

" 'The Executive Committee of the Board of Trustees has investigated Mr. Kohlberg's charges and found them inaccurate and irresponsible.'

"Raymond Dennett, your then secretary, has now sworn before the McCarran Committee that the above statement was untruthful, and known to you to be so.

"To Messrs. Eugene Staley, Herbert Eloesser, Galen M. Fisher, Mrs. Frank A. Gerbode, O. C. Hansen, Mrs. E. H. Heller, Rene A. May, Mrs. Alfred McLaughlin, Mrs. Harold L. Paige, Robert Gordon Sproul, Lynn White, Jr., and Ray Lyman Wilbur (all of California):

"On March 31, 1947, you issued a public letter of the same general tenor as the above, seeking proxies to oppose my Resolution for investigation.

"To Knight Biggerstaff of Cornell; John K. Fairbank, of Harvard; Harold H. Fisher of the Hoover Library; Kenneth Scott Latourette, of Yale; Raymond Kennedy, of Yale; Wm. W. Lockwood, of Princeton; Donald G. Tweksbury of Columbia:

"You signed statements in the same proxy fight, exonerating the I. P. R. of the slightest Communist bias.

"To Messrs. Edward W. Allen, Raymond B. Allen, Christian O. Arndt, J. Ballard Atherton, E. C. Auchter, George T. Cameron, Edward C. Carter, D. C. Clarke, Arthur G. Coons, George B. Cressey, Lauchlin Currie, John L. Curtis, Len de Caux, K. R. Duke, Clarence A. Dykstra, Rupert Emerson, Frederick V. Field, Charles K. Gamble, Carrington Goodrich, Henry F. Grady, Mortimer Graves, R. P. Heppner, John R. Hersey, Paul G. Hoffman, Benjamin H. Kizer, Daniel E. Koshland, Lewis L. Lapham, Owen Lattimore, Herbert S. Little, Boyd A. Martin, Charles E. Martin, Abbot Low Moffat, Donald M. Nelson, David N. Rowe, Gregg M. Sinclair, D. B. Straus, Donald B. Tresidder, Juan Trippe, Sumner Wells, Brayton Wilbur, Heaton L. Wrenn, Louise L. Wright and J. D. Zellerbach:

"You were the remaining members of the Board of Trustees of the IPR at the time my Resolution for investigation was voted on April 22, 1947. Not one of you voted for my Resolution to investigate.

"Since that time numerous qualified witnesses have testified under oath before the McCarran Committee that:

"1. Your organiaztion constantly and deliberately followed the Communist line in its publications.

"2. Some espionage activities were carried on.

"3. More than forty of your staff, Trustees and writers were actual Communists, or espionage agents, or both, and others leaned that way.

"4. That activities in infiltrating our government by such people were carried on both officially and unofficially in your name.

"The balance of this letter is addressed only to those of you who are not Communists, or pro-Communist in your sympathies. I suggest that you explain to the McCarran Committee your defense of the conspiracy in your midst; stating names of persons who induced you to protect the guilty, and reasons given; and reasons for neglecting the duty incumbent on you as Trustees. For example, which of you inveigled General Marshall into joining your Board?

"Such confession is the atonement for past injury to our country made by Louis Budenz and the other ex-Communists who testified. I hesitate to think you have less regard for our country's welfare than they."

Thereafter I received a letter from Dr. Roscoe Pound, dean emeritus of the Harvard Law School, and at present, visiting professor at the School of Law, University of California at Los Angeles, dated March 18, 1952, in which he said:

"Many thanks for your statement of date March 14 which I am rejoiced to have. One of the worst offenders in my experience is Professor J. K. Fairbank of Harvard. He is beyond redemption, but I take pleasure in showing him up on every occasion. I ran into him first in Nanking where the State Department information office was a fountain of misinformation."

I further state that the testimony on page 1085 of the MacArthur hearings of last May by Senator Knowland and General Bradley to the effect that we have no objectives in Korea; and the statement near the bottom of page 1556 of Part 5 of the McCarran hearings by Ambassador George Kennan to the effect that we have no over-all foreign policy, not even the Open-Door Policy and the Monroe Doctrine any longer, is conclusive proof either of incompetence on the part of the State Department, or neglect of America's interests by that Department.

ALFRED KOHLBERG.

Sworn to and subscribed before me this 16th day of April 1952.

[SEAL.]   PASQUALE J. FENICO,
                                                 Notary Public, State of New York.

Commission Expires March 30, 1954.

APPENDIX L

INSTITUTE OF PACIFIC RELATIONS
REPORT
OF THE
COMMITTEE ON THE JUDICIARY

SECOND SESSION

JULY 2 (legislative day JUNE 27), 1952.—Ordered to be printed

CONCLUSIONS

The Institute of Pacific Relations has not maintained the character of an objective, scholarly, and research organization.

* * *

The IPR has been considered by the American Communist Party and by Soviet officials as an instrument of Communist policy, propaganda and military intelligence.

* * *

The IPR disseminated and sought to popularize false information including information originating from Soviet and Communist sources.

* * *

A small core of officials and staff members carried the main burden of IPR activities and directed its administration and policies.

* * *

Members of the small core of officials and staff members who controlled IPR were either Communist or pro-Communist.

* * *

There is no evidence that the large majority of its members supported the IPR for any reason except to advance the professed research and scholarly purposes of the organization.

* * *

Most members of the IPR, and most members of its Board of Trustees, were inactive and obviously without any influence over the policies of the organization and the conduct of its affairs.

❋   ❋   ❋

IPR activities were made possible largely through the financial support of American industrialists, corporations, and foundations, the majority of whom were not familiar with the inner workings of the organization.

❋   ❋   ❋

The effective leadership of the IPR often sought to deceive IPR contributors and supporters as to the true character and activities of the organization.

❋   ❋   ❋

Neither the IPR nor any substantial body of those associated with it as executive officers, trustees or major financial contributors, has ever made any serious and objective investigation of the charges that the IPR was infiltrated by Communists and was used for pro-Communist and pro-Soviet purposes.

❋   ❋   ❋

The names of eminent individuals were by design used as a respectable and impressive screen for the activities of the IPR inner core, and as a defense when such activities came under scrutiny.

❋   ❋   ❋

Owen Lattimore was, from some time beginning in the 1930's, a conscious articulate instrument of the Soviet conspiracy.

❋   ❋   ❋

Effective leadership of the IPR had by the end of 1934 established and implemented an official connection with G. N. Voitinski, Chief of the Far Eastern Division of the Communist International.

❋   ❋   ❋

After the establishment of the Soviet Council of IPR, leaders of the American IPR sought and maintained working relationships with Soviet diplomats and officials.

❋   ❋   ❋

The American staff of IPR, though fully apprised that the Soviet Council of IPR was in fact an arm of the Soviet Foreign Office, was simultaneously and secretly instructed to preserve the "fiction" that the Soviet council was independent.

❁ ❁ ❁

IPR officials testified falsely before the Senate Internal Security Subcommittee concerning the relationships between IPR and the Soviet Union.

❁ ❁ ❁

Owen Lattimore testified falsely before the subcommittee with reference to at least five separate matters that were relevant to the inquiry and substantial in import.

❁ ❁ ❁

John Paton Davies, Jr., testified falsely before the subcommittee in denying that he recommended the Central Intelligence Agency employ, utilize and rely upon certain individuals having Communist associations and connections. This matter was relevant to the inquiry and substantial in import.

❁ ❁ ❁

The effective leadership of IPR worked consistently to set up actively cooperative and confidential relationships with persons in Government involved in the determination of foreign policy.

❁ ❁ ❁

Over a period of years, John Carter Vincent was the principal fulcrum of IPR pressures and influence in the State Department.

❁ ❁ ❁

It was the continued practice of IPR to seek to place in Government posts both persons associated with IPR and other persons selected by the effective leadership of IPR.

❁ ❁ ❁

The IPR possessed close organic relations with the State Department through interchange of personnel, attendance of State Department officials at IPR conferences, constant exchange of information and social contacts.

❁ ❁ ❁

The effective leadership of the IPR used IPR prestige to promote the interests of the Soviet Union in the United States.

A group of persons operating within and about the Institute of Pacific Relations exerted a substantial influence on United States far eastern policy.

*   *   *

The IPR was a vehicle used by the Communists to orientate American far eastern policies toward Communist objectives.

*   *   *

A group of persons associated with the IPR attempted, between 1941 and 1945, to change United States policy so as to accommodate Communist ends and to set the stage for a major United States policy change, favorable to Soviet interests, in 1945.

*   *   *

Owen Lattimore and John Carter Vincent were influential in bringing about a change in United States policy in 1945 favorable to the Chinese Communists.

*   *   *

During the period 1945–49, persons associated with the Institute of Pacific Relations were instrumental in keeping United States policy on a course favorable to Communist objectives in China.

*   *   *

Persons associated with the IPR were influential in 1949 in giving United States far eastern policy a direction that furthered Communist purposes.

A chief function of the IPR has been to influence United States public opinion.

*   *   *

Many of the persons active in and around the IPR, and in particular though not exclusively Owen Lattimore, Edward C. Carter, Frederick V. Field, T. A. Bisson, Lawrence K. Rosinger, and Maxwell Stewart, knowingly and deliberately used the language of books and articles which they wrote or edited in an attempt to influence the American public by means of pro-Communist or pro-Soviet content of such writings.

*   *   *

The net effect of IPR activities on United States public opinion has been such as to serve international Communist interests and to affect adversely the interests of the United States.

*   *   *

RECOMMENDATIONS

Legislation

The committee recommends speedy enactment of an adequate statute to permit congressional committees to require the testimony of a witness when it is determined such testimony is sufficiently important to justify extending to the witness immunity from prosecution with respect to the matters concerning which he testifies.

Investigations

The committee recommends:

(1) That a thorough study be made by the Committee on the Judiciary, in cooperation with the Department of Justice, of the Espionage Act and related legislation with a view to determining what revisions may be neecssary to deal effectively with present-day security problems.

(2) That the Committee on Government Operations undertake an investigation to determine the need for and proper scope of legislation to require departments and agencies in the executive branch to make available to congressional committees upon proper request material from their files.

(3) That consideration be given to investigation by some appropriate agency of the following:

(*a*) Possible Communist infiltration into and influence upon the Treasury Department and other agencies forming and administering fiscal and monetary policies and affairs of the United States;

(*b*) The role of Alger Hiss in foreign affairs and the formulation of foreign policy of the United States and his influence on personnel decisions in the State Department;

(*c*) The extent to which persons actively associated with the pro-Communist core of the IPR have been employed by any agency of the Government, and the activities and influence of any such persons still so employed; and

(*d*) The extent to which contributions by American charitable, scientific, and educational foundations have aided Communist or pro-Communist activity in the United States.

Departmental Activity

The committee recommends:

(1) That the Department of Justice submit to a grand jury the question of whether perjury has been committed before the subcommittee by Owen Lattimore.

(2) That the Department of Justice submit to a grand jury the question of whether perjury has been committed before the subcommittee by John P. Davies, Jr.

APPENDIX M

ALFRED KOHLBERG, INC.
Textiles
1 West 37th Street, Just Off Fifth Avenue
New York 18, N. Y.

April 22, 1954

To the President or Dean in Charge of Commencement Exercises,

My dear Doctor:

As everyone knows, this year's favorite subject for Commencement addresses will be "Opposition to Conformity in Thinking." This takes various forms, naturally, covering such matters as academic freedom, McCarthyism, investigations of subversives, etc., all presented on the highest intellectual level.

The names of Justice William O. Douglas, former Governor Adlai Stevenson, and Senator Herbert Lehman, immediately come to mind, along with such second-stringers as Henry Steele Commager and Robert M. Hutchins of the Ford Organization. You can't go wrong with any of them.

Should you not be able to secure one of these publicized stars for Commencement, may I be permitted to offer my services? So that you will know what to expect, I submit herewith a copy of my popular Commencement address, "Black Silence of Fear," which I'm sure you will appraise as a distillate of the combined wisdom of most name speakers of liberal persuasion.

As the demand for my services is likely to be overwhelming, I suggest that you wire your invitation without delay. Bookings will be made on a first-come, first-serve basis.

Very truly yours,
Alfred Kohlberg

AK:am

enc

P.S. Although I cannot endow you with a new Liberal Arts Building, dormitory, etc., for a honorary degree, I can, at least, present you with a Lobby.

The Black Silence of Fear[1]

Mr. President, Faculty Members, Alumni, Students and Friends:

I wish to address myself particularly to you young men and young women who are going forth today to make your way in the world.

Once, not many years ago, when I addressed young people at graduation time, I could assure them of a bright and attractive future. The sheepskins they bore raised them above the common herd, and the learning they had acquired was dedicated to the building of a new social order. Most of those who faced me at previous commencements went on to fight the good fight in government, while the rest fought in Europe, Asia, Africa, the South Pacific and Korea.

Now all that is changed. As we look about us what do we see?

Reaction is on the march to strip the Nation of its natural resources, to cripple our great social welfare programs, to undermine the rights of labor, and to eliminate government aids to the underprivileged. The Communists and the reactionaries find common cause in their opposition to the cause of freedom.[2]

There is a reign of terror abroad in the land, and only a few voices are raised against it. There is an inquisition into the views of scholars, writers, actors, editors and journalists, but we do not know what to do about it. Oh, my friends, we must rally to defend not only the innocents unjustly accused, but the cause of freedom itself. Instead we have given license to traveling troupes of congressional inquisitors to pry into the lives, the morals, the thoughts and the beliefs of scholars, teachers, writers and ministers, to detect whether they may not have had, in the distant past, some unorthodox thought, or some wrong or non-conformist belief.[2]

Yes, my friends, terror is abroad in the land, and liberals are the victims of a campaign of suppression and oppression aimed at chauvinistic thought control. It is a black fear fostered by so-called 100 percent Americans who want to impose their stupid mental regimentation on every liberal idea and smear every decent American as a communist.

The Bill of Rights is besieged, ancient liberties infringed, reckless words uttered, vigilante groups are formed, suspicion, mistrust and fear stalk the land, and political partisanship raises strange and ugly heads, the security of secret files is violated, and the specter of a political police emerges.[4]

What would Patrick Henry and Sam Adams and Thomas Paine and John Randolph and Benjamin Franklin and Alexander Hamilton and Thomas Jefferson say if they were here to witness today's spectacle? Those early American patriots welcomed new ideas from whatever source. We are in heroic company. However thin our ranks, they are thus strengthened by a mighty host.[2]

The Communist threat inside the country has been magnified and exalted far beyond its realities. The philosophy of strength through free speech is being forsaken for the philosophy of fear through repression. Character assassinations have become common. Good and honest men are pilloried.[1]

Those accused of illegal Communist activity—all presumed innocent of course until proved guilty—have difficulty getting reputable lawyers to defend them. Fear has mounted. This fear has even entered universities, great citadels of our spiritual strength, and corrupted them. We have the spectacle of university officials lending themselves to one of the worst witch hunts we have seen since early days. This is the Black Silence of Fear.[1]

Shame on them.

Look about you. Here on this very campus you will find victims of warmed-over charges made by character assassins.

I need not tell you how members of the teaching profession have suffered and the agonies they have endured at the hands of the Mc-

Carrans, the McCarthys, the Jenners, the MacArthurs and the J. Edgar Hoovers. Yet, I say, thank God the officials of this college had the backbone to stand up to those witch-hunters, and thereby vindicated not only academic freedom but civil liberties and the Fifth Amendment.

Education is impossible in many parts of the United States today because free inquiry and free discussion are impossible, . . . the teacher of economics, history or political science cannot teach. Even the teacher of literature must be careful. Didn't a member of Indiana's Textbook Commission call Robin Hood subversive?[6]

In many places it is unwise for a teacher to agree with Vice President Nixon about racial discrimination, or with Chief Justice Warren about health insurance. What teacher would dare to say what Secretary of State Dulles has said about the ultimate admission of Red China to the society of nations? Teachers are becoming second class citizens. In many states they are required to take special oaths that they have not been disloyal. Why not ask them to take oaths that they have not been robbers or prostitutes?[6]

Loyalty Oaths are a part of a rather fat-headed, feeble-minded, though not altogether depraved pattern peculiar to American life. By these oaths we put a premium on conformity. This results in a society of second-class citizens unable to voice their real opinions, although the only kind of advice a society needs is unpalatable advice.[3]

The teaching profession is being attacked by neurotics, the intellectually deprived, and common scolds. Any disagreement with my views is bound to be inconsequential, if not an actual display of lack of basic insight. They seek to tell us that our obligations include answering when spoken to, minding our own business, expressing admiration for all Senators and Congressmen, doing what we're told, staying out of politics, working quietly yet gaily for low pay, condemning Communism, being brave, fearless, outspoken and critical at the risk of disapproval by those who urge us to be fearless, rousing the moral enthusiasm of American Youth, providing them with spiritual values, teaching them to love their country and their parents, all under the happy stimulation of sneers, threats, insults and attacks. Authoritarianism is no sweeter in its effects on individuals, merely because it carries the backing of a government with a democratic constitution.[7]

These are times when nobody wants to be criticized by anybody for anything, for it is now almost as bad to be "controversial" as it is to be a spy or traitor.[6]

Each day some new name is pointed out in the press by a Congressional investigating committee as a person it is trying to prove is a Communist. I wonder whether this is really routing out dangerous people, or merely creating uncertainty about more or less harmless people?[8]

Opposed to these gentlemen and scholars what have you got? The answer, my learned friends, you all know—McCarthyism.

The black evil of McCarthyism has captured the imagination of the American people.[9]

An imposing array of imitators, admirers and supporters have gathered in their cause. The blind and bigoted purveyors of hate and prejudice in our land have joined the anti-Communist crusade as a likely caravan for their own evil designs. Neighbor has been set against neighbor. Fear and suspicion have replaced trust and confidence. They have invented the multiple untruth, the splattering smear, the trial by headline, the intimidation by innuendo, the grisly black-mail by threat of subpena. Freedom of association has been rubbed out in favor of guilt by association.[10]

The only danger we still face from the Communists is from possible espionage, sabotage and overt conspiracy. The detection of these activities is the responsibility of our security and police forces. This certainly is not a proper responsibility for Congressional committees sitting as judge, jury and prosecutor.[10]

And now we have McCarthy destroying the morale of the American Army into which many of you will shortly be inducted. By charging that the Army coddled Communists, McCarthy has accomplished what his fellow Fascists, Hitler, Mussolini, Syngman Rhee and Chiang Kai-shek failed to do.

But I am sure that the Army never coddled Communists at all deliberately. Not any more than previous Democratic Administrations ever coddled a single subversive, a single traitor or a single spy, deliberately.[13]

Meanwhile, as the inquisitors rant and rave, our beloved civil liberties are ground in the dust, the rights of man are violated, and the four freedoms guaranteed to us in our Constitution and Magna Charta are destroyed. So effective has been the work of the self-appointed vigilantes, flagwaving superpatriots and ultra-nationalists that today liberals cower in fear, not daring to open their mouths for fear that they will be hauled before reactionary browbeaters to be insulted and threatened.

But our illness goes deeper than any one man. It is a malady of the soul that summons all the evil forces of the Inquisition, of the Cheka, of Hitlerism, of Stalinism, of the Ku Klux Klan, and all those nauseous forces which claim dominion over the conduct and the souls of other men.[12]

The sinister significance of McCarthyism, the pro-fascist, anti-Communist crusade has an organic relationship with the frenzied preparations for aggressive war—the ringing of the Soviet Union and People's China with air bases, the sabotage of peace in Korea, the attempt to extend the war in Indo-China, McCarthyism points toward atomic war and national devastation.[11]

By confusing the masses with fantastic redbaiting and denouncing everything progressive as disloyalty, Dulles and Brownell are the blood brothers of Senator McCarthy. The attack upon Truman is in reality an attack upon the whole labor movement. Freeing ourselves from the Big Lie that the U.S.S.R. is a military menace, we must accept the realistic policy of international negotiations on the basis of the peaceful co-existence of the U. S. and the Soviet Union.[11]

The issue, believe me, is not communism. However, don't misunderstand me. I hate communism. Indeed, despite what McCarthyites may say, I am not now, I have never been and I would not think of becoming a Communist. Nor am I sympathetic with any totalitarian ideas, nazi, or fascist. If in the past my name was mistakenly connected with alleged communist front organizations it only proves that there is nothing more undemocratic than guilt by association, as was so eloquently pointed out not long ago by Professor Henry Steele Commager. Therefore I say to you that the real issue is not communism but academic freedom, guilt by association and book burning.

In making this statement, I realize that I incur the undying hatred of the native-born fascist storm troopers who like nothing better than to lynch liberals like myself. However, I scorn them and thus take my place alongside those six bold men, unterrified scholars all, who stood shoulder to shoulder as they wrote a book in which they proved conclusively that they found it was no longer possible for them to express a sensible idea.

Our present day wrecking-crew may knock out one of the props of our democratic system—the right of petition. After all, if a petition for clemency for the Rosenbergs, for example, or for the abolition of the Un-American Activities Committee is to expose men and women to investigation, to the charge of subversion, they will think twice before signing anything.[14]

And who wants to think twice?

Do you realize what this is doing to American prestige abroad? I recently returned from a tour of several months in Europe and Asia where I heard everyone expressing fear not of communism, but of McCarthyism.

Europeans think they recognize America's dominant mood in inquisitions, purges, book burning, repression and fear which have obscured the bright vision of the Land of the Free and the Home of the Brave.[15]

The United States will never win the peace until it has done away with the witchhunt and the merchants of hate. Men and women are being condemned today on the basis of hearsay, innuendo and guilt by association. Men are adjudged on the whispered accusations of faceless people not known to the accused. Anyone—a Communist, a Socialist, a liberal or just a plain Yankee who does not like this business of the witchhunt and who shouts his protest—are all put in the same classification. These actions have made us suspect abroad.[5]

How is the United States to fulfill the obligation which history has thrust upon her? Only a committee of experts in the broad and complex field of foreign policy could work out a specific blueprint. The Eisenhower Administration has adopted, almost in toto, the foreign policies of the Truman and Roosevelt Administrations. Those who think in terms of absolutes concoct Wall Street bankers to account for the first World War, a Roosevelt conspiracy to account for Pearl Harbor, a Yalta sell-out to account for the cold war with Russia, and an Acheson-Lattimore conspiracy to account for the triumph of Communism in China.[16]

Fifteen years ago, President Roosevelt, in a historic address said: "America hates war. America hopes for peace. Therefore America actively engages in the search for peace." This statement marked the birth of our present foreign policy. We are still pursuing those ends. They have led us through World War II and into Korea.[17]

This nation is being weakened by the excesses of our investigating committees, fantastic charges of treason against our most honored statesmen, the obscene spectacle of distorted denunciation, the hysterical fear of Communist subversion, the erosion of civil liberties, the daily affront to human dignity.[19]

The contagion of meanness growing from hysterical fear of Communism at home is being spread to the very shield of the republic, our foreign policy.[19]

I have just completed the manuscript of a new book. It is entitled: MORE FEAR ON THE CAMPUS. This is a sequel to my previous book FEAR ON THE CAMPUS, which was a best seller for many months and a selection of a well-known book club.

In this latest book I propound some wonderful ideas which I'd like to discuss briefly today. As we all know, since Senator McCarthy has been dictating our foreign policy we have alienated 800,000,000 progressive and peace-loving peoples of the world. We have lost not only the good will and the vast trade of Soviet Russia and the democratic nations of Europe, but also the 400,000,000 Chinese who work happily under the enlightened leader, Mao Tse-tung.

This we must stop. We must get back in step with the new social order in which there is no capitalist exploitation of the masses, no Wall Street imperialism, and in which academic freedom can flourish.

How can we do this? Let us take as our example the electrifying spectacle of people willing to avail themselves of the Fifth Amendment because they believe in the Constitution. Because, never let it be forgotten for one minute, that once the fascists finish with the communists, they will start in on Catholic priests, Protestant ministers, Jewish rabbis, college professors and innocent little babies.

The demagogs and irresponsibles have made such inroads upon our entire structure of liberties, and our entire fabric of moralities as will not be easily repaired for some time to come. Do I need to name these demagogs and irresponsibles? You know their leading spirits as well as I do—McCarthy, Jenner, Velde.[10]

I maintain that we must have a new way of doing things, to protect the rights of our mental minorities. We must of course do away with star chamber proceedings and kangaroo courts. Instead, I recommend that we have all hearings on alleged communists conducted by liberal radio commentators. In this way, not only civil liberties would be protected, but we would have a new birth of freedom of expression in the arts, sciences and professions.

That is my plan to protect people accused by primitives and flag-wavers. But how about fighting the lesser evil, communism?

The real answer to Communism is in the old fashioned phrase good works—good works inspired by love and dedicated to the whole man.[18]

This plan would have another great advantage, one that gives it great merit in the field of psychological warfare. By thus showing our confidence in communists we might well lull the justified suspicions of the Politburo, so that Molotov would be willing to join us in another conference.

Admittedly, of course, most of the tensions between east and west have been caused by American atom-rattling and threats, not to mention our McCarthy-like demagoguery abroad, which in the case of Korea caused the South Koreans to swarm across the border forcing the peace-loving North Koreans to defend themselves.

However, I am sure that if we can persuade President Eisenhower to impeach Senator McCarthy we can then go on to the next step of creating harmony at home.

It is from the British that we have inherited the concept that a man is innocent until he is proven guilty. Today crude and sinister men are trying to destroy this concept and to shake the very foundation of our freedom based on the due process of law. Witch hunters are on the loose again, often cloaked with immunity and armed with subpoenas and the cruel whiplash of unevaluated gossip.[20]

Let us have an end to the pussyfooting that has been going on about the use of the methods of tyranny in a democratic country.[19]

Let us join with peace-loving peoples around the world in bonds of true international brotherhood.

1—Justice Wm. O. Douglas, N. Y. Times, January 13, 1952
2—Senator Herbert H. Lehman, U. S. Senate, May 25, 1953
3—Henry Steele Commager, N. Y. Times, October 10, 1951
4—Gov. Adlai E. Stevenson, Philadelphia, December 12, 1953
5—Justice Wm. O. Douglas, N. Y. Times, November 25, 1953
6—Robert M. Hutchins, Look, March 9, 1954

7—Pres. Harold Taylor, Sarah Lawrence College, Minneapolis, June 21, 1953

8—Eleanor Roosevelt, N. Y. World, December 15, 1953

9—Senator Herbert H. Lehman, before A.C.L.U. panel, Washington, D. C. March 1, 1951

10—Senator Herbert H. Lehman, U. S. Senate, March 1, 1954

11—National Committee of the C.P. of U.S.A., Political Affairs, Dec. 1953, page 1

12—Mark F. Ethridge, The Nation, December 12, 1953, p. 499

13—Gov. Adlai E. Stevenson, Miami Beach, March 5, 1954

14—Henry Steele Commager, N. Y. Times, Nov. 8, 1953

15—Gov. Adlai E. Stevenson, Chicago, Sept. 15, 1953

16—Henry Steele Commager, N. Y. Times, Feb. 21, 1954

17—Senator Herbert H. Lehman, U. S. Senate, January 28, 1952

18—Gov. Adlai E. Stevenson, San Francisco, September 9, 1952

19—Averell Harriman, Albany, N. Y., April 10, 1954

20—Pres. Truman, Fulton, Mo., April 12, 1954

APPENDIX N

MEMORANDUM

From: New York State Office

Subject: Campaign of Struggle Against United States Imperialist Intervention in China

What is happening in China today is the most open expression of American imperialism at work.

The successful military intervention of Republican Spain by German and Italian imperialism in 1936 spearheaded the outbreak of the recent war. A people's victory in Spain would have resulted in the strengthening of the peoples' movements in each country against their own Municheers, would have weakened German and Italian fascism internally, would have re-stimulated the struggle of the German and Italian working classes, and could have laid the basis for the successful crushing of fascism on its own soil even prior to its invasion of other countries.

Today, American imperialism, by armed force, is intervening in the struggle of the Chinese people to establish a democratic Chinese Republic. Victory in China for the American monopolists, defeat for the Chinese people, will set back the anti-imperialist struggle of all colonial and semi-colonial peoples. It will strengthen American imperialism in its drive for domination of the world, and will intensify their attacks against the working class at home. It will sharpen the contradictions between the United States on one hand, and Great Britain, Holland and other imperialist countries with Far Eastern interests, on the other. It brings much closer the possibility of war against the Soviet Union.

However, this perspective is no more inevitable than was the defeat of Republican Spain. An aroused working class, together with its natural allies, guided by the Communist Party, can defeat these aims of American imperialism.

Therefore, the New York State Committee of the Communist Party proposes the following program of action:

A. *Independent Role of the Party—Mass Actions:*

1. Picket line demonstrations, city wide, organized by the State Committee, and in communities organized by County Committees and the Clubs.

2. Mass meetings or outdoor meetings, to be held by each Club (also forums for veterans, youth, etc.)

3. Shop gate meetings to be held in industrial concentrations.

4. Delegations to Congressmen by Clubs in Congressional districts to demand the reversal of United States imperialist policy of armed intervention in China.

5. Special mobilization of all Party members to distribute the Pearl Harbor edition of the Sunday Worker, on Sunday, December 9th. Securing maximum subs to the Sunday Worker on this day to be the chief aim of mobilization. Distribution as well of the language press.

6. Distribution to the people of New York—to the workers in the shops, to the youth, to the Negro people, to the veterans, etc.—of a series of five leaflets issued by the State Committee in connection with the campaign against armed intervention in China:

   a. The Truman administration, atom bomb diplomacy, and the role of the Soviet Union.

  b. Jobs and wages.
  c. Bourgeois democracy, democracy in the liberated countries, democratic China and the Chiang Kai-shek dictatorship.
  d. The Negro people and colonial struggles.
  e. The farmers.

7. Concentration during this campaign on the sale and distribution of the following pamphlets and books:

  a. Mass distribution of Gene Dennis' report to the National Committee meeting.
  b. Mass distribution of Foster's pamphlet. The Strike Situation.
  c. Mass distribution of Joe North's pamphlet on China—3¢—ready around December 15th.
  d. Books:
     1. Marxism and the National Colonial Question—by Stalin
     2. Leninism—by Stalin
     3. Foundations of Leninism—by Stalin
     4. China's New Democracy—by Mao Tse Tung, 25¢
     5. The Fight for a New China—by Mao Tse Tung, 25¢
     6. Challenge of Red China—by Gunther Stein, $3.50
     7. Report From Red China—by Harrison Forman, $3.00

8. Complete registration in the course of this campaign by the end of the year.

  a. Party mobilization day to complete the registration, December 23, 1945.

9. Party building and recruiting:

  a. Invite your friends and shop mates to all meetings held by the Party—organize small gatherings subsequently for recruiting.

10. All these activities to be linked with a mass turnout and overflow Lenin Memorial meeting on January 15, 1946.

B. *Coalition Activities*:

Initiated and spurred by the Communist Party Clubs and Counties, and including the Communists where possible, as part of all committees that are established, joint statements made, speakers at meetings.

1. Broad city wide delegation to Washington.

2. Organize conference of various groups (individual groups or jointly) in the community and set up committees to support the struggle for a democratic China (trade unions, CIO and especially AFL, national groups, women's groups, youth, veterans, settlement houses, civic clubs, the Communist Party Clubs, etc.)—to undertake action such as mass meetings, visits to Congressmen, issuing general educational material, urging the City Council to memorialize Congress to stop the American imperialist policy, picket lines, etc.

3. Organize mass meetings of national groups including trade union and Party speakers.

4. Mass meetings by trade unions in the garment center, the waterfront, Harlem, etc., including Party speakers where possible.

5. Resolutions of protest against American imperialist policy in China in all locals of trade unions (especially AFL), and mass organizations.

6. Joint Statements of leading people in the Counties and communities addressed to the Truman Administration.

AIMS AND OBJECTIVES OF CAMPAIGN

A. To mobilize the broadest unity of action of the American people of New York State and City in opposition to the Truman Administration and Republican Party policies of imperialist world domination in general, and the policy of imperialist intervention in China in particular.

1. To expose the role of American imperialism, aided by British imperialism, in its attempt to torpedo genuine international cooperation for the extirpation of fascism and the unity of the Big Three, to expose its role in fostering the resurgence of fascist and reactionary regimes in Europe and Asia, and the encouragement of blocs for an imperialist war against the Soviet Union.

2. To make the American people, especially the workers in the basic and key concentration industries, conscious of the fact that this imperialist foreign policy is inseparably linked with the reactionary offensive of the Truman Administration and Big Business on the

domestic front, which aims at weakening and smashing the trade unions, leading to increasing poverty of the American masses.

B. To create and advance the conditions for a broad labor-progressive coalition, based on the new relationship of forces and emerging re-alignments, with labor as the decisive key force in this coalition, exerting its independent role in opposition to the two major bourgeois parties.

    1. To achieve the maximum unity of action of the entire labor movement, (AFL, CIO, and Railroad Brotherhoods).

    2. To win the Negro people as an ally of labor.

    3. To win the middle class (especially the farmers) as an ally of labor in this struggle.

C. To cement the international solidarity of all peoples in the struggle for an anti-imperalist, anti-fascist united front against fascism and reaction.

    1. To expose the imperialist machinations of the United States and Great Britain in the Balkans, Greece, etc.

    2. To link the campaign against imperialist intervention in China with the struggles of the colonial peoples in Java, Indonesia, India, etc., to free themselves of the imperialist yoke and tyranny.

D. To advance the vanguard role of the Communist Party, through its independent actions, as well as through its initiative, in advancing and becoming an accepted part of a new, broad, anti-fascist coalition in New York City and State, and by showing in action that it is in the forefront of the struggle of this coalition.

    1. To eradicate all remnants of revisionist thinking and Browderism throughout the Party from top to bottom.

    2. To mobilize every member of our Party without exception in this struggle, which is only a forerunner of the crucial struggles facing the working class and the American people now and in the period ahead.

    3. To transform our Party, through this struggle, into the fighting, vanguard mass Party of New York State.

    4. To complete the registration by January 1st, to build and recruit into our Party in the course of this campaign.

NOTE: Please keep a record of all activities in the China Campaign in your County, so that we may subsequently be able to summarize all of them for the entire State.

APPENDIX O

The Communist Conquest of China
An address by John F. Kennedy, at Salem, Mass.,
January 30, 1949.
(Mr. Kennedy was then a Congressman.)
Over these past few days we have learned the extent of the
disasters befalling China and the United States. Our relationship
with China since the end of the Second World War has been a
tragic one, and it is of the utmost importance that we search
out and spotlight those who must bear the responsibility for our
present predicament.

When we look at the ease with which the Communists have
overthrown the National Government of Chiang Kai-shek, it
comes as somewhat of a shock to remember that on November
22, 1941* our Secretary of State, Cordell Hull, handed Ambassador Namuru an ultimatum to the effect that: (1) Government
of Japan will withdraw all military, naval, air and police forces
from China and Indochina; (2) the United States and Japan will
not support militarily, politically, economically, any government
or regime in China other than the National Government of the
Republic of China.

It was clearly enunciated that the independence of China and
the stability of the National Government was the fundamental
object of our Far Eastern policy.

That this and other statements of our policies in the Far East
led directly to the attack on Pearl Harbor is well known. And it
might be said that we almost knowingly entered into combat
with Japan to preserve the independence of China and the countries to the south of it. Contrast this policy which reached its
height in 1943, when the United States and Britain agreed at

---

* The correct date was November 26, 1941.

Cairo to liberate China and return to that country at the end of the war Manchuria and all Japanese-held areas, to the confused and vacillating policy which we have followed since that day.

In 1944 Gen. "Vinegar Joe" Stilwell presented a plan to arm 1,000,000 Chinese Communists, who had been carefully building their resources in preparation for a post-war seizure of power, and with them to capture Shanghai and clear the Yangtze. This plan was supported by some State Department officials, including Ambassador Clarence Gauss. Chiang Kai-shek refused to cooperate with this plan, which would have presented the Chinese Communists with an easy coup. Chiang requested that Stilwell be recalled, which caused such bitter comment in this country; and Gauss resigned. From this date our relations with the National Government declined.

At the Yalta Conference in 1945 a sick Roosevelt, with the advice of General Marshal and other Chiefs of Staff, gave the Kurile Islands as well as the control of various strategic Chinese ports, such as Port Arthur and Dairen, to the Soviet Union.

According to former Ambassador Bullitt, in *Life* magazine in 1948, "Whatever share of the responsibility was Roosevelt's and whatever share was Marshall's, the vital interest of the United States in the independent integrity of China was sacrificed, and the foundation was laid for the present tragic situation in the Far East."

When the armies of Soviet Russia withdrew from Manchuria they left Chinese Communists in control of this area and in possession of great masses of Japanese war material.

During this period began the great split in the minds of our diplomats over whether to support the government of Chiang Kai-shek, or force Chiang Kai-shek as the price of our assistance to bring Chinese Communists into his government to form a coalition.

When Ambassador Patrick Hurley resigned in 1945 he stated, "Professional diplomats continuously advised the Chinese Com-

munists that my efforts in preventing the collapse of the National
Government did not represent the policy of the United States.
The chief opposition to the accomplishment of our mission came
from American career diplomats, the embassy at Chungking, and
the Chinese and Far Eastern divisions of the State Department."

With the troubled situation in China beginning to loom large
in the United States, General Marshall was sent at the request
of President Truman as a special emissary to China to effect a
compromise and to bring about a coalition government.

In Ambassador Bullitt's article in *Life,* he states and I quote:
"In early summer of 1946 in order to force Chiang Kai-shek to
take Communists into the Chinese Government, General Marshall had the Department of State refuse to give licenses for
export of ammunition to China. Thus from the summer of 1946
to February 1948 not a single shell or a single cartridge was
delivered to China for use in its American armament. And in
the aviation field Marshall likewise blundered, and as a result
of his breaking the American Government's contract to deliver
to China planes to maintain eight and one-third air groups, for
3 years* no combat or bombing planes were delivered to China
—from September 1946 to March 1948. As Marshall himself
confessed in February 1948 to the House Committee on Foreign
Affairs, this "was in effect an embargo on military supplies."

In 1948 we appropriated $468,000,000 for China, only a frac-
tion of what we were sending to Europe, and out of this $468,-
000,000 only $125,000,000 was for military purposes. The end
was drawing near; the assistance was too little and too late; and
the Nationalist Government was engaged in a death struggle
with the on-rushing Communist armies.

On November 20, 1948, former Senator D. Worth Clark, who
had been sent on a special mission to China by the Senate Committee on Appropriations, in his report to the committee said,
"Piecemeal aid will no longer save failing China from commun-

---

* The actual duration of the embargo was about a year and a half.

ism. It is now an all-out program or none, a fish or cut bait proposition."

Clark said this conclusion was confirmed by Ambassador J. Leighton Stuart and top American Army officers in China.

On November 25, 1948, 3 years too late, the *New York Times* said: "Secretary of State George Marshall said today the United States Government was considering what assistance it could properly give to the Chinese Government in the present critical situation."

On December 21 a *Times* headline was "ECA Administrator Hoffman, after seeing Truman, discloses freezing of $70,000,000 program in China in view of uncertain war situation."

The indifference, if not the contempt, with which the State Department and the President treated the wife of the head of the Nationalist Government, who was then fighting for a free China—Madame Chiang Kai-shek—was the final chapter in this tragic story.

Our policy in China has reaped the whirlwind. The continued insistence that aid would not be forthcoming unless a coalition government with the Communists was formed, was a crippling blow to the National Government. So concerned were our diplomats and their advisers, the Lattimores and the Fairbanks, with the imperfections of the diplomatic system in China after 20 years of war, and the tales of corruption in high places, that they lost sight of our tremendous stake in a non-Communist China.

There are those who claimed, and still claim, that Chinese communism was not really communism at all but merely an advanced agrarian movement which did not take directions from Moscow.

Listen to the words of the Bolton report: "Its doctrines follow those of Lenin and Stalin. Its leaders are Moscow-trained (of 35 leading Chinese Communist political leaders listed in the report, over a half either spent some time or studied in Moscow). Its policies and actions, its strategy and tactics are Communist.

The Chinese Communists have followed faithfully every zigzag of the Kremlin's line for a generation."

This is the tragic story of China whose freedom we once fought to preserve. What our young men had saved our diplomats and our President have frittered away.

Index

A

Abel, Rudolf, 231
ABMAC (See American Bureau for Medical Aid to China)
Acheson, Dean, 11, 13, 96, 101, 105, 123, 124, 127, 128, 130, 131, 132, 138, 146, 154, 159, 187, 236, 290, 297, 298
A Curtain of Ignorance, 149
Adams, Sherman, 107, 228
Agronsky, Martin, 120
AJLAC (See American Jewish League Against Communism)
Albrecht, Charlotte, 25
Alert, 195
Alexander, Ruth, 260
Allied Syndicates, 144, 145
Al Mah, 63
Alsop, Joseph, 283
Amerasia, 95, 118, 147, 199, 200
American Bureau for Medical Aid to China, 54, 57, 58, 60, 61, 62, 63, 64, 68, 69, 70, 71, 75, 83, 163
American China Policy Association, 125, 154, 192, 216, 233-240
American Chinese Export Corporation, 151
American Jewish Committee, 251
American Jewish Congress, 251
American Jewish League Against Communism, 248, 249, 250, 251, 252, 268
American Legion, 182, 244, 262, 269
American Legion Magazine, 107, 194
American Red Cross, 60
America's Retreat from Victory, 107
Anderson, Jack, 150
Anslinger, H. J., 148
Anti-Semitism, 247, 248

A Program to Govern Our Foreign Relations, 228, 242
Arms, Brig. Gen. T. S., 66
Army-McCarthy Hearings, 106, 257
Ascoli, Max, 135, 146, 147
As He Saw It, 264
Asia Magazine, 74
Asiaticus (Hans Moeller), 172
Atkinson, Brooks, 110
Atlantic Charter, 110, 215
Avco Manufacturing Corporation, 144
Awakened China, 149

B

Bachman, Dr. George, 62, 67, 68
Bachrach, Selma, 21, 23
Badger, Vice Adm. Oscar Charles, 123
Baker, John Earl, 236
Ballantine, Joseph W., 182
Bank of China, 139, 140, 141, 144, 145, 151
Barnes, Joseph, 99, 167, 192
Barnett, A. Doak, 291, 292
Barnett, Frank, 260
Barrows, Maj. Gen. David O., 236, 291
Baruch, Bernard, 257
Batista, Fulgencio, 288
Bay of Pigs, 298
Bentley, Elizabeth, 259
Benton, Sen. William, 96
Berle, Adolf, 201
Bishop, Air Marshal Billy, 35
Bisson, T. A., 56, 76, 83, 89, 102, 174
Black and Conservative, 220
Blaine, James G., 69
Bluecher, Marshal, 30
Blueprint for World Conquest, 207
Blum, Robert, 291